Tort Law in Chile

Tort Law in Chile

Alfredo Ferrante

This book was originally published as a monograph in the International Encyclopaedia of Laws/Tort Law.

Founding Editor: Roger Blanpain
General Editor: Frank Hendrickx
Volume Editor: Britt Weyts

Wolters Kluwer

Published by:
Kluwer Law International B.V.
PO Box 316
2400 AH Alphen aan den Rijn
The Netherlands
E-mail: lrs-sales@wolterskluwer.com
Website: www.wolterskluwer.com/en/solutions/kluwerlawinternational

Sold and distributed by:
Wolters Kluwer Legal & Regulatory U.S.
7201 McKinney Circle
Frederick, MD 21704
United States of America
E-mail: customer.service@wolterskluwer.com

ISBN 978-94-035-4931-6

e-Book: ISBN 978-94-035-4692-6
web-PDF: ISBN 978-94-035-4453-3

This title is available on www.kluwerlawonline.com

The Author

Alfredo Ferrante, Doctor in Law at the University of Oviedo (Spain), with honours and awarded by Sancho Rebullida prize. He received his Bachelor of Laws from University of Pisa (Italy) and University of Oviedo, Spain.

He has been teaching all the main areas of private law in Spain, at the University of Oviedo, Spain (2004–2011) and at the University of Girona, Spain (2011–2015) where he has taught in Spanish, Catalan and English.

Former associate professor of private and comparative law at the University Alberto Hurtado (2015–2020) in Santiago de Chile (Chile) where he has been head of the private law department (2019–2020).

Since the end of 2020 he is associate professor of private comparative law at the University of Pavia in Italy. Admitted to Italian and Spanish Bar and Arbitrator.

He has been a visiting professor and has held several conferences in Europe and Latin America, being a member of several associations among which the European Law Institute (ELI). Part of the study group that elaborated the Principles of Latin American Contract Law. He has published more than 100 scientific contributions.

The Author

To my parents, from whom I must always learn.

Table of Contents

Table of Contents

List of Abbreviations

Art.	Article
CC	Chilean Civil Code
CCom	Chilean Commercial Code
CCF	French Civil Code
COT	*Codigo orgánico de Tribunales* (Ley 7.421/1943 (DO 9 Jul. 1943)
CP	Chilean Penal Code
CPC	Code of Civil Procedure (*Código de procedimiento civil*)
CPP	Code of Criminal Procedure (*Código procesal penal*)
CPR	*Constitución Política de la República de Civile*
CS	*Corte Suprema de la República de Civile* (High court)
D.	*Digesto*
DFL	*Decreto con Fuerza de Ley*
DL	*Decreto Ley*
DO	*Diario Oficial de la Repubública de Chile*
EA	*Estatuto Administrativo* (DFL 29/2004, of 16 Jun. (DO 16 Mar. 2005) refunde Ley 18334/1989, of 15 Sep. (DO 23 Sep. 1989)
GJ	Gaceta Jurídica
L	Ley (act)
LGUC	*Ley General Urbanismo y Construcción* DFL 458/1975, of 18 Dec. (DO 13 Apr. 1976)
LPC	*Ley sobre protección de los derechos de los consumidores.* Ley 19.496/1997, of 7 Feb. (DO 7 Mar. 1997). (Consumer Protection Act)
LPInd	*Ley propriedad industrial.* (Ley 19.039/1991, of 24 Jan. (DO 25 Jan. 1991), now DFL 3/2006, (DO 20 Jun. 2006).

List of Abbreviations

LMV	*Ley de Mercado de Valores* (Ley 18.045/1981, of 21 Oct. (DO 22 Oct. 1981)
LOCBGAE	*Ley Orgánica Constitucional de Bases Generales de la Administración del Estado.* DFL 1/2000, DFL 1/19653, of 13 Dic (DO 17 Nov. 2001). *Texto refundido de la Ley 18.575.*
LOCM	*Ley Orgánica Constitucional de Municipalidades* (DFL 1/2006, of 9 May 2006 (DO 29 Jul. 2006). Texto refundido de la Ley 18.695.
LT	*Ley de Tránsito* DFL 1/2009, of 27 Dec. (DO 29 Oct. 2009). Texto refundido de la Ley 18.290.
OGUC	*Ordenanza General de Urbanismo y Construcciones.* Decreto 47/2002, of 16 Abr (DO 5 Jun. 1992)
PUCV	*Pontificia Universidad Católica de Valparaíso*
RDJ	*Revista de Derecho y Jurisprudencia*
ROL	Identification number of the Judgment
SAP	Judgment of the Court of Appeals (Corte de Apelaciones)
STC	Judgment of the Constitutional Court (Tribunal Constitucional)
TDLC	*Tribunal de la Libre Competencia*
UF	*Unidad de Fomento*

§1 Handbooks

Abeliuk, *Las Obligaciones*	René Abeliuk Manasevich, *Las Obligaciones.* I (Santiago de Chile: Thomson Reuters, 6th ed., 2014).
Alessandri, *De la responsabilidad*	Arturo Alessandri Rodríguez, *De la responsabilidad extracontractual en el derecho chileno* (Santiago de Chile: Editorial Jurídica de Chile, 1943 reprint, 2011).
Barros, *Tratado*	Enrique Barros Bourie, *Tratado de Responsabilidad Civil Extracontractual* II vol. (Santiago de Chile: Editorial Jurídica de Chile, 2nd ed., 2020).
Corral, *Lecciones*	Hernán Corral Talciani, *Lecciones de Responsabilidad Civil Extracontractual* (Santiago de Chile: Legal Publishing, Thomson Reuters, 2nd ed., 2013).
Diez, *El daño*	José Luis Diez Schwerter, *El daño extracontractual. Jurisprudencia y doctrina* (Santiago de Chile: Editorial Jurídica de Chile, 1997, reprint, 2016).
Figueroa, *Curso*	Gonzalo Figueroa Yáñez, *Curso de Derecho Civil*, IV (Santiago de Chile: Editorial Jurídica de Chile, 2012).

Meza, *Manual*	Ramón Meza Barros, *Manual de Derecho Civil. De las Obligaciones* 2 vol. (9th ed., Santiago de Chile: Editorial Jurídica de Chile, 2010).
Ramos, *De la responsabilidad*	René Ramos Pazos, *De la responsabilidad civil extracontractual* (5th ed., Santiago de Chile: Legal Publishing, 2009).
Rodríguez Grez, *Responsabilidad extracontractual*	Pablo Rodríguez Grez, *Responsabilidad extracontractual* (Santiago de Chile: Editorial Jurídica, 2nd, 2010).
Tapia, *De la Responsabilidad*	Orlando Tapia Suárez, *De la Responsabilidad civil en general y de la responsabilidad delictual entre los contratantes* (Santiago de Chile: Legal Publishing, 3rd ed., 2007).

List of Abbreviations

General Introduction

§1. General Background

I. Geography

1. Chile[1] can be described as 'tricontinental'. In addition to being primarily located in South America, it has islands (Isla de Pascua and the Isla Salas y Gómez) located in Oceania, and it is also partially located in Antarctica. Chile is located in the extreme part of the Southern Cone, bordering the Pacific Ocean to the west, Peru to the north and Argentina and Bolivia to the east. The Southern Cone ends at the Drake Passage, which separates America from Antarctica. This is also where the Pacific and Atlantic Oceans meet.

2. Chile is long and narrow with a variety of territories and climates. The Andes mountains (decreases in height towards the south), and the Patagonia region are key features of the landscape. It is also characterized by a series of volcanoes located in a highly seismic zone. In fact, Chile is situated in the 'Pacific Ring of Fire', which is above the fault line that connects the Pacific, Nazca and South American tectonic plates.

3. Chile is known for its biodiversity and its various climates. This includes desert, microclimate (Elqui Valley) and glaciers. There are also four different macroforms that alternate: Coastal Plain, Cordillera de la Costa, Intermediate Depression and Cordillera de los Andes.

4. Chile is 4,329 kilometres long. It is the longest and narrowest country in the world, with 17,574,003 inhabitants.[2] However, 40.5% of the population is concentrated in the metropolitan region of Santiago del Chile.[3] Santiago del Chile city

1. For more detail, *see* Enrique Espinoza. *Jeografía descriptiva de la República de Chile* (Santiago de Chile Imprenta i Encuadernación Barcelona, 4d ed, 1897); Aimé. Pissis, *Geografía física de la República de Chile* (Paris: Instituto Geográfico de Paris Delagrave, 1875).
2. Instituto Nacional de Estadísticas. *Síntesis de resultados. Censo 2017.* (Santiago de Chile: Instituto Nacional de Estadísticas, 2018), at 5. The population density is 25.74 inhabitants per square kilometre. The last official census was conducted in 2017: for more information, *see* http://www.censo2017.cl/
3. In Santiago, the population density is 393 inhabitants per square kilometre.

(originally *Santiago del Nuevo Extremo*) was founded in 1541 by the Spanish conqueror Pedro de Valdivia (a native of Extremadura). It has been the capital since 1818, which is the same year that Chile declared independence.

5. For historical reasons, more than one language is spoken in Chile, but the official language is Spanish. The indigenous people speak other languages (*Mapudungun, Aimara, Quechua Sureño, Rapanui*; *Kawésqar* and *Yagan* are endangered). Although the indigenous languages are not considered official languages, they are considered worthy of protection in the territories where they are spoken and can be used for communication and education.[4] Since 2013, *Mapudungun* has been a co-official language in the municipality of Galvarino (approx. 12,000 inhabitants). In 2017, *Rapa Nui*[5] became the official language of Isla de Pascua.

II. History

6. The Chilean territories[6] were discovered in 1520 by Fernando de Magallanes, who managed to circumnavigate the strait (which was named after him).[7] After the first partially unsuccessful expeditions conducted by Diego de Almagro, and some struggles for the conquest between the latter and Francisco Pizarro, the actual conquest was conducted by Pedro de Valdivia. In 1541 he founded the current Santiago de Chile, called 'Captaneria general de Chile' (or *Nueva Extramadura*). He became its first governor, although everything depended on the Vicereinnado español of Peru.

This created a lot of friction with the indigenous community.[8]

4. Ley 19253/1993, of 28 Sep, *establece normas sobre protección, fomento y desarrollo de los Indigenas, y crea la corporación nacional de desarrollo indigena* (DO 5 Oct. 1993).
5. Decreto Municipalidad de la Isla de Pascua 1882/2017, of 26 Sept. (D. O. 14 Dec. 2017) establishes the *Rapa Nui* (*Vãnaŋa Rapa Nui*) language as the official language in the commune of Isla de Pascua.
6. *See* Diego de Rosales, *Historia general del reino de Chile. Indian Flandes*, ed. Benjamín Vicuña Mackenna, Valparaíso, Imprenta del Mercurio, 1877; Gonzalo Fernández de Oviedo, *Historia general y natural de las Indias* (Madrid: Real académica de Historia, 1851); Simón Collier & William F. Saeter, Historia *de Chile 1808–1994* (Cambridge: Cambridge University Press, 2nd ed., 1998); Eduardo Cavieres. *Sobre la Independencia en Chile. El fin del Antiguo Régimen y los orígenes de la representación moderna* (Valparaíso: Ediciones Universitarias de Valparaíso, 2013).
7. The pre-Hispanic period is known as the period of the 'chinchorra' culture that brought together indigenous people who inhabited the current Atacama Desert (between 1700 and 1500 BC). Afterwards, the Chilean territories have held various indigenous populations and cultures, which, however, still exist in part. It must be remembered that for a period of time the Inca Empire conquered the north of Chile (being part of the 'Qullasuyu' zone of the Inca Empire).
8. Significant is the residence of the Mapuche people under the reins of Lautaro. Two battles are significant: in 1533 the battle of Tucapel took place where Valdivia died; in 1557 in the battle of Mataquito Lautaro was killed.

After the battle of Curalaba,[9] from the period of conquest, next comes colonization and Christianization operated also by the Jesuits that partially lead to agreements with the Mapuche people.[10]

7. The departure of the last Spanish governor Francisco García Carrasco led to the first meeting of the Chilean government and the independence from Spain.[11] On 18 September 1810, the National Holiday was celebrated. The national government was first established on 4 July 1811.

There were three events from 1810 to 1823 that led to the conformation of the Republic of Chile: *La Patria Vieja* (1810–1014), *La reconquista* (1814–1817) and *La Patria Nueva* (1818–1823). During *La Patria Vieja*, Chile gained independence. But after the battle of Rancagua, its independence was lost again. This allowed the Spanish *reconquista* to continue until February 1817. The new independence (*La Patria Nueva*) was gained thanks to the victory in the battle of Chacabuco, which was led by the liberator Bernardo O'Higgins. Thus, on 11 January 1818, in the city of Concepción, independence from Spain was proclaimed. Albeit, the first formal register was not dated until 12 February 1818, via the signing of the *Acta de Declaración de Independencia*. Bernardo O'Higgins became governor until his abdication in 1823. From 1823 to 1826, General Ramón Freire was appointed Supreme Leader. In February 1827, Freire became the President of the Republic.

8. Although various constitutions were issued during the period of independence (1811, 1812, 1814, 1818, 1822, 1823, 1828) from Spain, there were three that clearly marked the modern constitutional process (1833, 1925, 1980). The year 1833 marked the end of a civil war between conservatives (*pelucones*) and liberals (*pipolos*). This created a Republic of conservative matrix, which led to the creation of the Constitution of the Republic of 1833, a text that lasted until the Constitution of 1925.

9. In the period leading up to the Constitution of 1925, civil wars occurred three times (1851, 1859 and 1891). This period of the Republic was essentially divided into three parts. First, the period from 1830 to 1861 ended with the conservative government of Manuel Montt Goberno who enacted the first Civil Code in 1855. Second, during the period of the Liberal Republic (1861–1891), Chile won the

9. This war sanctions the end of the period of the conquest, in this one dies the governador Marín García Oñez, it was in 1598.

10. In 1641, through the Parliament of Quilín, peace was established with the Mapuche asumento that the BioBio River as a frontier. Later on, it was not respected. *See* José Bengoa (ed.) *Procesos, políticas y culturas en el Chile del Bicentenario* (Santiago de Chile: Catalonia, 2017); José Bengoa, *Historia de los antiguos mapuches del sur. Desde antes de la llegada de los españoles hasta las paces de Quilín* (Santiago de Chile: Catalonia, 2003).

11. *See* Simon Collier, *Ideas and politics of chilean independence: 1808–1833* (Cambridge: Cambridge University Press, 1967); Gabriel Salazar, *Construcción de Estado en Chile (1800–1837): democracia de los 'pueblos', militarismo ciudadano, golpismo oligárquico* (Santiago de Chile: Sudamericana, 2007); Leonardo León, *Ni patriotas ni realistas. El bajo pueblo durante la Independencia de Chile, 1810–1822*) (Santiago de Chile: Centro de Investigaciones Diego Barros Arana, 2012); Eduardo Cavieres. *Sobre la Independencia en Chile. El fin del Antiguo Régimen y los orígenes de la representación moderna* (Valparaíso: Ediciones Universitarias de Valparaíso, 2013).

Pacific War (1879–1883) by defeating[12] Peru[13] and Bolivia.[14] As a result, the city of Antofagast was annexed and no longer had access to the sea. The expansion to the south was at the expense of the land that the indigenous Mapuche people lived on; not to mention the occupation of Araucania (1861–1883). This brought about conflicts of territorial revendication that still exist somewhat in Chile.

10. Third, the Congresista revolutionary army government (Parliamentary Republic) imposed its will when the Liberal Republic ended because of a new civil war which led to the suicide of President José Manuel Balmaceda. In this period the presidents of the República were tightly controlled by the Congreso until 1924.

11. In 1924 the clash was also manifested by the army, via the *Ruido de sables* ('sabre rattling'). This contributed to a major change and opened the door to a new period known as the 'presidential republic'. This led to the ratification of the Constitution of 1925 and the presidents began playing a more protagonist role.

12. The *coup d'état* of General Augusto Pinochet began on 11 September 1973. This caused the death of the current President Salvador Allende, ushering in a dictatorial period with repression of human rights and personal liberties until 11 March 1990. The new President, Patricio Aylwin Azócar, initiated the democratic transition. This came about through strong protests that led to the plebiscite of 1988 in which Chileans decided that they no longer wanted the Pinochetist military government. This resulted in a call for presidential and parliamentary elections, which led to the election of Patricio Aylwin on 14 December 1989.

13. The Constitution of 1980, although with some later modifications that led to a new consolidated text of 2005,[15] was clearly influenced by the Pinochet dictatorship. With regards to this, in recent years we have entered a new period that has seen strong social rebellions that have resulted in strong demonstrations that began on 18 October 2019. This led to the decision to elaborate a new Constitution,[16] an idea that was ratified by popular vote in October 2020.[17] The new Chilean constituent process began with the elections celebrated on May 15 and 16 in 2021. From the

12. This war is associated with Arturo Prat, depicted in the Chilean 10,000 pesos banknotes, who died in battle at the beginning of the Pacific War (May 21, 1879) during the naval battle of Iquique, sinking together with the Chilean corvette Esmeralda against the Peruvian ironclad Huascar (commanded by Miguel Grau).
13. Peru also includes the cities of Arica and Tacna. Tacna was reannexed to Peru in 1929.
14. Chile, Peru and Bolivia had instead fought together to expel the Spanish in the Hispano South American War (1865–1871).
15. Decreto n. 100/2005, of 17 Sept, *Texto Refundido, coordinado y sistematizado de la Constitución Política de la Republica de Chile* (DO 22 Sept. 2005). *See* Lautaro Ríos Álvarez. 'La reforma de 2005 a la Constitución chilena'. *Anuario iberoamericano de justicia constitucional*, Nº. 10 (2006): 617 et seq.
16. A first consensual agreement between the parties took place on 15 November 2019. The Ley 21.200, of 23rd of December (DO 24.12.2020) creates the basis for the new elaboration through the modification of Chapter XV of the Constitution of 1980 and the so-called Acuerdo por la Paz y la Nueva Constitución.
17. About 78.27% voted 'apruebo' in the *plescito* with which the citizens had to manifest themselves in 'approving' or 'rejecting' the process of a new Constitution.

Constituent Assembly, 155 members will have the task of drafting and proposing (in nine months, extendable by another three) the text of the new Constitution.[18]

III. Political System

14. Chile has three independent powers: executive, legislative and judicial.[19] It is a unitary presidential constitutional republic. As a result, the president is both the head of state and the head of government. Legislative power is exercised by the *Congreso Nacional*, which is a bicameral system with two chambers: the Senate (*Senado*) and the Chamber of Deputies (*Cámara de Diputados*). The judiciary is independent of the executive and the legislature of Chile. It is divided into sixteen regions, with the last one created in 2018,[20] and run by governors. The regions are further divided into provinces and *Communas*.

15. Due to the fact that Chile is a Presidential Democratic Republic, it is possible for the President of the Republic to be authorized, upon delegation by Congress, to issue the so-called Decretos con Fuerza de Ley. This is similar in all aspects to the rank of an Ordinary Law (Articles 32 and 54, 64 CPR), which is characterized by a temporary limitation of its authorization (one year, Article 54 CPR) and content, with the exception that it is unable to touch issues related to the first three types of laws analysed, among other subjects. However, since 2005 and following the reform of the constitutional text,[21] there has been a peculiar DLF with a rank inferior to the ordinary law, which is the one that deals exclusively with acting as a consolidated, coordinated and systematized text of the previous rules. In this sense, it cannot provide for derogations and any changes can only be formal and not substantial because the updating of the text cannot 'alter, in any way, its true meaning and scope' (Article 54 CPR).[22]

16. The President of the Republic can also exercise a regulatory power (Article 32 CPR) which is manifested through the so-called Supreme Decree issued by him and has exclusive jurisdiction in certain matters (e.g., Articles 11, 19 n. 24, 93 n. 16, 94, 105, 129, 130, etc.). This is associated with a regulatory power of other institutions.[23]

---

18. *See* Rodolfo Walter Díaz (ed.). *Hacia una Nueva Constitución. Estado Regional y otros temas, Universidad de Concepción* (Santiago de Chile: Thomson Reuters, 2021).
19. *See e.g.*, Carlos Huneeus & Octavio Avendaño (eds). *El sistema politico en Chile* (Santiago de Chile: LOM Ediciones, 2018).
20. As of September 2018, the Ñuble region is created (with capital Chillán and three provinces: Diguillín, Itata and Punilla): Ley 21.033/2017, of Aug. 19 (DO Sept. 5, 2017).
21. Ley 20.050, of Aug. 18 (DO Aug. 26, 2005).
22. An example is DFL 1/2000, of 6 May (DO 30 May 2000) which accomplishes this task with the text of the Civil Code.
23. For example, among others, the *Contraloría General de la República* (Arts 98 et seq. CPR, DFL 2421 of 2019), the Central Bank (Arts 108 109, Organic Constitutional Law 18.840), of the National Television Council (Art. 19, L: Organic Constitutional Law 18.838) have it.

17. It has only been since the Political Constitution of 1925 that the inapplicability of legal texts as unconstitutional before the Supreme Court was established. Constitutional supremacy has been fully established since 2005 with the reform of the Constitution in 1980. In fact, the Constitutional Court not only maintains preventive control (granted in 1970), but also acquires the repressive control (inapplicability) which was originally exercised by the Supreme Court. Regarding this, the Constitutional Court would exercise a *control concentrado*. This position, for some, would be opposed by a diffused control (legitimized by Article 6 CPR), meaning that the Supreme Court would sometimes declare the inapplicability of certain precepts.[24]

IV. Economy and Social Value

18. Mining is very important to Chile and its economy. In fact, Chile is the largest producer and exporter of copper in the world. It is also a leader in the production of iodine, and second in the production of lithium compounds.[25]

19. From an economic perspective, the influence of the Chicago School and the training of Milton Friedman and Arnold Harberger are also important. The first foreign exchange programme was initiated by an agreement signed in 1956 between the University of Chicago and the Pontifical Catholic University of Chicago. This was later expanded, and created the phenomenon of the so-called *Chicago Boys*, who upon their return, contributed to a radical change in the Chilean economy,[26] especially in the Pinochet dictatorship.[27] This model is still somewhat present today, and it is represented by a liberal economy and a privatized system. This has contributed to a high level of macroeconomic stability and a high level of capital market development. However, this is undermined by the unequal distribution of income.[28] In fact, after Costa Rica, Chile is the second most unequal country (in

---

24. For example, *see* CS Aug. 30, 2016 (rol 35,236-2016). *See e.g.*, Lautaro Rios Álvarez. 'El Control Difuso de Constitucionalidad de la Ley en la República de Chile'. *Ius et Praxis*. 2002/1, at 389 et seq.
25. *See*, Servicio Nacional de Geología y Minería. *Anuario de la Mineria de Chile* (Santiago de Chile, Ministerio de Mineria 2019), at 13 and 30.
26. A symbol of the economic policy used during this period can be found in the document 'el Ladrillo' drafted in 1972 by Andrés Sanfuentes, Juan Villarzú & José Luis Zabala Ponce: 'El *ladrillo': bases de la política económica del gobierno militar chileno, Centro de Estudios Políticos* (Santiago de Chile Alfabeta, 1992).
27. For example, during Pinochet's military government, these were some of the positions: Sergio De Castro was Minister of Economy and Minister de hacienda; Pablo Baraona, Minister of Economy and Minister de Mineria; Alvaró Bardón President of Banco Central del Chile and undersecretary of the economy; Rolf Luders, Minister de Hacienda y de Economia. Reference is made to Manuel Délano & Hugo Traslaviña. *La herencia de los Chicago Boys*, Santiago de Chile: ediciones Ornitorrinco, 1989).
28. *See e.g.*, the data from Banco Central de Chile: https://www.bcentral.cl/

terms of income inequality) of all OECD countries.[29] After Montevideo, Santiago de Chile is the second most expensive city in Latin America.[30]

20. The official currency is the *peso chileno*; its largest denomination is 20,000 pesos which depicts Andrés Bello, the mastermind of the Civil Code of 1855. Since 1967, the Unidad de Fomento (UF) has been used in Chile as an inflation-adjustable measure, which is updated daily.[31]

Until March 2020, the 'Gran torre Santiago', which was completed in 2014 and is located in Santiago del Chile in the Costanera Center complex, was the tallest skyscraper in Latin America (300.3 metres). It was later surpassed by the 'Torres Obispado' in Monterrey (305 metres).

§2. Legal System

I. Primacy of Legislation and Codification

21. Chile belongs to the civil law family. Noting that the Leyes Marianas (named after Mariano Egaña) of 1837 was the first prototype of civil codification,[32] it is significant that the current Constitution was enacted in 1980 (with standardized text of 2005[33]), the legal system is based on the Civil Code of 1855[34] (with consolidated text of 2000[35]) and commercial matters are regulated by the Commerce Code of 1865.[36] Additionally, the first consumer protection law was enacted in 1997[37] (LPC), the current Criminal Code dates back to 1874[38] and the reform of the criminal procedure was carried out with the *Código procesal penal* of 2000[39] (which

29. Calculated based on the GINI index: *see* Organisation for Economic Co-operation and Development (OECD) page: https://data.oecd.org/inequality/income-inequality.htm
30. Relative to the year 2020. In third place is São Paulo. *See* Numbeo's cost of living index: https://es.numbeo.com/coste-de-vida/iniciar-p%C3%A1gina
31. Decreto (Ministro de Fomento) 40/1967, of 2 Jan. (DO 22 Jan.1967). As of May 31, 2021, one UF corresponds to 29,582.77 Pesos Chileno, approximately 33.80 Euros.
32. Bernardino Bravo Lira, 'Los comienzos de la codificación en Chile: la codificación procesal'. *Revista Chilena de Historia del Derecho*, 1983/9: at 210.
33. Decree No. 100/2005, of 17 September, cit.
34. *See e.g.*, Alejandro Guzmán Brito. 'Ensayo de una bibliografía para la historia de la codificación civil chilena'. *Quaderni fiorentini per la storia del pensiero giuridico moderno* (Ejemplare dedicato a Emilio Betti e alla scienza giuridica del Novecento), 1978/1, at 601 et seq. Also Alejandro Guzmán Brito, 'El Código Civil de Chile en su ciento cincuenta años y crónica de un congreso internacional de conmemoración celebrado en Santiago de Chile'. *Anuario de derecho civil,* 2006/3: at 1283 es seq: Alejandro Guzmán Brito. 'El Código civil y sus primeros intérpretes', *Revista chilena de Derecho*, 1992/1: at 81 et seq.
35. DFL 1/2000, cit.
36. On the codification of the código de comercio Javier Barrientos Grandon. *Historia del código de comercio de la República de Chile. Sobre la cultura a través de un libro, estudio adjunto a la reimpresión del Código de Comercio con ocasión de la conmemoración del sesquincenario de la promulgación del Código de Comercio* (Santiago de Chile: Facultad de Derecho Pontificia Universidad Católica de Chile, 2015).
37. Ley 19.496/1997, of 7 Feb. (DO 7 Mar. 1997).
38. Ley 2.561/1874, of 12 Nov. (DO 12 Nov. 1874).
39. Ley 19.696/2000, of 29 Sep. (DO 12 Oct. 2000).

replaced the *Código de Procedimiento Penal de Chile* of 1906[40]), while the current *Código de Procedimiento Civil* dates back to 1902[41] (albeit a major reform may be underway, as several proposals have been presented in this sense[42]). The *Código orgánico de Tribunales of* 1943 governs the judicial power.[43] Other codes have been inserted[44] and modified with particular frequency.[45]

22. The Chilean legal system prioritizes written sources of law over verbal ones. The former has a hierarchical pro-Kelsenian categorization (besides what is in the Constitution) that is supplemented by certain provisions contained in the preliminary titles of the Civil Code (CC) and the Commercial Code (Ccom).

23. While drafting Article 1 CC, Andrés Bello took the classic definition of law based on the Digest[46] and added an explicit reference to the Constitution.[47] This clearly demonstrates that the role of sources and their hierarchy already existed when the Civil Code was created in 1855.

24. The executive message of 1855 regarding the approval of the Civil Code stated that 'following the example of almost all modern codes, the force of law has been taken away from customs'. Although, from the contrary interpretation of Article 2 CC, it can be inferred that it plays a relevant role as a source when directly established.[48]

25. It is significant that Article 1546 CC generally requires the execution and interpretation of contracts be carried out not only according to law, but also according to customs. However, this provision is often underestimated.

---

40. Ley 1853/1906, of 13 Feb. (DO 19 Feb. 1997).
41. Ley 1.552/1902, of 28 Aug. (DO 30 Aug. 1902).
42. On codification in procedural matters, *see e.g.*, Bernardino Bravo Lira. 'Los comienzos de la codificación en Chile: la codificación procesal'. *Revista Chilena de Historia del Derecho,* 1983/9: at 191 et seq.
43. Ley 7.421/1943, of 15 June (DO 9 Jul. 1943).
44. Currently, for example, the Código Sanitario (DFL 725/1968, of 11 Dec., DO 31 Jan. 1968), the Código Tributario de Chile de 1974 (DL 830/1974, of 27 Dec., DO 31.12.1974.), Código Aereonautico (Ley 18.916/1990, of 19 Jan., DO 8 Feb. 1990), the Código de Trabajo (DFL no. 1/2002, of 31 July, DO 16 Jan. 2003).
45. As in the case of the Labour Code, although it was not called Código del trabajo, the first legislation was that of 1931, approved by DFL 178/1931 of 28 May (DO 31 May 1931), followed by the labour codes of 1987 (Ley 18620/1987) and the consolidation of 1994 (DFL 1/1994, of 24 Jan).
    Also, the first tax code dates back to DFL 190/1960 of 26 Mar. (DO 5 Apr. 1960), and the first health code is from 1918 (Ley 3385/1931 of 22 May, DO 22 Jun. 1931) while the second is from 1931 (DFL 226/1931 of 15 May, DO 29 May 1931) to then give way to the current one of 1968.
46. D. 1.3.7: '*Legis haec virtus est: imperare, vetare, permittere...*'.
47. Art. 1 CC: 'La ley es una declaración de la voluntad soberana que, manifestada en la forma prescrita por la Constitución, manda, prohíbe o permite' (*The law is a declaration of the sovereign will which, manifested in the form prescribed by the Constitution, commands, prohibits or permits*).
48. This is the case, for example, with Art. 1188, 1198, 1938, 1940, 1944, 1951, 1954, 1986 CC, and expressly subordinated to the Law as per Art. 2117 CC.

As previously mentioned, from a territorial point of view, local customs prevail over general customs. In commercial relations, customs assume the role of a subordinate and subsidiary source (Article 4 Ccom). This effectively establishes the possibility of being subjected to verification (Article 5 Ccom), as well as its subsequent interpretative role (Article 6 Ccom). The important reference made in the commercial sphere to international and local customs (e.g., Articles 854, 1092 Ccom)[49] should also be noted.

II. Position of the Judiciary

26. The judiciary (*see* Articles 76 et seq. CPR, COT) is independent of the executive and legislative branches. The basic structure is formed by the ordinary (or special[50]) *Juzgados*, the *Cortes de Apelaciones* (divided into seventeen jurisdictional territories) and a Supreme Court.[51] The latter has the 'superintendencia directiva, correccional y económica' (*supervisory, remedial and economic supremacy*) (Article 82 CPR) with respect to the former. In 2019, the Supreme Court heard 41,327 cases; 12005 are pending and 36,953 have been decided.[52]

27. Although they are overseen by the Courts of Appeal, they are not technically part of the *poder judicial*, Local Police Judges (*Jueces de Policia Local*) that adjudicate minor disputes and most consumer disputes.[53]

28. The Judicial Branch Administrative Corporation (*Corporación Administrativa del Poder Judicial*, CAPJ) is an institution at the service of the courts of justice, administering the human, corporal, financial and technical affairs of the Judicial Branch. It is composed of the Chief Justice of the Supreme Court, who heads it, and four justices of the highest court, elected by their peers for a period of two years.

---

49. *See* Alfredo Ferrante, 'Chile', in *International Contract Manual*, edited by Albert H. Kritzer, Sieg Eiselen, Francesco G. Mazzotta, Vikki Rogers (New York: Thomson Reuters, 2020), at 50-2.
50. Such as Juzgados de Fmilia, Juzgados *de Cobranza Laboral,*i *Juzgads Laborales, Juzgados de Garantía. See* Poder Judicial de Chile, *Estructura y descripciones de Cargo Tribunales del País* (Santiago de Chile: Poder Judicial de Chile, 2020).
51. This has been envisioned since the Constitution of 1823, *see* Bernardino Bravo Lira, 'La Corte Suprema de Chile 1823–2003, cuatro caras en 180 años'. *Revista Chilena de Derecho*, 2003/3: at 535 et seq.
52. Instituto Nacional de Estadisticas, *Estadísticas judiciales 2019* (Santiago de Chile: Instituto Nacional de Estadisticas, 2020), at 9. More extensively, *see also* la memoria istituzionale: Poder Judicial, *Memoria Institucional 2019* (Santiago de Chile: Poder Judicial, 2020).
53. *See* Ley 15.231/1963, of 30 July (DO 8 Aug.1963) then consolidated in Decree 307/1978, of 3 Mar. (DO 28.5.1978). In relation to procedural aspects, *see* Ley 18.287/1984, of 18 Jan. (DO 7 Feb. 1984). *See* Ministerio de Justicia y Derechos Humanos. *Diagnostico de funcionamiento de los Juzgados de Policía Local en Chile* (Santiago de Chile: Ministerio de Justicia y Derechos Humanos, 2020); María Rebeca Ahumada, *El procedimiento aplicado ante los Juzgados de Policía Local desde una mirada teórica y práctica* (Santiago de Chile: Universidad Finis Terrae, 2017).

III. Distinction Between Public and Private Law

29. As a country belonging to the civil law legal tradition, Chile can be described as having a macro-division between public and private law. In this sense, administrative law acquires a specific autonomy.[54]

Notwithstanding, there are currently no specific Tribunals for Administrative Law Disputes (*Tribunales del Contenciosos Administrativos*), despite being provided for in the Constitution (Article 38.2 CPR).[55] Therefore, the third section of the Supreme Court performs this function.[56]

30. In the context of public and administrative[57] law, it is important to highlight the *Constitutional Organic Law on the General Bases of State Administration*[58] and the regulation of municipalities.[59] There are various agencies (*Superintendencias*) that are responsible for taxing and supervising certain regulations.[60]

31. The General Accounting Office (*Contraloría General de la República*) plays an important role in public and administrative law. It is the superior fiscal body of the State Administration, which was formally established in 1927[61] and it is currently protected under the Constitution (Articles 98–100 CPR).

32. As noted above, domestic law is essentially based on a codified system (civil, commercial and penal code) in which B2C is added to the relations of the

54. *See* Alejandro Vergara Blanco, *El Derecho Administrativo como sistema autónomo. El mito del código civil como Derecho Común* (Santiago de Chile: AbeledoPerrot-Legal Publishing, 2010).
55. *See* Ezio Costa Cordella. 'Los Tribunales Administrativos especiales en Chile'. *Revista de derecho (Valdivia)*, 2014/1, at 151 et seq.
56. For an in-depth study *see* Sandra Ponce de León Salucci. *Jurisdicción contenciosa administativa. El control de la administración por los tribunales ordinarios y especiales y procedimientos aplicables.* (Cuadernos Académica Judicial, Santiago de Chile: Académica Judicial, 2020).
57. *See* Eduardo Soto Kloss, *Derecho Administrativo Temas Fundamentales* (Santiago de Chile AbeledoPerrot-Thomson Reuters, 3rd ed., 2012).
58. *Ley Orgánica Constitucional de Bases Generales de la Administración del Estado*: Ley 18.575, fijada por el texto refundido de DFL 1/2000, of 13 Dec. (DO 17 Nov. 2001). *See e.g.*, Juan Carlos Ferrada Bórquez, 'La responsabilidad patrimonial del Estado de Chile: una revisión panorámica después de casi veinte años de jurisprudencia de la Corte Suprema'. *Revista de Administración Pública*, 2020/211: at 373 et seq.
59. Ley 18.695, *Orgánica Constitucional de las Municipalidades*, consolidated by DFL 1/2006, of 9 May (DO 26 Jul. 2006).
60. Superintendencia de Seguridad Social (SUSESO, 1953); Superintendencia de Electricidad y Combustibles (SEC, 1985); Superintendencia de Servicios Sanitarios (SISS, 1990); Superintendencia de Salud (SuperSalud, 2005); Superintendencia de Casinos de Juego (SCJ, 2005); Superintendencia de Pensiones (SP, 2008);Superintendencia del Medio Ambiente (SMA, 2010); Superintendencia de Educación (SEE, 2012); Superintendencia de Insolvencia y Reemprendimiento (SIR, 2014), Comisión para el Mercado Financiero (CMF, 2018), Superintendencia de Educación Superior (SES, 2018). In the area of consumption, the Servicio Nacional del Consumidor (SERNAC, 1990) assumes a particular role.
61. DFL 400-bis/1927, of 12 Mar. (DO 26. Mar. 1927).

Ley 19.496 of 1997 for consumer protection. Chile ratified the CISG[62] in 1990[63] pursuant to Article 96, in connection with Article 12.[64]

IV. Sources of Private Law in General and of Tort Law in Particular

33. The traditional classification for the sources of private law or obligations can be traced back to Article 1447 CC, a provision that inaugurates Book IV of the Civil Code. The article is collocated in Title I ('definitions') of the section dedicated to 'Obligations in general and contracts' (*De las obligaciones en general y de los contratos*). For this reason, there are five sources of a legal obligation:[65] the contract, the quasi-contract, the crime, the quasi-delict and the law. Recently, unjustified enrichment has emerged as a source of obligation.[66]

34. Confronted with this approach, the doctrine has taken three alternative positions. Based on the notion that the law is the only legitimate source of immediate obligation (or the mediated source of all the others),[67] it submits that a legal obligation arises only from contract and the law, thus classifying the sources of obligation according to the will or the unwillingness to oblige.[68]

35. A third interpretation[69] considers the classification of obligations to be threefold. In this sense, it is important to consider the debtor's intention to be bound (with a subdivision into voluntary sources - for example the unilateral declaration of intent - and non-voluntary sources - for example criminal offences and quasi-delicts), distinguishing from those situations in which the debtor is legally bound in *stricto sensu.*

62. On a general overview of contract law in Chile and other signed conventions: Ferrante, 'Chile', cit., at 50-4 et seq.
63. Chile signed it in 1980, and ratified in 7 Feb. 1990: *See* Decreto 544/1990, of 31 May (DO 3 Oct. 1990).
64. *See* Francisco José Grob Duhalde. 'La reserva de Chile a la "Convención de Viena" de 1980'. *Revista de Derecho (PUCV)*, 2011/36, at 37 et seq.
65. René Abeliuk Manasevich, *Las Obligaciones.* I (Santiago de Chile: Thomson Reuters, 6th ed., 2014, at 51; Ramón Meza Barros, *Manual de Derecho Civil. De las Obligaciones* (9th ed., Santiago de Chile: Editorial Jurídica de Chile, 2010), at 10.
66. Enrique Barros Bourie, *Tratado de Responsabilidad Civil Extracontractual. I.* (Santiago de Chile: Editorial Jurídica de Chile, 2nd ed., 2020), at 22. Barros, *Tratado, I,* cit., at 23. In relation to the possible interrelated extension to the theory of abuse of rights, unjust enrichment or the unilateral declaration of will, *see e.g.*, Rodrigo Barcia Lehmann, *Lecciones de derecho civil chileno. II. De las Fuentes de Obligaciones* (Santiago de Chile: Editorial Jurídica de Chile, 2010), at 12 et seq.
67. Gonzalo Figueroa Yáñez, *Curso de Derecho Civil,* IV (Santiago de Chile: Editorial Jurídica de Chile, 2012), at 49.
68. Meza, *Manual, I,* at 15. Thus, for example, it is considered that in quasi-delicts 'the commission of the act is voluntary but its consequences are not' and that 'the obligations resulting from the illicit act are not intended by the author and are imposed by the law in order to repair the damage caused', the same applies to quasi-contracts whose obligation derives from the law. In support of this and the classification between *ex lege* and *ex contractu* vendría, Art. 578 CC: cf. Barcia, *Lecciones II,* at 12.
69. Abeliuk, *Las Obligaciones, I,* at 55–56.

36. From this perspective, it is clear that civil liability must be considered a general principle of private law, and it should have the same traditional sources as obligations.[70] In this regard, a distinction must be made between contractual liability and extracontractual or aquiline liability (tort), which refers to criminal offences or quasi-delicts. Thus, if the source of contractual liability arises from an agreement, in tort liability the law imposes limits of a pecuniary nature which have an impact on the individual's volition.[71]

37. More concretely, as concerns tort liability, Article 1437 CC must be understood in conjunction with Articles 2284 and 2314 CC;[72] articles which expressly state that obligations which are not established by contract are established by law or a voluntary act of the party which, by causing damage, generates compensation. Thus, tort liability arises from the law, as in the case of strict liability from a criminal offence or quasi-delict[73] (although tort liability arising from the law would be exceptional[74]).

38. Traditionally, Chilean Tort Law is codified primarily in Articles 213–2326 CC (Book IV, Title XXXV). Except for an amendment to Article 2320,[75] this field of law has not changed since its approval in 1855. The following is an excerpt of the principal tort law provisions from the Civil Code.

Article 2314 CC. El que ha cometido un delito o cuasidelito que ha inferido daño a otro, es obligado a la indemnización; sin perjuicio de la pena que le impongan las leyes por el delito o cuasidelito (*Whoever has committed a crime or quasi-delict that has caused damage to another is obliged to pay compensation, without prejudice to the penalty imposed by law for the crime or quasi-delict*).

Article 2315 CC. Puede pedir esta indemnización no sólo el que es dueño o poseedor de la cosa que ha sufrido el daño, o su heredero, sino el usufructuario, el habitador o el usuario, si el daño irroga perjuicio a su derecho de usufructo o de habitación o uso. Puede también pedirla en otros casos el que tiene la cosa con obligación de responder de ella; pero sólo en ausencia del dueño (*Compensation may be claimed not only by the owner or possessor of the thing that has been damaged, or by his heir, but also by the usufructuary, the tenant or the user, if the damage is prejudicial to his right of usufruct or of habitation or use. In other cases, the possessor may also claim damages, but only when the owner fails to do so*).

70. Orlando Tapia Suárez, *De la Responsabilidad civil en general y de la responsabilidad delictual entre los contratantes* (Santiago de Chile: Legal Publishing, 3rd ed., 2007), at 14.
71. *See* Barros, *Tratado, I*, cit., at 18.
72. *E.g.*, Tapia, *De la responsabilidad*, at 144–146; René Ramos Pazos, *De la responsabilidad civil extracontractual* (5th ed., Santiago de Chile: Legal Publishing, 2009), at 35; Hernán Corral Talciani, *Lecciones de Responsabilidad Civil Extracontractual* (Santiago de Chile: Legal Publishing, Thomson Reuters, 2nd ed., 2013), at 21–22 and 175.
73. Barros, *Tratado, I*, at 28.
74. Arturo Alessandri Rodríguez, *De la responsabilidad extracontractual en el derecho chileno* (Santiago de Chile: Editorial Jurídica de Chile, 1943 reprint, 2011), at 13; cf. Meza, *Manual, II*, at 349.
75. Art. 4 of Law 18.802/1989, of 23 May (DO 9 Jun.1989) derogates from the original fourth paragraph of Art. 2320, which provided that: 'As such, the husband is responsible for his wife's driving.'

Article 2316 CC. Es obligado a la indemnización el que hizo el daño, y sus herederos.

El que recibe provecho del dolo ajeno, sin ser cómplice en él, sólo es obligado hasta concurrencia de lo que valga el provecho.

(*Whoever did the damage is liable for compensation, and his heirs.*

Whoever receives benefit from the malice of another, without being an accomplice in it, is only liable up to the amount of the value of the benefit).

Article 2317 CC. Si un delito o cuasidelito ha sido cometido por dos o más personas, cada una de ellas será solidariamente responsable de todo perjuicio procedente del mismo delito o cuasidelito, salvas las excepciones de los artículos 2323 y 2328.

Todo fraude o dolo cometido por dos o más personas produce la acción solidaria del precedente inciso.

(*If a crime or quasi-delict has been committed by two or more persons, each of them shall be jointly and severally liable for any damage arising from such crime or quasi-delict, except for those cases provided for in Articles 2323 and 2328.*

In the event of fraud or malice committed by two or more persons, the joint and several liability of the preceding paragraph shall apply).

Article 2318 CC. El ebrio es responsable del daño causado por su delito o cuasidelito (*An intoxicated person is liable for the damage caused by his crime or quasi-delict*).

Article 2319 CC. No son capaces de delito o cuasidelito los menores de siete años ni los dementes; pero serán responsables de los daños causados por ellos las personas a cuyo cargo estén, si pudiere imputárseles negligencia.

Queda a la prudencia del juez determinar si el menor de dieciséis años ha cometido el delito o cuasidelito sin discernimiento; y en este caso se seguirá la regla del inciso anterior.

(*Minors under seven years of age or mentally ill persons are not punishable for a crime or quasi-delict; however, the persons entrusted with their care shall be liable for the damages caused by them, if negligence can be imputed them.*

The judge may determine at his discretion whether a minor under sixteen years of age shall be liable for a crime or quasi-delict; if the judge deems the minor has committed the crime or quasi-delict, the preceding paragraph shall apply).

Article 2320 CC. Toda persona es responsable no sólo de sus propias acciones, sino del hecho de aquellos que estuvieren a su cuidado.

Así el padre, y a falta de éste la madre, es responsable del hecho de los hijos menores que habiten en la misma casa.

Así el tutor o curador es responsable de la conducta del pupilo que vive bajo su dependencia y cuidado.

Así los jefes de colegios y escuelas responden del hecho de los discípulos, mientras están bajo su cuidado; y los artesanos y empresarios del hecho de sus aprendices o dependientes, en el mismo caso.

Pero cesará la obligación de esas personas si con la autoridad y el cuidado que su respectiva calidad les confiere y prescribe, no hubieren podido impedir el hecho (*Everyone is responsible not only for his own actions, but also for the acts of those who are under their care.*

Thus, the father, and in his absence the mother, is responsible for the acts of the minor children who live in the same house.

Likewise, the guardian or curator is responsible for the conduct of the dependent ward under his or her care.

Thus the heads of colleges and schools respond to the fact of the disciples while they are under their care, and the entrepreneurs of the facts of theirs apprentices or dependents.

However, such persons shall be released from their obligation if, with the authority and care that their respective capacity confers and prescribes, they were unable to prevent the act).

Article 2321 CC. Los padres serán siempre responsables de los delitos o cuasidelitos cometidos por sus hijos menores, y que conocidamente provengan de mala educación, o de los hábitos viciosos que les han dejado adquirir.

(*Parents will always be responsible for the crimes or quasi-delicts committed by their minor children, which are known deemed to be the result of poor upbringing or of the bad habits that they have allowed their children to develop*).

Article 2322 CC. Los amos responderán de la conducta de sus criados o sirvientes, en el ejercicio de sus respectivas funciones; y esto aunque el hecho de que se trate no se haya ejecutado a su vista.

Pero no responderán de lo que hayan hecho sus criados o sirvientes en el ejercicio de sus respectivas funciones, si se probare que las han ejercido de un modo impropio que los amos no tenían medio de prever o impedir, empleando el cuidado ordinario, y la autoridad competente. En este caso toda la responsabilidad recaerá sobre dichos criados o sirvientes.

(*Masters are responsible for the acts of their housemaids or servants in the exercise of their respective duties, even if the act in question has not been carried out in their presence.*

However, masters shall not be liable for what their housemaids or servants have done in the exercise of their respective duties if it is proved that said duties have been improperly performed such that the masters had no means of foreseeing or preventing them, using ordinary care and the competent authority. In such cases, all liability shall be borne by the respective housemaids or servants).

Article 2323 CC. El dueño de un edificio es responsable a terceros (que no se hallen en el caso del artículo 934), de los daños que ocasione su ruina acaecida por haber omitido las necesarias reparaciones, o por haber faltado de otra manera al cuidado de un buen padre de familia.

Si el edificio perteneciere a dos o más personas proindiviso, se dividirá entre ellas la indemnización a prorrata de sus cuotas de dominio.

(*The owner of a building is liable to third parties (other than those referred to in Article 934), for the damage caused by its ruin due to the omission of the necessary repairs, or for having failed in any other way to exercise the care of a reasonable head of household.*

If the building belongs to two or more persons in joint ownership, the indemnity shall be divided among them pro rata in proportion to their respective ownership interests).

Article 2324 CC. Si el daño causado por la ruina de un edificio proviniere de un vicio de construcción, tendrá lugar la responsabilidad prescrita en la regla 3.a del artículo 2003.

(*If the damage caused by the ruin of a building is due to a construction defect, the liability prescribed in Rule 3.a of Article 2003 shall apply*).

Article 2325 CC. Las personas obligadas a la reparación de los daños causados por las que de ellas depende, tendrán derecho para ser indemnizadas sobre los bienes de éstas, si los hubiere, y si el que perpetró el daño lo hizo sin orden de la persona a quien debía obediencia, y era capaz de delito o cuasidelito, según el artículo 2319.

(*Any person required to repair the damage caused by their dependents is entitled to be indemnified with their property, if any, and if the person who has committed the damage has done it without the order of the person to whom he owed obedience, and such dependents were punishable for a crime or quasi-delict, in accordance with Article 2319*).

Article 2326 CC. El dueño de un animal es responsable de los daños causados por el mismo animal, aun después que se haya soltado o extraviado; salvo que la soltura, extravío o daño no pueda imputarse a culpa del dueño o del dependiente encargado de la guarda o servicio del animal.

Lo que se dice del dueño se aplica a toda persona que se sirva de un animal ajeno; salva su acción contra el dueño, si el daño ha sobrevenido por una calidad o vicio del animal, que el dueño con mediano cuidado o prudencia debió conocer o prever, y de que no le dio conocimiento.

(*The owner of an animal is responsible for the damages caused by such animal, even after it has been released or lost; unless the release, loss or damage is not attributable to the fault of the owner or of the person charged with the custody or use of the animal.*

The same applies to any person who makes use of an animal belonging to a third party; the action against the owner is barred if the damage has occurred due to a defect or quality of the animal, which the owner with ordinary care or prudence should have known or foreseen, and of which he has not disclosed).

Article 2327 CC. El daño causado por un animal fiero, de que no se reporta utilidad para la guarda o servicio de un predio, será siempre imputable al que lo tenga, y si alegare que no le fue posible evitar el daño, no será oído.

(*The damage caused by a fierce animal that does not generate any utility in the surveillance or service for the land is always imputable to the owner, and if he alleges that it was not possible for him to avoid the damage, he will not be heard*).

Article 2328 CC. El daño causado por una cosa que cae o se arroja de la parte superior de un edificio, es imputable a todas las personas que habitan la misma parte del edificio, y la indemnización se dividirá entre todas ellas; a menos que se pruebe que el hecho se debe a la culpa o mala intención de alguna persona exclusivamente, en cuyo caso será responsable esta sola.

Si hubiere alguna cosa que, de la parte superior de un edificio o de otro paraje elevado, amenace caída y daño, podrá ser obligado a removerla el dueño del edificio o del sitio, o su inquilino, o la persona a quien perteneciere la cosa o que se sirviere de ella; y cualquiera del pueblo tendrá derecho para pedir la remoción.

(*The damage caused by a thing that falls or is thrown from the top of a building, is attributable to all the people who inhabit the same part of the building, and the compensation shall be divided among all of them; unless it is proven that the fact is due to exclusively the fault or bad intention of one person, in which case this person alone will be* liable.

If there is a thing that, from the top of a building or from another elevated area, threatens to fall and damage, the owner of the building or site, or its tenant, or the person to whom the thing or property belongs or make use of it, may be forced to remove it; and any of the people will have the right to request removal)

Article 2329 CC. Por regla general todo daño que pueda imputarse a malicia o negligencia de otra persona, debe ser reparado por ésta.

Son especialmente obligados a esta reparación:

1º. El que dispara imprudentemente un arma de fuego;
2º. El que remueve las losas de una acequia o cañería en calle o camino, sin las precauciones necesarias para que no caigan los que por allí transitan de día o de noche;
3º. El que, obligado a la construcción o reparación de un acueducto o puente que atraviesa un camino lo tiene en estado de causar daño a los que transitan por él.

(*As a general rule, any damage that can be attributed to malice or negligence of another person must be repaired by the latter.*

The following are specifically obliged to indemnify:

1º. Whoever imprudently shoots a firearm;
2º. Whoever removes the slabs of a ditch or pipe on a street or road without the necessary precautions so that those who travel therein during the day or night do not fall;
3º. Whoever undertakes to build or repair an aqueduct or bridge that crosses a road and keeps it in such a state as to cause damage to those in transit thereon).

Article 2330 CC. La apreciación del daño está sujeta a reducción, si el que lo ha sufrido se expuso a él imprudentemente.

(*The assessment of the damage is subject to reduction if who suffered it recklessly exposed himself to it*).

Article 2331 CC. Las imputaciones injuriosas contra el honor o el crédito de una persona no dan derecho para demandar una indemnización pecuniaria, a menos de probarse daño emergente o lucro cesante, que pueda apreciarse en dinero; pero ni aun entonces tendrá lugar la indemnización pecuniaria, si se probare la verdad de la imputación.

(*The injurious accusations against the honor or the credit of a person do not give the right to demand a pecuniary compensation, unless consequential damage or loss of profit is proven, which can be appreciated in money; but not even then will the pecuniary compensation take place, if the statement is proved to be true).*

Article 2332 CC. Las acciones que concede este título por daño o dolo, prescriben en cuatro años contados desde la perpetración del acto.

(*The remedies for damage or malice provided under this Title are barred in four years starting from the commission of the deed*).

Article 2333 CC. Por regla general, se concede acción popular en todos los casos de daño contingente que por imprudencia o negligencia de alguien amenace a personas indeterminadas; pero si el daño amenazare solamente a personas determinadas, sólo alguna de éstas podrá intentar la acción.

(*In general, a people's action may be brought for any incidental damage resulting from the imprudence or negligence of any person that jeopardizes an indefinite number of persons; if the injury affects only specific persons, the action may be brought only by one of these persons*).

Article 2334 CC. Si las acciones populares a que dan derecho los artículos precedentes, parecieren fundadas, será el actor indemnizado de todas las costas de la acción, y se le pagará lo que valgan el tiempo y diligencia empleados en ella, sin perjuicio de la remuneración específica que conceda la ley en casos determinados.

(*If the people's actions referred to in the preceding articles appear to be sufficiently supported, the plaintiff shall be entitled to recover the costs of the action, including the value of the time and effort expended thereon, without prejudice to any special compensation available under the law in specific cases*).

39. This general scheme envisaged by Andres Bello in the Civil Code must be integrated by the progressive enactment of special laws which, in certain cases, have also contributed to the shift in the view of liability from a fault-based system to a strict-liability system.[76]

40. In this context there is a production of legislation which attempts to regulate compensation in specific areas and which at times must be coordinated with the provisions of the Civil Code. Thus, over the years, the laws for work-related accidents and occupational injuries have been established,[77] as well as the liability for damages caused by motorized vehicles[78] and infringements of intellectual property laws.[79] The law also provides for the liability of construction defects[80] or in matters of consumption, with particular reference to sales and services.[81]

76. An extensive discussion can be seen in chapter X of the second tome of Barros, *Tratado*, at 703–972; more systematically Corral, *Lecciones*, cit., at 249 et seq.
77. Ley 16.744/1968, of 23 Jan. (DO 1 Feb. 1968). In relation to responsibility in the work environment *see* the Laboral Code (DFL 1/2003, of Jan. (DO 16 Jan. 2003).
78. Ley 18.290/1984, of 23 Jan. (DO 8 Feb. 1984), now consolidated in DFL 1/2007, of 27 Dec. (DO 29 Oct. 2009). In relation to the establishment of compulsory insurance: Ley 18.490/1986, of 2 Jan. (DO 4 Jan. 1986).
79. Ley Nº 17.336/1970, of 2 Aug. (DO 2 Oct. 1970), with important modifications in 2010 (Ley 20435/2010, of 23 Apr., DO 04 May 2010).
80. D.F.L. 458/1975, of 18 Dec. (DO 13 Apr. 1976).
81. Ley 19.496/1997, of 17 Feb. (DO 7 Mar. 1997).

41. It should also be noted that liability may be established for damages caused by the performance of periodic activities[82] or those which relate to the right to privacy.[83]

42. In a broader and more general context, liability for damages caused by airplanes,[84] damage caused by the environment[85] (having already established criminal and administrative liability for hydrocarbon fumes in the sea[86]) or damage caused by exercising nuclear activities[87] are envisaged.

43. Over the years, liability for damages caused by the public administration,[88] liability for lack of service on the part of municipalities,[89] liability for the acts of the Public Ministry,[90] health liability of the State[91] and protection of patients' rights have been progressively regulated.[92]

44. Attention should also be drawn to the administrative and criminal liability for unfair competition in antitrust matters;[93] in the contractual sphere, reference should be made to the liability of managers of joint-stock companies.[94] The express recognition of moral damage in the law instituting the National Service for Special Protection of Children and Adolescents (*Servicio Nacional de Protección especializada a la niñez y adolescencia*) is also particularly significant.[95]

§3. Function of Law of Tort Law

I. The Legal Basis of Liability

45. Justice is one of the legal foundations (*fundamentos*) that prompts change in the law. As concerns civil liability, justice translates (according to the ideals of

82. Ley 19.733/2001, of 18 May (DO 4 June 2001).
83. Ley 19.628/1999 of 18 Aug. (DO 28 Aug. 2001) also in consonance with the processing of personal data: Ley 21096/2018, of 5 June (DO 16 June 2018).
84. Ley 18.916/1990, of 19 Jan. (DO 4 Feb. 1990).
85. Ley 19.300/1994, of 1 Mar. (DO 4 Mar. 1994).
86. Ley 2222/1978 of 21 May (DO 31 May 1978).
87. Ley 18.302/1984, of 16 Apr. (DO 2 May 1984).
88. Ley 18.575/1986, now in the Consolidated Text: DFL 1/2000, DFL 1/19653, of 13 Dec. (DO 17 Nov. 2001). In relation to the liability of companies that are concessionaires of public works: DFL 164/1991, now recast text Supreme Decree 900/1996, of 18 Oct. (DO. 18 Dec. 1996).
89. Ley 18.575/1986, now recast text DFL 1/2006, of 9 May (DO 26 Jul. 2006).
90. Ley 19.640/1998, of 8 Oct. (DO 15 Oct. 1998).
91. Ley 19.966/2005, 25 Aug. (DO 3 Sep. 2004).
92. Ley 20.584/2012, of 13 Apr. (DO 24 Apr. 2012).
93. DL 211/1973 recast in DFL 1/2004; of 18 Oct. (DO 7 Mar. 2005).
94. Ley 18.046/1981, of 21 Oct. (Ley Sobre Sociedades Anonimas, DO 22 Oct. 1981).
95. Ley 21.302/2020, of 22 Dec. (DO 5 Jan. 2021).

Aristotle and in part those of Saint Thomas[96]) into distributive and corrective (or commutative[97]) justice. Thus, it would move away from retributive justice, which is partly related to criminal law[98] and partly to be abandoned.[99] If distributive justice moves in proportion geometrically, corrective justice moves arithmetically.[100]

46. Although the doctrine identifies these two ideas of justice as relevant, positions are not unambiguous in their application.

Some scholars[101] associate subjective liability with corrective justice, because strict liability is based on distributive justice.

Other scholars[102] argue that both forms of justice (without specifying) are relevant, while still others submit that the two forms of justice are inseparably linked to tort liability. Although it is affirmed that 'la justicia correctiva es el principio que mejor explica la responsabilidad extracontractual'[103] (*corrective justice is the principle that best explains tort liability*) both because modern risks make this inadequate and because 'es imposible separar la responsabilidad extracontractual de las demandas de la justicia distributiva y correctiva'[104] (*it is impossible to separate tort liability from the demands of distributive and corrective justice*).

It is interesting to note that the presumption of fault of the entrepreneur for the actions of his employees is used to defend this inseparability[105] or to justify only

---

96. On this point in the Chilean doctrine in connection with civil liability: Alberto Pino Emhart, 'Entre reparación y distribución: La responsabilidad civil extracontractual como mecanismo de distribución de infortunios', *Revista Chilena de Derecho Privado*, 2013/21, at 92 y ss; Barros, *Tratado, I*, at 57 et seq.
97. Pino, in Chilean doctrine, observes how Saint Thomas preferred to use the term 'commutative justice' although Aristotle defined it as 'corrective justice': Pino, *Entre reparación*, cit. at 94.
98. Cf. Pino, 'Entre reparación', cit., at 95.
99. Hence, part of the doctrine refers to a 'decaimiento' (*decline*) of the idea of retributive justice, affirming that to accept it would imply linking the extent of compensation to the degree of fault when in fact this graduation should be ignored in order to fulfil the principle of integral reparation. Barros, *Tratado, I*, at 42.

    It should be noted, however, that case law provides for the award of greater amounts in cases of malice.
100. In this sense, the findings of Pino are interesting: Pino, 'Entre reparación', cit., at 93 y ss.
101. Gian Franco Rosso Elorriaga, 'El principio de la responsabilidad civil objetiva limitada: un elemento de equilibrio sistémico que no contradice al denominado principio de la reparación integral del daño', *Revista de Derecho Privado (Universidad Externado de Colombia)* 2014/26, at 464. On the association between strict liability and the distributive function (sic): Ruz, *Explicaciones*, cit., at 437.
102. Corral, *Lecciones*, cit., at 67–68. This author considers that distributive justice is contemplated in constitutional rights which, even if limited, are directed towards essential services, such as 'the right to social security (Art. 19. 18º Constitution)': Corral, *Lecciones*, cit., at 67.
103. Pino, 'Entre reparación', cit., at 91, especially p. 98 et seq.
104. Pino, 'Entre reparación', cit., at 90, especially at 101 et seq. The author writes that the two forms of justice are 'inseparable' and makes a reconstruction based on the influence of English doctrine (passim).
105. Pino, 'Entre reparación', cit., at 116 et seq. Other examples of this inseparability would be, in addition to the presumption of fault of the entrepreneur, the intervention of the role of insurance companies, the protection of the right to honour. A more critical approach is taken in relation to moral damage, *see* Pino, *Entre reparación*, cit., at 110 et seq. On moral damage, *see also* Alberto Pino Emhart, 'Justicia distributiva, responsabilidad civil y terremotos. Reflexiones en torno a los fundamentos de la responsabilidad civil'. *Derecho y Justicia*, 2011/1, at 16 et seq.

distributive justice by associating the presumption of fault with an objectification of responsibility.[106]

Finally, another viewpoint considers a dominant role of corrective justice that is the basis both in the case of subjective[107] liability and in that of strict liability.[108] This affirms[109] that the function of the law of civil liability is *compensatory* (or corrective) and not distributive, even if there is an exception in cases of vicarious liability.[110]

II. Principle of Repair

47. If one of the basic principles of civil liability is corrective justice.[111] then it is clear that a consequence of this is the principle of repair, whereby the party responsible for the damage must repair the harm.[112] Thus, Articles 2314 and 2329 CC reflect this principle by adopting, on the one hand, Gaius's dictum of *alterum non laedere*,[113] and on the other, by drawing on Domat's[114] teachings by modelling Article 2314 CC on the norm which establishes such the principle in the French Code (Article 1382 CCF of 1804).

106. Gonzalo Ruz Lártiga, *Explicaciones de Derecho Civil. Contratos y responsabilidad extracontractual*, IV (Santiago de Chile: Abeledo Perrot, Legal Publishing, 2011), at 437.
107. Barros, *Tratado, I*, cit., at 475 et seq.
108. Barros Bourie, Enrique, 'El contrato y el hecho que causa daño como antecedentes de la responsabilidad', *Estudios de Derecho Civil IV*. 297–313 (Carlos Pizarro Wilson ed.) (Santiago de Chile: Legal Publishing, 2009), at 301. On the problems relating corrective and distributive justice, *see also* Enrique Barros Bourie, 'Justicia y eficiencia como fines del derecho privado patrimonial', in *Estudios de Derecho Civil Código y dogmática en el Sesquicentenario de la Promulgación del Código Civil* (Juan Andrés Varas & Susan Turner, coords.) (Santiago de Chile: LexisNexis, 2005), at 15 et seq.
109. Barros, *Tratado, I*, cit., at 291. Likewise, 'el papel esencial del derecho civil es establecer reglas de responsabilidad por las consecuencias que se siguen de nuestros actos conforme a la justicia correctiva, pero no deberes positivos para asegurar el bienestar de los demás (según un concepto de justicia distributiva)' ('the essential role of civil law is to establish rules of responsibility for the consequences that follow from our acts in accordance with corrective justice, but not positive duties to ensure the welfare of others (according to a concept of distributive justice)') at 130.
110. According to the author, this is because vicarious liability includes corrective and distributive aspects. Barros, *Tratado, I*, cit., at 481.
111. *See* Enrique Barros Bourie, '¿Qué justifica imponer esponsabilidad civil por daños? l', *Estudios de Derecho Privado. En homenaje al prof. Daniel Peñailillo Arévalos*, (Santiago de Chile: Thomson Reuters, 2019), p. at 705 et seq.
112. Barros, *Tratado, I*, cit., at 225.
113. In fact, although Chilean doctrine also notes that a true general principle of responsibility was foreign to Roman law because restorative and sanctioning actions were not well separated (Ramón Domínguez Águila, 'Aspectos contemporáneos de la responsabilidad civil'. *Revista de Derecho Concepción*, 1989/185, at 111), it should be noted that the Digest Ulpianus enshrines the principle of *alterum non laedere* in one of the three main rules. Thus, 'Iuris praecepta sunt haec: honeste vivere, alterum non laedere, suum cuique tribuere' (D.01.I.10.1), that is, 'The precepts of law are these: to live honestly, not to harm others, to give to each his own.' An open access translation of the Digest has been realized by the Institute of Computational Linguistics 'Antonio Zampolli' of the CNR and by the Department of Legal Sciences of the University of Sapienza and is available here: https://.dbtvm1.ilc.cnr.it/digesto/Digesto_Home.html.
114. As Domínguez notes, 'Aspectos contemporáneos', cit., at 111–112.

48. Here the principle of repair aims to fully repair the damage[115] as 'corrective justice requires that the reparation of the damage be equivalent to the harm caused to the injured party'.[116] Thus, 'the purpose is to reintegrate the injured party's estate with the loss suffered as a consequence of the illicit act',[117] despite this not always possible. When this is not possible, the restorative function will become compensatory, since it will only be partial with respect to the total damage created.

It should be noted[118] that the principle of full compensation prevails in cases of pecuniary damages, while non-pecuniary damages (or moral harm) calls for compensatory principles to be applied. In fact, even if the monetary amount were increased, it would never be possible to return the injured party to the situation he was in prior to the occurrence of the harm, such as in the case of permanent damage to physical integrity.

Thus, making the injured party whole or compensating him to the extent possible is the 'primordial' principle[119] of civil liability. As such, this system of repairing damages would also be implicitly assumed by the Chilean Constitution[120] and associated with other functions. Some scholars support the dualistic principle of compensation by stating that contractual liability and tort liability have different functions.[121]

49. Last, although the 'sole objective of liability is the reparation of damage',[122] given the intrinsic limitations that may be experienced when compensating, this will 'not only be reparative but also compensatory or satisfactory'.[123] What is certain is that it is a single function that can be called indemnification, reparation, compensation, or satisfaction. However, taking on different nuances depends on whether one can obtain full reparation for the damage caused, since the intention is not to

115. *See* Carmen Domínguez Hidalgo, 'El principio de reparación integral del daño: sus contornos', in *Estudios de Derecho Civil VIII*, (Domínguez Hidalgo, Carmen; González Castillo, Joel; Barrientos Zamorano, Marcelo; Goldenberg Serrano, Juan Luis, coord..), (Santiago de Chile: Legal Publishing, 2013), at 561 et seq.; Ruz, *La reparacion*, cit., at 661 et seq.; Barros, *Tratado, I*, cit., at 267; Corral, *Lecciones*, cit., at 377; Ruz, *Explicaciones*, cit., at 445; Cristián Aedo Barrena, *Responsabilidad extracontractual* (Santiago de Chile: Librotecnia, 2006), at 22.
116. Barros, *Tratado, I*, cit., at 224.
117. Tapia, *De la responsabilidad*, cit., at 313.
118. Barros, *Tratado, I*, cit., at 224.
119. Corral, *Lecciones*, cit., at 60; Barros, *Tratado, I*, cit., at 43.
120. As Corral, *Lecciones*, cit., at 69 et seq. observes and analyses.
121. Adrían Schopf Olea, 'Las diferencias funcionales entre la responsabilidad civil contractual y extracontractual'. in *Presente y futuro de la responsabilidad civil* (Rodrigo Barría Díaz & Alfredo Ferrante & Lilian San Martín Neira ed.) (Santiago de Chile: Thomson Reuters, 2017), at 61 et seq. Thus, the extracontractual responsabilidad would externalize negative duties of conduct oriented to the 'protection of our most fundamental goods' and the contractual one in 'positive duties of conduct oritati to implement for the benefit of other people' (*supra*, at 71).
122. Alessandri, *Responsabilidad*, cit., at 29.
123. Alessandri, *Responsabilidad*, cit., at 167.

award an amount that is less than the damage suffered.[124] Nevertheless, it is also true that insurance policies have contributed to a partial revision of the liability structure.[125]

III. Other Functions

A. *Economic Analysis of Law and the Punitive Function*

50. It should be noted that discussing the functions of liability, many Chilean authors have made general considerations that were not necessarily in line with the Chilean context, meaning they have spoken of various functions[126] in the abstract. Thus, reference has been made to the conception that this plays in the economic analysis of law or to the punitive function.

51. The Chilean doctrine has been critical of the economic analysis of law, which would have a general prevention in administrative law and a special prevention in private law.[127] It has been clearly stated that the economic analysis of law would encourage a shift from the indemnification function to the 'preventive social function',[128] or that 'it would move away from corrective justice'.[129]

52. The punitive function[130] must be distinguished from the sanctioning function. If the punitive one 'excede el perjuicio efectivo sufrido por la víctima y que cumplen una función vindicativa y preventiva'[131] (*exceeds the actual damage suffered by the victim and fulfils a punitive and deterrent function*), the sanctioning one is not necessarily over compensatory.[132]

The recognition of the punitive function in foreign jurisdictions has been abstractly[133] considered. A part of the doctrine declines to accept this function in a

124. Tapia, *De la responsabilidad*, cit., at 311.

125. On the point Domínguez, 'Aspectos contemporáneos', cit., at 126 et seq., also Pino, 'Entre reparación', cit., at 113 et seq. *See* para. 532.

126. In riferimento alla polifunzionalità della responsabilità civile si é evidenziato che avrebbe anche una funzione sociale o assistenziale. With reference to the polyfunctionality of civil liability, it has been highlighted that it would also have a social or welfare function Lilian San Martín Neira, '¿Hacia una función social o asistencial de la responsabilidad civil?', *Estudios de Derecho Privado, II Jornadas Nacionales de Profesoras de Derecho Privado* (María Elisa Morales Ortiz, Pamela Mendoza Alonzo ed.) (Santiago de Chile: DER, 2020), at 29 et seq.

127. Barros, *Tratado, I*, cit., at 51–52.

128. Barros, *Tratado, I*, cit., at 225.

129. Pino, 'Justicia distributiva'. cit., at 5 et seq. For others the económico analysis of law would lead to an *institutional function of* civil responsibility: Corral, *Lecciones*, cit., at 65.

130. *See* paras 547 et seq.

131. Ramos, *De la responsabilidad*, cit., at 2.

132. Apart from the punitive damages, this doctrine notes that a kind of sanctioning function would be manifested in certain norms such as Art. 1768 CC in relation to fraud and wilful abduction in the conjugal society; Art. 1693 CC; the deprivation of the action of nullity by concealing the contract knowing the defect that invalidates it (Art. 1683 CC) or the incapable who acts with malice to induce to contract (Art. 1685 CC): Corral, *Lecciones*, cit., at 64.

133. For example, *see* Aedo, *Responsabilidad*, cit., at 43 et seq. Barros, *Tratado, I*, cit., at 226.

national context, stating that 'non deve ser importada'[134] (*it must not be imported*) and that 'debe tenerse mucho cuidado de copiar conclusiones que son ajenas a nuestro sistema legal, especialmente las de Estados Unidos'[135] (*we must take great care to copy conclusions that are alien to our legal system, especially those of the United States*).

Another part of the doctrine[136] recognizes this general tendency and abstractly justifies it in the evolution of fault. Although it is clearly established that the function of damages is strictly compensatory and restorative,[137] it has been observed that the Chilean case law incorporates the punitive element when assessing immaterial harm.[138]

53. Although at present one must consider with caution the affirmation that 'in Chile, no existen las llamadas indemnizaciones punitivas'[139] (*in Chile, there are no punitive damages*), since it is possible to identify a punitive function in matters of consumer protection where, in the event of unjustified suspension or termination of the provision of basic services (such as, for example, drinking water, gas, energy, telephone, etc.) compensation equivalent to 'ten times the daily average of that billed in the previous bill' (Article 25 Ley 19.496) is provided for each day of default. cf. Article 25 Ley 19.496).[140]

B. Demarcation and Expressive Function

54. Generally speaking, among the complementary functions of civil liability, it has been considered to have a demarcation function with regards to the freedom of private individuals, establishing what is permitted and what is not.[141] In the wake and influence of the English doctrine, the 'expressive' or 'communicative' function has also been advocated. This 'would not only be aimed at obtaining compensation for damage, but would also manifest or communicate a specific message such as the claim of violated rights or liability by damaging party'.[142] Civil liability 'should place the victim in a position as close as possible to being able to forgive his or her

134. Corral, *Lecciones* cit., at 64.
135. Abeliuk, *Las Obligaciones. I,* cit., at 202.
136. Dominguez, 'Algunas consideraciones', cit., at 599. In this sense for this doctrine considers que estrattamente the functions would be the punitive, preventive and compensatory.
137. Barros, *Tratado, I*, cit., at 226.
138. Barros, *Tratado, I*, cit., at 226, note to pié no. 9 & at 326 et seq.
139. Ramos, *De la responsabilidad,* cit., at 2.
140. Note also the possibility of increasing the amount of compensation by 25% in certain cases (*see* Arts 24.5 and 53 C Ley 19.496). On the compensatory regime in the event of suspension of the supply of electricity, also in relation to special legislation, *see* Carrasco Astudillo, Gonzalo, *El régimen compensatorio por suspensión del suministro eléctrico* (Santiago de Chile: Rubicón, 2020).
141. They highlight this function in these terms: Corral, *Lecciones*, scit., at 60; Ruz, *Explicaciones*, cit. at 436.
142. Alberto Pino Emhart, 'No sólo quieren dinero: La función expresiva de la responsabilidad extracontractual', in *Presente y futuro de la responsabilidad civil* (Rodrigo Barría Díaz & Alfredo Ferrante & Lilian San Martín Neira ed.) (Santiago de Chile: Thomson Reuters, 2017), at 176.

offender',[143] so the communicative function could manifest itself through the different concessions in relation to the economic situation of the injured party.[144]

C. Preventive Function

55. The deterrent function has also been highlighted as complementary, although it has always been cited in abstract terms.[145] With this in mind, there are only a few studies that have taken a clear and detailed position on compliance with a general character[146] or in relation to specific norms or concrete laws.[147] To better understand this, it is necessary to make some general reflections and analyse the unusual aspects of the Chilean system.

56. To this end, it is necessary to highlight a peculiarity of the Chilean codification in the drafting of the civil liability structure. Not only does it draw on French influence,[148] but the presence of Articles 2333, 2334 CC (peculiar innovations of Andrés Bello) should also be highlighted. For these provisions, a class action is allowed when certain people may be harmed due to imprudence or negligence. Those who have studied the subject in detail[149] will note its preventive

143. Pino, 'No sólo quieren', cit., at 175
144. Thus it is stated that 'debería por ejemplo tener una nueva relevancia de la situación económica como criterio para determinar el monto de compensación material requerida en un caso particular' (*should, for example, have a new relevance of the economic situation as a criterion for determining the amount of material compensation required in a particular case*): Pino, 'No sólo quieren', cit., at 174.
145. Aedo, *Responsabilidad*, cit., at 22; Corral, *Lecciones*, cit., at 61; Carmen Domínguez Hidalgo, 'Algunas consideraciones en torno a la función de la responsabilidad civil', *Estudios de Derecho Civil Código y dogmática en el Sesquicentenario de la Promulgación del Código Civil* (Juan Andrés Varas & Susan Turner, coords.), (Santiago de Chile: LexisNexis, 2005), at 599; Ruz, Explicaciones, cit., at 438.
146. Aldo Molinari Valdés, *De la responsabilidad civil al derecho de daños y tutela preventiva civil*, (Santiago de Chile: LexisNexis, Ia edición, Santiago, 2004).
147. Rodrigo Barría Díaz, 'La función preventiva o disuasoria de la responsabilidad civil, a propósito de las leyes de Propiedad Intelectual y de Propiedad Industrial'. *Presente y futuro de la responsabilidad civil* (Rodrigo Barría Díaz & Alfredo Ferrante & Lilian San Martín Neira ed, Santiago de Chile: Thomson Reuters, 2017), at 177 et seq., José Luis Diez Schwerter, 'La acción de daño contingente del artículo 2333 del Código Civil chileno: sus elementos y ámbito de aplicación', *Revista de Derecho de (PUCV)* (2016/46), at 151. *See also* paras 355 et seq., 416.
148. Having been influenced, for example, not only by Roman sources, but also by García Goyena's draft Spanish code, the Louisiana code, and the Prussian code: Javier Barrientos Grandón, *El código civil. Su jurisprudencia e historia. Edición crítica, concordada y anotada* I y II (Santiago de Chile: Thomson Reuters, 2016); Amunátegui Perelló, *Carlos Código Civil de Chile, Edición anotada, concordada y con fuentes*, (Valencia: Tirant Lo Blanch, 2019, at 589 et seq.).
149. On Art. 2333 and 2334 CC: Schwerter, *La acción*, cit.; José Luis Díez Schwerter, & Verónica Delgado Schneider, 'Algunas útiles herramientas olvidadas en nuestra práctica del Derecho de Daños', Revista *de Derecho Universidad de Concepción,* 2005/214, at 144–148; José Luis Díez Schwerter, 'Notas sobre la acción preventiva de daños del artículo 2333 del Código Civil, Revista de Derecho Universidad de Concepción, 2005/217–218, at 317; José Luis Díez Schwerter, 'La acción de daño contingente del artículo 233 del Código Civil: sus elementos y ámbito de aplicación', *Revista de Derecho* (PUCV,Valparaíso), (2016/46), at 133 et seq. José Luis Díez Schwerter, 'La aplicación de

function.[150] This is why the provisions on civil tort liability contained in the Chilean Civil Code convey two functions: the (predominant) sanctioning function and the preventive function of Articles 2333 and 2334 CC.

57. Alternately, if the tort liability framework was traditionally circumscribed in a limited number of articles of the Civil Code (Title XXXV of Book IV, Articles 2314–2334), new special laws should modify the perspective. This should be done by introducing ad hoc norms that have influenced the classic concept of subjective fault, and the possible functions of liability.

58. Here the doctrine defends a 'preventive or dissuasive'[151] position regarding offences relating to intellectual[152] or industrial[153] property. The preventive function of Article 85 E (in conjunction with Article 85 D)[154] of the Law on Intellectual Property and Article 108[155] of the Law on Industrial Property is noted. Thus, on the one hand, it also relies on a minority opinion[156] of a Constitutional Court decision, which clearly affirms a deterrent function of Article 108.[157]

59. On the other hand, there are some reflections on the possibility that the protection established by these two articles is compensation or restitution. If the action

---

la acción por daño contingente en Chile, Colombia y Ecuador: del modelo de Bello a nuestros días', *Revista de Derecho Privado (Universidad Externado de Colombia)*, 2016/30, at 257 et seq.

150. Molinari, *De la responsabilidad,* cit., at 201 et seq., e.g., Schwerter, *La acción de daño contingente,* cit., at 151; Lilian San Martín Neira, 'Desastres naturales y responsabilidad civil. Identificación de los desafíos que presenta esta categoría de hechos dañinos', *Revista de Derecho* (*Valdivia*), 2019/2, at 135. Some hold that the action provided under these two articles has consonance with the figure of injunctions in the common law system: Barría, *La función preventiva*, cit., at 189, footnote 23.
151. Although sometimes used as synonyms, the author himself clarifies and is aware that deterrent effects can also be attributed to the *sancionadora* (sanctioning) function of civil liability: Barría, *La función preventiva*, cit., at 178.
152. Ley 17.336/1970, of 28 Aug. (DO 2 Oct. 1970) as amended.
153. Ley 19.039/1991, of 24 Jan. (DO 25 Jan. 1970), as amended.
154. As introduced by Law 20.435/2010, of 23 Apr., amending the Law on Intellectual Property (DO 4 May 2010).
155. As introduced by Ley 19.996/1996, of 25 Feb. that modifies the Industrial Property Law (DO 11 Mar. 2005).
156. Barría, *La función preventiva*, cit., at 212–213.
157. STC 14Jan. 2014 (rol 2365-12-INA) https://www.camara.cl/verDoc.aspx?prmTipo=SIAL&prmID=10787&formato=pdf.

   Effectively, the minority vote of Ministers Raúl Bertelsen Repetto and Juan José Romero talking about the responsibility of the Industrial Property Act that 'puede también contribuir a la disuasión de conductas violatorias de la ley en este tipo de materias. Por consiguiente, el artículo 108, letra b), consagra la obligación del infractor de pagar una suma de dinero que va más allá de una finalidad meramente compensatoria de los daños que a la víctima pudo ocasionarle la infracción' ('*can also contribute to the deterrence of conduct in violation of the law in this type of matter. Therefore, Art. 108, letter b), enshrines the obligation of the infringer to pay a sum of money that goes beyond a merely compensatory purpose for the damages that the infringement may have caused to the victim*').

   The judgment of the Constitutional Court affirms that the penalty imposed by the Supreme Court under Art. 108 b) was excessive in view of the constitutional principle and the principle of proportionality.

pursuant to Article 108 is clearly established,[158] there should be no doubt as to whether it is an action of indemnification or restitution. Additionally, there is a possibility for 'conceptual confusion'[159] in relation to Article 85 E.[160] It could be interpreted that this is externalized in an action of indemnification or restitution, but opting for restitution in this case.

Last, it is ultimately found that merely because interpretations of this nature are possible does not prejudice the function of the two norms, which continues to serve a preventive protection (remaining aware that such could be interpreted as a punitive action[161]) since in both situations the amount to be returned or compensated may exceed what actually needs to be compensated or returned.[162]

60. The preventive function of liability in other specific contexts (to which general liability rules would apply) has also been generally defended.

Thus, those who have dealt with climate change liability have considered that the mere presence of a general liability rule (such as that of Articles 2314 et seq. CC) would realize preventive function in relation to climate change liability in connection with the emission of greenhouse gases (GEI).[163]

More open is the position that liability should be greater in cases of natural disasters, especially earthquakes, which are a common occurrence in Chile.[164] In these cases, distributive justice would be 'a good example to put into practice'.[165] For others,[166] it must be observed, the 'gestión y *prevención* de los desastre naturales' (*management and prevention of natural disasters*) would be preventive and compensatory in nature.

To prevent environmental damage, some scholars argue in favour of the preventive protection of Articles 2333 and 2334 CC.[167]

158. Barría, *La función preventiva*, cit., at 208.
159. Barría, *La función preventiva,* cit., at 203.
160. Cf. paras 426 and 544.
161. Barría, *La función preventiva,* cit., at 211–212.
162. Barría, *La función preventiva,* cit., at 209.
163. Cristián Banfi del Río, 'Sobre la responsabilidad civil por cambio climático en Chile', *Acta Bioethica*, 2019/2, at 155.
164. *See* San Martín, 'Desastre naturales', cit., at 123 et seq.; Lilian San Martín, 'Desastres Naturales y responsabilidad civil: posible concurso causal entre actividad humana y fenómeno natural', *Estudios de derecho civil XIV* (Maricruz Gómez de la Torre Vargas, Gabriel Hernández Paulsen, Fabiola Lathrop Gómez, Mauricio Tapia Rodríguez ed.) (Santiago de Chile: Thomson Reuters, 2019) at 1149 et seq.; Lilian San Martín Neira, 'Algunos problemas de causalidad en la jurisprudencia sobre el 27F', *Estudios de derecho civil XV* (Fabian Elorriaga De Bonis ed.) (Santiago de Chile: Thomson Reuters, 2020) at 995 et seq.
165. Pino, 'Justicia distributiva', cit., at 1 et seq., especially pp. 23 et seq.
166. San Martín, 'Desastre naturales', cit., at 126.
167. According to Corral, *Lecciones*, cit., at 414, these provisions could be applied to the *Ley de Bases generales del Medio Ambiente* (Ley 19.300) in function of the supplementary role attributed to the Civil Code by Art. 51.3 of that law.

61. Ultimately there has been an effort to redeem the function in specific areas such as intellectual property liability, while analysing the criticisms[168] against this approach and implementing them.[169]

However, it should be noted that the preventive function operates before[170] the damage occurs.

With this in mind, speaking about preventive liability in relation to civil liability would not be adequate. If it is assumed that damage is a requirement of liability, then by definition civil liability cannot perform a preventive function given that its establishment presupposes damage and hence does not avoid it. This is why the legislative technique associated with regulating a liability case can prevent damage, but not civil liability (*stricto sensu).* Furthermore, the actual preventive value of Articles 2333 and 2334 CC can be understood, provided the damage is not presumed to exist and is instead considered to be an eventual[171] consequence of the risk. There is also another norm with an exclusively preventive function in the Chilean Civil Code. Sharing the opinion of those who have already observed it,[172] another example may be found in the second paragraph of Article 2328.2 CC, which, drawing[173] from the ancient Roman action *actio de positis vel suspensis*, states that an action may be brought to remove an asset from the possession of its holder in order to avoid its ruin or any damage it may cause.

§4. Relationship Between Tort and Criminal Law

62. Legal responsibility is not the same as moral responsibility.[174] Although the two can sometimes interact and civil liability[175] may also arise from the latter, there are differences just as there are differences between civil and criminal responsibility (although they are intimately related in some cases).

---

168. On the analysis of the criticisms which in general (not only in Chile) have been made of preventive protection: Barría, *La función preventiva*, cit., at 190–193. Some of these criticisms, however, would also be applicable to the compensation function and not only the preventive function (such as those in relation to the fact that the extent of compensation does not always bear relation to the actual damage caused, the limited function in the case of the fact that the payment is made by the insurance company, the fact that the function would persuade those with fewer assets, or the fact that it would be less practicable in cases where the damage is due to errors or mistakes, or the fact that the preventive effects could not be achieved in the case of malicious damage).
169. The author rebuts the criticism: Barría, *La función preventiva*, cit., at 194–200.
170. Ruz, *Explicaciones*, cit., at 438.
171. Hence, the doctrine considers that the '*daño contingente*' (incidental damage) pursuant to Art. 2333 CC is potential and not a future damage, therefore arguing that '*what characterizes incidental damage is the likelihood that the event constituting it will later result in actual damage*': Tapia, *De la Responsabilidad*, cit., at 196.
172. On the analysis of the criticisms that in general (not only in Chile) have been made of preventive protection: Barría, *La función preventiva*, cit., at 189.
173. Reference is made to Barría's study on this topic: Rodrigo Barría Díaz, 'Actio de efusis vel deiectis y actio depotis vel suspensis: antecedentes, contenudo y protección en la moderna responsabilidad contractual', *Revista de Estudios Histórico-Jurídicos*, 2018/XL, in particular at 571–572. Ramos, *De la responsabilidad Civil*, cit. at 75.
174. Tapia, *De la responsabilidad*, cit., at 5.
175. Abeliuk, *Las Obligaciones*, I, cit., at, at 203.

63. Title XXXV of Book IV of the Civil Code (Articles 2314 CC et seq.), which traditionally represents the section on tort liability, is entitled 'De los delitos y de los cuasidelitos' (crime and quasi-delicts). What is certain, however, is that it considers the difference between crime and quasi-delict to be 'idle'[176] and in a certain sense 'useless'[177] since as the illicit nature of both[178] gives rise to an obligation to repair the damage caused.[179] For this reason, part of the doctrine had already preferred to use the expression 'illicit facts',[180] even if would not be exhaustive, given the recent phenomena that can be generated in the case of liability for lawful acts.[181]

64. It is considered that tort liability arises (also combining it with Articles 1437 and 2284 CC) when damage has been caused intentionally (in which case the act is a *delito*) or accidentally (in which case the act is a *cuasidelito*[182]). Therefore, if the crime is characterized by an *animus nocendi*, the quasi-delito is related to imprudence, negligence or carelessness (*imprudencia, negligencia, descuido*).[183] Consequently, the psychological element, i.e., whether one intends to cause damage,[184] is the determining factor in classification of the act.

As a result, tort liability has also been defined as 'delictual liability', and as such is considered a source of legal obligation to pay compensation for damage caused wilfully or culpably.[185]

---

176. Meza, *Manual, II,* cit., at 246.
177. Alessandri, *De la responsabilidad*, cit., at 15.
178. Alessandri, *De la responsabilidad*, cit., at 15. Notwithstanding this distinction, it would be useful in the case of clauses that limit liability since, in the case of contractual liability, the condonation of future malice is not valid in accordance with Art. 1465 CC while, alternately, it can be excluded in the case of fault on condition that this is not *culpa grave* (gross negligence) (op. cit., p. 16).
179. Meza, *Manual, II*, cit., at 246.
180. For Tapia, this expression would also include the difference between acts and torts since the genre would be the facts, of which the acts would constitute a special category: Tapia, *De la responsabilidad*, cit. at 152. Similarly, Figueroa, *Curso IV*, cit., at 56.
181. As in the case of state liability: CS 20 Nov. 2012 (Rol 9924-2010), *see* with commentary by Luís Cordero Vega, 'Las Vacas Locas y la responsabilidad del Estado por acto lícito', *Mercurio Legal* 22.12.2012); Álvaro Quintanilla Pérez, '¿Responsabilidad del Estado por actos lícitos?' *Revista de Ciencias Sociales*, 1999/44, at 28i et seq. Chilean doctrine has dealt with 'lawful damage':

    Carlos Céspedes Muñoz, 'El daño lícito reparable y su proyección en el sistema chileno: concepto y naturaleza', *Ius et Praxis*, 2018/1, at 129 et seq., Carlos Céspedes Muñoz, 'Notas sobre la denominada "responsabilidad" por acto lícito en el derecho civil.: Reconociendo a las compensaciones por sacrificio', *Ius et Praxis*, 2021/2, 2021, at 114 et seq.; more generally Carlos Céspedes Muñoz, *El daño lícito* (Madrid: La Ley, 2016), *passim*.

182. Alessandri, *De la responsabilidad*, cit., at 14.
183. Alessandri, *De la responsabilidad*, cit. at 14, in the same sense Tapia, *De la responsabilidad*, cit. at 146.
184. Figueroa, *Curso, IV*, cit., at 95. Meza, *Manual, II*, cit. at 245–246, mentioning the psychological element.
185. Tapia, *De la responsabilidad*, cit. at 358.

65. Essentially, civil law doctrine adopts in part the concepts of *delito,*[186] which can be inferred from Articles 1 and 2 of the penal code.[187] Despite this, there is a clear position that the definition would not coincide since, in the criminal sphere, these situations can refer to the typified cases, while the spectrum is broader in the civil sphere. In this sense, if only the criminal cases are sanctioned *ex lege*, there is no case history in the civil field.[188] Although it has been appropriately pointed out that in the presence of a failure to act, liability for omission is essentially triggered by a statutory provision imposing the obligation to perform the omitted act,[189] as may be the case, for example, in certain instances of liability arising from the failure to comply with the administrative law (*culpa infraccional por omisión*).[190] In addition, an important differentiation between a civil and criminal offence and quasi-criminal offence is highlighted by the doctrine in the case of Article 2314 CC.[191]

66. In any case, it is evident that criminal responsibility and civil responsibility are clearly different.[192] For instance, the protected interest is different: in the criminal context, a 'social order'[193] is protected, while civil law aims to protect private interests related to any damage incurred.[194]

67. A crime or quasi-delict may result in a civil or criminal conviction, or both. What is relevant here are the hypotheses in which quasi-delicts give rise to the legal

---

186. The word 'delito' in Arts 2314 et seq. CC includes all criminal offences resulting from intent and is translated hereinafter as 'crime' also in relation to Art. 1 CP. If these offences are committed by negligence, they are associated with *cuasidelito*.
187. Art. 1 CP 'Es delito toda acción u omisión voluntaria penada por la ley' (*Any wilful act or omission punishable by law is a crime*).

 Las acciones u omisiones penadas por la ley se reputan siempre voluntarias, a no ser que conste lo contrario (*Actions or omissions punishable by law are always presumed to be voluntary, unless there is evidence to the contrary*).

 El que cometiere delito será responsable de él e incurrirá en la pena que la ley señale, aunque el mal recaiga sobre persona distinta de aquella a quien se proponía ofender. En tal caso no se tomarán en consideración las circunstancias, no conocidas por el delincuente, que agravarían su responsabilidad; pero sí aquellas que la atenúen (*Whoever commits a crime shall be responsible for it and shall incur the penalty prescribed by law, even if the injury falls upon a person other than the one whom he intended to offend. In such a case, circumstances not known to the offender that would aggravate his liability shall not be taken into consideration, but those that mitigate it shall be taken into consideration*).

 Art. 2.2 CP: 'Las acciones u omisiones que cometidas con dolo o malicia importarían un delito, constituyen cuasidelito si sólo hay culpa en el que las comete' (*The actions or omissions that are committed with intent or malice shall constitute a crime, or a quasi-delict if only offender has committed the crime*).
188. *See* Meza, *Manual, II*, cit. at 247; Alessandri, *De la responsabilidad*, cit. at 18.
189. Tapia, *De la responsabilidad*, cit. at 148.
190. Barros, *Tratado, I*, at 133–135.
191. Javier Barrientos Grandon, 'De la presunción general de culpa por el hecho propio. A propósito de los artículos 2314 y 2319 de nuestro "código civil imaginario" (II)', *Revista Chilena de Derecho Privado*, (2009/13, at 9.
192. For a parallel between the two forms of liability in general, *see* Abeliuk, *Las Obligaciones*. I, cit., at 203–204; Figueroa, *Curso IV*, cit., at 71–72; Corral, *Lecciones*, cit., at 43–44.
193. E.g., Meza, *Manual... de las obligaciones, II*, cit., at 247; Figueroa, *Curso, IV*, cit., at 67.
194. E.g., Figueroa, *Curso, IV*, cit. at 68.

obligation to pay damages and abstractly constitute a crime or a criminal offence (or quasi-delict), and whether an *ex delicto* civil liability may be established in either civil or criminal[195] courts (in the terms that will be discussed below).

The possibility of being able to condemn for compensation pertaining to damages also in the criminal court (Article 24 CP) creates this circumstance. Therefore, the foundation of civil responsibility *ex delicto* is based both on Article 2324 CC, the parallel norm in the civil court, and Article 24 CP.[196] This considers that the plaintiff has an 'alternative right'[197] to take recourse to the civil or criminal court for compensation for damages, even if it seems to give priority to the civil court. Due to being affirmed, it would be admitted for 'reasons of procedural economy' to take recourse to the criminal court as well.

68. Despite time bars for bringing criminal action being longer than those for civil action (*see* Article 94 CP), the statute of limitations for claiming compensation for damages in criminal proceedings is the same as those in in civil proceedings.[198] There are some peculiarities that pertain to the interruption of the limitation period.

Thus, on the one hand, the criminal action suspends the statute of limitations of the civil action provided a claim is made within sixty days of the suspension or termination of the criminal proceedings (Articles 68.1 y 68.2 CPP). On the other hand, if there is a claim for compensation in the criminal proceedings, it is considered that the 'preparation of the civil claim' interrupts the limitation period (*see* Article 61.3 CPP). Notwithstanding the literal wording of the provision, doctrine[199] has argued that notice must be given of such a claim.

69. An important role is played by the application of the procedures established which come from a combination of non-homogeneous rules, which intentionally refer to various texts. Thus, in addition to the Civil Code, the Penal Code,[200] the Code of Civil Procedure (*código de procedimiento civil*),[201] the Code of Criminal Procedure (*código procesal penal*)[202] and the Organizational Rules of Courts

195. On the concrete process of formulating the claim of civil liability in criminal proceedings, *see* Barros, *Tratado, II*, at 1068 et seq.
196. Similar to Figueroa, *Curso, IV*, cit., at 68–69.
197. CS 27 June 2007 (rol 45/2006).
198. The Penal Code expressly states that 'the statute of limitations for civil responsibility arising from an offence is governed by the Civil Code' ('*La prescripción de la responsabilidad civil proveniente de delito, se rige por el Código civil*': Art. 105.2 CP). In this case, if the liability is in tort, it will be four years (cf. Art. 2332 CC).
199. Barros, *Tratado, II*, at 1069.
200. *See e.g.*, Arts 1,2, 24, 59–68 CP.
201. *See e.g.*, Arts 167, 178–180 CPC.
202. *See e.g.*, Arts 59–68, 108, 242–246 CPP.

(*Código orgánico de tribunales*)[203] play a role, as does the Law on the Criminal Responsibility of Adolescents.[204] An important role was also played by the reform of the Penal Code in 2005.[205]

70. Before analysing liability claims, and therefore the possibility of receiving compensation for damages, it should be noted that, in criminal law, there are two other actions that are civil in nature but not strictly compensatory.

The first is the action for restitution which functions to regain possession of property.[206] This action can only be exercised in the criminal courts (Articles 59.1 CCP, 171 COT) since it is not possible to bring action alternatively in either to the civil or criminal courts (unlike in the *ex delicto* civil liability action).

The second is provided by another category of civil action[207] (other than the action for restitution pursuant to Article 59.2 CCP), which can be exercised in either civil or criminal proceedings. It has been carefully observed that if the action of the restitution of an object must be exercised strictly in the criminal court, the action for the restitution of the value of an object would instead fall into this second category; as a result, it could be claimed both in civil and criminal courts.[208]

71. The 2005 reform[209] of the code of civil procedure has played an important role in this matter and has shifted the focus from the criminal to the civil[210] sphere, which can be seen[211] from the fact that in the criminal sphere compensation can only be made in the ordinary procedure, allowing only restitutionary action in the simplified procedure (Article 393 CPP). This is not possible in the summary proceedings (Article 412 final paragraph CPP).[212] Despite this, and in accordance with the reform of Article 680 N. 10 CPC, part of the doctrine affirms that although it is not possible to have recourse to summary proceedings (as such are not an ideal way to discover the truth), the admission of facts in the summary judgment could be used

---

203. *See* Arts 171, 173, 174 COT.
204. Ley 20.084(2005, of 28 Nov. establishes a system of adolescent responsibility for criminal law infractions (DO 7 Dec. 2005):, *see e.g.*, Arts 1, 6, 10, 52.
205. The reform of the *Código procesal Penal* of 2000 (Ley 19.696) was carried out in 2005 by Ley 20.074/2005, of 9 Nov. de 2005 (DO 14 Nov. 2005). It should be recalled that the *Código de procedimiento penal* de 1906 (Ley 1853) still exists but with limited application. In this sense, *see* Arts 10–17.
206. On this point, *see e.g.*, Barros, *Tratado, II*, at 1062 et seq.; Corral, *Lecciones*, cit., at 48.
207. For example, Arts 370, 389, 410, 438 CP; on this point, *see* Barros, *Tratado, II*, at 1066.
208. In this sense Barros, *Tratado, II*, at 1066–1067.
209. For an analysis of the system prior to the reform, *see e.g.*, Carlos Achiardi Echeverría, 'Sobre la procedencia de la responsabilidad civil ex delicto en ciertas hipótesis penales', *Revista de Derecho de la Universidad Católica de Valparaíso* (1999/20), at 195 et seq.
210. Juan Carlos Marín González, 'La acción civil en el nuevo código penal procesal chielno: su tratamiento procesal', *Revista de Estudios de la Justicia*, 2005/6, at 12. Carlos Pizarro Wilson, 'Acción civil en el nuevo proceso penal. Legitimación activa. Víctimas por rebote', *Revista Chilena de Derecho Privado*, 2005/3,at 155 et seq.
211. As submitted by Marin, *La acción civil*, cit., at 12.
212. Marín observes, moreover, that this primacy is found in the possibility of continuing the civil liability proceeding in civil court even if it has been initiated in criminal court and the latter proceeding concludes before commencing the hearing (170 CPP) or the case is suspended (Art. 237 CPP): Marin, *La acción civil*, cit., at 12.

as an extrajudicial confession in the civil trial summary under certain circumstances.[213] Another factor that has given priority to civil jurisdiction is the limitation of standing in criminal proceedings, which is more extensive in civil[214] proceedings. Therefore, the proceedings that are brought against a person other than the accused must take place in civil proceedings (Article 59.3 CPP). Additionally, the passage from criminal to civil jurisdiction has effectively been carried out when compensation for moral damage (initially only awarded in criminal proceedings for moral damage deriving from a crime, a criminal offence or quasi-delict),[215] was allowed.

72. In terms of the right to bring proceedings (or 'active procedural legitimacy'), the 2005 reform entitles only the 'victim'[216](Article 59 CPP), although this concept can be considered in a broad sense given that the victim must be considered the person 'offended by the crime' (or criminal offence) (*ofendido por el delito*: Article 108 CPP). Thus, in the event of death, there is a pre-emptive order for certain family members that specifically excludes other parties.[217] It is interesting to note that despite that paragraph (a) of the provision 'spouse or civil partner and children' (*al cónyuge o al conviviente civil y a los hijos*) is mentioned, in some cases the preposition 'and' (*y*) is not considered to be cumulative (notwithstanding a spouse (or civil partner) and children included – and not excluded – under the same letter (a)). Thus, if compensation is granted to the spouse, it cannot be granted to the children or grandchildren.[218] If there is no doubt that grandchildren can be in another category or identified by another letter, then the children's case is more

213. This is the thesis of Ried, for whom a sort of validated 'verdad negociada' (*negotiated truth*) exists as an out-of-court confession under Art. 398 CPC: Ried, Ignacio Ried Undurraga, 'El efecto de la sentencia condenatoria del procedimiento abreviado en el juicio indemnizatorio por responsabilidad civil ex delicto'. *Ius et praxis*, 2017/1, at 579 et seq., especially pp. 608 et seq. Art. 680 n. 10 CPC was reformed by Law No. 20.192 de 2007 (DO 26.06.2007). Said provision makes applicable to the summary judgments the judgments related to Art. 59 CPP on condition that there is an enforced condemnatory criminal judgment ('*sentencia penal condenatoria ejecutoriada*'). The problem arises when there is a partial agreement in the presence of a plurality of defendants (pp. 614 et seq.). In civil proceedings against a third party civilly liable, alternately, the criminal conviction will serve as simple proof since the third party was not a defendant in the proceedings (p. 612).

214. Marin observes, moreover, that this primacy is found in the possibility of continuing the civil liability proceedings in civil proceedings even if they have been started in criminal proceedings and these proceedings are concluded before starting the oral judgment (170 CPP) or the case is suspended (Art. 237 CPP): thus, opportunely: Marin, *La acción civil*, cit., at 12 and 21 et seq.

215. Carlos Pizarro Wilson, 'Mirada de un civilista a la reparación en el nuevo proceso penal'. *Gaceta Jurídica*, 2003/296, at 59 et seq.

216. Figueroa, *Curso, IV*, cit., at 69.

217. *See* Arts 108.2 and 108.3 CPP. Art. 108.2 CPP: 'En los delitos cuya consecuencia fuere la muerte del ofendido y en los casos en que éste no pudiere ejercer los derechos que en este Código se le otorgan, se considerará víctima: a) al cónyuge o al conviviente civil y a los hijos; b) a los ascendientes; c) al conviviente; d) a los hermanos, y e) al adoptado o adoptante' ('*In crimes that result in the death of the victim and in cases where the victim is unable to exercise the rights granted in this Code, the following shall be considered victims: a) the spouse or civil partner and children; b) ascendants; c) cohabitant; d) siblings; and e) adopted or adoptive parents*').

218. CS 2 June 2004 (confirms Tribunal de juicio criminal hearing Valparaiso 3 May 2004); the judgment is commented by Pizarro, *Acción civil*, cit., at 155 et seq.

objectionable.[219] Another problem is the direct and indirect action associated with the death exercised by family members (*iure proprio* and *iure hereditatis),* which is analysed elsewhere.[220]

73. In relation to passive procedural legitimacy, the action can only be directed at the defendant (Article 59.3 CPP). In this regard, two limitations must be clarified in the criminal proceedings. Since there is no criminal liability of legal persons (Article 58 CPP), their civil liability can only be invoked in civil proceedings. The potential liability of third parties will also have to be invoked in the civil courts (i.e., liability for the actions of others). This includes certain problems in relation to the possible validity of the judgment on joint liability of parties who are not defendants but are civilly responsible (cf. Article 2317 CC).

74. Even if two or more cases are the same, the independence of civil and criminal responsibilities must be noted. With this in mind, criminal and civil responsibilities are distinct and different.[221] This is because the causes of justification provided for in criminal law[222] are not in agreement with those in civil law, even though part of the doctrine allows for some agreement.[223] Furthermore, the concepts of fault, malice, or capacity as a requirement for imputability[224] are not necessarily the same. The latter does not prevent the possibility of claiming (in civil law) the responsibility of the persons on whom the damage was done.[225] The lack of responsibility in the criminal process does not preclude the possibility of assessing civil responsibility *ex delicto*[226] in civil court.

219. But *see* paras 485 et seq.
220. *See* paras 483 et seq. and 517 et seq.
221. Just as the civil action is different from the criminal one: *see* Art. 67 CPC and SCS 28 July 2005 *Gaceta Jurídica* 2005/301, at 120.
222. Cf. Arts 10 nos. 4–11 CP. Notwithstanding the actions have an indirect relationship in part because it is expressly provided (Art. 66 CPP) that the sole exercise of the civil action in a case of civil liability *ex delicto* shall render the criminal action moot (except in cases that are prosecutable *de oficio*).
223. For example, problems could be those in the case of a different concept of legitimate defence or the one who acted driven by an irresistible force or an insuperable fear (*miedo insuperable*) (Art. 10 N. 9 CP). On the causes of justification, *see e.g.*, Pizarro, *Mirada*, cit.; Barros, *Tratado, I*, cit., at 138 et seq. Criminal legal doctrine has noted that some of these (such as that indicated in Art. 10 N. 11 CP) have not been studied in depth by civil law scholars: Ignacio Ried Undurraga, 'El efecto de la cosa juzgada de la sentencia penal absolutoria y del sobreseimiento definitivo en el proceso chileno de responsabilidad civil'. *Revista Chilena de Derecho Privado*, 2015/24, at 24.
224. For example, in the case of a mentally ill or intoxicated minor: *See* Art. 10 N. 1 y 2 CP, Art. 1 Ley 20.084; Art. 1447, 2318 and 2319 CC. On this point: Corral, *Lecciones,* cit., at 43; Barros, *Tratado, I*, cit., at 70 et seq.
225. *See e.g.*, Art. 2320, 2321 also in relation to Art. 10 Ley 20.084. On a civil liability *ex delicto*, for example, *see*: CS 22 Aug. 2012 (rol 2830/2012) commented by Carlos Pizarro Wilson, 'El caso de Aaron Vásquez y la responsabilidad por el hecho ajeno. Supreme Court, Santiago, 22 de agosto de 2012. Rol 2830/2012 y Corte de Apelaciones de Santiago, 19 de enero de 2012, rol 6427/2010', *Revista Chilena de Derecho Privado*, 2012/19, at 205 et seq.
226. SCS 26 Nov. 1998, GJ, no. 221, at 69; in a conforming sense, SAP Concepción 23 Apr. 1985 *RDJ*, 83, 1ª, at 96.

75. With regards to what has been stated above, the legislator expressly takes a position on the impact that the criminal judgment may have in the civil sphere; both in relation to the condemnatory judgment (Article 178 CPC), as well as with the acquittal judgment or final *sobresentimiento* (Article 179 CPC).

76. As concern convictions, Article 178 CPC clearly states that 'In civil courts, judgments issued in criminal proceedings may always be invoked when they condemn the defendant' (*En los juicios civiles podrán hacerse valer las sentencias dictadas en un proceso criminal siempre que condenen al procesado*). Hence, whether the conviction in criminal proceedings is *res judicata* (final) with respect to the intent and fault in the civil judgment should be assessed.

For some, it is noted[227] that civil and criminal fault are different, since the standard of culpability in penal law is potentially lower than in civil law (in penal law various graduations of guilt are not foreseen).[228] It must be noted that in the case of tort liability the graduation of fault is irrelevant (this is relevant in contractual law). Therefore, the doctrine in which criminal and civil fault coincide must be considered.[229] It has also been debated whether the concepts of civil and criminal intentions are different.[230]

What is certain is that – without prejudice to the fact that it will be necessary to prove a higher standard of fault in civil proceedings when required (because nothing prevents one from also bringing action in civil court liability *ex delicto of a* contractual nature) – the fault and malice proven in criminal proceedings are considered proven in civil proceedings.

77. One of the issues concerning a conviction judgment is whether it can also be enforced in cases of the third party alone. If *jus iudicata* were to be admitted, the fact that the third party can be subjected to the civil trial and not to the criminal trial would undermine *debido proceso* (due process) by virtue of the separate trials.[231] In this case, although the fact, the fault and defendant's offence[232] are proven, with

227. *See generally* Ried, *El efecto de la cosa juzgada,* cit., at 18 et seq., también Barros, *Tratado, I,* cit. at 88–89.
228. The degree of fault will not always coincide in civil and criminal law: Ried, *El efecto de la cosa juzgada,* cit., at 18.
229. Alessandri, *De la responsabilidad*, cit., at 33; Tapia, *De la responsabilidad*, cit., at 162
230. In relation to intent, *see* Art. 1 CP and Art. 44 CC. For example, in favour of difference: Ried, *El efecto de la cosa juzgada*, cit., at 19; in favour of comparability: Alessandri, *De la responsabilidad*, cit., at 33; Tapia, *De la responsabilidad*, cit. at 161. On the various concepts of intent, *see* Tapia, *De la responsabilidad,* cit., at 164 et seq.; Ramón Domínguez Águila, 'Fraus Omni Corrumpit. Notas sobre el fraude en el Derecho Civil', *Revista de Derecho, Universidad de Concepción*, 1991/189, at 7 et seq.; Alfredo Ferrante, '¿Hacia un concepto unitario de dolo u otra identidad? Sobre los deberes de información y el dolo en el contrato de seguro', *Estudios de Derecho Comercial, VIII Jornadas chilenas de Derecho Comercial, 7 y 8 de septiembre de 2017* 43–58 (Lorena Carvajal Arenas, Ángela Toso Milos coord.) (Santiago de Chile: Thomson Reuters, 2018), at 43 et seq.
231. The reflections of Felipe De la Fuente Hulaud, 'La acumulabilidad de la acción en el proceso penal', *Derecho de daños*, (Santiago de Chile: Lexis Nexis, 2002) at 138–140 are important.
232. SCS 7 May 1935, *RDJ*, 32, s. 1º, at 347; Barros, *Tratado*, *II,* cit., at 1075.

respect to the third party, the other elements of responsibility should be discussed (e.g., the existence of the damage and its quantification[233]).

78. The situation in acquittals is different since civil liability may be established (as expressly provided in Article 67 CPP) despite an acquittal in the criminal proceedings. For example, there are cases that can give rise to strict liability under civil law. It must therefore be mentioned[234] that the criminal judgment which acquits the accused (in relation to malice or fault) cannot operate as *res judicata* in civil proceedings, because this would mean that such party could be convicted before the civil courts. There are, nonetheless, additional issues that must be resolved as concerns the acquittal judgment.

As a general rule, the law expressly establishes the contrary in the event of conviction judgments and opts to invalidate the acquittal or definitive *sobreseimiento* judgment (*sentencia absolutoria penal o un sobreseimiento definitivo fundado*) in civil proceedings, except for three expressly sanctioned exceptions.

Without prejudice to certain clarifications (*see* Article 179 CPC[235]), *a juzgada* will be produced only when the judgment is based on: (1) the absence of a delito or quasi-delito;[236] (2) the absence of a relationship between the accused and the facts of the case; (3) a lack of evidence against the accused.

In these three circumstances it has been affirmed[237] that the fundamental right of *non bis in idem* (no double jeopardy) of the acquitted and remanded defendant outweighs the injured party's interest in obtaining damages.

Ultimately, it is important to preserve factual integrity to avoid generating contradictory judgments.[238] At the same time, it must be noted that there are a greater number of illicit conduct (it is important the difference between illegal and harmful conduct) are broader in civil than in criminal law.[239]

79. In the case of death of the accused, amnesty or pardon, there are those who believe that the judgment is not considered quashed.[240] Doubts arise in the case of

233. SCS 18 Mar. 2008 (Rol 369/2007); SCS 9 July 2001 (rol 915/1999), Barros, *Tratado, II,* cit., at 1074–1075.
234. As noted by Alex Carocca Pérez, 'Algunas consideraciones sobre los efectos de las sentencias penales absolutorias en los procesos civiles'. *Revista Procesal Penal* 2006/54, at 35 et seq.
235. For an overview on the case law, *see also*: Barros, *Tratado, II,* cit., at 1077 et seq.; Ried, *El efecto de la cosa juzgada*, cit., at 9 et seq.
236. It has been debated whether by 'no existencia del delito o cuasidelito' should be understood with reference to the 'delito or cuasidelito' or whether one should disregard the literal tenor and rather interpret the norm to refer to the 'inexistencia del hecho'. In favour of the latter position: Barros, *Tratado, II*, cit., at 1077 et seq.; a position that is attempted to be dismantled by Ried, *El efecto de la cosa juzgada*, cit., at 28 et seq.
237. *See* Ried, *El efecto de la cosa juzgada*, cit., at 32 et seq. In particular, on the application of the *cosa juzgada* in the civil sphere, with a reconstruction of a scheme of coincidence of the civil and penal elements, *see* pp. 25–26. On this point, *see also* Carocca, *Algunas*, cit., at 35 et seq.
238. On this point: Ried, *El efecto de la cosa juzgada,* cit., at 52.
239. *See* Ried, *El efecto de la cosa juzgada,* cit., at 22.
240. For example, in favour of this position is Corral, *Lecciones*, cit., at 46.

judgments granting amnesty. The doctrine is divided: one part of the doctrine submits that the amnesty would also extinguish its effects,[241] while another part[242] supports the possibility of a continuance to request compensation on the grounds that the State cannot eliminate the right to be compensated. Jurisprudence embraces the latter position in favour of the possibility of compensation despite the granting of amnesty.[243]

80. The doctrine is not homogeneous regarding the extensive effect on third parties of the favourable effect of the definitive acquittal and acquiescence judgment. A favourable position[244] is opposed by another part of the doctrine, which even relates it to a certain unconstitutionality.[245] From an intermediate perspective, however, there are those who[246] believe it will depend on the exemption invoked in criminal proceedings.[247]

81. It should be recalled that a civil trial can be continued for the purpose of establishing certain facts in relevant criminal proceedings (Article 167 CPC). For example, a claim for compensation against third parties for the unlawful behaviour of others. The criminal proceedings may also be continued for *acuerdo reparatorio*[248] (cf. Articles 242–246 CPP) or in the case of requests for civil actions other than compensation (Article 174 COT).

§5. Relationship Between Contractual and Delictual or Tortious Liability

I. Dual Regime

82. The Chilean Civil Code embraces a dualistic statute of liability, contractual and extracontractual (tort). On the one hand, the former is essentially regulated and founded in Articles 1545 et seq., while the latter is regulated in Title XXXV 'De los delitos y cuasidelitos' of Book IV (Articles 2314 et seq.). It has been stated that

241. These are the arguments of Rafael Fontecilla Riquelme, 'La responsabildad civil derivada de delito', *Revista de Derecho y Jurisprudencia*, 1945/42, at 134.
242. Corral, *Lecciones*, cit., at 46.
243. 'The obligation that generates this right is not extinguished by amnesty': SAP 14 Jan. 1963, *RDJ*, LX, s. 4ª, at 47. As already noted by Barros, this is also confirmed by CS 30 Mar. 1962, RDJ, LIX, s. 4ª, at 25; CS 1 Sept. 1967, *RDJ*, LXIV, s. 4ª, at 243. *See* Barros, *Tratado, II*, cit., at 1075 et seq.
244. Barros, *Tratado, II*, cit., at 1077.
245. *See* Carocca, *Algunas*, cit., at 46.
246. Ried, *El efecto de la cosa juzgada*, cit., at 43–44.
247. On the jurisprudential point of view, *see* Ried, *El efecto de la cosa juzgada*, cit., at 45 et seq.; Barros, *Tratado, II*, cit., at 1979 et seq.
248. Although the reparatory agreement may provide for the payment of sums of money to the victim, this does not necessarily exclude greater compensation in civil proceedings (unless one considers that the principle of good faith requires a tacit renunciation of the agreement), what is certain is that such sums must be imputed to compensation since, according to the last sentence of Art. 243 CPP, '*El acuerdo reparatorio no podrá ser dejado sin efecto por ninguna acción civil*'. On reparatory agreements (which can also derive not necessarily from a civil tort but in relation to other civil actions in the criminal proceedings) *see* Barros, *Tratado, II*, cit., at 1083–1084.

'there is no absolute equality between contractual liability and tort liability; but neither is there a fundamental differentiation between them. There are undoubtedly numerous differences between the two, but these only refer to their technical organization'.[249] There are those who support the dualistic principle by stating that contractual and tort liability serve different functions.[250] So, undoubtedly, the distinction between contractual and tort liability is based on the dual regime.[251]

83. Tort liability is also defined as *aquilana, responsabilidad delictual* or *cuasidelictual.*[252] Considering new trends in legal terminology, between the expression 'daños' (damages) and 'responsabilidad civil',[253] the latter should be preferred.

II. Common Regime Applicable to Quasi-contract and *Ex Lege* Obligations

84. Obligations arising from contracts generate contractual liability, and those arising from crimes/offences or quasi-delicts generate non-contractual (or tort) liability. We have seen[254] that obligations also arise from quasi-contract and from law, but in this case there is no express provision as to which statute should apply to these types of obligations.[255] This will then help to answer the question of which statute is applicable in the case of a unilateral declaration of will or action *in rem verso.*[256]

The recognition of the dual system of civil responsibility (contractual and tort) has entailed evaluating which regime between these two is primary so that it can be applied in a supplementary manner to other types of responsibility.

85. On the one hand there is a position that argues contractual responsibility should prevail and apply to quasi-contracts and legal obligations, relegating responsibility in tort as an exception to the former.[257] There are a couple of justifications for this effect: noting that the gradation of fault foreseen for contractual liability (cf. Article 1547 CC) is taken up in various provisions of the code and therefore assumes an expansive effect.[258] It also invokes an issue related to the geography and structure of the Chilean code and pointing out that the contractual liability of Article

249. Tapia, *De la responsabilidad*, cit., at 335.
250. Schopf, 'Las diferencias funcionales', cit., at 61 et seq.
251. *See* Carmen Domínguez Hidalgo, 'Responsailidad civil y principio de reparación integral del daño', *El Principio de Reparación Integral en sus Contornos Actuales. Una Revisión desde el derecho Chileno. Latinoamericano y Europeo* (Carmen Domínguez Hidalgo, ed.) (Santiago de Chile: Thomson Reuters, 2019), at 24 et seq.
252. On these points: Figueroa, *Curso, IV*, cit., at 57.
253. Corral, *Lecciones*, cit., at 19–20.
254. *See supra* paras 33–37.
255. In this sense, the imposition of the *Code Napoleon*: Tapia, *De la responsabilidad*, cit., at 425, and especially at 446 and 447.
256. As noted by Figueroa, *Curso, IV*, cit., at 62.
257. Alessandri, *De la responsabilidad*, cit., at 43–44.
258. Thus, if we observe this for example in Arts 250, 391 427, 2308, 2288: Alessandri, *De la responsabilidad*, cit., at 44–45, también Claro, Explicaciones, Tomo XI, 'Obligaciones', 2a. Parte, N°

1545 CC is in title XII (Book IV) of *los efectos de la obligación* and therefore would not apply only to contractual obligations.

86. The contrast to this view, what seems to be the majority view today is based on the writings of certain traditional authors[259] and is confirmed by more modern scholars who proport that contractual liability cannot be applied extensively.[260] This position's argument is based on the notion that an obligation *ex lege* cannot clearly derive from a contract, and also that some provisions relating to tort liability, such as Article 2316 CC, make express reference to the law. Additionally, the contrary argument would be unconvincing and literal.

87. Finally, there is a hybrid opinion.[261] Despite the fact that the regime of tort liability should be admitted, and given that it considers contractual liability to be an exceptional regime, in practice it will be necessary to reason by analogy and apply the most analogous statute (contractual or tort). This depends on the circumstance, thus admitting that in some cases the analogy between certain contracts and quasi-contracts is evident.

88. Classifying a statute as general does not necessarily imply that we can apply the rules of one statute to another. Alternatively, part of the doctrine considers that the provision on contractual liability is more common and therefore it can be applied to tort[262] or vice versa.[263] This latter approach should be completely excluded if we think that one of the two statutes is exceptional; and as we have seen, some people have considered contractual[264] or tort to be special.[265] If one accepts the maxim *lex specialis derogat generali*, then the analogical application between these two statutes would be self-excluding. This does not prevent a norm which is not strictly related to liability (i.e., contractual) but it can be broader in scope. For example, it has been considered that Article 2319 CC is broadly applicable to liability (both contractual and tort), to differentiate it from Article 2314 CC.[266]

1063, pág. 518 & N° 1067, pp. 522 and 523; Abeliuk, Las *Obligaciones. II*, cit., at 909. The application of the contractual regime to quasi-contracts is also found because of the profound similarities between the quasi-contract of *agencia oficiosa* and the contract of mandate; Claro notes that Art. 2287 states that, the obligations of the *agenti oficioso* are the same as those of the mandatory, that is, a contractual obligation.

259. Tapia, *De la responsabilidad*, cit., at 454 y ss which in turn embraces the position of Carlos Ducci Claro, *Responsabilidad Civil (Ex-Contractual)*, Memoria de Prueba, 1936. At 8; Carlos Ducci Claro, *Responsabilidad Civil*, (Santiago de Chile: Editorial Jurídica de Chile, 1971), at 22–23.
260. Corral, *Lecciones*, cit., at 37.
261. Barros, *Tratado, II*, cit., at 1170–1172. Although it subsequently seems to admit the statute of non-contractual liability as general and suppletory (op. cit. at 1174).
262. Ruz, *Explicaciones*, cit., at 446.
263. As in the case of the application of Art. 2329 CC, in order to grant moral damages in contractual matters, since the article relating to contractual responsibility (Art. 1558) referred only to damages and loss of earnings: Figueroa, *Curso, IV*, cit., at 62–63. This last aspect is outdated given that moral damages are also commonly granted in contractual matters *see* paras 452 et seq.
264. Barros, *Tratado, II*, cit., at 1171.
265. Corral, *Lecciones*, cit., at 23.
266. Tapia, *De la responsabilidad*, cit., at 528 et seq.; on the judgments that allow it at 531 et seq.

Other provisions prohibit application by analogy. For example, Article 2320 CC states that liability for the actions of third parties cannot be applied by analogy to contractual liability for the actions of third parties.[267]

89. From a practical perspective, recognizing contractual liability as a general statute instead of tort liability would mean (besides the different terms of prescription)[268] promoting the application of the presumption of fault under Article 1547.3 CC, thereby limiting compensation to only foreseeable damages (except for cases in which it is possible to establish malice, in accordance with Article 1558 CC) and excluding the joint liability imposed in tort cases (Article 2317 CC). The only exceptions to this application would be those expressly provided for in the black letter text of the law. Furthermore, certain liability agreements could be considered valid.

90. Despite it being clearly stated that the regime of contractual liability is general in scope, we must remember that the application of the tort regime is possible in some instances.[269] Thus, it should also be noted that although the provision on contract constitutes the general statute applicable to quasi-contracts or *ex lege* obligations, this does not mean that tort law provisions should be applied to other cases (as is the case of obligations relating to nullity).

91. Therefore, the finding of a dual regime requires not only evaluating which of the two is preponderant (i.e., general and applicable by default to other cases). It is also necessary to assess (a) whether the status of contractual and tort liability can be accumulated (*cumul/no cumul*) and (b) which of the two has applicable status in the case of precontractual liability.

III. *Cumul/No Cumul*

92. In certain cases, it may be possible to establish the existence of the requisites of both contractual and tort liability. This possibility is clearly the result of French influence. The issue of accumulation *(cumul)* of these two forms of liability relates to the possibility of bringing legal action in accordance with Articles 1545 CC

267. Sergio Fuenzalida Puelma, 'Los terceros en la responsabilidad contractual', Doctrinas esenciales. Derecho Civil. I. Obligaciones, (Raul Tavolari Oliveros ed.) (Santiago de Chile: Editorial Jurídica, 2009), at 573–574.
268. The general terms of prescription in the case of contractual liability are five years after the obligation becomes due and payable (Arts 2514 and 2515 CC) or of nullity, four years from the time the act or contract is concluded (Arts 1683 y 1691 del *CC*), whereas in the case of tort it is four years 'desde la perpretación del acto' (*from the performance of the contract*) (Art. 2332 CC): *see* Ramón Dóminguez Águila, *La prescripción extintiva: doctrina y jurisprudencia* (Valparaiso: Prolibros, 2nd ed, 2020).
269. Like all areas of the special regime of medical liability and others. This is the position of Carlos Pizarro Wilson, 'Responsabilidad contractual y extracontractual: Desde el problema de la opción al dilema del derecho común y especial'. *Presente y futuro de la responsabilidad civil* (Rodrigo Barría Díaz & Alfredo Ferrante & Lilian San Martín Neira ed.) (Santiago de Chile: Thomson Reuters, 2017), at 58–59.

et seq. or Articles 2314 CC et seq. It has been noted by the doctrine that it is not correct to call the phenomenon a 'cumulation of responsibility' because the accumulation would allow the injured party to obtain a double compensation for the damage suffered, generating problems of unjustified[270] enrichment;[271] the aggrieved party may choose between one or the other regimes. Thus, with reference to the problem, it has been preferred to frame it as[272] *concurrencia* or 'concurrence'[273] of contractual and tort liability. During these approaches, it should be pointed out (as correctly observed by the doctrine) that if cumulation represents the *genre* and the concurrent claim represents the *species,*[274] the correct denomination is 'intervention of the responsibility of the contract between the contracting parties'[275] since 'the real problem of the cumulation of responsibilities is nothing more than determining which intervention is possible or not for tort liability between the contracting parties'.[276] In other words, whether or not in the end one of the contractual obligations can also be configured as tort.[277]

93. Since the problem does not exist if all the conditions for establishing the relevant liability are not met,[278] in a way, it is a matter of the possible extension of tort liability to contractual matters. This is due to the advantages of taking legal action in a contractual context.

94. The problem is not suing the same party in both contract and tort when the facts ('*supuesto de hecho*') are different.[279] Neither is it when the same facts generate contractual compensation for the other contracting party and compensation for

270. In an analogous sense: Alessandri, *De la responsabilidad*, cit., at 61; Tapia, *De la responsabilidad*, cit., at 431 et seq.
271. Alessandri, *De la responsabilidad*, cit., at 62; Abeliuk, *Las Obligaciones. II,* cit., at 933; *see also* Carmen Domínguez Hidalgo, 'La concurrencia de responsabilidades o el mal llamado cúmulo de responsabilidades en el derecho chileno: estado actual', *Estudios de Derecho Civil III* (Alejandro Guzmán Brito ed., Santiago de Chile: Legal Publishing, 2008), at 717.
272. Domínguez, 'La concurrencia', cit. at 717; Carlos Pérez Bravo, 'Concurrencia de responsabilidades', *Art boni et aequi,* 2000/4, at 111 et seq.; Hernán Corral Talciani, 'Concurrencia de acciones de responsabilidad civil contractual y extracontractual en los daños causados por accidentes del trabajo', *Rev. Chilena de Derecho Privado*, 2010/14, at 69 et seq.
273. Hernán Corral Talciani, 'El concurso de responsabilidades en el derecho de daños chileno: defensa y delimitación de la teoría de la opción', *Estudios de Derecho Civil V* (Departamento de Derecho Privado Universidad de Concepción ed.) (Santiago de Chile: Abeledo Perrot Legal Publishing, 2010), at 639 et seq.
274. Tapia, *De la responsabilidad*, cit., at 434–435.
275. Tapia, *De la responsabilidad*, cit., at 435.
276. Tapia, *De la responsabilidad*, cit. at 431 and 627.
277. Cf. Meza, *Manual, II,* cit., at 252.
278. As opportunely. Noted by Tapia, *De la responsabilidad*, cit., at 434.
279. In this sense, it is not a hypothesis of cumulation that generates tort liability between two contracting parties for a reason different from the contract, as in the case of the tortfeasor who runs the injured party over with a car. In this case, the responsibility in tort is due to the material act (i.e., the car accident) and does not relate to any contractual relationship between the parties. Therefore, it is evident that responsibility in contract and responsibility in tort are distinct: Alessandri, *De la responsabilidad,* cit., at 50; Tapia, *De la responsabilidad*, cit., at 432; Abeliuk, *Las Obligaciones. II*, cit., at 917. Thus, it is noted that 'two persons do not always generate contractual liability merely because they are united by a contract': Abeliuk, *Las Obligaciones. II,* cit., at 912.

third parties. For example, family members or indirect victims of an accident harming the former.[280] Instead, it is a matter concerning when the facts[281] are considered hybrid, meaning a situation from which liability in both contract and tort arise as a result of all the conditions for such actions being fulfilled.

95. Medical malpractice is one area of law where liability may be established in both contract and tort. Consider, for example, the liability of a physician performing a surgical procedure in a 'host' hospital (i.e., one other than his/her normal place of practice). In the event of malpractice, a claim may be based in either contract or tort, depending on the defendant (i.e., the healthcare facility/hospital or the medical practitioner) and the facts of the case. Indeed, if the facts of the case determine the relationship between the injured party and the responsible party is established, it may be said that a fine line exists between contractual liability and tort liability. Thus, the problem[282] may arise in situations where there is a debate on the contractual or tort nature of the relationship, such as in the case of benevolent transportation[283] or other instances in which accessory obligations may be included in the contractual relationship despite lack of an express provision (e.g., *obligaciones de seguridad*, the obligation to ensure the health of the subject in the context of transportation or in the work environment). It should be noted that although the problem pertaining to *obligaciones de seguridad* remains broader,[284] these last two problems, previously discussed by the doctrine,[285] are in part resolved by the legislator. In relation to the contract of carriage, one is also liable for damages to the person (cf. Article 2015 CC[286]). In relation to the contract of employment, the employer is obliged to take all necessary measures to effectively protect the life and health of the workers (Article 184 of the *Código del Trabajo*[287]). There are those who identify cases of concurrence in cases of *culpa in contrahendo.*[288]

---

280. As already noted by Abeliuk, *Las Obligaciones. II,* cit., at 934 and confirmed, for example, by Corral, 'El concurso', cit., at 639. In this sense, cumulation of compensation or concurrence of responsibility should be considered two different matters: Barros, *Tratado, II,* cit. at 1158; Domínguez, 'La concurrencia', cit., at 717. Thus, in this sense, it would be a different problem when, in the event of the death of a worker, one wishes to claim damages *iure propio* or *iure hereditatis* (*see* paras 483 et seq. and 517 et seq.).
281. For example, Abeliuk, *Las Obligaciones. II,* cit., at 933; Corral, 'El concurso', cit., at 639.
282. On the interaction between contractual and tort liability in relation to *pure economic loss see* Schopf, 'Las diferencias funcionales', cit., at 82–84.
283. Thus, for example, there are those who consider that it is not a contract and therefore generates tort responsibility: Abeliuk, *Las Obligaciones. II,* cit., at 934; or those who consider it to be an unnamed contract: Tapia, *De la responsabilidad,* cit., at 62 and 609, more extensively at 59–72.
284. For a more extensive analysis in relation to these problems also in relation to the security of the person in relation to the contract of lease, loan, mortgage, deposit, mandate and company: Alessandri, *De la responsabilidad*, cit., at 52 et seq. Also Abeliuk, *Las Obligaciones. II*, cit., at 917 et seq.; María Teresa Alonso Traviesa, *El problema de la concurrencia de las responsabilidades* (Santiago de Chile: Lexis Nexis, 2006), especially the second chapter.
285. In relation to the employment relationship, *see* Alessandri, *De la responsabilidad*, cit., at 57.
286. As noted, also in relation to Art. 207 Chilean Commercial Code: Abeliuk, *Las Obligaciones. II,* cit., at 914; Alessandri, *De la responsabilidad*, cit., at 84.
287. Abeliuk, *Las Obligaciones. II,* cit., t 914.
288. This doctrine would also consider that they would be incorrectly called cases of precontractual liability: Domínguez, 'La concurrencia', cit. at 725.

96. Doctrine is divided on whether it is possible to allow concurrence:[289] part of the doctrine denies this possibility, while another (more recent) part accepts it.[290] In any case, what is clear is that there is indeed confusion,[291] and that the only point which is agreed within the doctrine as of late is that the problem has not been clearly framed until now[292] and it has not been clarified with the passage of time.[293]

97. The argument in favour of the viewpoint that denies[294] this concurrence is based on the need to give priority to the obligatory effect of the contract. Alternately, those in support of this position submit[295] that there is nothing to prevent Articles 2314 et seq. (traditionally considered applicable to torts) from also being applied in cases of contractual liability. In the perspective of the latter view, Article 2319 CC, for example, is applicable both to cases of contractual and tort liability, given that the provision makes a general reference to fault or intent.[296] Regardless of whether the theory is accepted, both positions recognize limits and exceptions.

98. Those who oppose this position suggest[297] there is another exception.[298] Namely, when the breach of the contractual obligation also constitutes a crime.[299] This option is offered by the regulations of criminal procedure which allow compensation to be claimed in tort. Part of the doctrine points out that this position is no longer[300] valid following the reform of criminal law as, in criminal proceedings, it is possible to bring action in contract. For other doctrines, however, the continuation of the system currently in force would entail the possibility not of making the

289. For example, Alessandri, *De la responsabilidad*, cit., at 63, 63–65; Ducci, Responsabilidad civil (*1933*), cit., at 13, Ducci, *Responsabilidad civil (1971)*, cit., at 24; Leslie Tomasello Hart, *El Daño Moral en la Responsabilidad Contractual* (Santiago de Chile: Editorial Jurídica de Chile, 1969), at 266. In this sense 'the rejection of the concurrent claim is the most coherent response to the dualist system of responsibility': Domínguez, 'La concurrencia', cit. at 726.

290. E.g., Tapia, *De la responsabilidad*, cit., at 525–526; Corral, 'Concurrencia' cit., at 639 especially 648 et seq. Rodrigo Barcia Lehmann, 'Algunas consideraciones sobre el principio de la responsabilidad. *Instituciones modernas de Derecho Civil: Homenaje al Profesor Fernando Fueyo Laneri* (Santiago de Chile: Editorial Jurídica ConoSur, 1996), at 562 et seq.

291. Consider that referring to the usual author (Barros, *Tratado, II,* cit. at 1157 et seq.) for some he would be in favour (according to Abeliuk, *Las Obligaciones*. II, cit., at 933) while for others (according to Corral, *Lecciones*, cit., at 30). The confusion can also be seen for example from the fact that the same author, in two different writings, states quoting the same work (Alonso, *El problema*, cit) that Alonso is against (Corral, 'Concurrencia' cit., at 644) even if he then states that he is partially in favour (Corral, *Lecciones*, cit., at 30).

292. Tapia, *De la responsabilidad*, cit., at 429.

293. Domínguez, 'La concurrencia', cit. at 717.

294. E.g., Alessandri, *De la responsabilidad*, cit. at 63, 63–65.

295. E.g., Tapia, *De la responsabilidad*, cit., at 526.

296. This also justifies the simultaneous presence of Arts 2314 and 2319 CC, otherwise the seocndo would be for the author a mere repetition of the first: Tapia, *De la responsabilidad*, cit., at 526–527.

297. Alessandri, *De la responsabilidad*, cit., at 68–69.

298. It is noted that it would not be technically an 'exception' since it is a simple implementation of the principle of autonomy: Abeliuk, *Las Obligaciones. II*, cit. at 933; también Domínguez, 'La concurrencia', cit. at 727.

299. For example, under Arts 450 and 491 CP.

300. Corral, 'El concurso', cit., at 647.

concurrent claim disappear but of limiting it[301] (only to cases of *ofendido directo* cf. Articles 59 and 108 Code of Criminal Procedure) from the crime/offence and not for indirect victims (*víctimas por repercusión o rebote*).

For those who accept the possibility to present concurrent claims, this would be limited to cases where 'the damage is the product of risks whose assumption was the object or subject of the contract'.[302]

99. It is incorrect to affirm[303] that a wilful act does not justify the exclusion of concurrent actions. However, stressing the principle of unity of act and intent only limits the effect: cumulation is still possible, since this is a tort case involving the parties to a contract which allows them to base a claim on wilful misconduct (which is regarded as a tort) or to rely on another claim under contract which is unrelated to said misconduct.[304]

100. It is interesting that the principle of contractual autonomy is used to justify the possibility of excluding the applicable system, both for those who defend competition[305] (when autonomy would exclude it) and for those who refuse it[306] (when autonomy would allow it). It should be noted that the position taken in the first case is accepted with limitation since those who support it submit that the agreement is valid only in cases not involving wilful misconduct or gross negligence.[307] But this is also possible in adhesion contracts.[308] Although some scholars have confirmed that this aspect is questionable[309] in contracts of adhesion, it must always be kept clear that the clauses of an adhesion contract are not necessarily unfair (or 'vessatory').[310]

101. Surely, admitting the possibility of opting between one of the two regimes has advantages.[311]

These can be divided in two categories: those arising from the differences in contractual and tort liability and those which (due to procedural issues involving the choice of one regime or another) entail presenting the claim before a different judicial body.

---

301. This is based on Arts 59 and 108 Code of Criminal Procedure: Domínguez, 'La concurrencia', cit. at 727.
302. Corral, 'Concurrencia, cit., at 651.
303. Corral, 'Concurrencia, cit., at 640.
304. In this sense one must interpret the reasoning of Tapia, *De la responsabilidad*, cit., at 565.
305. Corral, El concurso', cit., at 650.
306. Alessandri, *De la responsabilidad*, cit., at 65.
307. Corral, 'Concurrencia, cit., at 650.
308. Corral, 'Concurrencia, cit., at 650.
309. Domínguez, 'La concurrencia', cit. at 727.
310. Barros, *Tratado*, *II*, cit., at 1160–1061.
311. For a general overview, *see, e.g.*, Tapia, *De la responsabilidad*, cit., at 483 et seq.; Corral, 'Concurrencia, cit., at 641–642.

Traditionally, the tort route was advantageous since it was the only way to be awarded moral damages.[312] However, since such form of indemnification also allowed in claims under contract,[313] this question is no longer relevant.

Assuming that the question emerges from the possible extension of tort liability in cases involving contractual liability, admitting such an extension implies that the party that brings acting under tort initially be at a disadvantage. Namely, the plaintiff must prove that the claim falls within the scope of claims in contract, which as a basic rule is presumed. However, in some cases this is presumed also in the case of tort liability (e.g., responsibility of parents with respect to minor children).

In return, tort liability offers other benefits. As to the quantum of compensation in the event of a prior fault-related loss there is no limitation foreseen by the contract not to indemnify unforeseen damages arising from fault (Article 1558 CC).

102. Although fault must be proven, the advantage in tort matters will be that the party can be held liable regardless of the degree of fault. Whereas in contractual matters it would be possible to foresee a different fault, which would be more burdensome.[314] So would excluding the application of any clauses limiting contractual liability, such as, one which foresees a penalty clause.[315] Additionally, it will be possible to count on a longer limitation period for the action.[316] For those who do not accept the application of Article 2317 CC to all hypotheses of liability, there is also the advantage of a presumption of joint liability of the debtors,[317] which would not be the case if it is accepted that this provision is general in nature.[318]

103. From a procedural point of view, it has been noted[319] that in the event of an automobile accident or a labour dispute, choosing the contractual or tort route means choosing to file a claim before the ordinary judge (if in tort) or the competent authority (i.e., the local court or the *ad hoc* judge) for labour law proceedings (Article 420 of the Chilean Labour Code).[320]

Before analysing in greater detail the procedural limits relating to concurring claims,[321] it should be noted that part of the doctrine (both in favour and against concurrent claims) has been against the principle *iura novit curia* and the possibility of only invoking the claim for compensation and the facts on which it is

312. *See, e.g.*, Tapia, *De la responsabilidad*, cit., at 436; Domínguez, 'La concurrencia', cit. at 718.
313. *See* paras 452 et seq.
314. *See* Meza, *Manual, II*, cit., at 253.
315. For example, *see* Tapia, *De la responsabilidad*, cit., at 437; Corral, 'Concurrencia, cit., at 642.
316. The general rule is that contract claims are prescribed in four years and claims in tort in five years (cf. e.g., Art. 2320 CC). This could be beneficial, according to the doctrine, with respect to redhibitory vices or the contract of carriage: Corral, 'Concurrencia, cit., at 642.
317. Tapia, *De la responsabilidad*, cit., at 436.
318. For a general application of Art. 2317 CC: Manuel Somarriva Undurraga, *Tratado de las Cauciones*, (Santiago de Chile: Editorial Nacimiento, 1943, at 43.
319. As appropriately observed by Corral, 'Concurrencia, cit., at 642.
320. With the relevant reform of Art. 420 letter f): *See* para. 486.
321. *See* Barros, *Tratado, II* cit., at 1166 et seq.; Corral, 'Concurrencia, cit., at 652–653. *See also* Abeliuk, *Las Obligaciones. II*, cit., at 933.

based.[322] In reality, the opposite should be considered. More specifically, allowing a concurrence of actions (contractual and tort) is advantageous as it allows the judge to decide the applicable statute based on the facts presented, given both provisions are abstractly applicable in the case of concurrent actions. In this regard, the principle *iura notvit curia* is in perfect harmony with the possible concurrence of actions. Alternately, should the plaintiff bring action based on only one of the two possible statutes (for example, by invoking contractual liability), the other consequence would be the inability of the judge to decide the matter according to the canons of the other statute (thus invoking tort liability), as this would not reflect the option exercised by the plaintiff.

104. Although part of the doctrine argues that the *petitum* includes an action for principal and subsidiary responsibility (cf. Article 17.2 code of civil procedure),[323] this hypothesis presupposes the absence of the right to choose whether to file a claim in contract or in tort because it assumes that the judge may decide not to apply the chosen form of action to the relevant facts. Despite subsidiary responsibility theoretically suggesting that the judge is against the plaintiff's right to choose which action to bring, in practice it may benefit the party whose claim is uncertain as it allows the court to decide, based on the facts, which liability to impose (if any).

105. In the past, case law[324] has been reluctant to allow concurrent claims, tending to allow them in cases of medical malpractice by virtue of a *pro damnato*[325] approach. Currently, however, following an important decision[326] in 2016 on medical malpractice, there is a trend to allow concurrent claims, including those involving other types of liability (e.g., misleading advertising[327]).

106. As a brief digression, the problem with the concurrent claim can also be found in the case of a single category of liability, such as contractual liability. In this case, the possible competition between applicable norms is resolved according to the rule of subsidiary or the *bromcardo lex specialis derogat generali.* Despite this, it is possible that (by virtue of the protection of a particularly weak subject such as the consumer) the consumer is offered the choice of the most favourable protection between the general and special regimes in order to always guarantee the best

322. While in favour of the opposing opinion, Corral, 'Concurrencia, cit., at 652. Also against those who do not admit it, by criticizing it in favour of the principle of 'due process': Domínguez, 'La concurrencia', cit. at 732.
323. Barros, *Tratado, II,* cit., at 1167; Corral, 'Concurrencia, cit., at 652.
324. For an overview of the position that denies it *see* Barros, *Tratado, II,* cit., at 1062–1063; Corral, *Lecciones,* cit., at 31–32. Son an overview of the older position with some favourable judgments: Ramos, *De la responsabilidad,* cit., at 30–31.
325. Domínguez, 'La concurrencia', cit. at 730. En relación con la responsabilidad medica e.g., Pérez, 'Concurrencia', cit., at 111 et seq. In relation to the pronouncements on work accidents e.g., Alonso, *El problema*, cit., at 290 et seq.
326. CS Mar. 21, 2016 (rol 31061/2014).
327. CS 18Jan. 2018 (rol 73907/2016). For commentary *see* Patricia Verónica López Díaz, 'Publicidad engañosa. Indemnización de daños. Concurrencia de responsabilidad civil. Opción de responsabilidades. Responsabilidad extracontractual. Comentario a Corte Suprema, 18 de enero de 2018', *Revista chilena de Derecho Privado*, 2018/50, at 195 et seq.

protection in the event of any discrepancies or inconsistencies between the two regimes. The possibility of a real choice presents itself, for example, between the remedy system foreseen for purchase and sale in the code, the remedy as set out in Ley 19.496 for the protection of consumer rights,[328] and the possibility of referring to the general remedies under contract law, such as Article 1489 CC.[329]

This does not mean that by protecting the weaker party there is also a real choice between liability deriving from non-fulfilment of the contract and civil liability deriving from the administrative contravention in consumer law;[330] e.g., relating to the non-conformity of goods. Thus, it will be possible to choose between remedies due to the lack of conformity or compensation for damages: Articles 3, 20 and 21 Ley 19.496) to that of an administrative violation that gives rise to a right to compensation by virtue of a breach of contract, such as the refusal to grant a remedy chosen by the consumer in the event of a lack of conformity of the good (Articles 23 and 26 Ley 19.496).

However, it should not be forgotten that precontractual liability might also derive from other administrative sanctions, such as false or misleading advertising. According to the doctrine, this constitutes a tort,[331] a hypothesis (that also in this case, since it may overlap with the hypotheses provided for in common law) which allow the consumer to choose between the two forms of action. For instance, the common law legislation is more favourable, by virtue of the *pro-consumer*[332] principle.

---

328. *See* Bruno Caprile Biermann, 'Las acciones del comprador insatisfecho: el cúmulo actual y la tendencia al deber de conformidad', *Estudios de derecho civil II*, 629–650 (Hernán Corral Talciani & Mª Sara Rodríguez Pinto ed.) (Santiago de Chile: Thomson Reuters y La Ley, 2007), at 629 et seq.; Bruno Caprile Biermann, 'Las acciones del comprador insatisfecho: el cúmulo actual (ley de protección al consumidor, vicios redhibitorios, error sustancial, resolución por incumplimiento), y la tendencia al deber de conformidad en el derecho comparado', *Estudios de derecho privado en homenaje a Christian Larroumet*, 561–602 (Fabricio Mantilla Espinosa & Carlos Pizarro Wilson, ed.) (Santiago de Chile: Fundación Fernando Fueyo Laneri, 2008), at 561 et seq.; Pedro Zelaya Etchegaray, 'El cúmulo de responsabilidad en la nueva ley de protección al consumidor. Estudios sobre la ley N° 19.496 y las principales tendencias extranjeras', *Cuadernos de Extensión de la Universidad de los Andes. Derecho del consumo y protección del consumidor*, (Hernán Corral Talciani ed.).1999/3, at 213 et seq.
329. Alfredo Ferrante, 'Una revisión de los remedios del consumidor chileno en la compraventa con disconformidad a partir de la diferencia entre obligación y garantía', *Revista de derecho privado*, 2018/35, at 191.
330. Corte Concepción 29 Jan. 2003 (rol 20.455-2001). On the preponderance of civil liability for administrative infringement in front of contractual liability, *see* Alfredo Ferrante, 'La devolución de la cantidad pagada en la jurisprudencia: desencaje con la garantía legal', *Revista de Derecho (Valdivia)*, 2020/1, at 141 et seq.
331. On this point, *see* María Sara Rodríguez Pinto, 'Responsabilidad precontractual en la Ley N° 19.496 de 1997 sobre Protección de los Derechos de los Consumidores', *Estudios de Derecho Civil, Jornadas Nacionales de Derecho Civil, Santa Cruz 2012* (Carmen Domínguez Hidalgo, *et al.* ed.) (Santiago de Chile: Legal Publishing Thomson Reuters, 2013), at 493 et seq.; López, *La responsabilidad precontractual en la Ley 19.496 2019*, cit., at 399 et seq.
332. *See* Patricia Verónica López Díaz, 'La tutela precontractual en la Ley 19.496: su configuración, alcance y eventual convergencia con aquella propia de la contratación civil', *Revista Chilena de de Derecho*, 2019/2, at 417 et seq.

107. Finally, in relation to the above-analysed phenomenon, it is also necessary to note the tendency to consider norms traditionally considered applicable in tort liability as indistinctly applicable also in contract disputes. The problem with concurrent claims can be avoided by extrapolating a general principle from the applicable rule. The concept of civil liability partially blurs the distinction in this dualistic regime. It has already been seen in relation to Article 2317 CC in the context of joint and several liability. Recently, it has also been accepted by the case law in relation to Article 2330 CC, considering that the principle of mitigation of damage traditionally found in tort liability is also applicable to contractual[333] liability.

IV. Precontractual Liability

A. Special or Derivative Nature

108. Establishing contract law as the general regime does not mean applying it also to cases of precontractual liability. In dealing with precontractual liability, it is necessary to highlight a Chilean phenomenon. On the one hand, the Civil Code (of 1855) does not provide a discipline for precontractual liability. However, it also does not regulate the formation of the agreement (or meeting of the minds), which is why the later regulation (which the Commercial Code of 1865 provided for in Articles 98 et seq.) is still applied today.[334] Therefore, the code expressly provides for two legal hypotheses of precontractual responsibility that were prior to the debates that arose from the theories of Jhering,[335] Faggella[336] or Saleilles.[337]

---

333. CS Mar. 3, 2020 (rol 12,473-2018).

334. On this point, *see e.g.*, Ramón Domínguez Águila, *Teoría general del negocio jurídico* (Santiago de Chile: Prolibros 3rd ed., 2020), at 65 et seq.; Ducci, *Derecho Civil, IV*, cit. at 248 et seq.; Victor Vial del Rio, *Teoría general del acto jurídico* (Santiago de Chile: editorial jurídica de Chile, 5th ed., 2006), at 62 et seq.

335. The theory of responsibility for *culpa in contrahendo,* transposed then in the German Civil Code of 1900, dates back to 1861: Rudolf Von Ihering, 'Culpa in contrahendo oder Schadensersatz bei nichtigen oder nicht zur Perfektion gelangten Verträgen', *Jherings Jahrbucher fur die Dogmatik des heutigen romischen und deutschen Privatrechts*, 1861/4, at 1 et seq.

336. Faggella is the first who, in 1906 who broads the scope of action of precontractual responsibility and also considers the possibility of imposing liability for unjustified interruption of negotiations. (Gabriele Faggella, 'Dei periodi precontrattuali e della loro vera ed essata costruzioni scientífica', *Studi giuridici in onore di Carlo Fadda pel XXV anno del suo insegnamento,* III, (Napoli: Luigi Pierro e figlio, 1906), at 271 et seq.).

As Bersani observes, after the Saleilles paper of 1907, he responded with the essay of 1908 (Gabriele Faggella, *'Fondamento giuridico della responsabilità in tema di trattative contrattuali'*, *Arch. giur. Filippo Serafini,* 1909/82, at 128–150) and adhered to the hypothesis of the early existence of precontractual responsibility. The essay would later be incorporated into the second edition of 1918 of the work of 1906 (Gabriele Faggella, *I periodi precontrattuali e la responsabilità precontrattuale* (Rome: Società Cartiere Centrali, 2nd ed., 1918). Véase Carlo Bersani, Carlo, 'Gabriele Faggella', in 44 *Dizionario Biografico degli Italiani* (Rome: Istituto della Enciclopedia italiana, 1994) *ad vocem*).

337. The term 'precontractual responsibility' dates back to 1907: Raymond Saleilles, 'De La Responsabilité Précontractuelle. A propos d' un étude nouvelle sur la matière', *Revue Trimestrielle de Droit Civil*, 1907/6, at 697 et seq.

109. In concrete terms, Article 98 CCom envisages acceptance of an offer even after the deadline for acceptance has expired (*aceptación extemporanea*). But if the other party is not notified, liability for damages will arise.

Additionally, the possibility of withdrawing the offer once it has been formulated but before it has been accepted is foreseen; withdrawal is considered possible provided it is timely (*retractación tempestiva*), but it gives rise to the obligation for indemnity and liability under Article 100 CCom.

110. These are two typical hypotheses of precontractual responsibility[338] that must distinguished from the atypical hypotheses of breach of preliminary negotiations.[339] While the former, although not strictly a hypothesis of contractual responsibility, falls within the scope of contractual responsibility, the unjustified termination of negotiations is considered subject to the laws on tort responsibility.[340]

Therefore, without prejudice to what will be discussed in terms of the grounds or source of precontractual liability, it should be clear that there are two typical hypotheses, the source of which is the law.

111. Given the above, it is clear that the discussion on contractual liability began only after these codes were adopted.

As it is not expressly regulated, over the years various monographs[341] have covered the subject. Except for a few specific cases where it could be a *tertium genus*[342] of liability, the debate has been based on the dualist theory of liability and whether tort or contract law applies.

112. However, it must be clarified that the general and abstractly applicable rule on responsibility is not necessarily applicable to in hypotheses of precontractual

338. Alessandri, *Tratado,* cit., at 45.

339. For a comparative analysis (between Germany, France, Chile, and England and Wales) on these topics *see* the very interesting book of Isabel Margarita Zuloaga Rios, *Reliance in the Breaking-off of Contractual Negotiations. Trust and Expectation in a Comparative Perspective* (Cambridge: Intersentia, 2019).

340. Alessandri, *Tratado,* cit., at 45.

341. *See* Manuel Risueño, *De las obligaciones precontractuales* (Santiago de Chile: Litografía Universo, 1933); Hugo Rosende Álvarez, *Algunas consideraciones sobre la responsabilidad precontractual* (Valparaíso; Valparaíso editorial Universitaria, 1979); Isabel Margarita Zuloaga Ríos, *Teoría de la responsabilidad precontractual. Aplicaciones en la formación del consentimiento de los contratos*, (Santiago de Chile: Legal Publishing, 3rd ed, 2008); Marcelo Barrientos Zamorano, *Daños y deberes en las tratativas preliminares de un contrato* (Santiago de chile, Editorial Legal-Publishing, 2008); Rosario Celedón Förster, & Patricia Silberman Veszpremi, *Responsabilidad precontractual por ruptura de negociaciones contractuales (*Santiago de Chile: Editorial Jurídica de Chile, 2010); Roberto Ríos Ossa, *El deber precontractual de declaración del riesgo en el seguro de daños* (Santiago de chile, Editorial Legal-Publishing, 2008); Patricia Verónica López Díaz, *La tutela precontractual del acreedor* (Santiago de Chile: Thomson Reuters, 2019). Also Zuloaga Rios, *Reliance in the Breaking-off …* , cit.

342. He discusses the theoretical existence of a third type of liability: Figueroa, *Curso, IV*, cit., at 55. In concrete terms, this position is embraced by Zuloaga, *Teoría de la responsabilidad,* cit., at 124 et seq.

liability. For example, some scholars state that the provision on contractual liability is generally applicable, but precontractual liability gives rise to tort liability.[343]

113. Apart from isolated positions that are influenced by Jhering[344] and which advocate precontractual liability falls within the scope of contract law,[345] the preponderant view is that the statute on contractual liability is applicable only when the statute on tort liability[346] that the statute on tort liability is the suppletory regime in this case and applies to precontractual liability.[347]

However, even though the tort statute is supreme,[348] it must be assumed that the position of Chilean doctrine is to embrace a broad concept of precontractual responsibility that covers not only the phase subsequent to the offer but also the previous one relating to preliminary negotiations.[349] Accordingly, a more careful analysis is required, which entails considering precontractual responsibility in various stages that would sometimes be associated with contractual responsibility and sometimes with tort liability, depending on the stage of the process.

114. The first phase relates to the breakdown of negotiations. Here, the doctrine[350] agrees that precontractual liability has a tortious nature. Clearly, a breakdown of negotiations does not automatically impose liability, but will do so when negotiations are unjustly terminated and there has been certain reliance by the other party on the conclusion of the transaction, generating certain expenses or costs. A further possibility should be added to this whereby[351] such liability could be subject to contractual liability if there is a prior agreement of the parties that provides for the consequences in the event of a breakdown.

115. Once the offer has been formulated, a second phase begins, in which Articles 98 and 100 CCom come into play. These articles specifically establish a

343. For example, Abeliuk, *Las Obligaciones. II,* cit., at 909 and 912.
344. One of Jhering's first translations to French, a language more understandable to Chilean jurists, is from 1893: Ihering, Rudolf Jhering, 'De la culpa in contrahendo ou des dommages -interdi dans les conventions nulls ou restées imparfaites', *Ouvres choisis de Rudolf Von Jhering, II,* (Octave De Meulenaere trad., París: Marescq, 1893), at 1 et seq.
345. Thus Risueño, *De las obligaciones precontractuales,* cit.
346. *See* Barros, *Tratado, II,* cit., at 1115; Barrientos, *Daños,* cit., at 117 et seq. It is also noted that one of the foundations is primarily linguistic since, being precontractual, it cannot derive from the fulfilment of the contract in the same way as the contract: Figueroa, *Curso, IV,* cit. at 60.
347. *See* Barros, *Tratado, II,* cit., at 1174; Barrientos, *Daños,* cit., at 117 et seq. It is also noted that one of the foundations is primarily linguistic since, being precontractual, it cannot derive from the fulfilment of the contract in the same way as the contract: Figueroa, *Curso, IV,* cit. at 60.
348. In this sense and making general considerations: Domínguez, *Teoría general,* cit., at 95; Abeliuk, *Las Obligaciones. II,* cit. at 912.
349. Thus, for example, citing Barros, precontractual responsibility is that which occurs during the negotiation of the contract, at the time an agreement has been reached or in the event of the breakdown of negotiations. In this sense, the torts in the phase subsequent to the negotiations would be based on Arts 98 and 100 Ccom: Barros, *Tratado, II,* cit., at 1117.
350. Alessandri, *De la responsabilidad,* cit., at 45.
351. Hugo Rosende Álvarez proposes this in his work entitled 'La responsabilidad precontractual en la formación del consentimiento en los contratos reales y solemnes', *Instituciones modernas de derecho civil: Homenaje al profesor Fernando Fueyo Laneri* (Santiago de Chile: Conosur, 1996), at 345.

legal source of liability, which in cases of *aceptación extemporanea* and *retratación tempestiva* the compensation of costs incurred, including damages, is expressly provided. In this regard, if one part of the doctrine considers that both relate to a contractual responsibility,[352] another part of the doctrine argues that Article 98 (*aceptacion extemporanea*) applies to tort liability and Article 100 to contractual liability.[353]

In the case of contracts in rem and contracts requiring a certain format (e.g., written by parties or by deed of a notary public), with consensual contracts[354] there could be an additional hypothesis of precontractual responsibility related to the phase between the formal acceptance of the offer and the execution of the contract. There is no consensus among scholars as to whether this phase generates tort[355] or contractual[356] liability.

116. The so-called precontract phase is the final stage preceding the conclusion of the agreement. The doctrine essentially agrees that this phase gives rise to contractual liability.[357]

117. The case law also supports the tort nature of precontractual liability.[358] This trend is further confirmed in accordance with the liability of an employee,[359] subject

352. Alessandri, *De la responsabilidad*, cit., at 45.
353. Rosende, 'La responsabilidad precontractual', cit., at 337 and 345–346; contra Corral, Lecciones, cit., at 39. The latter author would consider that for Rosende the *omisión de retractación tempestiva* would be a case of tort liability.
354. Rosende overcomes the initial argument that the provisions of Art. 97 y ss CCOM do not apply to contracts in rem and contracts requiring a specific format: Rosende, *La responsabilidad precontractual,* cit., at 346. Rosende, 'La responsabilidad precontractual', cit., at 346. If this were not the case, he says, one would have to refer to the contract of promise which has the disadvantage of being formalized in these contracts: Rosende, *La responsabilidad precontractual,* cit., at 339.
Given that contracts in rem and contracts requiring a specific format differ also in terms of the formation of the agreement and the execution, it is not possible to accept the definition of precontractual responsibility offered by the part of the doctrine which considers precontractual liability as that which is generated by the damage caused in the preparatory phases without resulting in the formal execution of the same: Corral, *Lecciones*, cit., at 38.
355. Rosende, 'La responsabilidad precontractual', cit., at 337 et seq.
356. It is considered that this responsibility cannot be in tort since there is an offer that has already been accepted. Therefore, this author submits that a contractual responsibility exists, provided that the offer is considered an *unnamed* agreement: Corral, *Lecciones*, cit., at 39. As mentioned in the previous footnote, acceptance of this form of liability would partially contrast with his definition of precontractual liability.
357. Así se afirma que 'Debe advertirse, por último, que el contrato preliminar, como una promesa de contrato, dado que es contrato, origina ya responsabilidades netamente contractuales': Abeliuk, *Las Obligaciones. II*, cit., at 912. In the same sense e.g., Rosende, *La responsabilidad precontractual*, cit. at 347.
358. CS 29 Dec. 2011 (rol 1872/2010,); CS 12 Apr. 2012 (rol 218/2011,) comentada por Marcelo Barrientos Zamorano, 'Culpa in contrahendo en mutuo hipotecario', *Revista Chilena de Derecho* 2012/3, at 829 et seq.
359. Here we convict the bank for employee liability (due to precontractual liability) Supreme Court – Sala Primera Civil, 13 Dec. 2018 rol 45515-2017.

to proof that the relevant party acted in bad faith.[360] If bad faith cannot be proven, the action will be dismissed based on lack of evidence that the defendant unjustly interrupted the negotiations.

If the party has claimed the specific performance or compensation for damages on the basis of contractual liability (cf. Article 1489), it will not be possible to have precontractual liability even where it can be proved.[361] Nonetheless, it should be noted that there is a dissenting opinion of the Supreme Court in favour of the application of the contractual statute instead of tort provisions.[362]

B. *Basis and Attributing Factor*

118. As concerns the basis for precontractual liability, a number of aspects may be identified. On the one hand, the law appears to establish *(ex lege)* instances of precontractual liability in certain cases (Articles 98 and 100 CCom).

More generally, the theories whether precontractual liability derives from fault[363] according to Jhering's theory or whether it relates to the abuse of rights[364] have not taken root. It is believed that liability is generated by a transmutation of good faith and a violation of the canons of fair play and fair dealing to which the party should be bound during preliminary negotiations,[365] which for some is clearly wilful misconduct[366] in the event of a breakdown in negotiations. Thus, the parties are bound by the duty of loyalty even after the formulation of the offer.[367] Accordingly, case

360. CS 6 Jun. 2017 (rol 8481/2017). This confirms the judgment of appeal); también queda demostrato that the party attuó with good faith in CS 12 Jul. 2004 (rol 2622-2000, VLEX-32104576): confirms the judgment of appeal).
361. In this case the Supreme Court estimates that the Court of Appeal erred in having granted, equivocally, a precontractual responsibility since compensation was not solicited under this heading: CS 22 Nov. 2001 (rol 2217/2000, Resolución n° 18502 – Id. vLex VLEX-32103581- and Resolución n° 18503 Id. vLex VLEX-32103585).
362. In this sense the vote of Muñoz for which 'La responsabilidad precontractual, si bien participa de la extracontractual en la inexistencia de vínculo, adquiere sus contornos más apropiados en la de carácter contractual, que, además, en concepto de quien previene constituye el régimen de responsabilidad general y subsidiario en el derecho civil' CS 29 Dec. 2011 (rol 1872/2010,). For a commentary on the judgment *see* Lilian San Martín Neira, 'Responsabilidad precontractual por ruptura injustificada de negociaciones', *Rev. Chil. Derecho*, 2013/1, at 317 et seq.
363. In this sense Risueño, *De las obligaciones precontractuales,* cit.
364. *See* Ramón Domínguez Benavente & Ramón H. Domínguez Águila, & Carmen Domínguez Hidalgo, Responsabilidad precontractual. Responsabilidad extracontractual. Retiro immotivado de las negociaciones preliminares. Comentario de jurisprudencia: Corte de Apelación Concepción 5 de junio de 1996', *Revista de Derecho (Universidad de Concepción)* 1996/199, at 182; Alessandri, *De la responsabilidad*, cit., at 196.
365. Rosende, 'La responsabilidad precontractual', cit., at 344.
366. Barros, *Tratado, II* cit., at 1117.
367. Barros, *Tratado, II* cit., at 1117.

law also links liability with good faith, with criteria relating to fairness and bona fides,[368] reinforcing a trend that began in 1996[369] and was consolidated in 1998.[370]

119. As noted,[371] the duty and importance of good faith derives from the influence of canonists, and is extended to the phase preceding the formation of the contract. Therefore, one should refer to a duty of loyalty and correctness rather than the association of this responsibility with Article 1546 CC; an article which establishes the duty to behave in accordance with principles of good faith and fair dealing in relation to the contract.[372] Thus, if one assumes that the statute's applicability to this is contractual, one should not refer to this norm (as the doctrine does[373]) to justify the duty of fairness and loyalty, given that this norm is associated with contractual liability and not with precontractual liability (unless one assumes in general the applicability of the contractual regime to this).[374] Otherwise there may be a contradiction in terms. For that reason, at one point it was suggested to add a new paragraph dedicated to precontractual liability to Article 1546 CC.[375] In this way, duties

---

368. For example, CS 29 Dec. 2011 (rol nº 1872/2010, Id. vLex VLEX-436726158).
369. SCA Concepción 5 June 1996 (rol 374-1993) later ratified by the Supreme Court. This was a preliminary negotiation with a sudden breakdown of negotiations. The judgment is commented by Domiguez et al, *Responsabilidad extracontractual (1996)*, cit., at 179 et seq.
370. In connection with a lease agreement: SCA Concepción 30 June 1998 (rol 1530/96). As noted, no appeal has been filed with the Court of Cassation: Ramón Domínguez Benavente & Ramón H. Domínguez Águila, & Domínguez Hidalgo, Carmen, 'Responsabilidad precontractual. Ruptura injustificada de Negociaciones Avanzadas. Daño Causados. Comentario a Corte de Apelaciones de Concepción, 30 de junio de 1999, rol 1530/96', *Revista de Derecho Universidad de Concepción*, 1998/204, at 186–187.
371. Domínguez, *Teoría general,* cit., at 87.
372. Art. 1546 CC: 'Los contratos deben ejecutarse de buena fe, y por consiguiente obligan no sólo a lo que en ellos se expresa, sino a todas las cosas que emanan precisamente de la naturaleza de la obligación, o que por la ley o la costumbre pertenecen a ella' (*Contracts must be executed in good faith, and therefore are binding with respect not only to what is expressed therein, but also to all matters which arise precisely from the nature of the obligation, or which by law or custom belong to it*)
373. *E.g.,* Patricia Verónica López Díaz, 'La indemnización precontractual y contractual: Divergencias y eventuales zonas de confluencia'. *Presente y futuro de la responsabilidad civil* (Rodrigo Barría Díaz & Alfredo Ferrante & Lilian San Martín Neira ed., Santiago de Chile: Thomson Reuters, 2017), at 94–95; Domínguez, Teoría *general*, cit., at 86; Ducci, Derecho *Civil, IV*, cit., at 255.
374. Thus, it is interesting to note the *obiter dictum* of that judgment which states that Art. 1546 CC, relating to the principle of good faith, cannot be applied to precontractual responsibility, since this is not a form of contractual responsibility: CS 12 Jul. 2004 (rol 2622-2000, VLEX-32104576). The judgment is commented by Ramón Domínguez Águila, 'Comentario de jurisprudencia: Responsabilidad precontractual. Principio de buena fe, aplicación del art. 1546 sólo a la ejecución del contrato. Casación en el fondo por infracción de ley', *Revista de Derecho* (Universidad de Concepción) 2005/217-218, at 305 et seq.
375. It was proposed to add that: 'Las partes en el desarrollo de las tratativas en la formación del contrato deben comportarse según la buena fe' (*The parties must behave in good faith in the course of the negotiations during the formation of the contract*): Rafael Gómez Balmaceda, & Hugo Rosende Álvarez, 'Comentario crítico presentado por los profesores Rafael Gómez Balmaceda y Hugo Rosende Álvarez (a la ponencia principal presentada por el profesor don Álvaro Puelma Accorsi)'. *Estudios sobre reformas del Código Civil y Código de Comercio*, (Santiago de Chile: Editorial Jurídica, 1999), at 305. Other doctrine has proposed introducing a second paragraph to Art. 1545 CC, relating to contractual liability: 'Los interesados en las negociaciones preliminares tendientes a celebrar un contrato deberán actuar de buena fe y deberán indemnizar de todo perjuicio a la otra

of fairness and loyalty not strictly relating to Article 1546 CC could be based on the general principle of good faith; the legal basis would not be founded on a specific provision, but rather on the general principle of good faith and in the trust placed in the other party.[376]

C. Business to Consumer Contracts

120. What is certain is that consumer legislation and the business-to-consumer relationship have contributed to the evolution of precontractual responsibility[377] by providing for precise duties relating to the negotiation phase, which are typified[378] in the Consumer Protection Act.

Thus, specific disclosure obligations require true and appropriate information to be provided (Article 3 letra c) Ley 19.496), and non-compliance can also lead to liability for omission.[379] It is also important to remember the role of wilful misconduct in relation to precontractual obligations in insurance contracts.[380] Or, as will

---

parte en caso contrario', Álvaro Puelma Accorsi., 'Ponencia principal presentada en Seminario sobre contratos preparatorios'. *Estudios sobre reformas del Código Civil y Código de Comercio*, (Santiago de Chile: Editorial Jurídica, 1999), at 290.

376. On good faith and the protection of trust (*confianza tutelable*) *see* Patricia Verónica López Díaz, 'La confianza razonable y su relevancia como criterio fundante de la tutela de ciertas anomalías o disconformidades acaecidas durante el iter contractual: una aproximación desde la doctrina y la jurisprudencia chilenas', *Revista de derecho privado (Universidad Externado de Colombia)*, 2019/36, at 127 et seq.; Iñigo De la Maza Gazmuri, 'El retiro unilateral como un caso de responsabilidad precontractual', *Cuadernos de análisis jurídico. Temas de Contratos* (Iñigo De la Maza Gazmuri ed.), 2006/3, at 147 et seq.

377. The topic of precontractual liability in the field of consumer law has been discussed in María Sara Rodríguez Pinto, 'Supuestos de responsabilidad civil precontractual en la ley N° 19.496, de 1997, sobre protección de los derechos de los consumidores', *Gaceta Jurídica*, 2012/384, at 7 et seq.; María Sara Rodríguez Pinto, 'Responsabilidad precontractual en la Ley N° 19.496 de 1997 sobre Protección de los Derechos de los Consumidores', *Estudios de Derecho Civil, Jornadas Nacionales de Derecho Civil, Santa Cruz 2012* (Carmen Domínguez Hidalgo, *et al.* ed.) (Santiago de Chile: Legal Publishing Thomson Reuters, 2013), at 493 et seq.; Marcelo Barrientos Zamorano, 'Tendencias de la jurisprudencia reciente por danos en estacionamientos y el deber precontractual de seguridad en el consumo', *Estudios de Derecho Civil, Jornadas Nacionales de Derecho Civil, Santa Cruz 2012* (Carmen Domínguez Hidalgo, *et al.* ed.) (Santiago de Chile: Legal Publishing Thomson Reuters, 2013), at 429 et seq.; Patricia Verónica López Díaz, 'Por una modulación reequilibradora del ámbito de aplicación subjetivo de la Ley 19.496: su expansión a las tratativas preliminares y al período de prueba del bien o producto y su improcedencia frente al abuso del consumidor', *Revista de Derecho Universidad de Concepción*, 2018/244, at 91 et seq.; Patricia Verónica López Díaz, 'La tutela precontractual en la Ley 19.496: su configuración, alcance y eventual convergencia con aquella propia de la contratación civil', *Revista Chilena de de Derecho*, 2019/2, at 399 et seq.

378. On the typicity and atypicality of disclosure obligations, *see* Inigo De la Maza Gazmuri, 'Tipicidad y atipicidad de los deberes precontractuales de información', *Revista de Derecho (PUCV)*, 2010/34, at 75 et seq.

379. Figueroa, *Curso, IV*, cit., at 60. More specifically, we refer to Inigo De la Maza Gazmuri, 'Buena fe, el reverso de la moneda. A propósito del dolo por omisión y el deber precontractual de informar', *Revista Chilena de Derecho Privado*, 2008/11, at 43 et seq.

380. Ferrante, ¿Hacia un concepto, cit., at 43 et seq.

be discussed *infra*, certain disclosure obligations relating to defects.[381] Precontractual liability also occurs in the consumer sphere, based on duties of loyalty and disclosure.[382]

121. The existence of a law in favour of the weaker party supports to notion that precontractual liability is based on law (*ex lege*). Accordingly, claims for compensation for damages arise from non-compliance with disclosure obligations in violation of the principles of protection, transparency and confidence that are generated for example in the case of products dangerous to health and physical integrity (cf. Articles 44–46 Ley 19.496), or in the case of false or misleading advertising (Articles 28 and 28 A Ley 19.496). As concerns for others kinds of contracts, here precontractual liability might arise in the event of an unfair sale (Article 13 Ley 19.496), whereas administrative sanctions may be applied that would warrant compensation for damages (cf. Articles 3, 23, 26, 50, 50H Ley 19.496).

Scholars that accept the application of 'relative nullity' as a remedy and not a sanction have considered extending this solution to cases of precontractual responsibility and unfair terms (or clauses).[383] Basing their argument on the assumption that precontractual responsibility is subject to the rules of tort, this part of the doctrine supports the admissibility of concurrent consumer claims including remedies of customary law.[384] However, it appears[385] that an administrative sanction is not necessarily a consequence of tort liability; administrative sanctions may be contractual in nature (e.g., when a merchant fails to allow the remedy chosen by the consumer in the event of non-conforming goods, cfr. Articles 21, 22, 23, 26 Ley 19.496).

D. Frustrated Contract and Nullity: Nature of Liability Arising from Nullity

122. Part of the doctrine has explained that cases of precontractual responsibility (called frustrated contract)[386] must be distinguished from situations in which the contract was formed but then declared invalid due to specific circumstances (e.g., lack of consent). it follows that compensation does not technically derive from the

381. *See* para. 126.
382. Patricia Verónica López Díaz, 'Los supuestos y el alcance de la indemnización de daños como medio de tutela precontractual en el Código Civil chileno y su eventual confluencia con la indemnización por incumplimiento contractual', *Ius et Praxis* 2018/1, at 282.
383. López, *La responsabilidad precontractual en la Ley 19.496*, cit., at 409 et seq.
384. Patricia Verónica López Díaz, '*La tutela precontractual y contractual del acreedor en el código civil chileno: dos sistemas estructuralmente diversos pero, ¿plenamente coherentes y convergentes'*, *Rev. Chilena de Derecho Privado*, 2017/29, at 9 et seq., López, *Las relaciones, supra*, at 66; López, *La responsabilidad precontractual en la Ley 19.496*, cit., at 413 et seq.; López, *Los supuestos*, cit. at 282, López, *La tutela (2019)*, cit., *passim*.
385. *See* paras 92 et seq.
386. Tapia, *De la responsabilidad*, cit., at 426 y 467 et seq.

nullity itself but rather from the application of the general principle of *neminem laedere*, which is non-contractual[387] in nature. Therefore, claims for damages are non-contractual and accordingly independent from the action of nullity.[388]

123. Therefore, with some exceptions,[389] the hypotheses of nullity are not intimately related to precontractual responsibility. The doctrine essentially agrees that compensation in such cases relates to tort liability. These hypotheses are analysed in detail.

124. In relation to the sale of an object (or part of it) that is known not to exist (Article 1814.3 CC), tort liability arises since *nulidad* operates retroactively and therefore cannot be associated with contractual liability,[390] also because it would be associated with a malicious hypothesis of the seller that would generate tort liability.[391]

Even though it is generally accepted that liability for defects of consent (error, force, malice) is non-contractual in nature,[392] it is stated that the legislator has expressly sanctioned this form of liability in certain cases (e.g., the case of error *in persona*). In these circumstances, compensation unrelated to contractual liability is recognized in the case of an error regarding the other contracting party (Article 1455.2 CC)[393] and when an error *in persona* is made during a transaction (Article 2456 CC).[394]

125. Conversely, contractual liability could arise when a mandate is declared null and void, as the provision states that where the agent executes a null contract

387. Domínguez, *Teoría general*, cit., at 407–408.
388. Domínguez, *Teoría general*, cit., at 408.
389. Rejecting the concept of nullity as a sanction, an isolated doctrine has considered nullity not only related to tort liability but has considered it to be a remedy in the precontractual phase. In this sense, it would have admitted the possibility of being able to opt between such hypotheses of extracontractual liability (as for example in the case of *vizio del consentimiento*, or defect of consent) with contractual remedies, such as that of termination for non-performance: Patricia Verónica López Díaz, 'La nulidad como un medio de tutela precontractual en el Código Civil chileno: configuración, modalidad de ejercicio y eventual concurrencia con la resolución por incumplimiento', *Revista de Derecho (Coquimbo)*, 2019/26, e3597.
390. Alessandri, *De la responsabilidad*, cit., at 45–46, retmado también por Abeliuk, *Las Obligaciones. II*, cit., at 912–913.
391. Tapia, *De la responsabilidad*,cit., at 541; Arturo Alessandri Rodríguez, *De la Compraventa y de la Promesa de Venta I-1* (Santiago de Chile: Editorial Jurídica de Chile, 2017, re-edition of work of 1917), at 195.
392. Alessandri, *De la responsabilidad*, cit., at 45–46.
393. Alessandri, *De la responsabilidad*, cit., at 45–46; Abeliuk, *Las Obligaciones. II,* cit., at 912–913; Tapia, *De la responsabilidad*, cit., at 540. Isolating the part of the doctrine that argues the provision includes a presumption of fault, attributing precontractual responsibility to a *culpa in conrahendo* based on the teachings of Ihering and which would essentially adopt the principle of presumption under Art. 1547.3 CC: Augusto Fuentes de la Sotta, *La responsabilidad por el hecho de otro en material contractual* (Santiago: Universidad de Chile, 1938), at 43 et seq.
394. In this sense, the tort liability would apply to him to 'apply the general principle of art. 1455 CC': Tapia, *De la responsabilidad*, cit., at 540.

in good faith he becomes a bona fide agent (Article 2122 CC).[395] If this is so, it should follow that performing the mandate with malice gives rise to tort liability.

E. Certain Disclosure Requirements and Hidden Defects in the Object or Property Sold, Leased, or Borrowed

126. In relation to certain disclosure obligations indirectly provided for by the code,[396] it should be recalled that in relation to hidden defects in the purchase and sale, Article 1861 CC recognizes compensation for damages 'if the seller knew of the defects and did not disclose them' or 'if the defects were such that the seller should have known of them by virtue of his profession'.

This interpretation is more varied since it appears to consider that such compensation is linked to the precontractual phase and therefore of an extracontractual nature.[397] Another approach distinguishes the two hypotheses in the sense that if the first derives from a situation of malice (and therefore is of an extracontractual nature), the second instead is related to gross negligence and should be associated with a contractual responsibility since the negligence does not necessarily (as opposed to malice) derive from a behaviour prior to the formation of the contract.[398] A third position instead suggests that since the contract has been executed, the bad faith or negligence that has concealed the defects is of contractual nature.[399]

127. Following this reasoning, all forms of compensation resulting from an executed contract are contractual, notwithstanding, as in the case of the lease (*arrendamiento*), the defect exists prior to the establishment of the contract (Articles 1932–1933 CC).[400] This would offer greater support to the theory since Article 1933 CC expressly provides for compensation for actual damage, while precontractual liability entitles the injured party only to recover the so-called negative interest. Still, part of the doctrine[401] argues this falls within the scope of precontractual

---

395. Corral, *Lecciones*, cit., at 42.
396. As is the case, for example, also in the situation of an immaterial error under Art. 1454 no. 2 CC, Domínguez, *Teoría general*, cit., at 89. On the duty to disclose any unapparent or hidden defects, *see also* Barros, *Tratado, II*, cit., at 1119 et seq.
397. A part of scholars differentiates nature (contractual or non-contractual) depending on the remedy chosen in these cases. So the compensation related to hidden defects in this cases in related to a non-contractual liability: Patricia Verónica López Díaz, 'Las relaciones entre la tutela precontractual y contractual del acreedor: la conexión y la proyección-absorción', *Revista de Derecho (PUCV)*, 2018/30, at 69 y ss; cf. Patricia Verónica López Díaz, 'La protección del acreedor por vicios redhibitorios en el Código Civil chileno: entre la fase precontractual y contractual', *Revista de Derecho (PUCV)*, 2016/47, ap. 57 et seq.
398. This is the position of Ferrante, *Consideraciones*, cit., at 883–884.
399. Ducci, *Derecho Civil, IV*, cit. at 255–256.
400. Ducci, *Derecho Civil, IV*, cit. at 255–256. The author also finds similar reasoning for Arts 1928 and 1959.
401. López, *Las relaciones 2018*, *supra*, at 69 et seq.

responsibility and is as such non-contractual. Similar reasoning is applied for undisclosed defects of objects of a loan agreement (Article 2183 CC).[402]

F. Quantum

128. In relation to the *quantum* (or extent) of precontractual liability, it is necessary to differentiate from the stage in which one fines oneself. The distinctive feature of this situation is that if there is an unjustified breakdown in negotiations, the negative interest (i.e., the indirect expenses incurred by the party for which blame cannot be imputed) may be compensated,[403] although some argue that compensation may be awarded for the *perdida de chance* (loss of chance).[404]

129. In the case of Articles 98 and 100 CCom, compensation is due for the negative interest as well as any actual loss, including lost profits.[405]

130. What is unusual is that the Court of Cassation seems to confuse the two criteria in certain situations, combining negative interest with actual damage (or the so-called positive interest) and lost profit.[406]

131. It has been established that the 'relative interest' should also be compensated in cases of nullity.[407] However, as explained above, this would require considering each and every type of case since the indemnification could also have a broader scope (although it does not appear possible to compensate for lost profits in this case).[408]

402. Contract theory (also in relation to Art. 2188 CC): Ducci, *Derecho Civil, IV*, cit., at 255–256; *contra* López, 'Las relaciones' cit., at 69 et seq.
403. Domínguez, *Teoría general*, cit., at 95. In a nearly analogous sense: Barros, *Tratado, II* cit., at 1118; Patricia Verónica López Díaz, 'La indemnización precontractual y contractual: Divergencias y eventuales zonas de confluencia'. *Presente y futuro de la responsabilidad civil* (Rodrigo Barría Díaz & Alfredo Ferrante & Lilian San Martín Neira ed., Santiago de Chile: Thomson Reuters, 2017), at 100. *See* Francisco Segura Riveiro, 'El interés contractual indemnizable en las hipótesis de responsabilidad precontractual', in *Estudios de Derecho Civil II. Jornadas Nacionales de Derecho Civil, Olmue, 2006* (Hernán Corral Talciani & María Sara Rodríguez ed., Santiago de Chile, Abeledo Perrot, 2007) at 345 et seq.
    For case law, *see e.g.*, the indemnification of operating expenses in connection with a mortgage contract: SCS 12 Apr. 2012 (Rol 218/2011) commented by Barrientos, 'Culpa in contrahendo en mutuo hipotecario', cit., at 829 et seq.
404. Corral, *Lecciones*, cit., at 43.
405. For Rosende, it is also possible to compensate for moral damage. In the timely retraction of Art. 100, the limit on compensation consists of compensating without making the injured party better off than he would have been had the contract been correctly executed: Rosende, 'La responsabilidad precontractual', cit. at 345–346.
406. CS 29 Dec. 2011 (rol 1872/2010).
407. Domínguez, *Teoría general*, cit. at 137.
408. On this point, *see* Barros, *Tratado, II* cit., at 1125–1126.

§6. Protected Interests

132. The CPR protects individuals by providing a range of actionable rights. In this sense, Article 19 CPR lists a considerable number of rights.

Among these, several stand out: 'the right to life and to the physical and mental integrity of the person' (Article 19 n. 1 CPR), equality between individuals and groups must be guaranteed before the law, stating that 'in Chile there is no privileged person or group' (Article 19 n. 2 CPR), making it necessary to safeguard 'Equal protection under the law in the exercise of their rights' (Article 19 n. 3 CPR), 'Respect and protection of private and public life and the integrity of the individual and his or her family' (Article 19 n. 4 CPR); 'The right to personal liberty and security of person' (Article 19 n. 7 CPR).[409]

133. The right to property in all its forms is also protected, within the meaning of Article 19 n. 24 CPR: *the right of ownership in its various forms over all kinds of tangible or intangible property.*[410]

134. Since 1999,[411] the protection of private life (*protección de la vida privada*) has been governed, consolidating the approach taken by the case law that has gradually led to the awarding of damages for violation of the right to privacy and damage to reputation.[412]

The compensation related to the respect for private life and honour[413] has been effectively protected by the courts since 2008 through the inapplicability of the

409. On the constitutionalization of private law Barros, *Tratado*, I, cit., at 259 et seq. On the limits that in contractual matters may entail the specific performance or in non-pecuniary damage: Claudia Bahamondes Oyarzún & José Luis Ugarte Cataldo, 'Hacia una distinción conceptual entre la afectación de los derechos fundamentales y la provocación del daño moral', *Fundamentos Filosóficos del Derecho Civil Chileno* (Esteban Pereira Fredes, ed9 (Santiago de Chile, 2019) at 413 et seq.; Claudia Bahamondes Oyarzún, 'La ejecucion personal como límite al cumplimiento específico del contrato: un acercamiento a partir de los derechos fundamentales del deudor', *Estudios de Derecho Civil XIII* (Claudia Bahamondes Oyarzún, Leonor Etcheberry Court, Carlos Pizarro Wilson ed.) (Santiago de Chile: Thomson Reuters, 2018), at 799 et seq.; Claudía Bahamondes Oyarzún, *El cumplimiento específico de los contratos* (Santiago de Chile: Der, 2019), at 213 et seq.

410. *See* paras 213 and 530.

411. Ley 19.628/1999, of 18 Aug. (DO 28 Aug. 2018). *See* Emilio Pfeffer Urquiaga, Emilio, 'Los derechos a la intimidad o privacidad, a la honra y a la propia imagen. Su protección frente a la libertad de opinión e información', *Ius et Praxis*, 2000/1, at 465 et seq.; Pablo Contreras Vásquez & Pablo Trigo Kramcsák, 'Interés legítimo y tratamiento de datos personales: antecedentes comparados y regulación en Chile'. *Revista Chilena de Derecho y tecnología*, 2019/1, at 69 et seq.; Carlos Benussi Díaz, 'Obligaciones de seguridad en el tratamiento de datos personales en Chile: Escenario actual y desafíos regulatorios pendientes', *Revista Chilena de Derecho y tecnología*, 2020/1, at 227 et seq.

412. *See* paras 237 et seq.

413. Carmen Domínguez Hidalgo, 'El principio de reparación integral del daño y su proyección en materia de daño moral causado por afectación al honor de la persona en Chile', *El Principio de Reparación Integral en sus Contornos Actuales. Una Revisión desde el derecho Chileno. Latinoamericano y Europeo* (Carmen Domínguez Hidalgo, ed.) (Santiago de Chile: Thomson Reuters, 2019), at 123 et seq.; Carmen Domínguez Hidalgo, 'La tutela al honor: una mirada presente y hacia el futuro', *Estudios de derecho civil VII*, (Fabián Elorriaga De Bonis ed.) (Santiago de Chile: Thomson Reuters, Abeledo Perrot, 2012), at 797 et seq.; Gonzalo Linazasoro Campos, 'Artículo 2331

limitations of Article 2333 CC[414] and the consequent possibility of indemnifying the injured party in such cases. Hence, it is considered that 'the rule is disproportionate, by absolutely and a priori precluding the award of compensation for moral damages when the credit or honor of a person is deemed to have been damaged by unjust remarks. Thus, the essence of a right protected by the Constitution (Article 19, No. 4) is affected)'.[415]

135. This view was consolidated in 2012 with the law that establishes the principle of finality of personal data.[416] The reform of 2018[417] is fundamental in that it constitutionally consecrates the right to the protection of personal data,[418] although its final text was substantially reduced compared to what was envisaged during its preparation.[419] In this sense, the progressive protection of these situations can be framed as contractual or tort liability.

---

del Código Civil: Las razones de su inaplicabilidad por inconstitucionalidad', *Estudios de Derecho Civil V. Jornadas Nacionales de Derecho Civil, Concepción, 2009.* (Derecho de Derecho Privado, Universidad de Concepción ed.) (Santiago de Chile: AbeledoPerrot, 2010), at 763 et seq.; Manuel Nuñez Poblete, 'Desaplicación e inaplicación jurisdiccional de las leyes en chile: ejercicio de la jurisdicción y control concreto de constitucionalidad', *Revista de Derecho Universidad Católica del Norte*, 2012/ 2, at 191 et seq. Cristián Andrés Larrain Páez, 'Algunas cuestiones relevantes sobre el derecho al honor y la responsabilidad civil, en partícular sobre el daño moral, el art. 2331 del Código Civil y la legitimación activa'. *Revista Chilena de Derecho Privado*, 2011/17, at 143 et seq.

414. STC 10 June 2008 (rol 943), STC 15 Apr. 2014 (rol 2513/2014), STC of 29 Jan. 2014 (rol 2255/ 2014), STC 29 Mar. 2011 (rol 1798/2011); STC 24 May 2011 (rol 172310/2011); STC 15 Mar. 2011 (rol 1741/2011); STC 15 Mar. 2011 (rol 1679/2011); STC 9 Nov. 2010 (rol 1419/2010); STC 23 Sept. 2010 (rol 1463/2010), STC 16 Apr. 2009 (Rol 1185/2009).
415. SCS 24 Oct. 2013 (rol 2422/2013).
416. Ley 20.575/2012, of 14 Feb. (DO 17 Feb. 2012). Carlos Peña González, 'Informe sobre el proyecto de Ley de Protección del honor y la intimidad de las personas'. *Cuadernos de Análisis Jurídico*, 2004/1, at 75–104.
417. *See* paras 237 et seq.
418. Ley 21096/2018, of 5 June (DO 16 June 2018).
419. The current Art. 19.4 CPR states that the CPR establishes the individual right to 'El respeto y protección a la vida privada y a la honra de la persona y su familia, y asimismo, la protecciónde sus datos personales. El tratamiento y protección de estos datos se efectuará en la forma y condiciones quedetermine la ley' (*The respect and protection of the private life and honour of the individual and his family, as well as the protection of their personal data. The processing and protection of this data shall be carried out in the manner and under the conditions determined by law*).

    The draft law provides for the introduction of the following *ad hoc* clause: Art. 19.4 CPR 'Toda persona tiene derecho a la protección de sus datos personales y obtener su rectificación –, complementación y cancelación, si estos fueren – erróneos o afectaren sus derechos, como asimismo a manifestar su oposición, de acuerdo con las disposiciones establecidas en la ley. Su tratamiento sólo podrá hacerse por ley o con el – consentimiento expreso del titular' (*Every person has the right to the protection of his personal data and to correct, supplement and cancel such data if it is incorrect or affects his rights, as well as to express his opposition, in accordance with the provisions established by law. The processing may only be carried out in accordance with the law or with the express consent of the data subject*). *See* Alfredo Ferrante, 'Lesión del Derehco al honor y tratamiento de datos referidos al incumplimiento de la obligación dineraria', *Revista Chilena de Derecho Privado*, 2014/23, at 300–305.

136. Protection of one's reputation has also found important protection in various forms.[420]

137. In the realm of consumer law, the LPC expressly provides for the protection of individual 'dignity' in the context of consumer relations (Article 15 Ley 19.496). Accordingly, 'la integridad física o psíquica de los consumidores e la su dignidad' (*the physical or psychological integrity of consumers and their dignity*) are also worthy of protection and prejudice to one's dignity may give rise to increased administrative sanctions (Articles 24 and 37.7). This was established by the 2018 reform[421] by implicitly allowing claimants to seek damages for violations in these cases (Article 51.2 LPC).

138. Contractual liability may also arise in response to the infringement of fundamental labour rights.[422]

420. The relevant references are found in: Cristián Larraín Páez, 'Responsabilidad por vulneración de derecho al imagen: análisis comparado y propuestas para el derecho chileno', Revista Chilena de Derecho Privado, 2016/26, at 119–185; Alfredo Ferrante, 'La protección a la imagen y sy materialidad en el ordenamiento chileno', *Rev. Boliv. de Derecho* 2017/23, at 134 et seq.; Jorge Allapán Quinteros, 'El derecho a la propia imagen: ¿Derecho personalísimo? ¿Derecho Fundamental? Precisiones terminológica para el ordenamiento jurídico chileno', *Revista Chilena de Derecho*, 2016/2, at 433 et seq.

421. Ley 21.081, of 13 Jul. (DO 13 Sept. 2018).

422. Cf. e.g., Arts 485, 489 DFL 1/2003 On this point: Corral, *Lecciones,* cit., at 255 et seq.; Bahamondes Oyarzún & Ugarte Cataldo, 'Hacia una distinción conceptual entre la afectación de los derechos fundamentales y la provocación del daño moral', cit., at 413 et seq.

Part I. Liability for One's Own Acts

Chapter 1. General Principles

§1. Unlawfulness and Fault

I. Overview

139. Part of the doctrine has traditionally identified personal responsibility (liability for one's own acts) with the terminology *responsabilidad simple* to distinguish such liability from the so-called complex liability (*responsabilidad compleja*) associated with liability for things, animals or 'acts for others'.[423]

140. The system of civil liability set out in the Civil Code (Articles 2314 et seq. CC) is divided into three categories: liability for one's own actions (Articles 2314, 2329 CC), liability for the actions of others (Articles 2320–2322) and liability in cases where an object is involved in causing damage due to its operation or its flaws (Articles 2323, 2324, 2326, 2328 CC).[424]

II. Structure of Liability for One's Own Actions

141. The liability scheme set out in the Civil Code has traditionally been regarded as a system of subjective liability for fault. Therefore, this is the general system and in the absence of express provision, the subjective system must be adhered to. However, there is a lack of standardization in the way it defines the so-called elements[425] or foundations that differentiate it from strict liability,[426] including the 'requirements'[427] for establishing such liability. Some believe that it is necessary to distinguish between a 'general prerequisite' (known as capacity), and the other 'requirements or elements'.[428]

423. Alessandri, *Responsabilidad*, cit., at 70
424. Alessandri, *Responsabilidad*, cit., at 211.
425. Alessandri, *Responsabilidad*, cit., at 95; Ruz, *Explicaciones*, cit., at 455; Tapia, *De la responsabilidad*, cit., at 155; Rodriguez Grez, *Responsabilidad extracontractual*, cit., at 119.
426. Ramos, *De la responsabilidad Civil*, cit., at 36, although he then uses requirements and elements indistinctly at 46. Recently the doctrine has begun to differentiate more clearly the existence of two systems, subjective and objective, within the Chilean system: Barros, *Tratado*, I, cit., at 31–37.
427. Aedo, *Responsabilidad* cit., at 155.
428. Corral, *Lecciones*, cit., at 99.

142. Traditionally, these elements include: (1) capacity of the wrongdoer, (2) malice or fault,[429] (3) damage, (4) causation,[430] sometimes replacing capacity with the concept of *hecho imputable*.[431] In this sense, capacity seems to be a synonym for imputability. This position is illogical given that some consider fault and imputability to be synonyms,[432] while some regard them as separate elements,[433] and others still consider imputability as the combination of fault/malice and capacity.[434] Additionally, a less traditional theory also includes the concept of unlawfulness without specifying what to associate it with.[435] Speaking of unlawfulness,[436] as it refers to either unlawful conduct[437] or an unlawful fact (*hecho*),[438] unlawful, illicit or unjust means contrary to law (*derecho*) and therefore objectively goes against a practice, norm or principle of the legal system.[439] While in other cases the unlawful nature of the damage may be eliminated if it can be proved the damage was justified. Ultimately, the concept of unlawfulness is not an independent element, as it is in criminal law,[440] whereby the illicit nature of the act is essentially understood. For this reason, there has been a plurality of evolutionary creations and reconstructions, which has led to the mixing of these elements, sometimes chaotically.

143. Deferring to later aspects relating to causation[441] and damage/prejudice,[442] an action or an omission may give rise to liability[443] whenever an action that should have been or could have been carried out was omitted.[444] This omission may be

---

429. There are those who consider that *culpabibilidad* (other than fault) should also be added, which would be identified as a '*juicio de reproche personal':* Enrique Alcalde Rodríguez, 'El error de derecho como causal eximente de la responsabilidad extracontratual', *Actualidad Jurídica*, 2013/28, at 237. Sobre la culpabilidad y su derivación desde el derecho penal e.g., *see* Claudia Marcela Cárdenas Aravena, 'El principio de culpabilidad: estado de la cuestión', *Revista de Derecho, Universidad Católica del Norte,* 2008/2, at 67 et seq. On 'reprochabilidad' as a synonym of 'culpabilidad' and essentially also of fault instead: Corral, *Lecciones*, cit., at 202 et seq. As has already been pointed out, the doctrinal constructions are fluctuating and innumerable in this area: for example, for others, 'reproachable' is synonymous with 'imputable': Figueroa, *Curso, IV*, cit., at 95.
430. Alessandri, *Responsabilidad*, cit., at 95; Ruz, *Explicaciones*, cit., at 455.
431. Barros, *Tratado*, I, cit., at 69 et seq.
432. Ramos, *De la responsabilidad* cit., at 41.
433. Tapia, *De la responsabilidad*, cit., at 156.
434. Figueroa, *Curso, IV*, cit., at 89; Hugo Rosende, 'Algunos aspectos acerca de las nuevas tendencias sobre la responsabilidad civil extracontractual', *Actualidad Jurídica*, 2000/2, at 278.
435. Aedo, *Responsabilidad*, cit., at 155 et seq.
436. Aedo, *Responsabilidad*, cit., at 241 et seq.
437. Figueroa, *Curso IV*, cit., at 89; Hugo Rosende, 'Algunos aspectos', cit., at 278.
438. Corral, *Lecciones,* cit., at 99, more generally at 111 et seq. Rodríguez Grez, *Responsabilidad extracontractual*, cit., at 117, 129 et seq.
439. Corral, *Lecciones,* cit., at 99.
440. *See* Ried, 'El efecto de la cosa juzgada', cit., at 21.
441. *See* paras 396 et seq.
442. *See* paras 435 et seq.
443. For example, Figueroa, *Curso, IV*, cit., at 89. Alessandri discusses *culpa in ommitendo* in relation to Arts 2320–2323, 2326, 2327, 2339, 2333: Alessandri, *Responsabilidad*, cit., at 143.
444. In this sense, omission is produced when a provision imposes the obligation to perform an action that one has omitted to carry out: Tapia, *De la Responsabilidad*, cit. at 148.

intentional or related to *culpa infraccional* (related to an infraction).[445] This means that the wrongdoer's *behaviour* and the *standard* of reference that was or should have been adopted (fault and duty of care) must be analysed. This is also related to the *voluntariness* in the commission of such fact, and as a result they will reveal the *capacity and imputability* of the subject (imputability and capacity).

§2. Concept of Fault

I. Fault and Diligence

144. Traditionally,[446] fault[447] has been associated with a lack of diligence.[448] Over time, however, in the wake of the French approach and the term *faute,*[449] fault and malice have been used in a broad sense, noting that the terminology of the code refers to the canon of negligence rather than to fault[450] (Articles 2319, 2329, 2333 CC). Although there are those who note that there is no distinction between the concepts of fault, negligence and imprudence,[451] fault is more broadly framed as *ilicitud de la conducta.*[452] This leads some to identify fault with unlawfulness,[453] or to see fault as opposed to legality.[454] Liability may also be established for the violation of customs.[455]

445. Barros, *Tratado,* I, cit., at 129 et seq. In this case, for example, there is a duty to rescue a person, although this is only manifested in cases of extreme necessity and to the extent it does not presuppose danger for the person being rescued (*see* Art. 494 nos. 13 and 14 CP).
446. It is noted that this stems from the fact that the classical or subjective theory of liability is traditionally followed in Chile: Ramos, *De la responsabilidad Civil*, cit., at 48. In general *see* Cristián Aedo Barrena, 'El concepto normativo de la culpa', *Estudios de derecho civil IX* (Juan Andrés Varas Braun, Susan Turner Saelzer ed.) (Santiago de Chile: Thomson Reuters, Legal Publishing, 2014) at 485 et seq.; Pablo Rodríguez Grez, 'Apreciación de la culpa en materia civil', *Revista Chilena de Derecho Privado*, 2004/2, at 95 et seq.
447. Extensive reference is made to Cristián Aedo Barrena, *Culpa Aquiliana. Una conjunción de aspéctos historicos y dogmáticos* (Santiago de chile: Thomson Reuters, 2018).
448. Galvarino Moreno Araya, *La teoría de la culpa en el código civil,* (Santiago de Chile: memoria de prueba: Universidad de Chile, 1927), *passim*; Figueroa, *Curso, IV*, cit., at 95.
449. Tapia, *De la Responsabilidad,* cit., at 157.
450. Figueroa, *Curso, IV,* cit., at 100.
451. Corral, *Lecciones*, cit., at 212, critically *see* Gian Franco Rosso Elorriaga, 'Negligencia, imprudencia e impericia como conceptos negativos integradores de la culpa: un intento di conceptuación', *Estudios de derecho civil III*, (Alejandro Guzmán Brito ed.) (Santiago de Chile: Thomson Reuters, 2008) at 693 et seq.
452. Barros, *Tratado*, I, cit., at 83 et seq.; *see* Cristián Aedo Barrena, 'La culpa como ciriterio de distribución de riesgos sociales ¿Hay en la culpa una infracción de deber de cuidado?', *Estudios de derecho civil X* (Álvaro Vidal Olivares, Gonzalo Severín Fuster, Caludia Mejías Alonso ed.) (Santiago de Chile: Thomson Reuters, 2015) at 811 et seq.
453. Barros, *Tratado*, I, cit., at 102.
454. Cristián Aedo Barrena, 'El concepto normativo de la culpa como criterio de distribución de riesgos. Un análisis jurisprudencial'. *Revista chilena de Derecho*, 2014/2, at 707; Corral, *Lecciones*, cit., at 211.
455. In this case, the judge will have wider margins of interpretative action: Alessandri, *Responsabilidad*, cit., at 146; Barros, *Tratado*, I, cit., at 108–112.

145. Influenced by the German doctrine, there are those who[456] have analysed the confluence of certain aspects of fault in causation. It has also been pointed out that the foreseeability of the damage can operate both in relation to the attribution of fault to the wrongdoer, or a possible mediation of the compensation in relation to causation for the objective imputation of the consequences of the initial damage.[457]

II. Possible Presumptions of Fault

146. The general principle of *neminem laedere*, which is subjective in nature, is incorporated in two general rules: Articles 2314 and 2329 CC.[458] For the first, it is considered that: *Whoever has committed a crime or quasi-delict that has caused damage to another is obliged to pay compensation, without prejudice to the penalty imposed by law for the crime or quasi-delict.* Article 2329 states: 'Por regla general todo daño que pueda imputarse a malicia o negligencia de otra persona, debe ser reparado por ésta' (*As a general rule, any damage that can be attributed to the malice or negligence of another person must be repaired by the latter*). The similarity of these provisions – combined with the fact that in its second paragraph, Article 2329 provides three cases in which it is stated that the authors 'are specifically obliged to indemnify' – has prompted various interpretations.[459]

147. Three macro interpretations are possible in interpreting the difference from Article 2329 CC.[460] The first interpretation essentially states that Article 2329 includes a 'presumption of fault'. The second one finds there is a presumption of a causal[461] link.

The third[462] suggests there is a difference between Articles 2329 and 2314, but it is not based on any type of presumption (neither of fault nor of causality). According to a historical reconstruction, there is no presumption of fault, but Article 2314

456. Cristián Aedo Barrena, 'La recepción de la creación de riesgos no permitidos en el Derecho chileno, como criterio de imputació objetiva, ¿puede distinguirse de la culpa?', *Revista Chilena de Derecho Privado*, 2020/ 35, at 117–145; Ramos, *De la responsabilidad*, cit., at 55.

457. Barros, *Tratado*, I, cit., at 97; Corral, *Lecciones*, cit., at 210–211.

458. Corral, *Lecciones,* cit., at 90. *See* Joaquín Polit Corvalán, '¿Qué ha hecho realmente la jurisprudencia sobre la presunción general de culpa por el hecho propio?', *Estudios de derecho civil X* (Álvaro Vidal Olivares, Gonzalo Severín Fuster, Caludia Mejías Alonso ed.) (Santiago de Chile: Thomson Reuters, 2015) at 827 et seq.

459. The doctrine has observed that if in Chile the debate is open (whether to admit the presumption of guilt or not), in the analogous case Colombian prefers the presumption *see* Fabricio Mantilla Espinosa, Carlos Pizarro Wilson, 'La responsabilidad civil por actividades peligrosas: aplique primero y explique después', *Revista de Derecho* (Escuela de Postgrado Universidad de Chile), 2013/ 4, at 17 et seq.

460. In the sense that Art. 2329 is not a mere repetition of Art. 2314: Tapia, *De la responsabilidad*, at 527, 540

461. Corral, *Lecciones*, cit., at 223 and 226.

462. Javier Barrientos Grandon, 'De la presunción general de culpa por el hecho propio. A propósito de los artículos 2314 y 2329 y de nuestro 'Código Civil imaginario' (II)', *Revista Chilena de Derecho Privado* 2009/13, at 9 et seq. In part, this nuance is also observed by Rodriguez Grez, *Responsabilidad extracontractual*, cit., at 211–212.

refers to crimes and criminal offences, e.g., *delitos* or *cuasidelitos* (*responsabilidad civil ex delicto*), while Article 2329 refers to civil liability pertaining to damages for civil offences (*delitos civiles*).

148. To understand the first interpretation and the corollaries that have emerged from it, it must be premised that, as a general rule (also in accordance with Article 2314 CC in cases of extracontractual responsibility), it is the victim who must prove the *culpa* (fault) of the damaging party. This is consistent with the general rule (Article 1698 CC) which places the burden of proof for establishing the existence of a right on the person who alleges it.[463]

Among those who support the notion that Article 2329 expresses a presumption of fault, various possibilities are discussed with a more or less expansive effect: (1) some scholars consider Article 2329 CC (although in the first part it substantially reproduces Article 2314 CC) as providing for a 'presumption of fault' in the three specific cases that the second paragraph envisages.[464] Since this provision states that they 'are specifically obliged to indemnify', it is argued[465] that there are three exceptions to the general rule and that there is a presumption of fault limited to the cases explicitly indicated in Article 2329: (i) whoever imprudently shoots a firearm; (ii) whoever removes the slabs of a ditch or pipe on the street or road without the necessary precautions so that those who travel therein during the day or night do not fall; (iii) whoever undertakes to build or repair an aqueduct or bridge that crosses a road and keeps it in such a state as to cause damage to those in transit thereon; (2) which not only provides for these three possible cases, but also raises this presumption of fault to all the hypotheses in which the case would presuppose, according to the rules of experience that normally there should be no fault in the production of damage;[466] and (3) who extends said presumption to more cases than

463. For example, C.S. 26 Sept. 2000, RDJ, t XCVII, s. 1ª, at 169; CS 16 Oct. 2000, *GJ*, 244, at 61, CS 18 Jan. 2012 (rol 3391/2009).

464. Meza, *Manual, II*, at 277.

465. Meza, *Manual, II*, at 277.

466. Arturo Alessandri Rodríguez, 'Une nouvelle interprétation de l'art. 2329 du Code civil chileen', *Études de Droit Civil à la mémoire de Henri Capitant* (Paris: Dalloz, 1939) at 9 et seq.; Alessandri, *Responsabilidad*, cit., at 212–213. The author, in addition to giving some arguments of a literal nature, also gives a systematic justification by stating that this is due to the fact of providing a general presumption rule after some specific presumptions in the case of liability for the fact of the third party or things (Arts 2320–2328 CC). In relation to a presumption of Art. 2329 but with some nuances in relation to a presumption of a circumstantial nature also Barros, *Tratado*, I, cit., at 163–164; cf. Enrique Barros Bourie, 'Análisis histórico y comparado de la presunción de la responsabilidad por el hecho proprio del artículo 2329 del Código Civil', *El código civil de chile (1855–2005),* (Alejandro Guzmán Brito ed.) (Santiago de Chile: Lexis Nexis, 2007), at 619 et seq. Recall that Ducci already spoke of dangerous activity as an indication of fault Ducci, *Responsabilidad Civil*, (1971), at 99.

those provided for by the second paragraph of Article 2329 CC but only in the case of dangerous activities,[467] concept that has recently been broadened.[468]

149. Although traditionally the courts have not raised any particular objections and have associated Article 2314 with Article 2329 CC.[469] Since then (as previously mentioned),[470] a split position has emerged. From one point of view Article 2329 is a reinforcement of Article 2314 without further elaboration,[471] From onother point of view, instead, the two provision are partially different and Article 2329 contains a presumption.[472]

150. When assessing damage, it will be seen that sometimes the concept of unlawfulness, or conversely the nature of the damage, are used to presume fault.[473]

§3. Duty of Care

151. The application of the triple classification of contractual fault – provided for in Article 44 (*culpa leve, levisima, lata*)[474] – is also accepted by some doctrines[475] in tort matters, considering that tort liability is established automatically,

467. Ducci, *Responsabilidad Civil*, (1936), at 134: with a partial nuance in Ducci, *Responsabilidad Civil*, (1971), at 99. In favour of this limitation of the presumption of fault and against a general application also Tapia who is in favour of a restrictive application and limited to cases of dangerous activity not already regulated in special laws, because of the danger of an extreme objectification of responsibility: Mauricio Tapia Rodríguez, 'Contra una presunción general de culpa por hecho propio', *Estudios de Derecho Civil IV. Jornadas Nacionales de Derecho Civil, Olmué 2008* (Carlos Pizarro Wilson ed.) (Santiago de chile: Abeledo Perrot, 2009), at 689 et seq., esp. at 694 et seq.
468. On the concept of dangerous activity of 2329: Mantilla Espinosa, Pizarro Wilson, 'La responsabilidad civil por actividades peligrosas: aplique primero y explique después', cit. at 39 et seq. Recently for a broad in-sense jurisprudential overview and also in consumer matters: María Paz Gatica Rodríguez, 'Atividades peligrosas y tecnología: delimitando categorías y repensando reacciones desde la responsabilidad civil extracontractual', *Estudios de derecho civil XV* (Fabian Elorriaga De Bonis ed.) (Santiago de Chile: Thomson Reuters, 2020) at 957 et seq.
469. Alessandri, *Responsabilidad*, cit., at 214.
470. Carolina Schiele Manzor, Josefina Tocornal Cooper, 'Artículo 2329 del Código Civil. La interpretación de presunción por hechos propios existe en la jurisprudencia', *Revista Chilena de Derecho* 2010/1, at 123 et seq.
471. For example, CS 15 Jan. 2008 (rol 3070/2006) CS 28 May 2007 (rol 312/2006); CS 31 July 2006 (rol 1212/2004).
472. For example, CS 3 Nov. 1998 (rol 4420/1998; CS 2 Nov. 2000 (rol 1386-1999); CS 28 Dec. 2000 (rol 4335/2000): CS 14 Nov. 2002 (rol 3436/2002); CS 5 Jan. 2009 (rol 2380/2008); CS 2 Jan. 2013 (rol 7086/2010). *See* Barros, *Tratado*, I, cit., at 147–153.
473. *See* Art. 2330 CC and paras 376 et seq.
474. On the contrary, it would not be possible to consider applicable the criterion of distribution of the categories of fault, based on the utility of the parties, which is sanctioned for contractual responsibility by Art. 1547 CC. More extensively Gian Franco Rosso Elorriaga, 'Probelmas de graduación de la culpa y algunas implicacias prácticas', *Estudios de derecho civil VI*, (Gonzalo Figueroa Yañez, Enrique Barros Bourie, Mauricio Tapia Rodríguez ed.) (Santiago de Chile: Abeledo Perrot, Legal Publishing, 2011) at 475 et seq.
475. Barros, *Tratado*, I, cit., at 86 and bibliography cited. Here we observe that the traditional doctrine has come to this conclusion based on the concept of the unity of fault.

for '*colpa leve*'[476] and therefore assuming a standard of diligence that a normal person would have held in a similar situation. Accordingly, foreseeability becomes a requirement for the establishment of fault.[477] It is based on the standard of an ordinary person,[478] or the notion that fault is linked to behaviour contrary to that of an ordinary person who, in similar circumstances, would have foreseen the occurrence of the event as a result of such behaviour.[479]

Another part of the doctrine[480] considers that *culpa* in tort does not admit graduation, but ends up attributing it, considering that in certain cases one must respond for *levisima* fault.

This is because in analysing the fault, both the standard of an ordinary person and the specific circumstances of the case are considered. This means that the standard of fault must be raised if that person belongs to a specialized category (e.g., the standard of a surgeon will not be that of a normal doctor) or if the event occurred in a situation or circumstance different from the normal canons.

152. It has been noted that fault also operates as a mechanism for allocating risk between the conduct that must or should be assumed by the perpetrator and the scope of attention used by the victim.[481]

153. Adopting an abstract point of reference[482] as an average standard makes it possible to justify the exclusion of fault based on the error, since it could be argued that anyone in the same circumstance would have committed the same mistake;[483] this view is applied with caution[484] and discussed with particular reference to the error of law.[485]

154. The standard of conduct should also refer to those standards that may be envisaged in *ad hoc* regulations, or in relation to certain patterns of conduct whose failure to comply leads to the violation of certain contraventions (*culpa infraccional*).[486] Despite this, the violation of a norm does not necessarily automatically establish fault in relation to the damage committed; this will be limited by *rationale* of the provision (the *fin de la norma.*)[487] Only when the norm is intended to avoid

476. Figueroa, *Curso, IV,* cit., at 100.
477. Fault was already considered to be the possibility of taking what was not foreseen: CS 29 Mar. 1962, *RDJ,* 59, s. 4ª, at 21.
478. CS 2.11.2017 (Rol 4.839/2017).
479. CS 23.6.2015 (rol 26.534/2014), CS 26.2.2018 (Rol 37.434/2017). *See* Barros, *Tratado*, I, cit., at 95.
480. Alessandri, *Responsabilidad*, cit., at 38 and 143; Corral, Lecciones, cit., at 209–210.
481. Cristián Aedo Barrena, 'El concepto normativo', cit., at 705 et seq.
482. On the abstract acceptance of fault: Alessandri, *Responsabilidad*, cit., at 127–128; Gianfranco Rosso Elorrieaga, 'El buen padre de fmilia como criterio de apreciación de la culpa y su aplicación a la responsabilidad cuasidelictual', *Derecho de Daños*, (Santiago de Chile: Lexis Nexis, 2002), at 3–51.
483. Barros, *Tratado*, I, cit., at 98–99.
484. In relation to the error of sending documentation by the bank to the correct address: CS 4.9.2002, RDJ, 94, s. 1ª, at 186.
485. On the concept of '*culpabilidad*': *see* Alcalde, 'El error de derecho', cit., at 235 et seq.
486. For example, Barros, *Tratado*, I, cit., at 104 et seq.
487. *See* Barros, *Tratado*, I, cit., at 106–107.

the production of damage will the author of the offence be subject to the establishment of fault. Otherwise, this does not automatically mean that the person is at fault: this principle is established in certain areas, such as transit, where it is established that the administrative infraction relating to traffic does not generate an automatic cause and effect relationship between the administrative infraction and the damage produced by the accident.[488] Despite this, in general there is no precise automatism between *infraccional fault* and *culpa civil*, because a civil fault may exist despite the absence of the former, and vice versa.

155. *Culpa grave* (gross negligence) is equated with malice (Article 44 CC).[489] If it is true that in extracontractual matters, a tort is committed with fault or malice is less relevant, then it is also true that in the second case it may lead to an award for greater compensation.[490] In concrete terms, even malice in tort can be manifested through action and omission.[491]

We will return to the concept of malice in the context of the discussion on restitutionary obligations.[492]

§4. CAPACITY

156. Regarding liability for one's own acts, it has been observed that in order for there to be liability it is not sufficient that there has been a fault (or malice) on the part of the author, but it is necessary that this can be imputed to that person.[493] This gives rise to a concept of *imputabilidad* (imputability). Although it cannot be used as a synonym for tort liability,[494] it is partially linked to the willingness to commit the offence and to capacity. But once again, it does not necessarily coincide because the doctrine interprets these aspects in a variety of ways.

For some scholars, imputability must be associated with the voluntariness of the act and is therefore included in the concept of fault.[495] For others, imputability is a broader aspect since it includes the capacity and the culpability or the intent.[496] Still

488. Art. 166 Ley de Tránsito, DFL 1/2009, e.g., so the fact of being fined for driving without a licence does not generate culpable behaviour in relation to the accident that occurred CA Concepción 5.8.1980, *RDJ*, 77, at 105. Clearly, the infraction of the law contributes to the association of fault in other cases; such as those who travel at night with their lights off and drive on the opposite roadway, in the example of Alessandri, *Responsabilidad*, cit., at 129. Earlier, in favour of the binomial *culpa administrativa y culpa extracontractual*: Ramos, *De la responsabilidad*, cit. at 55.

489. On a jurisprudential study in extracontractual matters: Jorge Larroucau Torres, *Culpa y dolo en la responsabilidad extracontractual. Análisis jurisprudencial* (Santiago de Chile: LexisNexis, 2007).

490. Cf. *see* paras 489 et seq.

491. Ramos, *De la responsabilidad*, cit., at 51; Alessandri, *Responsabilidad*, cit. at 123. More generally in relation to fault and malice op. cit. at 119 et seq.

492. Cf. *see* paras 539 et seq.

493. Tapia, *De la Responsabilidad*, cit., at 169.

494. Abeliuk, *Las Obligaciones*, *I*, at 241.

495. Thus, it is stated that: '*imputability consists in the fact that the individual executing a harmful act has done it voluntarily, that is, that said act is the result of the free determination of its author*': Tapia, *De la Responsabilidad*, cit., at 169.

496. Figueroa, *Curso IV*, cit., at 89.

another part of the doctrine views capacity as a condition of imputability,[497] and there are some who assume that *imputabilidad* and capacity are synonymous.[498]

Apart from these conceptual nuances, it is clear that an act must be committed voluntarily in order to establish liability, and the concept of capacity required for the establishment of fault is different from that of legal capacity;[499] it is an *ad hoc* capacity, called *capacidad delictual*[500] applied to tort liability.

157. The rules governing capacity associated with the establishment of liability are defined in the negative[501] by systematizing the cases of incapacity in Articles 2318 and 2319 CC, with a clear differentiation of three categories: the intoxicated (Article 2318 CC), minors and the mentally ill (Article 2319 CC).

158. Delictual capacity (relating to contractual offences) is totally independent of criminal[502] and contractual capacity. The latter is much more limited as a presumption of the former type of capacity and 'toda persona es legalmente capaz, excpeto aquellas que la ley declara incapaces' (*everyone has legal capacity except those whom the law declares incompetent*) (Article 1446 CC). Similarly, although a 'sordomudo que no puede darse a entender por escrito' (*deaf-mute who cannot make himself understood in writing*) can be declared legally incompetent in relation to contractual effects (Article 1447 CC), he is fully capable of committing a non-contractual illicit act (*delito o cuasidelito*).[503] Another difference is that in the case of contractual capacity, reference is made between females and males in relation to their age;[504] here there is a generic reference to minors or those over 16 (cf. Articles 26 and 2319).[505]

497. Barros, *Tratado*, I, cit., at 70. The author speaks of 'imputable fact' (*hecho imputable*) (op. cit., at 69).
498. Lilian San Martín Niera, 'La imputabilidad o capacidad como elemento de la responsabilidad civil extracontractual. Un debate pendiente en la doctrina chilena', *Ius et praxis*, 2018/1, at 553.
499. This joints the '*capacidad de goce*' (the legal aptitude to acquire rights and be a subject of law, e.g., Art. 55, 74, 77 CC) and the '*capacidad de ejercicio*', which relates essentially to the contractual sphere: cf. Art. 1545–1547 CC): Domínguez Agúila, *Teoría general*, cit., at 197; Tapia, *De la Responsabilidad*, cit., at 170–171.
500. *See e.g.*, Alessandri, *Responsabilidad*, cit., at 86 et seq.; Barros, *Tratado*, I, cit., at 69 et seq.; Corral, *Lecciones*, cit., at 100 et seq.
501. *See* Barros, *Tratado*, I, cit., at 70.
502. *See e.g.*, Art. 10 CP which states that '"el menor de 18 años" y "el loco o el demente, a no ser que haya obrado en un intervalo lúcido"' (*the person under 18 years of age and the insane or mentally ill person, unless he has acted in a period of sanity*) are exempt from criminal liability. In the case of minors, it is considered that the Juvenile Criminal Responsibility Act (Ley 20.084) does not refer to the concept of discernment used in civil *law* but it uses 'different forms of application of punishment for minors' Figueroa, *Curso, IV*, cit., at 122.
503. Tapia, *De la Responsabilidad*, cit., at 173.
504. Here then there will be absolute incapacities and relative incapacities and prohibitions to contract called '*incapacidades epeciales*': Art. 1447 CC.
505. Tapia, *De la Responsabilidad*, cit., at 173. Art. 26 CC lists three categories: 'Llámase infante o niño todo el que no ha cumplido siete años; impúber, el varón que no ha cumplido catorce años y la mujer que no ha cumplido doce; adulto, el que ha dejado de ser impúber; mayor de edad, o simplemente mayor, el que ha cumplido dieciocho años; y menor de edad, o simplemente menor, el que no ha llegado a cumplirlos' ('*Infant, or child, is anyone who has not reached his seventh birthday; adolescent, a male who has not reached his fourteenth birthday and a female who has not reached*

159. The liability of a person who is *ebrio* (intoxicated) (Article 2318 CC) extends to various forms of intoxication, including drug addicts (cocaine addicts, morphine addicts, etc.)[506] If the norm is applicable without a doubt in cases where the condition is caused by one's own actions, the question is open in cases where the state is caused by a third party. Since the law is silent, there are those who argue that the intoxicated person is responsible in any case, since the culpability relates not just to becoming intoxicated, but also in allowing oneself to become intoxicated.[507] Opponents of this view base their arguments on the principle of the *actio libera in causa* and therefore contend that since the incapacity derives from an involuntary act, an exception of no imputability[508] could be applied, provided that the intoxication is not frequent.[509]

160. Article 2319 considers that a mentally ill person is not civilly liable for any wrongdoing he commits, provided: (1) that this incapacity exists at the time of committing the relevant wrongdoing; (2) is total; and (3) independent of the person's will.[510] It is not necessary, as in the case of civil incompetency, that the person be declared incompetent by decree of interdiction (Article 465 CC).[511]

161. In relation to the state of dementia, the denomination, nature or origin of the pathology[512] is indifferent. This can be applied to various situations such as cases of somnambulism or hypnotism.[513]

162. Concerning[514] to the incapacity of minors,[515] Article 2319 CC distinguishes between two categories: (1) minors under 7 years of age;[516] and (2) minors under 16 years of age 'without discernment'. On the contrary, the following always have capacity and are therefore liable in tort: (i) minors over 16 years of age; (ii)

---

her twelfth birthday; mature, one who has ceased to be an adolescent; adult, or grown-up, one who has reached his eighteenth birthday; and juvenile, or minor, one who has not reached his eighteenth birthday').

506. *See e.g.*, Alessandri, *Responsabilidad*, cit., at 101 et seq.; Barros, *Tratado*, I, cit., at 80.
507. Alessandri, *Responsabilidad*, cit., at 101. This author, however, assumes a different criterion in its application in relation to drugs; in this case, if he had been drugged against his will, he would not be liable.
508. Barros, *Tratado*, I, cit., at 80. Applying it interchangeably to the mentally ill and intoxicated: Abeliuk, *Las Obligaciones*, *I*, at 242.
509. In the case of alcoholism, some authors consider that this situation could be assimilated to the state of dementia: Corral, *Lecciones,* cit., at 103.
510. Corral, *Lecciones,* cit., at 101–102.
511. Abeliuk, *Las Obligaciones*, *I*, at 242. Thus, it is considered that the decree of interdiction does not necessarily entail proof of incapacity in tort since the act could have been committed during a period of sanity: Barros, *Tratado*, I, cit., at 72.
512. Figueroa, *Curso IV*, cit., at 121–122.
513. Así Alessandri, *Responsabilidad*, cit., at 100.
514. *See e.g.*, Abeliuk, *Las Obligaciones*, *I*, at 241–242; Barros, *Tratado*, I, cit., at 72–73; Corral, *Lecciones*, cit., at 103–105.
515. The age of adulthood is 18 years: Art. 26 CC.
516. In this case there is a presumption of entitlement to incapacity, no judgment of discernment is needed: Alessandri, *Responsabilidad*, cit., at 102.

minors between the ages of 7 and 16 whom, at the time of the event, had the capacity to understand the consequences of their actions (discernment).[517] The capacity for discernment is established by the judge.

Guardians of minors under age 7 and minors between the ages of 7 and 16 that lack discernment are liable for the actions of the undiscerning minor children.[518]

163. As regards the interaction and possibility of joint liability in relation to incapacitated persons.[519]

164. It is generally accepted that legal entities would be fully capable of being held responsible in tort, or even on the basis of infra-contractual liability (*responsabilidad infraccional*) from which civil liability can[520] also derive for acts committed by their employees.[521]

517. It is considered that discernment presupposes the capacity to understand that an act is illicit or manifests itself as a minimal appreciation of the risk in comparison with minors of the same age: Barros, *Tratado*, I, cit., at 73.
518. *See* para. 267.
519. *See* Art. 2330 and paras 376 et seq.
520. Abeliuk, *Las Obligaciones*, *I*, at 242; Barros, *Tratado*, I, cit., at 74–76. Part of the doctrine argues that civil liability in tort for legal persons is based on Art. 558 CPP: Corral, *Lecciones*, cit., at 109.
521. *See* paras 268 et seq.

Chapter 2. Specific Cases of Liability

§1. Liability of Professional

I. Overview

165. The Chilean legal system is not always characterized by a specific provision on liability for all professional activities. In such cases, reference should be made to the general rules of tort or contractual matters. In addition to this, it should be recalled that the criterion for establishing fault in contractual matters is governed by Article 1547 CC, which provides for a tripartition of fault and establishes a presumption in certain cases. If the general rule in tort matters is to be proven by the alleging party (Article 1698 CC), in contractual matters it is presumed since Article 1547.3 states that 'The burden of proof of diligence or care rests with the person who should have used it').

166. Further, it is particularly relevant that Article 1547.1 CC establishes a general rule whereby the standard of fault depends on the benefit that the parties obtain from the contract. Thus, it states that 'the debtor is only liable for culpa lata in contracts which by their nature are only useful to the creditor; he is liable for culpa leve in contracts made for the reciprocal benefit of the parties; and for culpa levísima, in contracts in which the debtor is the only one who brings benefit'.

167. Notwithstanding the wording of these provisions, in analysing and accepting the classification of obligations of means or results, scholars have changed their interpretations. Some consider[522] that the presumption of fault contained in Article 1547.3 applies only to obligations of result. Hence, it has been argued that the burden of proof in cases of obligations of means is split between Article 1547 CC and the general provision of Article 1698 CC (the latter applicable to torts). Thus, in a contractual context, it has been argued that the creditor must prove the existence of the obligation, while the debtor must prove the correct execution of the obligation and therefore his diligence in accordance with Article 1547.3 CC and Article 1698 CC.[523]

---

522. Hugo Cárdenas Villaroel, 'La cobertura dogmática de la recepción jurisprudencial de la distinción obligaciones de medios/obligaciones de resultado (una aproximación a través de casos de responsabilidad', *Cuadernos de análisis jurídico* (*ejemplar dedicado a la Responsabilidad medica*, Iñigo de la Maza ed.), 2010/6, at 49 et seq.

523. For this doctrine, this relates to the fact that in middle obligations performance would interrelate with fault, Pizarro. Carlos Pizarro Wilson, 'La culpa como elemento constitutivo del incumplimiento de las obligaciones de medio o de diligencia', *Revista de Derecho (PUCV)*, 2008/31, at 255 et seq.; cf. Pizarro, *Responsabilidad médica,* cit., at 91 et seq. In this context, if in the case of the obligation of means, the presumption of Art. 1547 would apply, in the case of those of results, responsibility would be objective, admitting only as excuses, for example, force majeure: Carlos Pizarro Wilson, 'El contrato médico. Calificación, contenido y responsabilidad', *Revista Chilena de Derecho*, 2014/3, at 840–841.

On the interrelation between Art. 1547 CC and 1698 in contractual matters without distinguishing between obligation of result and means: Daniel Peñailillo Arévalo, *Las obligaciones* (Santiago:

168\. *168.* Additionally, it should be noted that the application of Article 1547 CC can be excluded by party autonomy. At the same time, its application can be limited due to the fact that other provisions may be considered when the case involves professional activity, e.g., liability in the case of Article 2118,[524] or the hypothesis set out in Article 2158 CC relating to the severity of the fault, which must be proven.[525] Thus, these norms can interact, also because their applicability depends on the facts of the case. For example, Article 2158 is not applicable to all cases of medical malpractice, except when there is an obligation of result.[526] Furthermore, in the contractual sphere, the general rule on contracts for immaterial services[527] may also apply to for independent contractors (or freelance workers).

169. It will become clear in the following pages, especially when dealing with the liability for medical malpractice, that sometimes the distinction between an obligation of means or result produces the result as in tort. Other times it may blur the line between contractual and tort liability. The possible applications should be added to this whereby tort liability may be presumed in the case of certain dangerous activities.[528]

Evidently the panorama becomes even more complicated. One must bear in mind that the interpretations may vary depending on the applicability of the presumption pursuant to Article 1547.3 to any type of obligation, not assuming the differentiation between obligation of means and result.[529]

170. With regards to liability for medical malpractice, both with regard to the medical practitioner and the hospital, the judge plays a fundamental role. When

---

Editorial Jurídica, 2003). At 228 et seq. In a critical sense *see* Vidal, *Responsabilidad civil Medica*, cit., 2019, at 134 et seq. and 140 et seq.

524. Art. 2118 CC for which 'Los servicios de las profesiones y carreras que suponen largos estudios, o a que está unida la facultad de representar y obligar a otra persona respecto de terceros, se sujetan a las reglas del mandato' (*Professional services and careers that involve lengthy studies, or to which is linked the power to represent and bind another person with respect to third parties, are subject to the rules of mandate*).
525. Carmen Domínguez Hidalgo, 'El problema de la culpa presunta contractual y las obligaciones d emedio y obligaciones de resultado: sus implicancias para la responsabilidad médica'. *Cuadernos de análisis jurídico* (*ejemplar dedicado a la Responsabilidad medica*, Iñigo de la Maza ed.), at 23; Ramón Dóminguez Águila, 'La culpa en el derecho civil chileno. Aspectos generales', *Revista Anales de Derecho Universidad Católica*, 2008/3, at 124 et seq.
526. Cárdenas, 'La cobertura ', cit. at 83.
527. *See* Art. 1999 and 2006 CC: Corral, Lecciones, cit., at 284–285. The Chilean legal system differentiates between contracts of *arendamienot de cosas* (Art. 1915 et seq.), *de obra material* (Art. 1999 et seq.) and contracts of *servicios inmateriales* (Art. 2006 et seq.), where essentially the performance is intellectual. As concerns the latter, Art. 2006 expressly references the norm on compensation for damages already provided for contracts of *obra material.*
528. *See* paras 146 et seq.
529. This presumption, however, would not apply whenever the rule of the mandate (Art. 2158 CC) is applied, according to which it is the principal who must prove fault: As Alessandri, *Responsabilidad*, cit., at 42–43, footnote 3. Lorenzo De La Maza Rivadeneira, El contrato de atención médica', *Revista Chilena de Derecho*, 1989/1, at 11.

assessing the standards of conduct, he relies on the principle of *res ipsa loquitur* and the observation that the factual element often speaks for itself.[530]

171. Usually, independent contractors and freelance workers are excluded from the consumer relationship (B2C contract). Therefore, the LPC is inapplicable because a person who has a professional title and exercises the profession independently is not considered a *proveedor* (testator) for the purposes of this law (Article 1.2 LPC).[531]

II. Medical Practitioners

A. Overview

172. Liability of medical practitioners is not characterized by an adequate systematization in the Chilean legal system. Some characteristic features about how healthcare is developed should also be added to this.

Private organizations play a fundamental role in the Chilean social security system. The *Instituciones de Salud Previsional (*ISAPRES)[532] coexists with the national health system that operates through the *Fondo Nacional de Salud* (FONASA),[533] but in reality these institutions are major players in a system that operates essentially as health insurance funded by a minimum compulsory contribution (7% of taxable income) that can also be extended to provide more benefits or greater coverage by increasing minimum benefits that must be guaranteed by law, in accordance with the *Garantías Explícitas en Salud* (GES).[534]

In this system it is understood that healthcare – in practice –- is not public. On the contrary, usually access to healthcare services often requires not only advance payment, but sometimes also a co-payment in the event the patient's current coverage is insufficient or does not apply in respect to the treatment required.

173. For this reason, there is a tendency to outsource healthcare services to private clinics and not to public healthcare facilities. This implies that although there is a law regarding public healthcare, the reality is different. More specifically, the provision of healthcare service becomes a privately based insurance system (with the advantages and disadvantages that come from this) and leads to an outsourcing of medical services.

---

530. As highlighted by Jorge Larrocau Torres, '¿Cómo se prueba la responsabilidad civil médica en la justicia chilena?', *Revista de Derecho* (*Valdivia*), 2014/2, at 43 et seq. *See also* Jorge Larrocau Torres, '*Res Ipsa Loquitur*: quien habla es el juez, no la cosa', *Estudios de derecho civil VI*, (Gonzalo Figueroa Yañez, Enrique Barros Bourie, Mauricio Tapia Rodríguez ed.) (Santiago de Chile: Abeledo Perrot, Legal Publishing, 2011) at 491 et seq.
531. Cf. Art. 1999 and 2006 CC: Corral, Lecciones, cit., at 286.
532. Introduced with DFL 3/ 1981, of 27 Apr. 8 (DO 19 May 1981).
533. Introduced by Decree Ley 2.763, of 11 July 1979 (DO 3 Aug. 1979).
534. These already set out by decree in accordance with Art. 11 of Ley 19.966/2004, of 25 Aug. (DO 3 Sept. 2004).

174. In addition to this, there is a fragmentary and varied legislative landscape. To protect the constitutional right to health, which is guaranteed by artículo 19 N° 9[535] of the Political Constitution of Chile, from the perspective of public healthcare, there is a broad State responsibility whereby 'The State shall be liable for damages caused by the organs of the Administration in the exercise of their functions, without prejudice to the responsibilities that may affect the civil servant who caused them)'.[536]

There is also a specific law that guarantees health (i.e., the Law AUGE[537]) aimed at supporting the GES, which provides for certain minimum services through the 'Universal Access of Guarantees Explored' (*Acceso Universal de Garantías Explícitas*). Therefore, in this context, the organs of the State Administration are responsible for damages due to lack of service (Article 38 of Law 19.966), with a prescription period of four years from the action or omission that provokes the damage (Article 39); although the law explicitly provides for the compensation of moral damages in such cases (Article 41)[538] even if mediation is a precondition to the admissibility of any legal action.[539]

Accordingly, the programmatic norm of Article 38.2 CPR is implemented, according to which 'Any person whose rights are infringed by the State Administration, its agencies or municipalities, may file a claim before the courts as determined by law, without prejudice to the liability that may affect the official who caused the damage'.[540]

To some extent it has been discussed whether decentralized entities, i.e., the so-called *Establecimientos Autogestionados en Red*, may also be included as passive claimants in case of malpractice. However, this possibility has ultimately been negated.[541]

---

535. Art. 19 n. 9° Constitution: El derecho a la protección de la salud. El Estado protege el libre e igualitario acceso a las acciones de promoción, protección y recuperación de la salud y de rehabilitación del individuo. Le corresponderá, asimismo, la coordinación y control de las accionesrelacionadas con la salud. Es deber preferente del Estado garantizar la ejecución de las acciones desalud, sea que se presten a través de instituciones públicas o privadas, en la forma y condiciones que determine la ley, la que podrá establecer cotizacionesobligatorias. Cada persona tendrá el derecho a elegir el sistema de salud al que deseeacogerse, sea éste estatal o privado (*The right to health protection. The State protects the free and equal access to the actions of promotion, protection and recovery of health and rehabilitation of the individual. It shall also be responsible for the coordination and control of actions related to health. It is the State's preferential duty to guarantee the execution of health actions, whether they are provided through public or private institutions, in the form and conditions determined by law, which may establish compulsory contributions. Each person shall have the right to choose the health system to which he/she wishes to adhere, be it State or private*).
536. Art. 4 Ley 18.575/1986 cit.
537. Ley 19.966/2004, cit.; *see* Pizarro, *La responsabilidad civil medica*, cit., at 152 et seq.
538. Providing also an important study of the case law, *see* José Miguel Valdivia Olivares, 'La responsabilidad por falta de servicio en la administración hospitalaria en la jurisprudencia chilena', *Revista de derecho (Universidad de Concepción)*, 2019/243, at 213 et seq.; *see also* Carlos Pizarro Wilson, *La responsabilidad civil medica* (Santiago de Chile: Thomson Reuters, 2017), at 121 et seq.
539. Art. 43 et seq. of Ley 19.966/2004.
540. Cf. Art. 6 and 7 CPR.
541. These institutions were created in 2010: *see* Art. 31 D.F.L. N° 1/2005, DS 38/2005 on the point Hugo Cardenas Villarroel, 'La legitimación pasiva de la administración médico sanitaria en la era

175. In 2012, another law was added to this framework. Although it identifies the rights and duties of the patient,[542] the internal regulations of the institution in which the patient is located must be respected (Article 33 Ley 20.584), there is a specific duty to obtain information (Article 34) and to adopt appropriate and consensual behaviour (Article 35). Although there is no provision in relation to responsibility,[543] the law does establish certain duties of disclosure, security and protection. This is complemented by the criminal liability of the healthcare practitioner, which is expressly sanctioned (Articles 490 and 491 CP) in the event of *negligencia culpable*[544] (culpable negligence), which essentially are manifested in diagnostic or treatment errors.[545]

B. Medical Malpractice Liability

176. With regard to the liability of the practitioner,[546] alongside the potential application of contract law[547] and the reference to the provisions on mandates,[548] it is also accepted that a contract can be entered into through the tacit submission to treatment[549] or to the tacit acceptance by the third party benefiting from the treatment and the stipulation of an agreement in favour of third parties.[550] Despite this, the fact that it is an autonomous atypical contract is gaining ground.[551]

---

de los establecimientos autogestionados en red', *Revista Chilena de Derecho*, 2018/2, at 479 et seq. In this case, the doctrine concludes that such Establecimientos could not be legitimated passives for not having their own legal personality, and in that legitimated passive would be the corresponding *Servicio de Salud.*

542. Ley 20.584/2012 de 13 Oct. (DO 24 Oct. 2012). *See* the special issue on 'Derecho y deberes de los pacientes. estudios y texto legales y reglamentos', *Cuadernos de extensión jurídica* 2014/24 (Paulina Milos Hurtado & Hernán Corral Talciani ed.).
543. Although Art. 17 Ley 20.584 expressly provides for the absence of civil liability for the implementation of the ethics committees provided for by law.
544. This is expressly stated in Art. 491 of the CCpenal Code for 'médico, cirujano, farmacéutico, phlebotomico o matrona' in relation to the penalty provided for in Art. 490. On some cases of *responsabilidad civil ex delicto*: CS 2 Jun. 2004, *GJ*, 288, at 177; CS 19 Jan. 2005 (rol 9-2003). On Art. 491 CP *see* Pizarro, *La responsabilidad civil medica,* cit., at 177 et seq.
545. For example, CS 22 Aug. 2012 (rol 3240/2012); CS 6 Jul. 2018 (rol 38.838/2017); CS 18 Jun. 2018 (rol 6.549/2018); CS 17 Jun. 2019 (rol 2.468/2018); CS 4 Jul. 2017, (rol 95.114/2018); CS 1 Jul. 2019 (rol 7.755/2019);CS 2 Jul. 2019 (rol 4.272-2019): For an important study or and more extensively refer to Valdivia, 'La responsabilidad por falta de servicio', cit., at 23 et seq.
546. *See* Guajardo Carrasco, Baltazar, *Aspectos de la responsabilidad civil médica. Doctrina y* Jurisprudencia, Santiago de Chile: Librotecnica, 2002), Hugo Cardenas Villarroel & Jaime Moreno Molinet, *Responsabilidad médica. Estándares jurisprudenciales de la falta de servicio* (Santiago de Chile. Legal Publishing, 2011); Pizarro, *La responsabilidad civil medica*, cit.; Álvaro Vidal Olivares, *Responsabilidad civil Medica* (Santiago de Chile: Academia Judicial, 2019).
547. *See* De La Maza, 'El contrato de atención médica', cit., at 7 et seq.
548. Although the figure is rooted in the mandate, it excludes the evidentiary aspects of Art. 2158 CC, e.g., *see* CS. 10 Mar. 2016 (rol 213373/2015). On the existence of the *contrato de prestación de servicios médico*: *see also* CS 25 Apr. 2017 (rol 38151/2016).
549. Based on Art. 2124.2 CC: Barros, *Tratado*, *II*, at 705.
550. Guajardo Carrasco, Baltazar, *Aspectos de la responsabilidad civil médica. Doctrina y* Jurisprudencia, Santiago de Chile: Librotecnica, 2002), at 50 et seq.
551. Pizarro, 'El contrato médico', cit. at 825 et seq.; also Vidal, *Responsabilidad civil medica*, cit., at 21

This implies applying the relevant general norms. However, essentially (and for the reasons outlined above), the practitioner's liability is regarded by the doctrine as fundamentally contractual.[552] Tort liability only pertains to specific cases, such as the admission of an unconscious patient to the emergency room or in relation to indirect victims (*victima por rebote*).[553] Nevertheless, it is still possible to choose between contractual or tort liability, with decisive importance being given to the statute of limitations applicable to each type of liability.

177. The difference between contractual and tort liability is important for establishing the scope of liability of the healthcare staff and the joint liability of its members. In this regard, it is considered[554] that the individual practitioners should be liable where there is a contractual obligation to provide services, while only the physician (and not the entire team of practitioners) is responsible in situations that can be classified as tort. This is because Article 2320 relating to the subordination and dependence of the medical team is not applicable. Clearly, if it can be demonstrated that more than one practitioner is causally involved, that person will be jointly and severally liable under Article 2317. This would imply that where contractual liability is considered, such joint and several liability does not automatically apply and that joint and several liability can only be established if it can be proven that each agent contributed causally to the damage.

This interpretation opts for the traditional separation between the two positions which, without distinguishing between the contractual nature and tort nature, deems the physician to be responsible (as the head of the team and for not supervising). Alternatively, an antithetical position supports holding everyone liable.[555]

178. Insofar as liability is contract-based, the traditional approach has been to distinguish between obligations of means and obligations of results. This essentially means that the physician is responsible for the former, except in the case of cosmetic surgery[556] or simple or routine procedures, in which the risk is clearly reduced in relation to the desired outcome.[557] Together with the application of contract law, this implies a presumption of fault, as provided by Article 1547 CC.[558]

552. Pizarro, *La responsabilidad civil medica,* cit., at 20 et seq.; Barros, *Tratado, II,* at 704, Corral, *Lecciones*, cit., at 288.
553. Pizarro, *La responsabilidad civil medica,* cit., at 168 y ss; Barros, *Tratado, II*, at 715. Some also consider tort law to apply to the activity carried out with mere benevolence: Corral, *Lecciones*, cit., at 289.
554. Carlos Pizarro Wilson, 'Mal praxis en el equipo médico' *Revista medica de Chile*, 2011/5, at 667–671; cf. Pizarro, *La responsabilidad civil medica,* cit., at 108 et seq.
555. To this effect CS 20 Jun. 1996 (rol 33.393/1995); CS 31 Jan. 2018 (rol 9.189/2017).
556. For example, breast reduction must guarantee an aesthetically pleasing result: CS 28 Jan. 2011, (rol 5849/2009): cf. CS 10 Mar. 2016 (rol 21373/2015).
557. In this sense, the notorious disproportion between the risk taken and the result obtained becomes important: CS 25 Nov. 2013 (rol 8307/2012).
558. CS Apr. 25, 2017 (rol 38151/2916), CS. June 17, 2015 (rol 11078/2014), CS Jan. 19, 2015 (rol 7215/2014); cf. CS June 22, 2017, (rol 95138/2016).

However, liability is made more objective by applying the obligation of result.[559] It has evidenced three challenges related to medical responsibility: preparing a catalogue of conducts in relation to medical fault, assessing who correctly should be the burden of proof and the achievement of correct weighing of the judicial presumptions.[560]

179. The possibility of framing liability also in terms of tort therefore raises a number of issues in relation to the interaction between contractual liability and the burden of proof, an aspect that, as noted above, varies according to whether Article 1547 CC is applicable to obligations of means and results.

Thus, in addition to what has been mentioned above, it has been argued[561] that, in the case of obligations of means, the plaintiff must prove the violation of medical standards and protocols; the presumption of fault of Article 1547.3 CC[562] applies only if it is proven these standards and/or protocols have been violated, whereas this presumption does not appear to pose any problems in obligations of results when the desired outcome has clearly not been achieved. For others,[563] despite the theoretical operability of the presumption of fault, proving non-fulfilment (based on a standard of fault) requires the plaintiff to prove fault, not sufficing, for example, there mere claim of failure to restore health.

180. In some cases, depending on the relevant facts and interpretations, the difference between contractual and tort liability in medical malpractice cases, together with the difference between duties of care and outcome, become irrelevant since negligence in relation to the duty of care would lead to the demand for similar standards of proof to those of the duty of care in tort.[564] This is additionally so due to the establishment that normally the standard of *culpa* in the case of a contractual relationship for healthcare is that of *culpa leve*[565] given the contract usually entails mutual benefits[566] without prejudice to having set another contractual standard. In this regard, both abstract and concrete standards should be evaluated in relation to the conduct applicable to the concrete case.[567]

559. Carlos Pizarro Wilson, 'La obligación de resultado en el contrato médico. Hacia una responsabilidad objetiva', *Estudios de derecho civil IX* (Juan Andrés Varas Braun, Susan Turner Saelzer ed.) (Santiago de Chile: Thomson Reuters, Legal Publishing, 2014) at 625 et seq.; Pizarro, *La responsabilidad civil medica,* cit., at 96 et seq.

560. Hugo Cárdenas Villareal, 'Sobre la prueba de la culpa médica: tres consejos para la jurispridencia chilena', *Estudios de derecho civil IX* (Juan Andrés Varas Braun, Susan Turner Saelzer ed.) (Santiago de Chile: Thomson Reuters, Legal Publishing, 2014) at 550.

561. Barros, *Tratado, II*, at 710.

562. Barros, *Tratado, II*, at 708.

563. In this sense it is argued that 'it does not mean that the rule of Art. 547 does not apply, but that it is necessary to prove the breach by establishing negligence': Corral, *Lecciones*, cit., at 290.

564. As Barros notes, *Tratado, II*, at 707–709 and 716.

565. CS Nov. 25, 2013 (rol 8307/2012).

566. Art. 1547.I CC.

567. In this sense CS 27 Feb. 2018 (rol 21599/2017), CS 25 Apr. 2017 (rol 38151/2016), CS 19 Jan. 2015 (rol 7215/2014).

C. Lex Artis *and Information Duties*

181. The duty to act in accordance with the *lex artis medica* also implies a duty to follow certain standards or protocols. To this should be added certain obligations of information and guarantees, which must also be adopted so that the patient is aware of the service he is receiving and the risks involved. This includes the necessary informed consent[568] of the patient, which must be given freely[569] (Article 14 Ley 20.584). To this end, certain information duties are envisaged (Article 8 Ley 20.584), which must be proportioned in a 'clear and comprehensible manner' (Article 10). Additionally, a report on the activities and interventions carried out is required (Article 11). Although there is no automatism between civil liability relating to the *lex artis* and these duties, their violation certainly contributes at least to the formation of evidence regarding the former in the event of an injury. Thus, civil liability arises if the patient has not been properly informed of the results of the procedures carried out, the recommendations proposed by certain specialists,[570] or any illness that may recur.[571] Also important is the assessment of whether the violation of informed consent can give rise to an autonomous indemnification even without the occurrence of an injury. The doctrine has questioned whether it can be considered a morally indemnifiable damage or a loss of opportunity, with the latter[572] being the case.

D. Other Liabilities

182. It should be noted that liability may also be established in the event a healthcare practitioner fails to devote adequate attention a patient,[573] as well as in the event of faulty hospital administration.[574] For instance, Article 19 of the Regulation of Clinics and Hospitals[575] envisages liability of healthcare practitioners.

568. *See* María Graciela Brantt Zumarán, 'Los deberes de información y seguridad en el contrato de atención médica y la responsabilidad por su incumplimiento', *Colección de estudios de derecho civil en homenaje a la profesora Inés Pardo de Carvallo* (Alejandor Guzmán Brito ed.) (Valparaiso, Ediciones Universitarias de Valparaíso, 2008) at 505 et seq.; Iñigo De La Maza Gazmuri, 'Consentimiento informado, una visión panorámica', *Ius et Praxis*, 2010/2, at 89 et seq.
569. CS Aug. 1, 2018 (rol 16876/2018).
570. CS May 19, 2015 (rol 4388/2015).
571. CS, 23 Apr. 2014 (rol 5396/2014).
572. Carlos Pizarro Wilson, 'En oposición al consentimiento hipotético informado', *Revista de Derecho (PUCV)* 2015/ XLIV, at 119.
573. With ample reference to case law, *see* Valdivia, 'La responsabilidad por falta de servicio', cit., at 235 et seq.
574. *See* Valdivia, 'La responsabilidad por falta de servicio', cit., at 237 et seq.
575. Decree 161/1982, of 6 Aug. (DO 19 Nov. 1982.

III. Legal Practitioners

183. Changes in social relations are also reflected in the attorney-client relationship. In this sense, it is necessary to understand that difference between the relationship established with a traditional lawyer and the service provided by a large, structured firm with a team of experts; although both types of relationship are fiduciary in nature, the parameters change. If it is true that the traditional attorney-client relationship cannot be considered a B2C relationship, and therefore not governed by consumer legislation,[576] there are a number of doubts that arise with regard to the large firm that undertakes different obligations in favour of its clients, especially if they are natural persons. Therefore, also by virtue of the principle of good faith, the standards of the duty to provide information to the client[577] should be raised, and for some this could give rise to a genuine responsibility in its own right.[578]

While this sort of arrangement may constitute a contract of mandate, in the context of a legal proceeding or an action before the courts, it will have to meet certain formal requirements for its establishment,[579] in derogation of the general rules that define it as a consensual agreement.[580] The margins of mandate also serve to establish the limits of contractual versus tort liability of legal practitioners. Part of the doctrine[581] considers the liability for legal malpractice to be extracontractual in nature, performed in a spirit of friendship or liberality, and therefore subject to the laws of tort. The difference in activity between an appropriately licensed professional and one lacking such qualification is certainly significant.[582]

184. The Chilean legal system has a *Colegio de Abogados*, although membership has not been mandatory since 1981.[583] Since then, it has[584] not been a professional college *stricto sensu*, but it is considered an *associación gremial* and therefore subject to the relevant regulations.[585] Despite this, the courts have ruled that also non-member legal practitioners are bound[586] by the ethical rules of the

576. Art. 1.2 LPC, Corral, *Lecciones*, cit., at 286.
577. In this sense *see also* Sebastían Bozzo Hauri & Gonzalo Ruz Lártiga, 'El deber precontractual de información del abogado', Ius *et Praxis*, 2019/1, at 58–60.
578. Sebastían Bozzo Hauri & Gonzalo Ruz Lártiga, 'Responsabilidad por incumplimiento del deber de información del abogado', Ius. *Revista del Instituto de Ciencias Jurídicas de Puebla*, 2020/46, at 223 et seq.; Sebastían Bozzo Hauri & Gonzalo Ruz Lártiga, 'El deber contractual de información del abogado', Ius *et Praxis, 2021/1*, at 121 et seq.
579. This is done by means of a *mandato de patrocinio* (Art. 520–529 COT) or a *mandato di procaturela* (Art. 394–398 COT). On 'comparecencia en juicio' *see* Ley 18.120/1982, of 30 Apr. (DO 18 May 1982), in particular Art. 2.
580. For example, Art. 2116 and 2118 CC; Art. 528 COT.
581. Alessandri, *Responsabilidad*, cit., at 60–61.
582. Art. 520 COT et seq.
583. This was compulsory between 1928 and 1981 when the institution was a professional college a tenor of the *Ley Organica del Colegio de abogados* (DS 3274/1941, of 1 Sept.).
Prior to the *Colegio de Abogados* there was, as a private association, the *Instituto de Abogados* created in 1915. Technically the first *Colegio de Abogados* was established in 1862 and lasted only four years.
584. This is through the law on *Colegios profesionales*: DL 3261/1981 of 3 Feb. (DO 7 Feb. 1981),
585. DL 2.757/1979, of 29 Jun. (DO 7 Jul. 1979).
586. CS 24 Nov. 2014 (rol 23.134/2014).

Colegio de Abogados.[587] Although the administrative offence resulting from violation of the rules of professional colleges[588] does not necessarily involve compensation in civil court,[589] the ethical rules can be applied when assessing a lawyer's conduct and the standard of care exercised in the performance of his duties.[590]

185. Since an agreement for the provision of legal services is essentially considered an obligation of means,[591] an attorney's liability arises in the event of manifested error or negligence in the execution of his professional duties or in the incorrect application of procedural rules. Thus, claims for moral damages are granted when counsel for the appellant fails to appear at an appeal hearing, causing the action to be dismissed,[592] or when prior to the court order granting withdrawal from service, counsel has failed to act on behalf of his client.[593] An attorney who has negligently failed to make relevant evidentiary requests may also be found liable.[594]

186. Maliciously practising law without a licence for the purpose of deceiving a client is disciplined by the Penal Code and may give rise to civil liability.[595]

IV. Builders and Architects

187. To address the issue of civil liability of builders and architects,[596] it is necessary to simplify and clarify the interpretation of the law, given the various provisions involved. In this respect, not only are the norms of the Civil Code relevant,

587. There is now a new disciplinary regulation of 1 Aug. 2016 which amends the Code of Professional Ethics of 2011. Prior to this introduction, there was the Code of Professional Ethics for lawyers (*Código di ética professional del Abogado*) of 28 Oct. 1948. On the previous legislation *see* Alvaro Anríquez Novoa, 'Ética profesional del abogado. Normativa vigente en Chile', *Ius et Praxis*, 2016/2 at 331–372. *See also* Antonio Bascuñan Rodríguez, 'Deberes de Confidencialidad y secreto profesional del abogado, *Revista de Estudios de la Justicia*, 2011/ 15, at 221 et seq. For an initial framing Helena Carrera Bascuñan, '*El secreto profesional del abogado' estudio teórico y práctico* (Santiago de Chile: Editorial Jurídica de Chile, 1963). A series of resolutions on ethics judgments, from 1928 and updated until 2016, can be found on the official page of the *Colegio de Abogados*: https://colegioabogados.cl/
588. DL 3261/1981, cit.
589. SAP Antofagasta 11 Jan. 2011 (rol 674/2010). Contra and in favour of a tort liability for breach of the Code of Professional Ethics in favour of a client who was a legal entity: SAP Santiago 23 Nov. 2009 (rol 6875/2007).
590. CS 17.3.2017 (rol 6.059/2013); CS 13.10.2016 (rol 50.023/2016); Barros, *Tratado, I*, at 110.
591. Barros, *Tratado, II*, at 706.
592. CS Apr. 11, 2007 (rol 3291/2005).
593. CS 6 Dec. 2011 (rol 192/2010).
594. SAP Santiago 27 Jan. 2014 (rol 6744/2012).
595. *See* Arts 231 and 207 and 231 CP.
596. Barros, *Tratado, II*, cit., at 835 et seq.; In relation to the partly modified regimes *see* Patricio, Figueroa Velasco & Juan Eduardo Figueroa Valdés, *Urbanismo y Construcción (*Santiago de Chile: LexisNexis, 2006); Sergio Urrejola Santa María, La *responsabilidad profesional de los agentes de la construcción (*Santiago de Chile: LexisNexis, 2nd ed, 2007).

both in contractual matters (Articles 2003, 2004 CC) as well in tort (Articles 2323, 2324 CC) but also the special legislation, in particular the LGCU and its rules (OGUC).

In addition to this, it is necessary to consider the potential liability of other stakeholders, such as independent project managers and planners (who are not necessarily architects, but for example, engineers).

Another important factor is that Chile is a seismic country that also suffered a powerful earthquake in 2010 (8.8 MWW on the Richter scale). Therefore, an earthquake in this region is not necessarily considered a fortuitous event, despite being included by Andrés Bello in the definition provided in the Civil Code (Article 45 CC). This is because the building codes in seismic regions impose construction standards that must be higher than those imposed in in other regions.[597]

188. The Civil Code describes damage from 'ruin' (*ruina*) in non-contractual matters (2323 CC). In contractual matters, it is described as damage from 'ruin' caused by 'vicios de la contrucción'; 'vicios del suelo' and 'vicios materiales; falla de la contrucción'[598] (*construction defects; soil defects and material defects; failure of the construction*) for which the entrepreneur ('empresario') who has erected the building is responsible (Article 2003), since liability can also be extended to the architect (Article 2004 CC).

These concepts of ruin should be kept separate since Article 2324 CC itself makes a direct reference to contract law in the case of damage for 'ruin' due to construction defects.

Despite this, the introduction of special legislation raises the question of whether this can be compatible with the tort legislation of the code and whether the injured party can choose between the two. In relation to Article 2323 CC, 'ruin' is associated with a state of antiquity[599] and the action of fall or destruction of the asset. Therefore, it could include a state of degradation that leads to the decomposition of the building or a part of it.[600] The solution should be negative, also in consideration of the distinction made by Article 2424 CC. The doctrine is divided: part of the doctrine favours compatibility,[601] while another part opposes it in favour of a more restrictive interpretation.[602]

By compatibility it is meant the possibility of choosing between the regulations on contractual responsibility foreseen by the code (Article 2003, 2004 CC) and those provided in the special provisions of the LGCU. The interaction between the

597. On these effects, *see* the Chilean Standard (NCH 433) on 'Diseño sisismico de edificios' & (NCh2369) on 'diseño sismico de estructuras e instalaciones industriales'. *See* Arts 4.1.11, 5.4.5, 5.7.15, 5.7.20 OGUC. On the seismicity of theatres, auditoriums or places with a capacity of more than 1000 people Art.4.7.1 OGUC. On the obligation of the structural calculation of the construction project by an independent professional: Art.116 bis A OGUC.
598. Art. 2003.3 CC.
599. CS August 1, 1932, volume 29, 1ª s. at 542. Similarly, on this concept which for the doctrine would be taken from the verbs *caer* or *derribar* of Art.934 and Art.2003 CC: Alessandri, *Responsabilidad*, cit., at 307.
600. In this sense CS 18 Ag 1951, RDJ tome 48, 1st s., at 409.
601. Corral, *Lecciones*, cit., at 99.
602. Barros, *Tratado*, I, cit., at 69 et seq.

regulations is also supported by the fact of conceiving not only a material concept of ruin, but also an abstract one, (a *ruina funcional*),[603] as well as the broad concept of a construction defect.[604]

189. Currently the special system is based on Articles 18 and 19 LGCU. Although it establishes the liability of the various actors involved, primary reference is made to the liability of the 'primary seller owner' (*proprietario primer vendedor*) of the construction,[605] who is required to indicate[606] in the recorded sales contract: the name and contract information for the architect, the person who carried out the structural calculations of the building, the person responsible for the work, other persons responsible for the project, the technical inspector of the work (ìnspector técnico de obra') and the independent surveyor, if any; all of whom (as we will see) have potential subjective liability, compared to the strict liability of the seller.

190. It is important to note that although the code has remained unchanged, the special legislation relating to liability for construction defects has experienced various evolutions and modifications. Introduced in 1976, Articles 18 and 19 LGCU were modified in 1996 with the *Ley de Calidad de la Construcción*[607] (Law on the Quality of Construction), and then reformed in 2005,[608] 2010,[609] 2013[610] and 2017.[611]

Thus, the liability of those involved has changed over time. The original drafting of 1979 provides for a single system of strict liability of three actors involved: the manufacturer (*fabricante*), the planner (*proyectista*) and the builder (*constructor*), and a prescription period of five years from the date of the final approval by the *Dirección de Obras Municipales* (DOM).[612] The term 'planner' can include architects and engineers.[613]

603. Eduardo Court Murasso, 'Algunas Consideraciones en Torno a la Responsabilidad Civil por Vicios de la Construcción en las Legislaciones de España y Chile', *Estudios de Derecho Privado. Libro Homenaje al Profesor Gonzalo Figueroa Yáñez* (Fundación Fernando Fueyo, ed.) (Santiago de Chile: Editorial Jurídica de Chile, 2008), at 294,295; sobre este concepto y aplicación amplica del Art.2003 N°. 3, CC: Hernán Corral Talciani, 'La responsabilidad civil de los empresarios constructores y arquitectos por ruina o construcción defectuosa de edificios', *Revista de Derecho y Jurisprudencia*, 1995/92, pp. 56–57.
604. A favor Urrejola, *La responsabilidad profesional*, cit., at 27.
605. On the definition of 'propietario primer vendedor': *see* Art. 1.1.2 OGUC.
606. Art. 18.7 LGUC.
607. Ley 19.472/1996, of 4 Sep. (DO 16 Sept. 1996).
608. Ley 20.016/2005 of 6 May (DO 27 May 2005).
609. Ley 20.443/2010, of 16 Nov. (DO 23 May 2010).
610. Ley 20.703/2013, of 18 Oct. (DO 5 Nov. 2013).
611. Ley 21.014/2017, of 18 May (DO 26 May 2017).
612. *See* Bruno Caprile Biermann. 'Las modificaciones introducidas por la Ley n. 20.703, de 5.1.2013, a la responsabilidad civil del Director de obras municipales y otros profesionales de la contrucción y a la modificación y rectificación de deslindes de terrenos', *Estudios de Derecho Civil X*, (Álvaro Vidal Olivares, Claudia Mejías Alondo, Gonzalo Severín Fuster ed., Santiago de Chile: Thomson Reuters, 2015), at 999 et seq.
613. As can be deduced from the original wording of Art.19 LGUC.

191. Since 1996, two different liability regimes have been established. It introduces the figure of the 'primary owner seller' (*proprietario primer vendedor*), for whom strict liability is established (but who is entitled to make a claim against other potentially liable persons).[614]

For the builder (who also absorbs the notion of what was once the 'manufacturer') and the 'planners', a subjective liability is established because they are responsible only for their 'errors'. Conversely, the liability of the builder[615] is also extended to the subcontractor, thus making it possible to also comply with the provisions set out in the Civil Code (Article 2003 No. 3 CC).

It also establishes the civil[616] liability of legal persons,[617] jointly and severally with responsible parties, while also establishing the liability of their legal representatives if they are dissolved.

192. If the regime has been subject to the ordinary rules of procedure since 1996, with the possibility of initiating arbitration proceedings,[618] in 2010, procedural modifications were made. Although initially it was not possible to implement actions provided by consumer law, this was partially derogated from what was explicitly provided for in Article 2 letter (e) LPC. It was also established that it would be possible to benefit, albeit with certain limitations, from the protection of the collective and widespread interest of the LPC (unless at least six injured parties were involved[619]). In this context, the *Juez de letras* will have jurisdiction, while the ordinary judge will have jurisdiction over matters involving liability for violation of the norms of the Civil Code.

The 1996 reform compensates for the fact that Article 2 letter (e) LPC excludes this activity from being included in the B2C relationship, expressly providing that the advertising conditions must be included in the public sales contract.[620] This aspect was also reinforced in 2017, not only by establishing that all the 'information given to the buyer' must be included, but also by expressly providing that both are to be considered incorporated into the sales agreement.

---

614. In the regulation of the law the primary owner seller's is reiterated almost literally, with two nuances. On the one hand, it is specified that the liability related to 'fallas y defectos' (which in the law referred to construction in general) pertains not only to the construction itself, but also to the design (*diseño*). On the other hand, it is also specified that this responsibility refers both 'to the execution phase or after it has been completed'. In this sense, the broad scope of action is explained (Cf. Art. 18.1 LGCU, Art.1.2.3. OGUC).
615. Art. 18.2 LGCU cf. Art. 1.2.6. OGUC.
616. In the event of a criminal offence, since it is not possible for legal persons to be held criminally liable, the proceedings in the criminal courts and the corresponding civil liability *ex delicto* may be requested by natural persons.
617. Art. 18.6 LGCU. The regulation refers to solidarity of the legal persons involved, whether they are '*empresas proyectistas*' or '*empresas constructoras*' (Art.1.2.11. OGUC).
618. *See* Art. 223 COT, Juan Eduardo Figueroa Valdés, *Contrucción y arbitraje* (Santiago de Chile: Rubicon, 2019).
619. Cf. Art. 19 LGCU and Art. 54 H et seq. LPC.
620. On a probelma related to clauses, also in relation to advertising prepared in massive sales in constructions: SAP Santiago de Chile, 7 May 2020 (rol 16.078-2020) with commentary by Macarena Díaz de Valdés Haase, 'Nulidad de cláusulas abusivas en reservas, promesas de compraventa y compraventas suscritas por consumidores de viviendas comercializadas en verde', *Revista chilena de derecho privado*, 2020/35, at 273–285.

193. In 2005,[621] the civil liability scheme for the owner-builder was divided into two parts. In addition to contractual liability, a tort liability of the owner who has built a construction in favour of third parties is expressly provided for if he has not yet sold the asset.[622] It was also decided to establish an express categorization of construction defects and to set a different term for each of these for the exercise of liability action, eliminating the general five-year prescription period initially envisaged.

Thus, starting in 2005, there is a prescription of ten years for structural defects (*falla o defectos estructurales*);[623] five years for those relating to structural elements and installations (*elementos constructivos o de las instalaciones*) and three years for aspects related to the finalization of the work (*elementos de terminaciones o de acabado*). In the first two cases, the *dies a quo* of the original legislation is maintained,[624] while in the third case, a longer period is provided (i.e., from the time the property is entered in the property register).

194. The 2013 reform distinguishes among the other potentially involved actors by treating the architect separately and introducing reference to the *profesional competente que realice el proyecto del cálculo estructural* (competent professional who carries out the structural planning project) and the '*Inspector Técnico de Obra*' (ITO, technical inspector of the work).

The scope of the architect's liability is expressly broadened, as he will be liable not only for errors but also for non-compliance with the legal and regulatory standards relating to the project.[625]

A similar provision is made for the '*profesional competente que realice el proyecto del cálculo estructural*' or other activities related to the geotechnical or engineering report.[626]

This dual reference (to the violation of norms and to errors) would seem to change the initial liability regime (only related to errors) and predispose a mixed system of liability; strict liability related to the violation of certain laws (e.g., the building code for seismic regions) and subjective liability for errors (i.e., to non-structural defects). The technical inspector of the work (ITO) essentially supervises the construction and is therefore subject to a *culpa in vigilando* for the work of others. In this context, he is also responsible for the ensuring the work is performed in compliance with the building code and other applicable law, including that the proper permits are obtained and the project is approved and compliant in general.[627] At this time, an obligation is introduced whereby the primary seller owner (*propietario primer vendedor*) is required to expressly indicate in the public written sales contract: the names and contact details of the aforementioned persons.

---

621. On the 2005 reform, *see* Macarena Silva Boggiano, 'La responsabilidad civil de los profesionales de la construcción después de la modificación al artículo 18 de la LGUC', *Revista de Derecho Económico* 2005/15, at 113 et seq.
622. Art. 18.1 LGCU.
623. For the definition of structural element. *See* Art.1.1.2 OGUC.
624. From the date of final inspection by the DOM (Dirección de Obras Municipales).
625. Art. 18.2 LGCU cf. Art. 1.2.4. OGUC.
626. Art. 18.3 LGCU cf. Art. 1.2.4. OGUC.
627. Art. 18.5 LGCU cf. Art. 1.2.8. OGUC.

In addition to these players, in 2013 the liability of the *revisor independiente*[628] (independent surveyor) was introduced; it should be noted that his involvement is not required and that any liability is dependent on the establishment of liability of the architect.[629]

195. The provisions set out in the Civil Code address the liability of the builder (literally is the, entrepreneur or *empresario*) and the architect (2003–2004 CC), and with the tort liability for property in cases of ruin (2223–2234 CC). To this is added the possibility for neighbours to claim compensation for damages by filing a complaint and notifying the interested party of the need to repair the building in question, pursuant to Article 934 CC.[630]

196. The builder's obligation is framed as an obligation of result,[631] and therefore does not require proof of fault. Instead, it is based on imputation, which relates to the risk of the activity carried out; the defective product or the danger of the goods.[632] Article 2004 CC states that in the case of the architect, the canons of liability provided by Article 2003 CC for the builder apply.

The protection afforded by these is not affected by special legislation (Article 18.4 LGCU).

197. If the law does not expressly qualify the limitation period of the LGUC, then it would be inappropriate to state that it is a prescription. In the case of Article 2003, in the absence of an explicit reference, the doctrine is divided on whether it should be considered a limitation period or a guarantee term. There is also a part of the doctrine that has considered it both a limitation period and a guarantee term (i.e., a term within which the defect must manifest itself). Therefore, if the defect manifests during this period, the prescription period begins. Here the doctrine is divided as to whether the prescriptive term of four years related to tort liability should apply,[633] or if instead the five-year term for contractual liability is applicable.[634]

628. Ley 20.703/2013, of 18 Oct. (5 Nov. 2013).
629. Art. 116.3 bis LGCU cf. Art.1.2.5. OGUC.
630. On this provision and the interaction with Arts 2003, 2323 and 2330 CC, *see* Pablo Cornejo Aguilera, 'Incentivos para la convervación y reglas de responsabildiad: la responsabilidad del Dueño de la edificicación por los daños ocasionados por su ruina'. *Revista Chilena de Derecho*, 2012/1, at 33 et seq.
631. Carlos Pizarro Wilson, 'Daños en la construcción, fuerza mayor y terremotos'. *Revista de Derecho de la Universidad Católica de Valparaíso*, 2010/34, at 163.
632. Hernán Corral Talciani, 'Responsabilidad civil en la construcción de viviendas. Reflexiones sobre los regímenes legales aplicables a los daños provocados por el terremoto del 27 febrero de 2010', *Revista Chilena de Derecho*, 2010/ 3, at 460.
633. Hernán Corral Talciani, 'Daños causados por la ruina de edificios y responsabilidad civil del empresario y de los profesionales de la construcción', *Revista de Derecho y Jurisprudencia,* 1996/93, at 48; more generally on this point: Barros, *Tratado*, *II*, cit., at 851–852.
634. Carlos Pizarro Wilson, 'Daños en la construcción, fuerza mayor y terremotos'. *Revista de Derecho de la Universidad Católica de Valparaíso*, 2010/34, at 162.

Thus, part of the doctrine[635] contends that it is not necessarily a rule on liability. Rather, it is a general rule to protect the owner of the building from defects resulting from its ruinous state. In this sense, the doctrine states that in addition to the general rule in force for contractual liability (Article 1553 CC), it is possible to make a claim for the restoration of the building or repair in kind.

In contrast, another view proports that the term set out in Article 2003 is prescriptive[636] and its duration depends on the specific case, being that this rule may include third-party claims of contractual or tort liability.[637]

198. As concerns liability for the ruin of a building, it is important to note the deterrent function of liability. Thus, damage can be prevented by neighbours via a petition to require the owner to repair the building (Articles 932–934 CC), from which civil liability can arise in cases of inaction. Article 2323 CC is also relevant in that it entitles third parties with a legitimate interest to make a claim. This form of liability is based on a canon of culpability for having omitted the necessary reparations according to the *cuidado de un buen padre de familia* (care of a good father of a family).

199. Article 2323.2 CC proceeds to expressly recognize liability in the event that the building is owned by more than one person *proindiviso*, in which case the compensation is divided on a proportional basis for each share of ownership.

V. Others

A. *Notaries and Property Registrars*

200. The responsibility of notaries and property registrars ('*conservadores de bienes raices*') is yet to be addressed deeply. For this reason, a system reform is being discussed, also with a view to modernize[638] the system. It should be noted that little attention has been devoted to this subject, also because insurance policies and out-of-court settlements[639] play an important role. Still, it is interesting to observe that these professionals are currently not subject to precise duties of information, although it has been proposed to apply those relating to consumer reports.[640]

635. Carlos Pizarro Wilson, 'Daños en la construcción, fuerza mayor y terremotos', cit., at 164. SAP Santiago de Chile 9 Mar. 2009 (rol 4694/2008).
636. Alessandri, *Responsabilidad,* cit., at 379.
637. Alessandri, *Responsabilidad,* cit., at 315.
638. Proyecto de Ley Moderniza y fortalece el funcionamiento y la fiscalización del sistema registral y notarial Boletin 9059-07, Mensaje Nº 176 – 361, 6 Aug. 2013. Connected to Proyecto de Ley modifica régimen de nombramiento y funciones del sistema notarial y registral. Boletín 8673-07, Mensaje 171-360, 3 Oct. 2012 cf. Proyecto de Ley reforma el sistema registral y notarial. Boletín 5836-07, Mensaje 1234-355, Santiago, Chile, 3 Mar. 2008. On the early debates related to the reform see the special issue on 'Derecho Notarial y Registral: contribuciones académicas para su futura reforma,' *Cuadernos de extensión jurídica* 2018/30 (GianFranco Rosso Elorrieaga ed.).
639. Tapia, 'Responsabilidad civil de los notarios', cit., at 62.
640. Tapia, 'Responsabilidad civil de los notarios', cit., at 64; already Pizarro, 'La responsabilidad civil de los notarios', cit., at 141, manifests a concern about informational duties.

Article 452 COT is extended to all the provisions of the COT for notaries, including the regime of infractions and penalties.[641]

201. In the Chilean legal system, notaries and property registrars have a special status not only because of their role as auxiliares de la Admnistración de Justicia[642] and public servants,[643] but also because of their regular contact with the public (which is conducted within a certain scope and for which they receive remuneration). However, because their service is not a service in the strict sense of the word, remuneration consists of pre-established state tariffs with fixed limits (aranceles).[644] Furthermore, the practice of having the signature of several private entities on file contributes to establishing a certain fiduciary relationship. Notaries and property registrars must deposit the amount equal to 'one year of the base salary assigned to the office and for the other officials equal to the amount of the annual salary that the law fixes for the effects of their retirement'. In order to 'cover any fines, costs and damages to which they may be subject as a result of acts related to the performance of their duties, within 30 days after having assumed office'.[645]

202. This sui generis situation has left open the debate in the doctrine on the legal nature of the service, starting from the observation that both notaries and property registrars are directly appointed by the President of the Republic upon nomination by the respective courts of appeal.[646] In this sense, through the exercise of their respective functions, they fulfil an obligation sourced in the law.[647]

While some commentators limit their observations to noting that this is a 'complex' situation given the institutional function (without being public officials) of notaries and property registrars,[648] recent doctrine – in contrast to earlier scholarship that considered liability to be beyond the scope of contract, emphasizing the

641. Art. 440–445 COT.

642. Along with others such as I fiscales judiciales (Arts 350 et seq. COT); I Defensores Públicos (Arts 365 et seq. COT; Relatores (Arts 372 et seq. COT); Secretarios de las Cortes o Tribunales Superiores de Justicia y Juzgados (Arts 379 et seq. COT); Administradores de Tribunales con competencia en lo Criminal (Arts 389 A et seq. COT); Receptores (Arts 390 et seq. COT);, Procuradores del Número (Arts 396 et seq. COT), Archiveros Judiciales (Arts 453 et seq. COT), Consejos Técnicos (Art. 457 COT); y Bibliotecarios Judiciales (Art. 457 bis COT).

643. For *notarios*: (Art. 399–445 COT); *conservadores* (Art. 446–542 COT). *See also* Art. 58 342, 842 CPC, Art. 187 n. 3 CC: Carlos Pizarro Wilson, 'La responsabilidad civil de los notarios en Chile', *Revista de Derecho, Universidad Católica del Norte,* 2011/22, at 140–141.

644. Art. 492 COT.

645. Art. 473 COT.

646. Art. 459 COT. They are also subject to disciplinary control by these courts of appeal (Art. 553).

647. Art. 1437 and 2284 CC.

648. Art. 1.2 LPC, Corral, *Lecciones,* cit., at 286.

public function of the service[649] – has tended to suggest that liability is fundamentally contractual,[650] without discounting potential tort liability in cases where damage is caused to persons other than those soliciting the service[651] or in cases of criminal responsibility, since the law allows concurrent claims in contract and in tort.[652]

The contractual nature is also supported by the fact that there is a general regime of contractual liability,[653] as well as by the fact that 'although the notary cannot refuse to provide the service, this does not change the contractual nature, being nothing more than another contract of a compulsory nature as to the subject with whom it is to be contracted'.[654]

In this case, the contract is considered an agreement for the provision of professional services, to which the rules of the contract for the provision of services ('*contrato de arrendamiento de servicios*') and those of the mandate,[655] whereby liability for gross negligence arises on the grounds that the standard is higher in the case of a fee-based mandate (Article 2129 CC).[656]

203. Notwithstanding, the position of the courts is clear. And although there are few decisions, the approach adopted is that of tort liability,[657] based,[658] in the case of the property registrar, on 96 of the Reglamento del Conservador de Bienes Raíces.[659] In this sense, the general provisions of Articles 2314 and 2329 CC are applied, although for this purpose consideration is also given to the violation of their duties.

204. As far as the property registrar is concerned – that is, the person who prepares and maintains public records[660] – is presumed that he performs a formal and

649. Abeliuk, *Las Obligaciones, II*, at 918; Daniel Peñailillo Arévalo, *Los bienes: la propiedad y otros derechos reales*. (Santiago de Chile: Editorial Jurídica de Chile, 2nd ed., 2019), at 255 et seq.
650. Joel González Castillo, 'La responsabilidad civil de notarios y conservadores de bienes raíces: régimen de responsabilidad y culpa de que responden', *Revista de derecho (Coquimbo)*. 2019/26, e3595; Mauricio Tapia Rodríguez, 'Responsabilidad civil de los notarios en la jurisprudencia chilena', *Cuadernos de extensión jurídica* 2018/30 (ejemplar especial sobre Derecho Notarial y Registral: contribuciones académicas para su futura reforma, GianFranco Rosso Elorrieaga ed.)., at 64; for Notary Pizarro, 'La responsabilidad civil de los notarios', cit., at 141.
651. Pizarro, 'La responsabilidad civil de los notarios', cit., at 144; expanding it also to conservatives González, 'La responsabilidad civil de notarios', cit., e3595.
652. *See* Art. 260, 440 et seq. And 193 CP, Art. 59.2 and 109 letra c) CPP: Pizarro, 'La responsabilidad civil de los notarios', cit., at 143; expanding it also to property registrars González, 'La responsabilidad civil de notarios', cit., e3595.
653. Tapia, 'Responsabilidad civil de los notarios', cit., at 64. *See supra* paras 202 et seq.
654. Pizarro, 'La responsabilidad civil de los notarios', cit., at 145.
655. Joel González Castillo, 'La responsabilidad civil de notarios y conservadores de bienes raíces: régimen de responsabilidad y culpa de que responden', *Revista de derecho (Coquimbo)*. 2019/26, e3595.
656. González Castillo, 'La responsabilidad civil de notarios y conservadores ... ', cit., e3595.
657. CS 11.11.2011 (rol 3.016-2009); CS 23 Jun. 2016 (rol 19.661-16), CS 24 Oct. 2016 (rol 14.317-16).
658. CS 28 Nov. 2012 (rol 892/2011); CS 24 May 2016 (rol 10646/2015). This norm had already been highlighted by Alessandri, *Responsabilidad*, cit., at 148.
659. *Decreto sin numero*, of 24 Jun. 1857 (DO 24 Jun. 1857).
660. *See* Art. 49 *Decreto sin numero*, of 24 Jun. 1857.

substantial function. This is evidenced by his authority to refuse to record a deed in the register in the event the deed possesses an evident or invalidating defect.[661] This may also occur when a person does not appear to be the owner of the property to be sold,[662] therefore, the property registrar may be sanctioned.

In this context, doctrine[663] and the case law hold that the property registrar has an obligation to faithfully and diligently execute the duties required of him in the exercise of his functions.[664]

Therefore, tort liability is based on the general and legal duties of the property registrar in obvious cases such as the registration of a non-existent property.[665] The infringement of the regulation, just as the commission of an administrative tort, may also give rise to civil liability. Thus, an *ilícito infraccional* pursuant to Article 13 of the regulation may be established in the event a lien is placed on property for which the debtor has no title.[666] This aspect also allows the property registrar to exclude his liability if he is able to prove that he acted in accordance with the law in force as pertains to the duties required in the exercise of his functions, even though tort claims place the burden of proof on the claimant to prove fault or fraud.[667]

205. As far as notaries are concerned, although their responsibility is not explicitly provided for, it should be noted that their functions[668] and disciplinary sanctions[669] are expressly defined. For example, authorizing signatures only after having verified the identity of the person (Article 425 COT). To this end, Article 432 COT considers that 'the notary is responsible for any faults, defects or damage to the records, for as long as he keeps them in his possession', while Article 402.3 COT expressly states that the notary in the event of his absence may nominate an attorney to act as his substitute 'under his responsibility'.

Like the liability of property registrars, liability of notaries based on the general provisions of the civil responsibility (Articles 2314, 2329 CC), is associated with the previously mentioned rules, generally contending that civil liability arises from the irregular act of the notary when he fails to comply with duties required in the exercise of his function.[670]

---

661. Art. 13 *Decreto sin numero*, of 24 Jun. 1857 states: '*si es visible en el título algún vicio o defecto que lo anule absolutamente*'.
662. *See* Art. 14 *Decreto sin numero*, of 24 Jun. 1857.
663. Domingo Hernández Emparanza, Descripción y análisis dogmático', *Estudios sobre reformas al Código Civil y Código de Comercio. Cuarta Parte. Derecho Registral Inmobiliario* (Fundación Fernando Fueyo, ed.) (Santiago de Chile: Fundación Fernando Fueyo, Editorial Jurídica de Chile, 2003), at 198 et seq.
664. Under this perspective expressly CS 24 May 2016 (rol 10646/2015). It states – recalling also CS 4 May 1948 (*RDJ*, 54, s. 1ª, at 545) – that the property registrar cannot be a 'mere receiver' ('*mero receptor de títulos*').
665. CS May 24, 2016 (rol 10646/2015).
666. CS 11 Jan. 1935, CS 23 Sept 1935, *RDJ*, 32, s. 1ª, at 538, *see* Alessandri, *Responsabilidad*, cit., at 175–176.
667. In this case, Art. 13 *Decreto sin numero*, of 24 Jun. 1857 is not considered to have been infringed in the case of the registration of a copy which was not subsequently authenticated: CS 28 Nov. 2012 (rol 892/2011).
668. Art. 401 COT.
669. Art. 440 COT.
670. CS 24 Oct. 2016 (rol 14317/2016).

Consequently, the liability is evident in the case of failure to verify a person's identity, whereby the notary has failed to ascertain that the person appearing was 49 years younger than the person he claimed to be[671] or has pretended to be a deceased person,[672] or where the notary does not fully abide by the instructions given by the parties, behaving negligently so as to act in a manner not required of him.[673]

206. In analysing the lex artis for notaries, legal scholars have noted that they are bound to act in accordance with a general standard of practice of the 'buen notaio' (good notary).[674] This not only implies compliance with the laws in force, but also (in certain cases) compliance with established practices or customs.[675] In spite of this, for certain activities (e.g., the verification of identity), it is considered sufficient to check the identity document without requiring, in the absence of specific regulations, a thorough or more comprehensive check (such as control by electronic means).[676]

The absence of any mandatory control activity has prompted the doctrine to assert[677] that notaries are not required to go to any lengths, not even in the case of a mandate (or power of attorney), to ascertain the validity of the deed to be notarized. This view is primarily based on the fact that mandates/powers of attorney are not attached to public documents and are considered legitimate based on the statement made by the parties thereto to have read and understood the contents thereof. Regardless of this position and practice, it cannot be held that the notary is exempt or excused from his duties and should therefore demand that the mandate or delegation be attached also for the purpose of its review.

207. Particularly interesting is the discussion on the potential liability of the notary in the event of harm caused by the activity of the substitute notary. Case law has broadly interpreted Article 402.3 to protect injured parties and has established the joint and several liability of the substitute notary and the titular notary for having notarized a forged mandate despite having been informed by the notary and the *Conservador de Bienes Raices* (later found to be injured parties) that suspicious persons were attempting to sell their land unlawfully.[678] Article 402 of the COT states that the titular notary proposes 'under his own responsibility' the substitute notary without expressly stating whether he will be jointly liable. For this reason, part of the doctrine[679] has criticized this decision on the grounds that, although in tort liability joint and several liability may be established pursuant to Article 2317 CC,[680] it

671. CS 23 Jun. 2016 (rol 19.661/16).
672. SAP Rancagua, 21 Sep. 2001 (rol 17.508-2001).
673. In this case the notary paid a deposit relating to a bank cheque not requested by the party because it was associated with an invalid agreement which was never signed: CS 11 Nov. 2011 (rol 3016/2009).
674. Pizarro, 'La responsabilidad civil de los notarios', cit., at 141 and145.
675. Tapia, 'Responsabilidad civil de los notarios', cit., at 73–74.
676. Tapia, 'Responsabilidad civil de los notarios', cit., at 78–79.
677. Tapia, 'Responsabilidad civil de los notarios', cit., at 80–81.
678. CS 24 Oct. 2016 (rol 14317-2016).
679. González, 'La responsabilidad civil de notarios', cit., e3595.
680. If contractual liability were considered, the responsibility of the titular notary would be in the tenor of Art. 1679 CC for which 'en el hecho o culpa del deudor se comprende el hecho o culpa de las

is technically impossible to speak of joint and several liability when the behaviour is carried out by a single person (i.e., the substitute notary) and not by several authors.

However, another view argues that such joint liability is possible because the conduct of the titular notary and the substitute notary constitute two different forms of negligence: the first is a *culpa in eliiendo* while the second consists in the careless (and harmful) notarization by the substitute of a fraudulent deed.[681]

Part of the doctrine[682] holds that this is a situation of liability for the actions of others and that Article 2320 CC thus applies since the titular notary is responsible for the actions of the substitute notary. However, this theory is challenged by those who[683] argue Article 2320 is inapplicable, as 'it is a legal guarantee of the acts of the person who replaces him'.[684]

208. Damages are paid in the form of moral damage,[685] material damage[686] or both.[687] It has been noted[688] that economic damages can be paid in terms of actual loss or lost profits.

B. Auditors

209. The professional liability of auditors relates to an internal context of the audited company and its associates, as well as the extent and scope of the analysis and information provided to third parties. This second aspect is based on the fact that such information provided is capable of impacting third-party decisions, such as those of an investor to acquire the company or certain assets. For this reason, any interested party may bring suit (active legitimacy) on the grounds that external auditors are explicitly liable, also 'for *culpa leve*, for the damage caused in the provision of their services'.[689]

210. According to this second perspective, although liability is not strictly precontractual, the doctrine[690] suggests a general duty exists to inform the public, which arises from the benefit received by a qualified expert. Certainly, the standard

---

personas por quienes fuere 'esponsible' (*the fact or fault of the debtor includes the fact or fault of the persons for whom the debtor is responsible*): Pizarro, 'La responsabilidad civil de los notarios', cit., at 147, followed by González, 'La responsabilidad civil de notarios', cit., e3595'

681. Tapia, 'Responsabilidad civil de los notarios', cit., at 80–81.
682. Hernán Corral'Talciani, 'Responsabilidad civil de los notarios', *El Mercurio*. 11 Nov. 2016.
683. Alessandri, *Responsabilidad,* cit., at 282.
684. It is also considered that there is not a relationship of dependence between the two: Alessandri, *Responsabilidad*, cit., at 224.
685. CS 23 Jun. 2016 (rol 19661/2016). Here the inscription was later cancelled producing no material damage.
686. CS 11 Nov, 2011 (rol 3016/2009), sentence to pay damages in the amount of the check held that was sent for payment.
687. CS 24 oct. 2016 (rol 14317-2016)'
688. Tapia, 'Responsabilidad civil de los notarios', cit., at 84 et seq.
689. '*Responderán hasta de la culpa leve por los perjuicios que causaren*': Art. 249 LMV.
690. Barros, *Tratado, II*, at 1113 and 1144 et seq.

of the 'good family man' (*buon padre di familia*) in this case must be translated to that of the 'good financial-accountant professional' ('burn professional financier-contable')[691] that conforms to canons of objectivity and reliability. If an external auditor commits an error, the liability will be in tort.[692] It is important to note that while initially the violation of certain ethical or administrative rules was considered sufficient grounds for holding the audit firm liable,[693] there has since been an important change in opinion.

Initially, the claim for indemnity was rejected on the formalist observation that it had not been specifically claimed based on a general civil law provision (e.g., Article 2314 CC[694]), but only on an interim system of rules. Therefore, it was considered that the violation of the latter lacked a substantial influence in relation to civil liability in absence of an express provision.

Recently, however, there has been a radical change of orientation. Specifically, it is argued that the violation of certain standards of conduct – such as those laid down in the generally accepted Statements on Auditing Standards[695] – is in itself sufficient to establish a presumption on which to base the liability of the auditor and condemn him to compensation.[696]

Important is a compensation[697] regarding a liability related to pension funds.[698]

C. *Liability in the Securities Market Act (*Ley de Mercado de Valores*)*

211. In addition to the express provision for the liability of the auditors (Article 239), the *Ley de Mercado Valores (LMV)* (Stock Markets Act) provides for various forms of liability. Apart from a general rule that envisages civil liability for those who break the law,[699] there is also a joint and several liability for anyone who infringes,[700] in the case of two or more potential buyers, the rules on public offerings.[701]

The LMV also establishes liability for the *corredores de bolsa y los agentes devalores* (stockbrokers and securities dealers), not only for their activity but also for the

691. CS 26 abr 2021 (rol 79288/2020). Also in relation to Arts 246 and 248 LMV.
692. *See* Felipe Bahamóndez Prieto, 'Pricewaterhouse: responsabilidad de las empresas auditoras exteras por sus labores profesionales', *Sentencias destacadas*, 2007/3, at 15–27.
693. CS 20 Jul. 2006 (rol 3572/2005). For comment Bahamóndez, 'Pricewaterhouse', cit., at 15 et seq.
694. Thus expressly CS 20 Jul. 2006 (rol 3572/2005).
695. Normas de Auditoría Generalmente Aceptadas en Chile (NAGA's) 2017.
696. CS 26 abr 2021 (rol 79288/2020). The ruling traces the violation of various sections of the generally accepted rules violated in the instant case, specifically certain provisions recaptured in sections AU 230, AU 311, AU 314, AU 318, AU 236, AU334, AU 339, AU 411, and AU 722.
697. CS 3 Sep. 2021(rol 8.429-18): CS 3 sept 2021 (rol 7.888-19).
698. *See* paras 534 et seq.
699. Art. 55 LMV.
700. Art. 55.3 of the LMV. This establishes this responsibility for 'directors, liquidators, administrators, managers and auditors of public offerings that violate legal provisions, regulations and rules that govern their institutional organization will be jointly responsible for the damage they cause'. *See e.g.*, CS 11 Aug. 2015 (rol 964-2015); *see* Miguel Schurman Opazo, 'La realización de transacciones mediante mecanismos engañosos o fraudolentos como delitos de la Ley de Mercado de Valores', *Revista de Ciencias Penales*, 2015/ 4 (2015), at 209 et seq.
701. Arts 55.4 and 198 et seq. LMV.

persons that they contract or use in their activity;[702] directors, liquidators or the manager of a stock exchange who fail to exercise his or her oversight duties in accordance with its by-laws, internal regulations and other governing rules may be held liable even for *culpa leve* (*hasta la culpa leve*) (including even the slightest fault).[703] The standard of conduct required to establish *culpa leve* also applies to the *representante de los tenedores de bonos* (bondholders' representative), who must operate 'in the best interest of the represented parties' during the exercise of their functions;[704] the same standard also applies for special directors or experts.[705]

Furthermore, it is expressly stated that 'the persons and entities participating in the risk classifications shall use in the exercise of their functions the care and diligence that men ordinarily use in their own business and shall be jointly and severally be liable for the damages caused to third parties by their fraudulent or culpable actions'.[706]

It also provides for a liability of the directors in the event of the public offering of securities, in case of a known state of insolvency[707] and in general vis-à-vis civil liability to customers (or any funds) in case of negligence of financial advisory, administration and investment management services by intermediaries or economic operators.[708]

§2. Liability of Public Authorities

212. Structuring the civil liability of the State, there is talk of a liability for government activity, one for acts of administration and one for judicial activity.[709] This liability is rooted in the Chilean Constitution, first and foremost in Article 38.2 of the CPR, which clearly states that any person whose rights have been infringed upon by the State Administration, its agencies or municipalities (*Municipalidades*) may claim damages, without prejudice to the liability that may be incurred by the functionary. This gives rise to a broad possibility of indemnification and a possible recourse against the individual.

Hence, public authorities are expressly responsible for compliance with the rules which they are required to observe.[710] A general liability for judges is also provided for.[711] It will be shown that these programmatic norms[712] are then regulated in a variety of laws.

702. Arts 34 LMV.
703. Art. 56 LMV.
704. Art. 106 LMV.
705. Art. 117 LMV.
706. Art. 93 LMV.
707. Arts. 63.2 and 63.3 LMV, *see also* Art. 53 LMV.
708. Sections 169 and 172 LMV.
709. Corral, *Lecciones,* cit., at 311.
710. Arts 6 and 7 CPR.
711. Art. 79 CPR. This is also provided in Art. 324–331 COT.
712. On an autonomous and independent liability under public law and thus on the untying of civil law regulations: *See* Eduardo Soto Kloss, *Derecho Administrativo. Temas Fundamentales* (Santiago de Chile: Abeledo perrot, 3rd ed, 2012, at 429 et seq., 815 et seq., *passim*. *See also* José Miguel

213. Indemnification by the State in the event of expropriation is also expressly recognized.[713] In this sense, there has been talk of liability for a lawful act,[714] but it is fundamentally a form of indemnification that is not subject to the principle of full compensation.[715]

214. The right to personal freedom is also constitutionally protected. Hence compensation by the State is expressly recognized in cases where the Supreme Court unjustifiably or erroneously awards it in a final judgment.[716] Experience indicates that compensation for moral damage is also awarded in cases of wrongful imprisonment. For example, the State has paid compensation for moral damages for the unjust incarceration of minors who were accused of robbing a jewellery store,[717] or when a person was wrongfully condemned for a felony crime but then later released from prison thanks to DNA testing.[718] A study by the *Defensoría Penal Pública* (Public Defender's Office) found that more than 33,000 innocent people have been incarcerated in the last twenty years.[719] This is coupled with the expressly liability of the personnel of the Public Ministry,[720] its *fiscales,*[721] and the State for its erroneous or arbitrary conduct.[722]

Valdivia Olivares, *Manual de Derecho Administrativo* (Santiago de Chile: Tirant Lo Blanch, 2018), at 427 et seq.; Cf. for a general overview from a civil law perspective, e.g., Barros, *Tratado, I*, at 505 et seq.

See also Luís Cordero Vega, *Responsabilidad extracontractual de la administración del Estado* (Santiago de Chile: Der, 2017), Juan Carlos Ferrada Bórquez, 'La responsabilidad patrimonial del Estado de Chile: una revisión panorámica después de casi veinte años de jurisprudencia de la Corte Suprema'. *Revista de Administración Pública,* 2020/211, at 373 et seq.

Monographically: Hernán García Mendoza, *La responsabilidad extracotractual del Estado. Indemnización del error judicial* (Santiago de Chile: Conosur, 1997); Patricio Rondini Fernández-Dávila, *Responsabilidad patrimonial del Estado Juez en Chile* (Santiago de Chile: Lexis Nexis, 2008).

713. Art. 19.24° CPR cf. Art.45.2 CPR.
714. Carlos Céspedes Muñoz, 'El daño lícito reparable y su proyección en el sistema chileno: concepto y naturaleza', *Ius et Praxis*, 2018/1, at 137. *See also* Álvaro Quintanilla Pérez. '¿Responsabilidad del Estado por actos lícitos?'. *Revista de Derecho del Consejo de Defensa del Estado.* 2000/1, at 41 et seq.; Álvaro Quintanilla Pérez, 'Corte Suprema en caso Lolco: no hay responsabilidad estatal por acto lícito eel ocaso de la doctrina galletué'. *Revista de Derecho del Consejo de Defensa del Estado.* 2004/12, at 41 et seq.
715. *See* paras 133 and 530.
716. Art. 19.7(i) CPR.
717. SJC Santiago de Chile, 3ª s. May 25, 2020 (rol 28376/2016).
718. CS 27 Jan. 2021 (rol 14741/2020).
719. More than 33,000 innocent people were in pretrial detention in the last 18 years. For the statistic and more information, refer to the page of the Innocents Project of the Public Defender's Office: http://www.proyectoinocentes.cl/; A list of cases can be found at: http://www.proyectoinocentes.cl/casos/listado.
720. Art. 11 Ley 19.640/1998, of 8 Oct. (DO 15 Oct. 1998).
721. Art. 45 Ley 19.640/1998, cit.
722. Art. 5 Ley 19.640/1998, cit. *See, e.g.*, Carlos Dorn Garrido, 'Responsabilidad extracontractual del Estado por actos del ministerio público'. *Revista del Consejo de Defensa del* Estado, 2005/13, at 13 et seq.

215. It is interesting that the provision on the remuneration of a public official is attachable in the event he is found liable. Whereas initially no limit was established,[723] the *Estatuto Administrativo* currently[724] (Administrative Code) establishes that it is attachable at the limit of 50%.[725]

It should also be noted that the *Estatuto Administrativo*[726] sets out that officials have the right to be defended by the institution to which they belong against civil liability actions in the performance of their duties. This is also established by a specific rule in the case of the Public Prosecutor.[727]

216. The primary legislation governing public administration is set forth in the Organic Constitutional Law of General Bases of the Administration of the State (*Ley Orgánica Constitucional de Bases Generales de la Administración del Estado*), which implements the general provisions of Article 38.1 of the CPR, originally envisaged in 1986[728] and now included in a text that has been in force since 2001.[729] Similarly, the law regulating municipalities (*Ley orgánica Constitucional de Municipalidades*) was introduced for two years later (in 1988[730]) and has been reorganized in a text that came into effect in 2006.[731]

217. The general structure of the programmatic norms of the Constitution entails not only declaring the State liable for damages caused by its organs in the exercise of their functions,[732] but also clearly indicates that the personnel of the administration may be civilly liable.[733] The organs of the State administration may also be held liable for damages caused,[734] including in the case of municipal administrations.[735] It is also made clear that the *Carabineros* (Military Police Officers) are liable not only for their administrative responsibilities (in accordance with the regulations of the Police Force), but also civilly.[736] In addition to these provisions, which are broad and general in nature, there are some more specific ones.

---

723. The *Estatuto administrativo* (Administrative Code) of 1960 did not establish limits: Art. 56 (DFL 338/1960).
724. Estatuto Administrativo (DFL 29/2004, of 16 Jun. (DO 16 Mar. 2005) which reiterates Ley 18334/1989, of 15 Sept. (DO 23 Sept. 1989).
725. Art. 95 EA, formerly Art. 90 Ley 18334/1989, cit.
726. Art. 90 EA; formerly Art. 84 Ley 18334/1989, cit.
727. Art. 86 Ley 19.640/1998, of 8 Oct. (DO 15 Oct. 1998).
728. Ley 18.575/1986, of 12 Nov. (DO 5 Dec. 1986).
729. LOCBGAD: DFL 1/2000, DFL 1/19653, of 13 Dec. (DO Nov. 17, 2001).
730. Ley 18.695/1988, cit., (now DFL 1/2006, cit.). Prior to that, Art. 61–63 of the *Organic Law of the Municipalities* were in force: Decree Law 1289, of 12 Dec. (DO 14 Jan. 1976).
731. LOCM: DFL 1/2006, of 9 May (DO 26 Jul. 2006).
732. Art. 4 LOCBGAD.
733. Art. 18 LOCBGAD.
734. Art. 44.1 LOCBGAD.
735. Art. 152.1 LOCM.
736. Art. 36 Ley Orgánica de carabineros: Ley 18961/1990, of 27 Feb. (DO 7 Mar. 1990).

218. As far as the regional government is concerned, it should be noted that the rules governing the civil liability of public officials also apply to regional councillors,[737] whereas the *delegado presidencial* of the region will be subject to the civil liability of the public official, regardless of whether he is a member of the administration.[738]

219. Liability for medical malpractice on the part of the State[739] has already been discussed.[740] The liability of local governments and the tax authorities for accidents caused by the poor condition of the road surface or lack of adequate signage[741] is also provided for in the *Ley de tránsito* (Traffic Act).[742]

Explicitly providing for joint and several liability of those who commission and carry out such works on the public highway,[743] this last type of liability is also extended to companies that are concessionaires of public works; they are also potentially liable for damage (of any nature) to third parties produced in connection with the works.[744] This point will be discussed *infra* in the context of traffic accidents,[745] as well as in relation to – for example – concessions for the construction of highways. It must also be understood that the *Fisco* (i.e., the Chilean version of the IRS, or the treasury) is not liable under contract law for its contractual obligations in agreements with the concessionaire and contractors or subcontractors, but with the peculiarity that Treasury will attend to the payment of the damages caused by the unforeseeable event or force majeure, if so established by the bidding rules.[746]

Pertaining to traffic signs, however, it is established that the municipalities are responsible for the installation and maintenance of traffic signs (signage) unless it is the responsibility of the *Ministerio de Obras Públicas* (the Ministry of Public Works).[747]

220. The criterion of *imputación*[748] for State and municipalities is the *falta de servicio*[749] (lack of service). Although only expressly applicable in certain cases,[750] *falta de servicio* is generally regarded as the fundamental basis for State liability.[751] It is debated whether this form of liability is linked to negligence or strict liability. This is also because the word *falta* may refer to an 'absence' of service, or to a poor

737. Art. 35 DFL 1-19175/2005, of 8 Aug. (DO 8 Nov. 2005).
738. Art. 5 DFL 1-19175/2005, of 8 Aug. (DO 8 Nov. 2005).
739. Ley 19.966/2005, 25 Aug. (DO 3 Sep. 2004).
740. *See supra* paras 176 et seq.
741. Art. 169.5 LT.
742. LT: DFL 1/2007, of 27 Dec. (DO 29 Oct. 2009).
743. Art. 96-2 LT.
744. Art. 35 DS 900/1996, of 31 Oct. (DO 18 Dec. 1996. Which recasts DFL 164/1991.
745. *See* paras 305 et seq.
746. Art. 22.2 DS 900/1996, cit.
747. Art. 94 LT.
748. Cf. Corral, *Lecciones*, cit., at 314; Barros, *Tratado, I*, at 537–538.
749. *See e.g.*, Valdivia, *Manual*, cit., at 433 et seq.; Aavv, *La falta de servicio* (Raúl Letelier Wartenberg coord) (Santiago de Chile: Abeledo perrot, 2012).
750. Art. 44.1 LOCBGAD, Art. 152.1 LOCM.
751. Cf. Cordero, *Responsabilidad extracontractual*, cit., at 95–96; Barros, *Tratado, I*, at 512 and 531 et seq.

translation – now disproved[752] – of *faute de service* (*culpa del servicio*). This means that sometimes it is possible to establish liability irrespective of fault.[753] At any rate, what is certain is that given its extent, the foundation for establishing this type of liability may vary depending on the scope of application.[754] This does not exclude decisions that establish liability based on general rules of tort liability, which we have seen may be considered as fault-based (Article 2314 CC) or subject to various interpretations (Article 2329 CC).[755] This is especially the case when a general liability rule requires a party to behave in a manner such as not to commit certain infractions[756] or in compliance with the standards of conduct required by the duties related to the purposes or tasks performed.[757]

221. Essentially, three levels of regulations have been identified concerning the liability of the State, its organs and the individuals who perform the functions that give rise to civil responsibility. The recognition of a right to recourse against the State is precisely why it is possible to assess whether the State liability (or that of its organs) is distinct from the liability of the individuals who perform public functions, and who are responsible. In other words, there are two scenarios: one in which these types of liability operate coherently within a homogeneous nucleus, and another in which they stand alone. In this second case there may be two different types of liability: one relating to the State or a public authority (organ), and another relating to the individual that materially committed the damage and subject to a standard of conduct.

Whether it is possible to prove that the individual is or may be linked to the State (or one of its organs) depends on how the right to recourse operates.

752. For example, Eduardo Soto Kloss, 'Comentario a la sentencia Corte Suprema de 13 de septiemnre de 1990, *Ius Oublicum*, 2001/6, at 209; Eduardo Soto Kloss, Soto, 'Responsabilidad del Estado por los daños producidos por la inactividad municipal: falta de servicio/omisión: artículo 142 de la Ley N°18.965' *Gaceta Jurídica*, 2008/341, at 37 et seq.

753. For example, Osvaldo Oelckers Camus, 'La responsabilidad civil extracontractual del Estado administrador en la Cosntitución política de 1980 y su imputabilidad por falta de servicio', *Revista Chilena de Derecho*, 1998/1, at 351:, For an objective responsibility already Jorge López Santamaría, 'Responsabilidad por falta de servicio. Casuística reciente', *Cuadernos Jurídicos* Universidad Adolfo Ibáñez, 1998/10, at 31 et seq.

754. *See* Barros, *Tratado, I,* at 509–512.

755. For an overview of case law, which for reasons of space cannot be dealt with exhaustively, *see e.g.*, Barros, *Tratado, I,* at 505 et seq.; Ferrada, *La responsabildiad patrimonial,* cit., at 388 et seq. Valdivia, *Manual,* cit., at 427 et seq. *See supra* paras 146 et seq.

756. It should be noted, however, that the administrative sanction is expressly independent of civil and criminal liability: Art.120 EA; already provided for in Art.115 Ley 18334/1989, Art.175–176 DFL 338/1960.

757. It should be noted, for example, that there is no express provision relating to liability in the *Ley Orgánica di Gendarmeria* (DL 2858/1979, of 2 Sept. DO 15 Sept. 1979) or in its enactment (Decreto 557/2011, of 22 Aug. DO 20 Dec. 2011).

222. Indeed the law expressly establishes a right to recourse (*derecho a repetir*) for the State towards State bodies[758] or regional administrations towards officials[759] in the event of *falta personale* (i.e., in the event of breach of a regulatory or infractional standard).

Another point of reference, also based on conduct, regards the right to recourse (*derecho a repetir*) of the State administrative bodies against officials who have acted in connection with medical malpractice 'with recklessness or malice'[760] in the exercise of their functions, or of the State against the Public Ministry and other officials in case of gross negligence or malice.[761]

223. The separability of the two liability actions is evident *a fortiori* in cases in which there is an *ad hoc* limitation period for civil liability proceedings against the State. This is notwithstanding it is, in absolute terms, identical to tort liability in general; meaning it is separate and autonomous in scope – and therefore can be modified independently at a later date – as is the case, for example, of State liability before the Public Prosecutor.[762] However, it should be noted this issue has yet to be resolved. On the one hand, certain laws (e.g., the liability of healthcare providers) include an *ad hoc* statute of limitations that is applicable both to the individual professional and the State administration.[763] On the other hand, it is questionable whether, in the absence of a specific rule, the general statute of limitations for civil liability laid down in the Civil Code (as opposed to the statute of limitations for the civil liability of the State, insofar as this is a *sui generis* form of liability) should be applied.[764]

224. Another example of separability is found in the case law which considers that the claim for damages does not necessarily extend to the entire amount of the judgment against an official. Rather, absent additional actions or evidence, it is limited to 50% as only half of the damages are attributable to a lack of service (*falta de servicio*) by the State (with the other half being attributable to a failure to act by the official himself).[765] Although there is no doubt as to the liability in tort, this is why the two forms of liability operate separately (while offering the same level of protection to the victim). And it is also the reason Article 2317 CC on joint liability

---

758. Art. 42.2 LOCBGAD.
759. Art. 152.2 LOCM.
760. Art. 38.3 Ley *de Acceso Universal con Garantías Explícitas* (Ley 19966/2004, cit.).
761. Art. 5.3 Ley 19.640/1998, cit.
762. Four years from the date of the 'actuación dañina': Art. 5.2 Ley 19.640/1998, cit. The general term set out in Art.2332 CC is four years from the 'perpretación del hecho'.
763. Art. 40 Ley 19966/2003, cit. Here it is stated that 'the action will be four years from the action or omission', referring to Arts 38 and 39 (i.e., to all types of liability).
764. Especially in cases of crimes against humanity, given also the peculiar historical situation that Chile experienced during the era of the Pinochet dictatorship. For the debate, *see* Barros, *Tratado*, *I*, at 560–563.
765. CS 13 Jan. 2011 (rol 6.665/2008). The judgment relates to inappropriate medical treatment. *See generally*, Hugo Cárdenas Villaroel, 'La acción de repetición del Fisco en contra del personal médico-sanitario', *Estudios de Derecho Civil V (VII Jornadas Nacionales de Derecho Civil, Concepción, 2009)* (Santiago de Chile: Legal Publishing, 2010), at 527 et seq. *See also* Pedro Pierry Arrau, 'Repetición del Estado contra el funcionario', Revista de Derecho Universidad Católica de Valparaiso 1995/XVI, at 349 et seq. The latter author recalls that in the 1950s, there was an express

is inapplicable in the majority of cases; in some cases, however, the claim is construed as an application of the rules on subrogation[766] and as having a compensatory nature.[767]

§3. Abuse of Rights

225. The abuse of rights[768] in the absence of a general rule has been highlighted as a 'multi-thematic' issue in which 'fraud against the law, the theory of causation, good faith and morals, good customs, public order, the antisocial exercise of law, the interpretation and integration of the law and equity'[769] come into play.

226. Hence the doctrine's[770] desire to provide a general principle[771] for its discipline, collocating it the first part of the code,[772] despite the existence of a draft law[773] that was aimed at achieving the same purpose through the introduction of Article 5 bis CC[774] did not succeed.

227. In the absence of a legal definition, the doctrine has attempted to define the scope and content, noting that there is no abuse if the relevant interest lies within the limits of the norm.[775] In this sense, the abusive exercise is seen as a limit[776]

provision in Art. 121 Estatuto Adminstrato DFL 256/1953) whereby it was envisaged that the State employee was responsible to the tax authorities for the harm caused by his negligence or imprudence (op. it., at 350).

766. On legal action for liability in matters related to provision of healthcare: CS.12 Jun. 2007 (rol 2.954-2006): *see* Hugo Cárdenas Villarroel, "La acción de reembolso del Fisco. A propósito del caso Beraud'. *Revista de Derecho Administrativo Económico*, 2008/2 at 127 et seq.
767. Barros, *Tratado, I*, at 554 et seq.
768. *See* Barros, *Tratado, I*, at 655 et seq.; *see* Pablo Rodríguez Grez, *El abuso del Derecho y el Abuso Circunstancial* (Santiago de Chile: Editorial Jurídica de Chile, 1997), for a historical reconstruction Juan David Terrazas Ponce, 'Abuso del Derecho. Definiciones en torno a su orígen'. *Revista de Derecho* (Gabriela Mistral), 2009/1, at 95 et seq. ídem en *Estudios de Derecho Privado. Libro homenaje al jurista René Abeliuk Manasevich* (Santiago de Chile: Editorial Jurídica de Chile, Santiago, 2010, at 281 et seq.). In relation to B2C relations *see* Erikaa Siler Soto, 'La relatividad de los derechos subjetivos de los consumidores', *Revista de Derecho (Valdivia)*, 2011/2, at 65 et seq.
769. Fernando Fueyo Laneri, *Instituciones de Derecho Civil Moderno* (Santiago de Chile: Editorial Jurídica de Chile, 1990), at 295.
770. Alessandri, *Responsabilidad,* cit., at 188.
771. On the conception of abuse as a general principle also Terrazas, 'Abuse', cit., at 191.
772. Fueyo, *Instituciones,* cit., at 275.
773. Civil Code reform project on abusive exercise of rights (Boletín 11108-07), Legislature No. 364, introduced Jan. 25, 2017.
774. The wording would have been: Art. 5 bis: '*La ley prohibe el ejercicio abusivo de los derechos, entendiéndose por tal aquel que es contrario a las finalidades del ordenamiento jurídico, las buenas costumbres, la moral y la buena fe. El juez se encuentra dotado de las facultades necesarias para arbitrar todas las medidas necearias a fin de evitar los efectos del ejercicio abusivo del derecho y fijar una indemnización, cuando ello correspondiere.*'
775. CS 20 Oct. 2008 (rol 5137/2006).
776. Barros, *Tratado, I*, at 665 Enrique Barros Bourie, 'Introducción a la doctrina del abuso de Derecho. Límites a los derechos subjetivos privados', *Revista de Derechos Y Humanidades*, 1999/7, at 14 et seq.

determined by its content.[777] Therefore, it is essentially limited by the maxim for which *Neminem laedit qui suo iure utitur* (or *qui iure suo utitur neminem laedit*), meaning 'he who exercises a right injures no man'.[778]

228. In this context abuse of rights is also associated with tort. Thus, liability for a quasi-delict not only arises from material facts but also from the abusive exercise of claims alleging civil liability. Consequently, abuse of rights is elevated to a source of civil liability,[779] an aspect that is also embraced by the case law which holds that a tort may consist in the damage caused by the abusive exercise of a right.[780] Accordingly, rights must be exercised for the purpose of satisfying of a serious and legitimate interest, which does not injure another person.[781] Otherwise, the abuse of right functions as a remedy to the excessive or abnormal exercise of the right.[782] As such, it is noted that the abusive exercise of a right constitutes a 'delito civil' (Article 2284 CC) and it will suffice to apply Article 2314 CC to condemn the wrongdoer to repair the damage.[783] Instead a right is said to have been negligently abused, giving rise to a quasi-delict, whenever it is exercised recklessly.[784] This doctrinal vision is supported by the case law that establishes an injured party is entitled to damages deriving from the abusive exercise of an individual right when fault or malice may be established,[785] thereby linking the remedy with an *animus* to cause harm and an evident lack of care.[786]

229. In addition to being a general tort - since there is no general rule in the Chilean legal system - the abuse of rights is also associated with certain specific provisions[787] with restitutionary, compensatory or other effects.

230. A restitutionary duty related to the abuse of rights has been identified in the case of pledges pursuant to Article 2396 CC, which states that if the creditor misappropriates the pledged item, he will lose his right of pledge and the debtor may demand the immediate restitution of the item.

---

777. Barros, *Tratado, I,* at 662 et seq. Barros, 'Introducción', cit., at 14 et seq.
778. 'To no one shall offend who makes lawful use of a right exercised by law': CS 16 Sept. 1912, *RDJ*, t10, s. 1ª, at 7.
779. Alessandri, *Responsabilidad,* cit., at 183.
780. CS 28 May 1998, *RDJ*, 16, s. 1ª, at 57.
781. CS 9 Nov. 2004 (rol 228/2003), *GJ*, 293, at 114.
782. Barros, 'Introducción', cit., at 18.
783. Alessandri, *Responsabilidad,* cit., at 191.
784. Alessandri, *Responsabilidad,* cit., at 193. In this sense the denunciation could produce responsibility if formalized with bad faith or imprudence or grave levity: CS 21 Nov. 1942, RDJ, XLII, 2ª s. at 29.
785. In this sense CS 11 Oct. 2016 (rol 16535/2015, CS 22 Nov. 2004 (rol 521/2004), CS 9 Nov. 2004, *GJ*, 293, at 114.
786. CS 9 Nov. 1992, *GJ,* 149, at 58.
787. *See* Alessandri, *Responsabilidad,* cit., at 183–209, Fernando Fueyo Laneri, 'El ejercicio abusivo del derecho'. *Revista del Colegio de Abogados*, La Plata, 1988, at 15 et seq.; también Alessandri, *Responsabilidad*, cit., at 183 et seq.; Barros, *Tratado*, *I*, at 655 et seq.

231. A restitutionary and compensatory duty arises in the event that company directors exploit their knowledge to obtain a benefit. In this case, there is an obligation to restore the benefit to the company's coffers, as well as a potential claim for damages by anyone with a legitimate interest.[788]

232. Another abuse of right is associated with the status of a shareholder who acts 'in bad faith or untimely' (Article 2110 CC) given the potential harm caused by such an abuse to the company and its shareholders.

Specifically, the bad faith waiving of a right by a shareholder is considered a profit belonging to the company. Thus, the shareholder who has waived a right may be liable for any losses incurred by the company (Article 2111 CC). Furthermore, any partition detrimental to the company's social interests will be considered 'untimely' and consequently without effect until the conclusion of the unfinished business (Article 2112 CC).

233. In family law, there are some provisions whose excessively restrictive nature creates an abuse. For example, Article 197.2 CC establishes a right to damages in cases where somebody has made a bad faith claim of filiation for the purpose of infringing another's right to honour.

Additionally, liability is extended jointly and severally to all parties who participate in a fraudulent claim for alimony, thereby allowing an action for restitution as well as damages (Article 328).

Some scholars have also proposed allowing compensation for the abusive exercise of one-sided divorce against a spouse who has not breached a marital obligation.[789]

234. Some rules implicitly associated with abuse of rights may result in action to eliminate the relevant effect or administrative sanctions.

For instance, an action that is neither restitutionary nor compensatory is found in the provision whereby it is prohibited to extract water for domestic use or utilization for the purpose of depriving a third party, only to waste or not use it. In such a case, the law – originally established by the Civil Code,[790] but now found in the *Código de agua*[791] – entitles interested parties to file a motion to close the well in question.

788. Art. 85 Ley de mercado de Valores (Ley 18.045/1981, of 21 Oct. (DO 22 Oct. 1981).

789. Jimena Valenzuela Del Valle, 'Responsabilidad civil por el incumplimiento de obligaciones matrimoniales y por el ejercicio abusivo del divorcio unilateral. UN estudio sobre su adminisbilidad en Chile', *Revista de Derecho (Universidad Católica del Norte)*, 2012/1 241 et seq.

790. In relation to what was the now abrogated Art. 945 of the Civil Code: Alessandri, *Responsabilidad*, cit., at 187.

791. Art. 56.1 código de aguas DF 1122/1981, of 13 Aug. (DO 29 Oct. 1981). Cf. with Art. 125 for which, however, there is no liability for damage to the lands or buildings of third parties resulting from any work done to prevent the entry of water that is not obligated to receive.

Instead, a fine is imposed[792] when a tenant abuses his rights by compromising the safety and health of other residents or by making noise. In this case, it is evident that the rights of others constitute a limit of their own.

235. Two reflections can be made from the perspective of the general theory of contract law: one relating to the offer, and another to the remedies available for breach.

An offer may also be implicitly connected to a potentially abusive behaviour with compensatory effect. The Chilean legal system permits an offer to treat to be withdrawn prior to its acceptance, subject to any compensation for expenses incurred by the other party in good faith and compensation for damages.[793] Although this doctrine is partially connected to the doctrine of *venire contra factum propio*, it should not be confused with the tacit waiver of a right.[794]

236. In terms of contractual remedies, legal scholars have argued that the right to choose a contractual remedy is not limitless. In particular, it depends on the credit rights and interests involved. This is the case, for example, whenever the creditor chooses a contractual remedy for the purpose of prejudicing the debtor's interests (rather than to satisfy his own), as this creates an excessive imbalance between the interest of the holder and the prejudicial effect for the debtor. In this sense, the abuse of right functions as an extrinsic limit to the free choice of remedy under Article 1489 CC in relation to Article 1537 CC.[795]

237. From a procedural perspective, to prevent groundless requests for pretrial protective measures (*medida prejudicial precautoria*), the applicant[796] must provide a security deposit (*prestación de fianza*), which is lost in the event of a withdrawal or dismissal since such a request is presumed by law to be malicious.[797] The doctrine holds that the pretrial elements of judicial actions (*acciones judiciales*) should also apply to administrative proceedings.[798] The initiation of legal proceedings with the aim of hindering the activity of a market agent is considered unfair competition and therefore an abuse of right.[799]

---

792. This corresponds to a fine of 3 UTM, or double in case of reincidence: Art. 32 Ley 19.537/1997, of 5 Dec. (DO 12 Dec. 1997). Already Alessandri had made reference to the repealed Art. 8 Ley N° 6.071/1937, of 16 Aug.
793. Art. 100 CCOm.
794. Also in relation to Art. 1696, 2160.1, 2518 CC: *see* Barros, 'Introducción', cit., at 27 et seq.
795. This theory, the seeds of which can be seen in Barros, is expanded and defended in depth by López: Barros, 'Introducción', cit., at 24; Patricia Verónica López Díaz, 'El Abuso del Derecho de Opción del Acreedor y su importancia en la construcción de un sistema equilibrado de remedios por incumplimiento contractual', Revista Chilena de Derecho Privado, 2012/19, at 13–62, in particular 32 et seq.
796. Art. 279.2 CPC, Gonzalo Cortez Matcovich, 'Contribución al estudio de las medidas cautelares previas a la demanda en el proceso civil chileno', *Revista de. Derecho* (Valdivia), 2017/1, at 244.
797. Art. 280.2 CPC, Also more generally Juan Carlos Marín González, *Tratado de Medidas cautle lares. Doctrina, jurisprudencia, antecedentes históricos y derecho comparaado* (Santiago de Chile: Editorial Jurídica, 2nd ed., 2015), at 396 et seq.
798. Barros, *Tratado*, *I*, at 692.
799. Art. 4 letras g) Ley 20.169/2007, of 2 Feb. (DO 16 Feb. 2007).

238. It is important to note that in consumer affairs there is a practice that can be associated with the abuse of rights in the case of out-of-court claims for consumer debts (*reclamos de cobranzas extrajudiciales*) where companies claim payment of debts by simulating a copy of a court document. Consumer law thus provides for certain limitations on aggressive practices towards the consumer through the reform of the LPC.[800]

§4. Injury to Repudiation and Privacy

I. Privacy

239. Not only are the rights to privacy and honour[801] individual rights (*'derechos de la personalidad'*[802]), but they are expressly recognized as constitutionally protected rights by Article 19 N. 4 CPR.[803] The latter is exceptional to the former and therefore more limited in scope.[804] This is because an individual's private life, dignity and honour are considered values with a certain hierarchy that must be protected with respect to the right to information.[805] Nevertheless, the latter is not an absolute rule. As will be seen in the case of the so-called right to be forgotten on the Internet.[806]

240. It has been noted[807] a physical demarcation of intimacy is protected under civil law by the easement of light and view (*servidumbres de vista*). The protection of privacy is certainly inversely proportional to one's role in society, especially one is a famous person or holds a public office. In this case, the balancing act between

800. *See* Arts 37, 39 A, 39 B and 39C LPC as reformed by Ley 21.230/2021, of 14 Ab (DO 15 Apr. 2021).
801. *See* extensively Barros, *Tratado*, *I*, at 565 et seq.
802. *See e.g.*, Carmen Domínguez Hidalgo, 'Los derechos de la personalidad y el principio de reparación integral del daño', Vvaa, *El Principio de Reparación Integral en sus Contornos Actuales. Una Revisión desde el derecho Chileno. Latinoamericano y Europeo* (Carmen Domínguez Hidalgo, ed.) (Santiago de Chile: Thomson Reuters, 2019), at 83 et seq.
803. Art. 19 No. 4 CPR: *see* Pablo Contreras Vásquez, 'El derecho a la protección de datos personales y el reconocimiento de la autodeterminación informativa en la Constitución chilena' *Estudios constitucionales*, 2020/2, at 87 et seq.
804. As specifically heard from STC 29 Sept 2020 (rol 1463/2009).
805. Thus, the Supreme Court affirms CS 15 Jun. 1993, F. del M., 415, at 347, confirming Santiago Court 31 May 1993.
806. *See* paras 249 et seq.
807. Art. 874 CC, doctrine also adds reference to Art. 842 and 844 relating to 'demarcación' and 'cerramiento', and to the violation of domicile in the criminal sphere (Art. 144–145 CP): Barros, Tratado, *I, at* 578.

the right to privacy and the right to information may be based on different criteria.[808] Whether suicide is included in the right to privacy is a controversial topic, as acknowledged by the case law.[809]

241. When crimes are committed, there is a tendency in investigative journalism to emphasize the need to inform the public about such crimes, prioritizing the right to information over the right to honour or privacy.[810] Another aspect, as will be discussed below, involves determining how long this information should be available and via which channels it can be disseminated.[811]

242. The necessary balancing act between the right of access to public information[812] and that of the protection of personal data,[813] which in the meantime has been granted constitutional protection,[814] must be carefully considered. This will facilitate the reintroduction of the convicted criminal into society by eliminating certain data and criminal records, provided certain requirements[815] are met. The removal of such data from public records is different from the removal of information from social networks.

---

808. For example, STC 31.1.2013 (rol 2246/2012); STC 5.6.2012 (rol 1990/2011), STC 11.9.2012 (rol 2153/2011): *see* Salvador Mohor Abuauad, 'Acción de inaplicabilidad por inconstitucionalidad, artículo 5° inciso 2°, Ley N° 20.285 sobre acceso a la información pública', *Revista de Derecho público* 2013/78, at 225 et seq.; Gabriel Cuevas Gatíca, 'Pugna de derechos por el uso de medios tecnológicos: el supuesto carácter de información pública de los correos electrónicos y la inviolabilidad de correspondencia', *Actualidad Jurídica* (Universidad del Desarrollo), 2014/29, at 493 et seq.
809. CS 3.11.1998, GK, 221, at 32.
810. CS 6.7.2020 (rol 31817/2019), CS 18.8.2020 (rol 33079/2020), CS 13.5.2020 (rol 31815/2019), CS 28.1.2019 (rol 22162/2018), CS 22.2.2016 (rol 375050/2015), CS 9.8.2017 (rol 11746/2017).
811. More broadly *see* Marco Antonio Rosas Zambrano, 'Responsabilidad civil extracontractual de los medios de comunicación, un régimen especial', *Estudios de derecho civil XV* (Fabian Elorriaga De Bonis ed.) (Santiago de Chile: Thomson Reuters, 2020) at 975 et seq.
812. *See* the law regulating access to public information: Ley 20.285/2008, of 11 Aug. (DO 20 Aug. 2008).
813. *See* Enrique Rajevic Mosler, 'Protección de datos y transparencia en la administración pública chilena inevitable y deseable ponderación', en AAVV, *Reflexiones sobre el uso y abuso de los datos personales en Chile*. Santiago, Expansiva – Ediciones Universidad Diego Portales, 2011), at 150 et seq. *idem En Foco*, 2011/1, at 1 et seq.; Jessica MatusArenas, 'Derecho de acceso a la información pública y protección de datos personales', *Revista de Derecho y Tecnología*, 2013/1, at 197 et seq.; Daniel Álvarez Valenzuela, 'Accceso a la Información pública y protección de datos personales ¿Puede el Consejo para la trasparencia ser la autoridad de control en materia de protección de datos?', *Revista de Derecho, Universidad Católica del Norte*, 2016/1, at 51 et seq.
814. Flavio Quezada Rodríguez, 'La protección de datos personales en la jurisprudencia del Tribunal Constitucional de Chile, *Revista de Derecho y Tecnología*, 2012/1, at 125 et seq.
815. Art. 1 DL 409/1932, of 12 Aug. (DO 18 Aug. 1932), also Art. 21.1 Ley 19628/1999. *See also* Decreto Supremo N° 64, de 27 Jan. de 1960 (DO 27 Jan. 1960). *See* in general the monographic issue on the right to obligo of the '*Revista 93*', 2016/14 of *Difensoria penal pública*.

To provide greater protection also in relation to crimes involving minors, in 2012,[816] a special section is introduced in the *registro general de condena*[817] (General Registry of Penalties) related to crimes that disable the convicted person from educational functions.[818] By virtue of stricter and more extensive penalties, as well as the insertion of a new Article 39 ter CP, since 2017,[819] the special section has been expanded and divided into two subsections. Notwithstanding, the transmission of information is permitted within certain limits, and it is not possible to disclose prohibitions that are not in force.[820]

243. The covert recording of a call or conversation, regardless of whether the party has participated in the same, is regarded as illegitimate without the prior consent of those involved. This is because the absence of consent gives rise to a presumption that the conversation is private and confidential.[821] Thus, malicious or unauthorized interference is considered a *delito de acción pública* (crime of public access),[822] unless expressly allowed in criminal law[823] (e.g., permitting certain types of recording by municipalities for purposes of public or private security, such as the installation of video cameras in small hot air balloons).[824]

244. Except for the corresponding ethical and criminal provisions[825] applicable to the respective occupations, a professional is not obliged to testify in court about matters covered by duties of confidentiality or privilege. In this case, the legal system indirectly protects the right to privacy.[826]

---

816. This related section is called 'Inhabilitaciones para ejercer funciones en ámbitos educacionales o con menores de edad (artículo 39 bis del Código Penal)' This is done by introducing the third paragraph to Art. 1 DL 645/1925 by the reform operated Ley 20594/2012, of 13 Jun. (DO 19 Jun. 2012).
817. Regulated by DL 645/1925, of 17 Oct. (DO 28 Oct. 1925).
818. *See* Art. 372 CP.
819. New penalties are introduced into the Penal Code through Article 39 *ter*. Thus, they conceive a first special section referring to the '*Inhabilitaciones impuestas por delitos de connotación sexual cometidos contra menores de edad*' and the second one to the '*Inhabilitaciones impuestas por delitos contra la vida, integridad física o psíquica de menores de dieciocho años de edad, adultos mayores y personas en situación de discapacidad*', here the convictions following the violations of Arts 39 bis and ter CP. The reform is operated by Ley 21013/2017, of 29 May (DO 6 Jun. 2017).
820. Art. 6 bis DL 645/1925, cit.
821. CS 5/28/2015 (rol 22835/2014).
822. *See* Art. 36 B letra Ley 18168/1982, of 15 Sep. (Ley General fe telecomunicaciones DO 2 Oct. 1982).
823. For example, *see* Galvez, 1992. This aspect would be limited in the public divulgation of certain sensitive images in private domicile for the protection of the accused or his family members: CS 20 Aug. 2015 (rol 22835/2014).
824. These were deemed lawful by CS 1 Jun. 2016 (rol 18481/2016).
825. The *Ley de prensa* expressly provides for criminal liability for directors and editors of the media in case of violation of confidentiality rules: Art. 7.3 Ley 19.733/2001, of 18 May (DO 4 Jun. 2001). *See also* Arts 22 et seq.
826. Art. 360 N° 1 CPC; Art. 303 CPP. On specific duties or obligations of privacy in relation to confidential information also in special legislation *see* Barros, *Tratado, I*, at 585 et seq.

II. Data Processing

245. The need for a more general protection of personal data is found with the 2018 reform of Article 19 No. 4 CPR and the express introduction of the protection of this right, along with that of 'honour and a private and family life' (already contained in the same provision). In spite of this elevation to constitutional status, protection often remains essentially of a general or programmatic nature.[827] There is also a need for a more concise set of laws to such effect, also with regard to the protection of the right to privacy and the diffusion of personal information on social networks.[828] This is because consent is often given unknowingly[829] and individuals are not necessarily in control of their data.[830]

246. In this context, protection of personal data should be regarded[831] as a limit[832] to the constitutionally protected rights to freedom of information and opinion.[833] For some,[834] this protection should also apply to legal entities.

247. There is a provision for the possible erasure of data for commercial purposes.[835] The disclosure of sensitive data by banking entities is expressly envisaged by the law on personal data,[836] especially with regard to delinquent accounts. The publication of these data in the bulletin of arrears[837] has generated an abundance of

827. *See e.g.*, Art. 2 and 10 Ley 19628/1999, of 18 Aug. (DO 28 Aug. 1999).
828. Paloma Herrera Carpintero, 'El derecho a la vida privada y las redes sociales en Chile', *Revista de Derecho y Tecnología*, 2016/1, at 87 et seq., en particular at 109.
829. On the need for appropriate access to other people's data also in relation to a bill presented in 2014: Francisco Alvarado Ávalos, 'Las fuentes de acceso público a datos personales', *Revista de Derecho y Tecnología*, 2014/2, at 219 et seq.
830. *See* Daniel Solove, 'Autogestión de la privacidad y el dilema del consentimiento', *Revista de Derecho y Tecnología*, 2013/2, at 213 et seq.
831. Humberto Nogueira Alcalá, 'Pautas para superar las tensiones entre los derechos a la libertad de opinión e informacioń y los derechos a la honra y la vida Privada'. *Revista de Derecho. Universidad Austral de Chile*, v.17, 2004/17, at 139 et seq.
832. *See* Alfredo Ferrante. *El derecho al Olvido en Internet* (Santiago de Chile: Thomson Reuters, 2021); Carlos Reusser Monsálvez, Derecho al Olvido. *La protección de datos personales como límite a las libertades informativas*, (Santiago de Chile: Der, 2nd ed., 2021).
833. Art. 19 No. 12 CPR.
834. Ignacio Rostión Casas, 'Sobre la Ley de Protección de la Vida Privada: La importancia de una 'fuente legal' y su aplicación en las Personas Jurídicas', Ius et Praxis, 2015/2, at 499 et seq.
835. Art. 12 Ley 19628/1999, cit.
836. Art. 17 Ley 19628/1999, of 18 Aug. (DO 28 Aug. 1999), as reformed by Ley 21.214/2020, of 24 Feb. (DO 28 feb. 2020).
837. The reference is for esmpio to the *Boletín DICOM*, it is recorded that existe a expressa previsiones that legitimizes the compensation for damages in this case: Art. 23 Ley 19628/1999 cit.

case law whereby injured parties have been protected by the awarding of compensation for moral damages. This aspect relates particularly to the right to honour[838] and image,[839] with occasional controversial application of Article 2331 CC.

III. Right to Be Forgotten on the Internet

248. The protection of personal data and privacy in the Internet age is increasingly under threat.[840] This may also indicate that the publication of such data infringes a person's right to honour or reputation of the person, including in a medium to long-term perspective. Due to the absence of an express provision on the right to be forgotten in Chile, legal protection has not been based on compensation and founds essentially a constitucional protection. So, this new form of right to privacy is protected via protective measures (i.e., the request for the erasure of data) or *recurso de protección* before the Court of Cassation, in the corresponding constitutional section, for the violation of constitutional rights. The current position of the court is not homogeneous and judgments vary between those recognizing the right to erasure and others that deny it.[841]

249. As concerns requests for erasure of data, it is important to note that the court may grant[842] requests, or order the information to be updated, for example, by indicating that the person who was subject to criminal proceedings was found not guilty.[843] However, the rule in such cases is not absolute and many decisions are not unanimous. The parameters for evaluating the right to be forgotten in contrast with the right to information are essentially (although other factors come into play) the public interest of the information and the passage of time,[844] albeit there is no consensus on the *dies a quo* that must be calculated and how long this must be. Still, the court tends to examine each case individually; there are positions for which a fixed parameter of ten years[845] or six years[846] from the news or the acquittal is sufficient.

838. *See* Alfredo Ferrante, 'Lesión del derecho al honor y tratamientos de datos referidos al incumplimiento de la obligación dineraria', *Revista chilena de Derecho Privado*, 2014/n. 23, at 289 et seq.; Cristián Andrés Larrain Páez, 'Algunas cuestiones relevantes sobre el derecho al honor … ', cit., at 143 et seq.
839. Alfredo Ferrante, 'La protección a la imagen y su materialidad en el ordenamiento chileno', *Revista Boliviana de Derecho*, no. 23, 2017/23, at 134 et seq.
840. *See* Paula Jervis Ortiz, 'Internet de las cosas y protección de datos personales', *Revista de Derecho y Tecnología*, 2015/2, at 9 et seq.
841. *See e.g.*, CS 18 Jul. 2019 (rol 5489/2019).
842. CS 21Jan. 2016 (rol 22.243/2015). For a commentary on this ruling: Rodrigo Pica Flores, 'El Derecho fundamental al olvido en la Web y el Sistema Constitucional Chileno', *Estudios Constitucionales*, 2016/1, at 309 et seq.; Ángela Vivanco Martínez, 'El derecho al Olvido y el eventual poder que tenemos sobre nuestra propria Historia', *Sentencias Destacadas 2016*, at 349 et seq.; Hernán Corral Talciani, 'El Derecho al Olvído en Internet. Antecedentes y bases para su configuración jurídica' *Revista Jurídica Digital, Universidad de los Andes*, 2017/1, at 10 et seq.
843. CS 9.7.2018 (rol 8543/2018).
844. *See e.g.*, CS 22 Jan. 2019 (rol 19134/2019).
845. *See e.g.*, Opposing vote of Sr. Aranguiz CS 9 Aug. 2017 (rol 11746/2017).
846. *See e.g.*, Opposing vote of Sr Puga CS 15 Jan. 2019 (rol 23107/2018).

§5. INTEFERENCE BY THIRD PERSONS WITH CONTRACTUAL RELATIONS

250. The subject attracted little attention in relation to the Chilean[847] legal system and has essentially been framed from the perspective of the law of unfair competition[848] and foreign law, predominantly common law.[849]

Essentially, it is possible to observe the emergence of a phenomenon from two points of view: that of unfair competition, taking as reference the law of unfair competition[850] and that of liability arising from a tort that has violated perfect competition, taking as reference the decree on perfect competition (*Libre Competencia*),[851] aspects that can generate civil[852] liability.

I. Unfair Competition

251. The reference to unfair competition[853] law is based on the fact that the law considers an act of unfair competition 'any conduct aimed at inducing suppliers, customers or other contractors to violate their contractual obligations with a competitor and the manifestly abusive exercise of legal actions in order to hinder the activity of a market agent'.[854]

847. Pioneering is the thesis of Francisco González Hoch, *Elementos de la culpabilida de la interferencia contractual por terceros*, (Santiago de Chile: Universidad de Chile, 1995). For an overview Barros, *Tratado, II*, at 1104 et seq.
848. *See* Cristián Banfi del Río, 'Daño entre competidores: una aproximación desde el Derecho Inglés, *Revista Chilena de Derecho Privado* 2007/8, at 9 et seq.; Cristian Banfi Del Rio, 'Interferencia en contrato ajeno: limitando la responsabilidad civil del competidor', *Cuadernos de Análisis Jurídico* (Íñigo De La Maza Gazmuri ed.), 2011/7, at 313 et seq.; Mauricio Tapia Rodríguez, 'La Ley Nº 20.196 sobre competencia desleal: una hipótesis de responsabilidad civil extracontractial', *Cuadernos de análisis jurídicos,* (Carlos Pizarro Wilson ed.) 2008/4, at 181 et seq.; José Manuel Bustamante Gubbins & Enrique Urrutia Pérez, 'Competencia desleal: inducción al incumplimiento de contratos y ejercicio manifiestamente abusivo de acciones judiciales', *Cuadernos de Extensión Jurídica,* 2007/14, at 73 et seq.
849. *See also* Adrían Schop Olea, 'Responsabilidad civil por inducir el incumplimiento contractual ajeno,' *Estudios de Derecho Civil X*, (Susan Turner Saelzer, Juan Andrés Varas Braun ed.) (Santiago de Chile: Thomson Reuters, 2014), at 669 et seq.
850. Ley 20.169/2007, cited above.
851. DL 211/1973 recast in DFL 1/2004; of 18 Oct. (DO 7 Mar. 2005).
852. Tort On the interaction and liability for acts of competence Cristián Banfi del Río, 'El dolo como condición esencial para atribuir responsabilidad civil por actos de competencia desleal: breve revisión de la juripsrudencia nacional', *Estudios de derecho civil XI (*Departamento de Derecho Privado Universidad de Concepción, ed.) (Santiago de Chile: Thomson Reuters, 2016) at 598 et seq.; Cristián Banfi Del Río,'¿Debe ser risarcido quien, ejecutando un acto ilicito o prohibido en el contrato que celebró, es dañado por la conducta anticompetiva de su contraparte?', *Estudios de Derecho Civil XII* (Hernán Corral Talciani, Pablo Manterola Domínguez ed.) (Santiago de Chile: Thomson Reuters, 2017), at 596 et seq. For a general overview Barros, *Tratado, II*, at 956 et seq.
853. *See* para. 464.
854. Art. 4 letras f) andg) Ley 20.169/2007, of 2 feb (DO 16 Feb 2007).

For some scholars it should be noted, however, that the statute of contractual liability prevails over the rules established by the law of unfair competition.[855]

The same is true when a third party attempts to unjustifiably cause the party with whom he has relations to cease doing business, causing him damage. Essentially, the doctrine[856] has observed that such cases in the Chilean context are part of the parties' precontractual responsibility.

Despite everything it should be clarified that Article 5 of the Law of Unfair Competition[857] expressly provides not only the possibility of requesting an action of cessation /removal of the act of unfair competence but to exercise 'jointly or separately' also an action for compensation by making express reference to the rules of tort liability (Articles 2314 et seq. CC).[858]

II. Unlawful Infringement of Perfect Competition

252. There are two opposing positions when it comes to the behaviour that gives rise to liability for tortious acts relating to unfair competition. On the one hand it is argued[859] that wilful conduct (or gross negligence) is necessary, while on the other hand there are those who consider *culpa leve* sufficient.[860]

253. The violation of perfect competition can also generate competitive torts which can cause damage to third parties. In relation to this matter, it is important to note the evolution that has taken place in relation to DL 211 and competitive torts.

In this sense, the creation of the *Tribunal de la Libre Competencia* (TDLC), established in 2003, with a reform that also introduced a claim for damages.[861]

Faced with this legislation, the doctrine had expressed some concerns which have been partially resolved. Thus, they had highlighted the lack of clarity on the way to request the claim compensation and on standing.[862]

---

855. Commenting on SAP Santiago 29 Jun 2016 (rol 7423/2014) *see* Ricardo Reveco Urzúa, Ricardo Padilla Parot, 'Primacía de las reglas del Estatuto Contractual, por sobre las normas de responsabilidad civil establecidas en la Ley de Competencia Desleal', Revista Chilena de Derecho 2017/28, at 375 et seq
856. Banfi del Río, 'Daño entre competidores', cit., at 14 (with jurisprudential references).
857. Art. 5 Ley 20.169/2007, cited above.
858. Art. 5 Ley 20.169 states that the resettlement action must be carried out in accordance with 'Título XXXV del Libro IV del Código Civil', that is to say, with Arts 2314 et seq. CC.
859. *See* Cristián Banfi del Río, 'El dolo como condición esencial para atribuir responsabilidad civil por actos de competencia dsleal: breve revisión de la juripsrudencia nacional', *Estudios de derecho civil XI (*Departamento de Derecho Privado Universiad de Concepción, ed.) (Santiago de Chile: Thomson Reuters, 2016) at 865 et seq.
860. *See* Mauricio Tapia Rodríguez, 'Dolo y culpa en la responsabilidad civil por competencia desleal', *Estudios de Derecho Civil XII* (Hernán Corral Talciani, Pablo Manterola Domínguez ed.) (Santiago de Chile: Thomson Reuters, 2017), at 621 et seq.
861. By means of the Ley 19.911/2003, of 20 oct (DO 14 Nov. 2003). Initially the claim for damages was contained in Art. 17 Ñ.
862. Cosó Andrés Fuchs Nissin, Álvaro Vives Martens, 'Dos problemas en torno a la responsabilidad civil derivada de ilícito anticompetitivos', *Estudios de derecho civil X (*Álvaro Vidal Olivares, Gonzalo Severín Fuster, Claudia Mejías Alonzo ed.) (Santiago de Chile: Thomson Reuters, 2015) at 985.

254. The introduction of the action for damages was expressly introduced in 2003 by means of a system shared by the countries of common law based on the follow-on-action for which the claim for damages must be requested after the judgment of conviction.[863]

Since the system envisaged by the reform contemplated a different jurisdiction, the TDLC (for the competitive tort and the ordinary civil judge for the subsequent claim for damages), it was hoped that it would be the TDLC itself that would have to declare the compensation for damages.[864] This petition was heard by the legislator who, maintaining the system of the follow-on-action,[865] in 2016, attributed[866] competency for both to the TDLC, reforming the provision, which is currently contained in Article 30. Despite this, part of the doctrine has criticized the reform.[867]

255. In relation to active legitimacy (or standing), it should be noted that, in 2016, the possibility was introduced for consumer associations to promote actions for compensation for prejudices to collective and diffuse interests before the TDLC.[868]

The transcendence of the violation of competitive torts on consumer rights, which has resulted in judgments for compensation in many cases, including in the case of controlled prices and cartels,[869] is also important. For example, when several companies have been found to have committed torts related to collusion in matters of prices, or in relation to the sale of chicken, whose compensation was requested by a consumer association.[870]

---

863. *See also* Cristián Banfi del Río, 'Acerca de la imputación de responsabilidad civil por ilícitos anticompetitivos entre rivales en Chile', *Revista Chilena de Derecho,* 2014/1, at 37 et seq.; Cristián Banfi del Río, 'La responsabilidad civil como forma de aplicación privada del derecho de competencia *Revista Chilena de Derecho Privado*, 2013/21, at 221 et seq.
864. Proposed by Andrés Fuchs Nissin, Álvaro Vives Martens, 'Dos problemas en torno a la responsabilidad civil derivada de ilícito anticompetitivos', *Estudios de derecho civil X (*Álvaro Vidal Olivares, Gonzalo Severín Fuster, Claudia Mejías Alonzo ed.) (Santiago de Chile: Thomson Reuters, 2015) at 966.
865. In this sense, it is considered that the responsibility for anticompetitive illegal acts, in addition to fulfilling a compensatory function, must play a dissuasive role in the commission of the infringements: Andrés Fuchs Nissin, Álvaro Vives Martens, 'Dos problemas en torno a la responsabilidad civil derivada de ilícito anticompetitivos', cit., at 985.
866. Ley 20945/2016, of 30 Aug. (DO 30 Aug. 2016).
867. Thus a 'bet' by the legislator has been defined: *see* Cármen Domínguez Hidalgo, 'Efectos de la sentencia dictada en sede de lubre competencia en materia de responsabilidad civil: algunas notas en perspectivas evolutivas', *Estudios de Derecho Civil XII* (Hernán Corral Talciani, Pablo Manterola Domínguez ed.) (Santiago de Chile: Thomson Reuters, 2017), at 607 et seq.
868. Art. 51 LPC, Art. 30 DL 211. *See* Gabriel Hernández Paulsen, 'Indemnizaciones a consumidores por los daños derivados de un ilícito anticompetitivos', *Estudios de Derecho Civil XII* (Hernán Corral Talciani, Pablo Manterola Domínguez ed.) (Santiago de Chile: Thomson Reuters, 2017), at 648 et seq.
869. Also with jurisprudential references *see* Gabriel Hernández Paulsen, 'Indemnizaciones a consumidores por los daños derivados de un ilícito anticompetitivos', *Estudios de Derecho Civil XII* (Hernán Corral Talciani, Pablo Manterola Domínguez ed.) (Santiago de Chile: Thomson Reuters, 2017), at 639 et seq.
870. Thus, the Supreme Court mandó a resolver en tal sentido al TDLC (CS 12 Jan 2021 (rol 1181/2020).

It is additionally interesting to note that Article 30 expressly states that the compensation shall include all damages caused during the period of the anticompetitive infringement, and that the evidence shall be evaluated according to sound criticism.[871]

However, it must be noted that often the case ends in a settlement[872] -- as in the case of price cartels on toilet paper,[873] or in the case of collusion on the prices of certain drugs.[874] Thus, the compensation is often converted into a mere insignificant or symbolic sum,[875] which can be collected through an online procedure by the consumer.[876]

256. Interesting is the compensation in kind that has been established in an out-of-court settlement by the National Consumer Service (SERNAC). In this manner, the compensation related to the collusion on diaper prices was realized via the delivery of 6.5 million diapers to other vulnerable consumers of some associations.[877]

---

871. On damages and also on culpability *see* Gabriel Hernández Paulsen, 'Indemnizaciones a consumidores por los daños derivados de un ilícito anticompetitivos', cit., at 652 et seq.
872. Part of the doctrine considers that the out-of-court agreements that are entered into with the Fiscalía Nacional Económica, especially with agents of markets, has an autonomous utela cautelar function: *see* Alejandro Romero Seguel, 'Los acuerdos extrajudiciales en materia de libre competencia como tutela cautelar autónoma', *Revista de derecho* (Coquimbo), 2020/27, e4381
873. For example, as was achieved by SERNAC in a case involving a price cartel on toilet paper: the agreement of 27 Jan. 2017 can be consulted en https://www.sernac.cl/portal/604/articles-5247_archivo_01.pdf.
874. In relation to the infractional conviction, the TDLC applied a maximum fine, which was confirmed by the Supreme Court: TDLC 31 Jan. 2012 (rol 184/08); CS 7 Sep. 2012 (rol. 2578/2012). In this case the indemnity agreement with SERNAC is concluded as of Nov. 11, 2020. In this case, there is a compensation of 22,000 Chilean pesos (approx. 34 US dollars) to be delivered to the 53,000 consumers identified in relation to 26 pharmacies sold between December 2007 and March 2008. The judgment condemning damages of first instance was JPI 17 Dec. 2019 (rol 1940/2013) and had established an emerging damage (group 1 of consumers) of 1.736.961.314 Chilean Pesos, and, for loss of profits (group 2 of consumers) to a total of $ 284.916.956 Chilean Pesos.
875. Thus, in the case mentioned above, there was a 150 million dollar award for 11 dollars per user (7.000 Chilean Pesos).
876. Available at www.micompensacion.cl
877. For the news in English: Canal 13, 'Comienza compensación por colusión de pañales: ¿Quiénes serán los beneficiados?', 14 Oct. 2019 en www.t13.cl

Part II. Liability for Others

Chapter 1. Vicarious Liability

§1. Overview

257. Certain special laws clearly establish vicarious liability. For instance, the liability of the owner of a vehicle involved in an accident, in which case joint and several liability with the driver is envisaged.[878] In the hypotheses of the Civil Code analysed here, the doctrine is not entirely univocal. Part of the doctrine does not consider this type of liability as vicarious,[879] while another part considers it to be a mixture of vicarious liability and fault,[880] unanimously considering that vicarious liability must be understood as *extricta*[881] (using an anglicism) and *objetiva*[882] (strict) liability. This is established. However, as will be seen, the reconstruction of this liability is based on aspects relating to fault and conduct. Thus, although the jurisprudence also proceeds to construct such liability as strict liability, it finds that the fault of the claimant plays a role.

258. The liability being analysed is regulated differently depending on whether the person under guardianship is legally capable. Among the various provisions, it is important to note that while Article 2319 CC generically refers to the liability of persons who are incapable of understanding and minors who lack discernment, Article 2320 refers to persons who are capable.

Article 2020 provides, in various paragraphs, a non-exhaustive[883] list of the main cases of such liability. Generally, the law envisages this form of liability whenever there is a relationship of authority or care (*cuidado*) towards the other person, such as the case of parental responsibility (a case which is complementary to

878. *See* paras 305 et seq.
879. Barros, *Tratado*, I, cit., at 173.
880. Corral, *Lecciones*, cit., at 228.
881. Barros, *Tratado*, I, cit., at 173–174.
882. Corral, *Lecciones*, cit., at 228.
883. Ramos, *De la responsabilidad Civil*, cit., at 60; critico Corral, *Lecciones*, cit., at 228; Barros, *Tratado*, I, cit., at 181.

Article 2321 CC), that of the tutor or caretaker with respect to the person who lives with and depends on him (*bajo su dependencia y cuidado*), that in relation to pupils or in the case of the entrepreneur and artisan. The latter case is complemented by Article 2322 CC which establishes liability in the case of the 'master' (*amo*). Essentially, therefore, what must exist is a relationship of subordination or dependence that generates an authoritative hierarchy.

259. In the case of an able-bodied person committing the illicit act, it is debated whether there is joint and several liability between the two parties. In accordance with Article 2317 CC, the opposing position should prevail[884] based on the existence of two distinct obligations, despite being aimed at satisfying the same interest. Instead, *nulla quaestio* when various subjects are in charge of supervising the person under their control.[885] We will return to this point in relation to the responsibilities of parents when the child is a pupil.[886]

260. In the case of the liability of the entrepreneur with respect to his employees, it has been argued that although joint and several liability is not possible under Article 2317,[887] both the entrepreneur and the employee could be liable for the total extent of any damages, holding such circumstances to represent a case of

884. For example, Corral, *Lecciones,* cit., at 230; Barros, *Tratado*, I, cit., at 185. In the same sense: CS 27 Jun. 2018 (Rol 38.145/2017); CS 5 Aug. 2013 (rol 1.006/2012).
885. Alessandri, *Responsabilidad,* cit., at 235.
886. *See infra* paras 279 et seq.
887. More extensively Pamela Mendoza Alonzo, 'Pluralidad de causantes de un mismo daño. Régimen jurídico aplicable en Chile', *Revista de Derecho Privado*. 41/2021, at, 257 et seq.; Pamela Mendoza Alonzo. 'Los sujetos pasivos de la acción de responsabilidad del artículo 2317 del código civil chileno', *Estudios de derecho privado en memoria del profesor Nelson Vera Moraga* (Carlos Céspedes Muñoz dir.) (Santiago de Chile: Thomson Reuters, 2019), at 311 et seq.; Pamela Mendoza Alonzo, 'Pluralidad de causantes de un mismo daño. Régimen jurídico aplicable en Chile', *Revista de Derecho Privado*. 41/2021, at, 257 et seq.; Hernán Corral Talciani, 'La responsabilidad solidaria de los coautores de un ilícito', *Lo Público y lo Privado. Estudios en homenaje al prof. Enrique Barros Bourie*, (Santiago de Chile: Thomson Reuters, 2017), p. 657 et seq.; Pamela Mendoza Alonzo, 'Una aproximación a la responsabilidad por el daño causado por un miembro indeterminado de un grupo determinado', *Estudios de Derecho Privado, II Jornadas Nacionales de Profesoras de Derecho Privado* (María Elisa Morales Ortiz, Pamela Mendoza Alonzo ed.) (Santiago de Chile: DER, 2020), at 347 et seq.; Hernán Corral Talciani, 'La solidariedad pasiva derivada de responsabilidad civil'. *Presente y futuro de la responsabilidad civil* (Rodrigo Barría Díaz & Alfredo Ferrante & Lilian San Martín Neira ed.) (Santiago de Chile: Thomson Reuters, 2017), at 367 et seq.

obligaciones in solidum,[888] different from joint liability.[889] This position is also supported by the applicability of Article 2325 CC.[890]

261. In general, the code predisposes responsibility on a relationship of authority or *cuidado* (of attention, care, protection) over other persons by setting out, in some cases, certain presumptions.

The presumptions may be divided into essentially two categories: those which admit proof to the contrary (last paragraph of Articles 2320 and 2322 CC) and those which do not admit such proof (set out in Article 2321 CC, as will be seen).

The last paragraph of Article 2320 applies to all the hypotheses provided in the provision and states that the person who has the *autoridad* (authority) or *cuidado* of certain persons may only exonerate himself from liability if they 'could not have prevented the fact'. In the case of Article 2322 CC (relating to los *amos y sirvientes*), a reference is added to the 'cuidado ordinario', and therefore to a *benchmark of* diligence, since it is stated that it must be proved that 'they had no means of foreseeing or preventing, by resorting to ordinary care, and the competent authority'.

Doubts as to the nature of the liability are also due to the fact that, although the provision of Article 2320 CC refers to a type of evidence that is essentially neutral and therefore associated with liability for the actions of others (and not linked to a fault of their own), some passages make reference to the conduct of the supervisor. Thus, it is necessary to consider whether the supervisor's actions created reliance. In this sense, part of the doctrine associates certain obligations of vigilance to the *cuidado* from which would derive a fault of the supervisor. Accordingly, hypotheses of *culpa in vigilando*, culpa in *educando* or *culpa in eligendo* may be abstractly configured, although not literally referred to in the black letter of the provisions. Consequently, there are two possibilities. On the one hand, it may be possible to consider these provisions as presumptions of 'liability for the actions of others'. On

888. *See* Pamela Mendoza Alonzo. 'Responsabilidad del empresario por hechos dañosos de sus dependientes: ¿obligación concurrente o in solidum?', *Estudios de Derecho Civil XIV* – (Marícruz Gómez de Latorre Vargas, Gabriel Hernández Paulsen, Fabiola Lathrop Gómez, Mauricio Tapia Rodríguez ed.) (Santiago de Chile: Thomson Reuters, 2019), at 1083 et seq.

889. On the difference between joint and several liability and *obligaciones in solidum* (also called *obligaciones concurrentes* or *obligaciones por el total no solidarias*), *see* Andrés Kuncar Onero, 'Responsabilidad solidaria versus responsabilidad concurrente', *Estudios de Derecho Privado. En homenaje al prof. Daniel Peñailillo Arévalos*, (Santiago de Chile: Thomson Reuters, 2019), p. 779 et seq.; Cristián Eduardo Aedo Barrena, Renzo Munita Marambio, 'La obligación in solidum en el derecho francés. Su proyectada adopación por el sistema chileno', *Actualidad Jurídica* (Universida del Desarrollo), 44/2021, at 411–447, especially at 431 et seq.; Hernán Corral Talciani. 'Obligaciones por el total no solidarias u obligaciones concurrentes', *Estudios de Derecho Civil X*, (Álvaro Vidal Olivares, Claudia Mejías Alonso, Gonzalo Severín Fuster ed.) (Santiago de Chile: Thomson Reuters, 2015), at 455–471, esp. at 468 et seq.

890. *See infra* paras 262 et seq.

the other, they may be considered presumptions of 'fault'[891] relating to lack of vigilance or attention;[892] depending on whether liability is considered to be for the actions of others or liability for one's own actions, linked to the conduct and fault of the supervisor.

Article 2325 CC plays a fundamental role in interpreting the rule.

262. It is useful to note that Andrés Bello has drafted an interesting provision: Article 2325 CC. This norm envisages a kind of patrimonial protection before the person responsible for the fact of others, when the person who committed the damage has assets.

Thus, it is established that 'Any person required to repair the damage caused by their dependents is entitled to be indemnified with their property, if any, and if the person who has committed the damage has done it without the order of the person to whom he owed obedience, and such dependents were punishable for an offence or quasi-delict, in accordance with Article 2319'.

In this case, a sort of recourse action is established for the person on whom the presumed responsibility (or the presumed fault, depending of interpretation accepted) rests against the assets of the person who has caused the damage.

For ethical-moral reasons, its scope is limited in cases where a parental relationship exists, compared to others.

The existence of this norm could lead to the conclusion that this is actually a liability for the actions of others and not for one's own actions, since there is an action for repayment (recourse).[893] For this reason, the question arises as to whether this provision applies to all hypotheses or only to some specific ones, since, as we have seen, doctrine sometimes frames this type of liability as a case of liability for one's own doing, linked to the fault of the supervisor or person in authority.

263. On the one hand, Article 2325 CC itself makes it clear that it does not apply in the case of incapacitated persons or minors lacking in discernment, i.e., in the case of Article 2319 CC.[894] As such, this provision would open the door to liability for one's own act in such cases. Here, the proof would be linked to the conduct of that person.[895] Indeed, at 2319 stated that he will be liable only 'if negligence can

891. On presumptions of '*culpabilidad*' *see e.g.*, Alessandri, *Responsabilidad*, cit., at 211.

892. For example, CS 15 Nov. 2010 (rol 6109/2008); CS 1 Dec. 2016 (rol 70,396/2008), CS 26 Mar. 2018 (rol 21,652/2017), CS 6 Jun. 2018 (rol 38,145/2017); CS 5 Jul. 2018 (rol 31,974/2017).

893. In this sense it is argued that the rule would be contrary to a liability for own's own fault: Gian Franco Rosso Elorriaga. 'El sistema de la responsabilidad de los empresarios por el hecho de los dependientes en el Código de Bello y las dificultades en su interpretación y aplicación', *La vigencia del Código Civil de Andrés Bello* (Felipe Navia Arroyo y Carlos Chinchilla Iambett ed, Bogotá: Universidad Externado, 2019), at 404–405.

894. This can be deduced from the last paragraph of Art. 2325 CC which, in relation to the person who commits the damage, states that: '... *and such dependents were punishable for an crime or quasi-delict, in accordance with Article 2319*'.

895. Cf. Tapia, *De la Responsabilidad*, cit., at 182. For example, there are those who consider Art. 2319 liability for *culpa* and Art. 2320 liability for the actions of others: Ramos, *De la responsabilidad Civil*. cit. at 59. Alessandri, *Responsabilidad*, cit. at 106 also considers a case of liability for own fact attributable to the fault of the guardian within the meaning of Art. 2319.

be imputed to them', that is, in relation to 'persons in charge' of the subject ('persons entrusted with their care', literally 'a cuyo caergo estén').

264. It remains to be seen whether the provision applies to all other cases under the Civil Code.[896]

According to a first interpretation, on the one hand there would be reasons to limit its application. In fact, the rule only applies when there is an asset.

Furthermore, it could be argued that its application is limited only to cases relating to a relationship of authority (e.g., in relation to employees), since the proof releasing such liability derives from a given and unfulfilled order and does not refer to a broader liability arising from *cuidado*. Since liability is excluded when it is shown that the damage arises from the incorrect performance of instructions by the damaging party, it could be more accurately associated with authoritative roles. This is also true for cases in which specific orders have been given, as in the case of the entrepreneur,[897] although this opinion is not universally accepted by the doctrine.[898] Even so, if this were the case, it would be possible to identify a fault on the part of the person who must supervise or educate the subject, hence the elaboration of *culpa in vigilando, educando or eligendo.*

According to a second and broader interpretation, the rule essentially deals with hypotheses of liability for one's own actions based on fault, fault that is presumed at the time of committing the damage. Therefore, there will be two types of fault: that caused by the agent (which must be proven), and that of the individual who has authority or control over such agent, which is presumed in accordance with Article 2320 CC or Article 2322 CC (*see below*). The absence of proof of fault on the part of the agent of the damage means that it is impossible to charge the other party with fault under Article 2320 CC.[899]

As mentioned above, the case law objectively determines the responsibility also thanks to the application of presumptions (*presunciones judiciales*) for which the type of damage or behaviour is presumed to be culpable,[900] since the same circumstances in which the damage occurred can demonstrate the lack of vigilance or care.[901]

---

896. Cf. Arts 2320, 2321 and 2322 CC.
897. On the association of the relationship of dependency with the contractor and subjection to the orders of the employee: CS 19 Jun. 1954, RDJ, t. LI, s. 1ª, at 216; CS 11 Dec. 1958, RDJ, T. LV, s. 4ª, at 209.
898. In this sense, Art. 2325 CC is not considered applicable to the case where damage is caused by the employee based on the finding that there is fault on the part of the entrepreneur. This position leaves open the possible division of responsibility in proportional parts when the faults of both are demonstrated Barros, *Tratado,* I, cit., at 201.
899. *See* CS 4 Jul. 2012 (rol 1059/2010); CS 15 Nov. 2010 (rol 6109/2008). For the doctrine: Barros, *Tratado*, I, cit., at 184.
900. Barros, *Tratado*, I, cit., at 178.
901. Thus Alessandri, *Responsabilidad,* cit., at 105.

265. Notwithstanding, the application of Article 2325 CC is only eventual and depends on whether the damaging party has assets. In this sense, it has been defined as an 'illusory'[902] device, which does not univocally justify the nature of the liability set out in specific legal norms.

It should also be recalled that, at the time of its enactment, the scope of Article 2325 CC was undoubtedly broader -- for two reasons. First because an individual reached the age of majority at 25 and, therefore, the assumptions were justified given the greater number of cases involving responsibility for minors.[903] Second, the regulations on employment contracts were not as meticulous as they are today. In this sense, many situations have passed from cases of tort liability to cases of contractual liability.

266. However, if the hypotheses falling under the auspices of Article 2320 CC (or 2322 CC) are considered to be liability for the actions of others, the proof of exoneration will be more rigid as the exoneration will not relate to the conduct of the subject. Instead, the general exemptions will be applied, such as the breaking of the causal link, the actions of the third party or the victim, fortuitous events, or force majeure. It is curious that the process of construing such responsibility as strict liability in those cases where the liability for one's own actions is relevant has led to this form of liability being equated to the other.[904]

267. According to this general scheme, the burden of proof will be different depending on whether the person who has committed the damage is legally capable. The general scheme which applies in the case of the able-bodied has been briefly discussed. Article 2319 CC applies to the case of minors lacking discernment and incapable of understanding and wanting the consequences of their actions. Specifically, since there is no presumption, it is the victim who must prove the 'negligence' ('*negligencia*') of the person who is responsible for (*a cuyo cargo*) the specified individuals.

The provision applies where the damaging party is a child under 7 years of age, i.e., a *nino or infante* (under Article 26 CC) – or a '*demente*' *(mentally ill)*, providing that only the conduct of the supervising person is relevant. The concept of a *demented person* must be considered in a broad sense and include all cases of mental illness,[905] although it is limited in certain cases[906] and must be proved by the

902. Thus Alessandri, *Responsabilidad,* cit., at 235.

903. Alfredo Ferrante, 'Ilícito del menor ¿quién paga? '. *Presente y futuro de la responsabilidad civil* (Rodrigo Barría Díaz & Alfredo Ferrante & Lilian San Martín Neira ed.) (Santiago de Chile: Thomson Reuters, 2017), at 252.

904. Thus, the doctrine states that sometimes it is necessary to identify the occurrence of a fortuitous event or force majeure: Barros, *Tratado*, I, cit., at 187.

905. Tapia, *De la Responsabilidad*, cit., at 183, also Ramos, *De la responsabilidad Civil*, cit., at 42.

906. For part of the doctrine, the dissipator and the interdictor must be considered capable: Barros, *Tratado,* I, cit., at 176. More specifically, there are those who consider that even the demented person who is legally incapable is responsible if it is demonstrated that he has carried out the damage in a 'lucid interval': Tapia, *De la Responsabilidad*, cit. at 185; Alessandri, *Responsabilidad*, cit., at 99. In this sense, another part of the doctrine considers it relevant whether the interdiction is transitory or permanent: Alessandri, *Responsabilidad*, cit. at 97.

person who alleges it.[907] It has been said that the relevant person must be completely incapacitated at the moment the damaging act is committed,[908] which some scholars[909] argue applies also to the intoxicated and the drug addict who are not in control of their behaviour.

Here, the application of Article 2319 CC means that fault is not presumed[910] and must be proven.

The rule applies when damage is caused by demented persons or minors under the age of 7.

When the damaging party is between 7 and 16 years old, the judge will assess on a case-by-case basis whether the damaging party had discernment, and thus whether s/he may be considered capable under the law (second paragraph of Article 2319 CC). If the damaging party is older than 16 but has not yet reached the age of majority, the minor is considered capable as a *menor adulto* (Article 26 CC).[911]

The terminology used in relation to incapacitated persons and minors is outdated and requires updating also in relation to the current treaties and conventions in force, as well as the progressive capacity of the minor, as – for example – in the light of the *Convention on the Rights of the Child.*[912]

In cases where the minor lacks in discernment,[913] the rule does not require cohabitation with the minor,[914] as this may also be a factual situation that may occur.[915] In this sense, liability is incumbent on the guardian of the incapacitated child, for example the parents but also a temporary caregiver such as a babysitter.

§2. EMPLOYEE/EMPLOYER

268. Liability for damage committed by an employee may be configured both as contractual and tort liability. In these cases, it is the victim who must prove the

907. As such, the presumption of nullity provided for in contractual matters for acts carried out by the demented person in Art. 465 CC does not apply: Alessandri, *Responsabilidad*, cit. at 103.
908. Ramos, *De la responsabilidad Civil*, cit., at 41.
909. Ramos, *De la responsabilidad Civil*, cit., at 43.
910. Tapia, *De la Responsabilidad*, cit., at 179; Barros, *Tratado*, I, cit., at 174; más critico Corral, *Lecciones,* cit., at 104 y 231.
911. Alessandri, *Responsabilidad*, cit., at 106; Ramos, *De la responsabilidad Civil*, cit., at 44–45.
912. *See* Lucia Rizik Mulet. *Responsabilidad civil de los padres por los daños ocasionados por sus hijos menores de edad* (Santiago de Chile: Universidad Diego Portale, inédita, 2019), *passim.*
913. Some reflections on the imputability of minors can be seen in Lucía Rizik Mulet. 'Notas sobre la responsabilidad civil extracontractual de los niños. Especial referencia al requisito de imputabilidad civil y al estadar de diligencia', *Estudios de Derecho Civil XIII* (Claudia Bahamondes Oyarzún, Leonor Etcheberry Court, Carlos Pizarro Wilson ed.) (Santiago de Chile: Thomson Reuters, 2018), at 655 et seq.
914. Ramos, *De la responsabilidad Civil*, cit., at 66.
915. Corral, *Lecciones*, cit., at 104.

existence of a link of subordination or dependence between the parties. This link may also be *de facto*[916] and the rule does not require prior formal authorization,[917] as for example in a mandate.[918]

269. Without prejudice to application of contract law,[919] the above-mentioned situations can occur in relation to the relationship between artisans and their apprentices, entrepreneurs and their employees (third and fourth paragraphs of Article 2320 CC, respectively) or between *los amos* and their *criados o sirvientes, en el ejercicio de sus respectivas funciones*' (Article 2322 CC). The various burdens of proof depending on the relevant presumptions.[920]

The notion of master (*amo*) should be understood in the broadest sense,[921] as well as that of entrepreneur. Hence, the doctrine[922] posits that the common elements of these aspects are a direct and material agent of the damage, a relationship or bond with this subject and the entrepreneur or responsible person through a relationship of subordination or dependence or bond. A further requirement is that the damage must occur during the performance of the assigned function, which must be understood broadly, as also in the use of a company car by the employee.[923] However, this does not mean that the entrepreneur is responsible every time damage is caused by an asset belonging to him. That is, if the object is used for purposes unrelated to the employee's functions, the owner or the supervisor should not be liable.[924]

Those that associate such liability with the fault of the supervising party essentially assert the existence of *culpa in vigilando*[925] or *culpa in eligendo,*[926] even if this liability has sometimes been considered strict[927] on the grounds of liability for

916. CS 27 May 2019 (Rol 4350/2018); CS 20 Dec. 2016 (rol 99.845-2016).
917. CS 15 Nov. 2010 (rol 6109/2008); CS 10 Sep. 2012 (rol 1630/2010); Corral, *Lecciones,* cit., at 232.
918. Barros, *Tratado*, I, cit., at 180.
919. *See* paras 272–273.
920. *See* para. 281.
921. *See* Barros, *Tratado*, I, cit., at 189–190.
922. Ramos, *De la responsabilidad Civil*, cit. at 70; Pedro Zelaya Etchegaray, 'La responsabilidad civil del empresario por el hecho de su dependiente. Un intento por sistematizar la jurisprudencia chilena', *Revista de Derecho de la Universidad de Concepción*, no. 197/1995, at 110–111.
923. *See* Pedro Zelaya Etchegaray, 'Responsabilidad civil del empresario en el uso de vehículos de transporte. Un estudio de la jurisprudencia chilena', *Responsabilidad Civil del Empresario*, *Cuadernos de Extensión Jurídica*, (Federico McKay Alliende ed.), 1996, at 105 et seq. Recently on a fatal accident related to a transported for an employee with a company vehicle e.g CS 15 Mar. 2015 (rol 9496/2014).
924. Such as when an employee murders his wife with a company-owned firearm: CS 23 May 2017 (rol 4902/2017).
925. Alessandri, *Responsabilidad,* cit., at 261.
926. Ramos, *De la responsabilidad Civil*, cit., at 69; Pedro Zelaya Etchegaray, 'La responsabilidad civil...', cit., at 130.
927. The doctrine considers that although the responsibility of the entrepreneur is based on a system of fault, in fact the jurisprudence continues to treat it as if it were vicarious: Barros, *Tratado*, I, cit., at 192–193. More amply Osvaldo Lagos Villareal, 'Hacía una objedivización jurisprudencial de la responsabilidad patronal? Criterio para evaluar sus consecuecias', *Estudios de Derecho Civil III* (Alejandro Guzán Brito ed.) (Santiago de Chile: Thomson Reuters, 2008, at 845 et seq.

business risk.[928] It has also been asserted that the supervising party should be responsible for the actions of the party who actually committed the damage on the grounds of *culpa in omittendo,*[929] for example in the case where instructions have been given. In favour of the injured party, the circumstances surrounding the occurrence of the damage are irrelevant, including whether it is possible to identify the party who caused the damage. In this sense, it has been said that the rule provides for 'anonymous fault or fault of the unknown employee'.[930]

270. Notwithstanding, there has been talk of a 'historical'[931] and 'practical'[932] inadequacy as a result of changes in the socio-economic-political contexts have changed. Indeed these norms were designed for essentially undeveloped or rural economies without extensive labour laws or to change production or labour mechanisms.

271. In accordance with the above analysis, even here the law does not envisage solidarity of the entrepreneur and the employee,[933] although it has been argued that the fault of the entrepreneur would tend to exclude that of the employee.[934] Still, it is possible to sue both the entrepreneur and employee for total compensation by *obligaciones in solidum.*[935]

272. The Civil Code also provides for contractual liability in the case of actions of the employee. In addition to the legal presumptions in tort matters, there is a system of fault which must be proven.

Thus, in all cases, Article 1679 CC states that the debtor's deed or fault includes the deed or fault of the persons for whom he is responsible; this extends, by tenor of the Article 1590.1 CC, to the liability of auxiliaries when damage is caused to goods to be delivered as a result of negligence.

It should also be noted that under Article 2135 CC, the agent is liable for the deeds of the third party who has delegated, without authorization from the principal, in which case he would be liable for the acts carried out by the principal as his

928. Pedro Zelaya Etchegaray, 'La responsabilidad civil...', cit., at 124 et seq. Considers that it should be associated with *responsabilidad por culpa in eligendo y vigilando* and not with that for risk: CS 25 Jan. 2006 (rol 5079/2003).
929. Pedro Zelaya Etchegaray, 'La responsabilidad civil...', cit., at 115.
930. ('culpa anónima o del dependiente desconocido'): Pedro Zelaya Etchegaray, 'La responsabilidad civil ...', cit., at 122–123; This type of 'anonymous fault' is different from another one that can manifest itself as a justification of the liability of the entrepreneur: la *culpa organizacional*: Barros, *Tratado*, I, cit., at 197–198.
931. Pedro Zelaya Etchegaray, 'La responsabilidad civil...', cit., at 113.
932. Pedro Zelaya Etchegaray, 'La responsabilidad civil...', cit., at 115. The author also identifies a third type of inadequacy: the technical one.
933. Pedro Zelaya Etchegaray, 'La responsabilidad civil...', cit., at 127–128.
934. Barros, *Tratado,* I, cit., at 200. In relation to the possible joint and several liability between the company and the bodies from which the damage proceeds according to Art. 2317 CC, except when the application of the. Art. 2325 CC: Alessandri, *Responsabilidad*, cit. at 116 and 118.
935. *See* para. 260.

own. If the principal has authorized the deeds, a *culpa in eligendo* of the agent in the choice of the delegates could be configured.[936]

273. In relation to the liability of the entrepreneur for accidents occurring in the workplace,[937] there is an obligation to take out insurance on workers regardless of their conduct.[938] This obligation is complementary to the normal system of liability,[939] as it is expressly possible to compensate moral damage,[940] including in cases of unjustified dismissal.[941] The doctrine has noted that the law tends to favour a social security system for worker protection over a system of liability.[942]

274. It should be noted that there are also other cases of liability for the deeds of others established by special laws, not contained in the Civil Code. For example, the shipowner is liable for damages caused by his employees while at sea.[943] The same applies in aviation cases, where liability is established (both for the air carrier and for the person who benefits financially from the operation) for the acts of employees while performing their functions.[944]

936. Barros, *Tratado,* II, cit., at 1095.
937. Art. 209–211 *Codigo del Trabajo. See* José Luis Diez Schwerter. 'La culpa del empresario por accidentes del trabajo: modernas tendencias jurisprudenciales', *La responsabilidad por accidentes del trabajo Cuadernos de Extensión Jurídica,* (Jorge Baraona González, Pedro Zelaya Etchegaray ed.) (Santiago de Chile: Universidad de los Andes, 2005) at 73–98.
938. The exclusion applies only in case of force majeure: cf. Arts 1 y 5 Ley 16.744/1968, cit.
939. Art. 69 Ley 16.744/1968, cit., *see* José Luis Diez Schwerter, 'La reparación de daños derivados de infortunios laborales en Chile: entre derecho común y legislación especial. Etapas de la elección de un modelo', *Estudios de Derecho Civil V – Jornadas Nacionales de Derecho Civil, Concepción 2009* (Departamento de Derecho Privado de la Facultad de Ciencias Jurídicas y Sociales de la Universidad de Concepción ed.) (Santiago de Chile: Thomson Reuters, 2009) at 705 et seq.
940. Art. 69 Ley 16.744/1968, cit. Ramon Domínguez Águila, 'Responsabilidad civil del empresario por daño moral', en, *Responsabilidad Civil del Empresario, Cuadernos de Extensión Jurídica,* (Federico McKay Alliende ed.) (Santiago de Chile: Universidad de los Andes, 1996) at 19–34.
941. Claudia Bahamondes Oyarzún, 'Daño moral por despido injustificado', *Cuaderno de Análisis Jurídico I: temas de responsabilidad civil,* (Carlos Pizarro Wilson ed, Santiago de Chile: Universidad Diego Portales, 1996) at 253–270; Eduardo Court Murasso, 'La indemnización del daño moral por despido injustificado', *Derecho de daños* (Santiago de Chile: Lexis Nexis, 2002), at 229 et seq. Cf. Arts 160 y 168 *Codigo del Trabajo.*
942. Corral, *Lecciones,* cit., at 250. El autor sistematiza ampliamente il sistema descritto vid. op. cit., 249 et seq. *See* Ramón Domínguez Águila, 'Responsabilidad civil y seguridad social', *La responsabilidad por accidentes del trabajo Cuadernos de Extensión Jurídica,* (Jorge Baraona González, Pedro Zelaya Etchegaray ed.) (Santiago de Chile: Universidad de los Andes, 2005), at 31 et seq.; AAvv, *Responsabilidad Civil del empresario por accidentes del trabajo y enfermedades profesionales. Tendencias actuales, Cuadernos de Extensión Jurídica,* (María Sara Rodríguez, Francisca Barrientos Camus ed.) (Santiago de Chile: Universidad de los Andes, 2011); Alfredo Sierra Herrero, Marcelo Nasser Olea, 'La responsabilidad del empleador por enfermedades profesionales de sus trabajadores. Enfoque jurisprudencial', *Revista Chilena de Derecho,* 2012/1, at 57 et seq.
943. Art. 885 Ccom.
944. Art. 171 Código aereonáutico. *See* para. 353.

§3. Independent Contractors

275. It has been held[945] that there is no employee relationship when a person provides independent services to several persons, just as there is no employee relationship when the principal relies on the specialization and technical qualifications of others, implying that the work is performed in full autonomy. The relationship between the contractor and the subcontractor (*contratista* and *subcontratista*) is more complex,[946] as the law tends to exclude the liability of the principal.[947] Nonetheless, the contractor may be held liable if it is established that the principal has in fact given orders or instructions,[948] or when there is an evident *culpa in eligendo* in having chosen an incompetent subcontractor. However, the latter case is governed by the general provision relating to contractual liability (Article 2314 CC) and not that of Article 2320 CC.[949] In this sense, it is possible to apply the provisions of Article 2314 or 2329 CC, provided that the prerequisites are met.[950]

276. Without prejudice to the foregoing, it could be argued that the problem is partly solved with the introduction[951] of the new Title VII to Book I of the Labour Code and Article 183-A et seq. In particular, the reform establishes the liability relationship between the principal and the contractor, which may be interpreted as extending to contractual or tort liability.

945. Barros, *Tratado*, I, cit., at 194. Interesting in this sense considering that there is no supervisory control in this case of the company that constantly benefits from another company for the transportation of its goods: CS 29 Jan. 2008 (rol 4318-2006): for a comment Fabián Elorriaga De Bonis. 'La responsabilidad del empresario por el hecho de su contratista independiente por daños a terceros', *Estudios de Derecho Civil V – Jornadas Nacionales de Derecho Civil, Concepción 2009* (Departamento de Derecho Privado de la Facultad de Ciencias Jurídicas y Sociales de la Universidad de Concepción ed.) (Santiago de Chile: Thomson Reuters, 2009), at 742 et seq. Also, with jurisprudential references, Fabián Elorriaga De Bonis. 'De nuevo sobre la irresponsabilidad del empresario por el hecho del contratista independiente. Crítica a tres recientes sentencias', *Estudios de Derecho Civil VII* (Fabián Elorriaga De Bonis ed.) (Santiago de Chile: Thomson Reuters, 2011), at 719 et seq.

946. De Bonis, 'La responsabilidad del empresario..., cit., at 727.

947. For a historical reconstruction, *see* Fabián Elorriaga De Bonis. 'La responsabilidad del empresario..., cit., at 731 et seq.

948. On these aspects, also with jurisprudential references, *see* Elorriaga De Bonis. La responsabilidad del empresario..., cit., at 736 et seq.

949. As defended by Elorriaga De Bonis. 'La responsabilidad del empresario...,' cit., at 740.

950. In this sense, a kind of liability can be envisaged in relation to organizational aspects of the organs or representatives of the company: *See* Barros, *Tratado,* I, cit., at 201. Thus, there is a liability of legal persons related to certain incorrect choices made by its organs, such as directors, chairmen or board of directors; Alessandri, *Responsabilidad*, cit., at 110. More specifically: Osvaldo Lagos Villareal. 'El daño imputable al accionista o al director infractores como límite a la responsabilidad civil en conflictos de sociedades cotizadas', *Estudios de Derecho Civil VI – Jornadas Nacionales de Derecho Civil, Olmué 2010* (Gonzalo Figueroa Yañez; Enrique Barros Bourie, Mauricio Tapia Rodríguez ed.) (Santiago de Chile: Abeledo Perrot, Legal Publishing, 2010) at 707 et seq. However, it is not considered that there are supervisory duties on the part of the Stock Exchange with respect to stock resale managers or brokers: CS 26 Mar. 2018 (rol 15,568/2017).

951. This is thanks to Ley 20123/2006 of 5 Oct. (DO 16 Oct. 2006). On the point, *see* Pamela Prado López. 'Crítica a la configuración de la responsabilidad principal y de la empresa usuaria en la Ley 20.213', *Estudios de Derecho Civil III* (Alejandro Guzán Brito ed.) (Santiago de Chile: Thomson Reuters, 2008), at 857 et seq.

277. As far as the liability of the contractor is concerned, it is understood that both the party that undertakes the work and those who actually perform it are liable for damages caused by the maintenance of public roads.[952]

§4. Liability of Legal Entities for Deeds of Their Organs (and for Act of Persons Entrusted with Power to Act Without Being an Organ)

278. Although the doctrine conceives the liability in review as relating to a private law[953] relationship, part of the case law has extended its scope to administrative cases provided the damage caused by the employee occurred during the performance of his functions.[954]

952. Art. 69 LT, in generale *see* José Luís Diéz Schwerter, 'Reparación y prevención de daños derivados de deficiencias viales en Chile: panorama normativo y juripsrudencial', *Estudios de derecho civil III*, (Alejandro Guzmán Brito ed.) (Santiago de Chile: Thomson Reuters, 2008) at 817 et seq., and *see* paras 305 et seq.

953. As Alessandri, *Responsabilidad,* cit., at 232. Another part of the doctrine considers that in the case of the relationship with the State, this holds indirect and substitute responsibility: Pedro Zelaya Etchegaray, 'La responsabilidad civil...', cit., at 111.

954. CS 14 Aug. 2007 (ROL 6338/2002). They admit the principle although they do not apply it in the concrete case: CS 13 Jan. 1997, *G.J.*, 199, at 89, CS 17 Jan. 1985, *RDJ*, t. 82, s. 4°, at 11. Contra eD in favour of liability in the private law relationship only: e.g., CS 28 Jan. 1998, *RDJ*, t. XCV, s. 1°), Corral, *Lecciones,* cit., at 233–234.

Chapter 2. Liability of Parents, Teachers and Instructors

279. The liability of the minor is related to the two status that that person can have: a son or a pupil.

So liability for the illicit acts of minors relates to the responsibility of parents for the acts of their children (Article 2320, paragraphs 2 and 5 and Article 2321 CC), and teachers or instructors for the acts of their pupils (Article 2320, paragraphs 4 and 5, CC).[955]

In the latter case, the law does not envisage the direct responsibility of the teacher, who is the party charged with the direct supervision of the child. Rather, the *jefes de colegios y escuelas* are liable, thus placing a greater legal responsibility on the head of the institution. This rule clearly protects the injured party by guaranteeing greater solvency and legal security.

280. As concerns parental responsibility, it is worth mentioning that some aspects of the law are somewhat outdated given that the discipline has remained unchanged since its approval.

Although the second paragraph of Article 2320 provides that 'the father, and in his absence the mother' shall be liable, this should be considered derogated[956] or otherwise reinterpreted considering the 2013 reform,[957] which introduced the principle of parental co-responsibility (Article 225, second and third, paragraph CC). Hence, there would be a joint responsibility between both parents despite the black letter text of the provision, meaning that the concept of *cuidado* should be reinterpreted. The position appears more open in the case of divorced parents since, in the absence of an agreement, the courts essentially grant custody to the mother.[958] Such arrangement potentially allows for a distinction between liability based on custody (Article 2320 CC) and parental responsibility ('*responsabilidad parental*'). In the

955. Ferrante, 'Ilícito del menor ¿quién paga? ' cit., at 251 et seq.; Carlos Pizarro Wilson. 'La responsabilidad civil de los padres por los daños ocasionados por sus hijos menores', *Estudios de derecho privado. Homenaje al profesor Ramón Domínguez Águila* (Manuel Barría Paredes, Bruno Caprile Biermann, et al. ed.) (Santiago de Chile: Thomson Reuters, 2017), at 769 et seq.; Lilian San Martín Neira. 'La responsabilidad civil de los padres por los daños causados por los hijos menores', *Mercurio Legal*, 20 Jun. & 6 Jul. 2016; Lucia Rizik Mulet 'Modelos de responsabilidad civil de los padres por los daños ocasionados por sus hijos menores de edad. Ideas para su estudio dogmático en Chile', *Estudios de Derecho Privado, II Jornadas Nacionales de Profesoras de Derecho Privado* (María Elisa Morales Ortiz, Pamela Mendoza Alonzo ed.) (Santiago de Chile: DER, 2020), at 377 et seq.

956. In this sense, Barros, *Tratado,* I, cit., at 181. The doctrine has always been critical of the provision and in favour of applying it indiscriminately to both parents: Ramos, *De la responsabilidad Civil*, cit., at 65.

957. Ley 20,680 /2013, of 16 Jun. (DO 23 jun. 2013).

958. A favour of a compartmentalized custody also in these cases in the absence of legal provision, *see* Rodrigo Barcia Lehmann, 'La evolución de la custodia unilateral conforme a los principios de interés superior del niño y corresponsabilidad de los padres', *Revista Ius et Praxis,* 2018/2, at 469 et seq.

event the case falls under Article 2320 CC, it is possible to assert the existence of joint responsibility of both parents on the grounds of a *culpa in educando*, which may be attributable to the State before the separation or divorce. The dichotomy between a divorced parent and parental autonomy (and *cuidado*) no longer exercisable by one of them, raises questions that the jurisprudence will have to resolve. It should also be recalled that in Chilean law, the exercise of parental authority is related more to patrimonial aspects than to those relating to choices about how to raise and discipline the child.[959] Thus, it is held that Chilean law unequivocally distinguishes between parental responsibility and parental authority, which is not related to child-rearing or supervisory duties, up to the management of the minor's estate.[960]

Certainly, the issue still leaves many questions unanswered. Indeed, the responsibility of the parent is not only linked to the concept of cohabitation with the child, as required by Article 2320 CC, but also in case of abandonment of the child, as has been defended by the doctrine.[961]

281. Parental liability for the illicit acts of a minor involves three rules of the Civil Code. Article 2319 CC (analysed above) applies when the minor lacks in discernment[962] at the time of the act or is under 7 years of age.

If the minor is capable of discernment, two complementary[963] provisions (i.e., Article 2320 and Article 2321 CC), shall apply, but they are treated somewhat differently. In fact, unlike the presumption of Article 2320 which would be *simplemente legal*,[964] in the case of Article 2321 CC, the presumption would be *especial*[965] since the provision does not allow proof to the contrary[966] and therefore tends to give rise to strict liability in cases where the damage occurs due to repeated bad behaviour, manners or habits.

Thus, if these rules are related to *culpa in educando* and *culpa in vigilando*, it could be argued that (in the case of parents) if Article 2320 refers to *culpa in vigilando*, Article 2321 refers to *culpa in educando*, with the nuance that the latter case implies a stricter form of liability. It is also important to note that if Article 2320 refers to cohabitation with the minor, Article 2321 does not. In practice, this leads

959. Ferrante, 'Ilícito del menor ¿quién paga? ' cit., at 253 et seq.; also at 260 et seq.
960. *See* Ramos, *De la responsabilidad Civil*, cit., at 66.
961. Barros, *Tratado*, I, cit., at 177. Jurisprudence in indicating the various application requirements, paraphrasing Art. 2320 CC, instead states that cohabitation should be proved: CS 28 Dec. 2012 (rol 479/2011).
962. Tapia, *De la Responsabilidad*, cit., at 175.
963. On the complementarity of Art. 2320 and 2321 CC : CS 27 Jan. 1998 (Legal Publishing CL/JUR/2411/1997).
964. Ramos, *De la responsabilidad Civil*, cit., at 63; Barros, *Tratado*, I, cit., at 186; Corral, *Lecciones,* cit., at 237.
965. Barros, *Tratado*, I, cit., at 179.
966. It is argued that it would not admit exoneration: Corral, *Lecciones,* cit., at 238. This would be demonstrated by the adverb 'always' when it is stated in the provision that the subjects in such cases are 'always liable': thus Ramos, *De la responsabilidad Civil*, cit., at 63.

to a strict liability,[967] also in consideration of the interplay between the norms, irrespective of whether criminal proceedings may be a material consequence.[968]

282. First, there is an exception to the general rule. While the principle of joint and several liability under Article 2317 CC is limited by the joint interpretation of the analysed above rules,[969] it appears no joint and several liability exists between the head of the school (‘*jefe de colegio*’) and the parents if the pupil that has caused damage. Despite such a responsibility may be established on the grounds of the *culpa in vigilando* of the school and the *culpa in educando* of the parents, it does not appear to have been considered neither by the jurisprudence nor the doctrine. Instead, the issue appears to be constructed as a transfer of the situation of *cuidado* from one subject to another, with the exclusion of parental responsibility, subject to the application of Article 2321 CC. Therefore, essentially, the question is resolved by framing the case as a self-excluding liability between them.

However, it must be noted that – in relation to a sexual abuse of a student–- the responsibility *de manera simplemente conjunta* has a responsibility in equal parts between the direct author and the school.[970]

283. As far as the responsibility of the head of the institution (*jefe de colegio*) is concerned, the rule is applicable every time the minor is a pupil – from the moment s/he enters the institution until the moment s/he leaves the school or other related activities – and includes cases such as field trips or excursions, as well as obligations to transport (e.g., with school buses) minors home,[971] but not cases of self-harm.[972]

284. As concerns liability for pupils, the problems are certainly complicated by the fact that the institution may be liable both in contract and in tort,[973] based, for example, on the argument that the school has an implicit contractual obligation

967. CS 12 Jun. 2018 (rol 314/2018); CS 5 Jul. 2018 (rol 31,974/2017).
968. CS 9 Mar. 2015 (rol 9.573/14); CS 22 Aug. 2012 (rol 2830/2012), *see* Carlos Pizarro Wilson. ‘El caso Aarón Vásquez y la responsabilidad por hecho ajeno. Supreme Court, Santiago, 22 de agosto de 2012, rol 2830/12; Corte de Apelaciones de Santiago 19 enero de 2012 rol 6410’, *Revista Chilena de Derecho privado*, 19/2012, Arts 205 et seq.
969. Expressly in accordance with Art. 2317 CC, it is also encountered in the case of liability for inanimate objects (*see* Arts 2323 and 2328 CC).
970. CS 27 Jun. 2018 (rol 38145-2017).
971. Expressly clarified by Ramos, *De la responsabilidad Civil*, cit., at 67.
972. Thus Ramos, *De la responsabilidad Civil*, cit., at 67.
973. *See* Renzo Munita Marambio. ‘Daños derivados del Bullying: consideraciones sobre la naturaleza de la responsabilidad de los establecimientos privados de enseñanza y su estándar de diligencia exigible’, *Estudios de Derecho Civil XIV* – (Marícruz Gómez de Latorre Vargas, Gabriel Hernández Paulsen, Fabiola Lathrop Gómez, Mauricio Tapia Rodríguez ed.) (Santiago de Chile: Thomson Reuters, 2019), at 1116 et seq. For some general reflections Lucía Rizik Mulet. ‘La responsabilidad de los jefes de colegios por los daños ocasionados por sus alumnos’, *Estudios de Derecho Civil XII* (Hernán Corral Talciani, Pablo Manterola Domínguez ed.) (Santiago de Chile: Thomson Reuters, 2017), at 696 et seq.

to guarantee the pupil's safety.[974] What is undisputable is that a whole series of other provisions on the educational roles of schools[975] come into play, including those associated with bullying.[976]

974. Thus, clearly Ramos, *De la responsabilidad Civil*, cit., at 67.
975. *See* Patricia López Díaz. 'Responsabilidad civil extracontractual por bullying o acoso escolar. Infracción del art. 16 b de la Ley general de educación. Presunción de culpabilidad por hecho propio. Responsabilidad del guardían. Obligación concurrente. Indemnización de daños. Daños moral', *Revista de Derecho Privado*, no. 1/2018, at 321 et seq.; also Munita Marambio. 'Daños derivados del Bullying...', cit., at 1113 et seq.; Rizik Mulet, 'La responsabilidad de los jefes … ', cit., at 687 et seq.
976. CS 30 Aug. 2018 (rol no 8088/2018), CS 22 Nov. 2016 (58852/2016), CS 23 Jul. 2015 (rol 22,632/ 2014), CS 22 Abr 2015 (rol 11,418/2015).

Chapter 3. Liability for Things and Animals

285. Together with liability for one's own actions and those of others, a third distinction[977] provides for the liability for property, which is governed by dedicated provisions of the Civil Code, as well as complimentary special laws that have been introduced over time.

This type of liability can be divided into a responsibility for animate and inanimate objects. In fact, although in 2009 the law for the protection of animals defines them as 'living and sentient beings that are part of nature' ('*seres vivientes y sensibles que forman parte de la naturaleza*'),[978] they remain for all practical purposes movable things (Articles 567 and 571 CC) or even immovable in certain circumstances (*see* last paragraph of Article 570 CC). At the same time, the applicable law also depends on whether the animal is domestic.

Legal persons are additionally considered subject to these rules,[979] and the liability of the guardian (*guardían*) refers to the supervision of both a person and a thing,[980] although, as will be discussed further, in some instances a system of presumptions provides for strict liability since there is no provision that establishes a rule or general principle of this type of responsibility.[981] In this sense, the cases provided are regarded as exhaustive.[982]

§1. Things

286. The rules on liability for inanimate objects identified in the Civil Code essentially refer to damage caused in connection with things that have fallen or been thrown from buildings (Article 2328 CC) or damage relating to buildings or the ruinous state of the property (Articles 2323 and 2324 CC). This aspect has already been discussed in the context of the liability of builders and architects,[983] but it should be noted that the second paragraph of Article 2323 CC provides for a proportionate liability – and not joint and several liability in accordance with Article 2317 CC – divided among the co-owners according to their share of ownership interest.

Following the literal wording of the provision, to consider the liability of the owner in accordance with Article 2323, it must be proved that he has acted negligently (i.e., that the repairs have not been performed in accordance with the standard of diligence expected by a 'good father': *buen padre de familia*), which may

977. This systematization is relative, given that within the scope of liability for things there are also hypotheses of liability for damage caused by another person. In fact, Art. 2326 provides for the liability relating to the 'dependiente encargado de la guarda o servicio del animal'.
978. Art. 2 Ley 20.380/2009, of 11 sept (DO 3 Oct. 2009).
979. Alessandri, *Responsabilidad*, cit., at 117.
980. Figueroa, *Curso IV*, cit., at 122.
981. Barros, *Tratado*, I, cit., at 220, Corral, *Lecciones*, cit., at 245.
982. Ramos, *De la responsabilidad Civil*, cit., at 71; Alessandri, *Responsabilidad*, cit., at 117.
983. *See* paras 187 et seq.

be deduced from the same facts that caused the damage and, thus, lead to a reinterpretation of the literal nature of the rule.[984]

287. Article 2328 CC refers to two types of damage: that caused by the thing 'thrown' ('*que se arroja*') or that 'falls' ('*cae*') from the building. Again, also in this case, there is an exception to the joint and several liability sanctioned by Article 2317 CC, albeit the exception is only potential. The literal wording of Article 2328 CC states that 'the compensation shall be divided between all the parties, unless it is proved that the fact is due exclusively to the fault or bad intention of one person',[985] in which case that person alone will be liable. In this sense the liberating proof of some will be achieved by identifying the true responsible person(s).[986]

288. As regards the nature of this liability, there are two opposing positions. One argues there is a presumption of fault,[987] while the opposing argument[988] submits this provision establishes strict liability, an interpretation which is supported by a historical reconstruction of the norm[989] and the association with a presumption of causality.[990]

289. Despite the rule referring to the liability of the persons living in the part of the building that is enclosed, a broad interpretation is preferred to include the liability of the persons who could have used the property at the time of the damage.[991]

290. Article 2328 CC is inapplicable when the item is a part of the same building, as such cases fall under Article 2323 CC[992] or Article 2424 CC, depending on the circumstances.[993]

---

984. Alessandri, *Responsabilidad,* cit., at 283.
985. The 'bad intention' must be considered as malice: Tapia, *De la Responsabilidad*, cit., at 165.
986. Rodrigo Barría Díaz. 'La responsabilidad objetiva del artículo 2328 del código civil', *Estudios de Derecho Civil VI – Jornadas Nacionales de Derecho Civil, Olmué 2010* (Gonzalo Figueroa Yañez; Enrique Barros Bourie, Mauricio Tapia Rodríguez ed.) (Santiago de Chile: Abeledo Perrot, Legal Publishing, 2010) at 521 and 528
987. E.g., Alessandri, *Responsabilidad*, cit., at 117; Ruz, *Explicaciones*, cit., at 498; Corral, *Lecciones,* cit., at 248.
988. Barría, 'La responsabilidad objetiva...', cit. at 521 et seq.; Jorge Larrocau Torres, *Culpa y dolo en la responsabilidad extracontractual. Análisis jurisprudencial* (Santiago de Chile: Lexis Nexis, 2007), at 182; en parte también Barros, *Tratado*, I, cit., at 220 & 222.
989. Barría, 'La responsabilidad objetiva...', cit. at 522.528. More amply Rodrigo Barria Díaz, 'Actio de effusis vel deiectis y actio de positis vel suspensis : antecedentes, contenido y proyecciones en la moderna responsabilidad extracontractual', *reviata de estudios históricos-jurídicos,* 2018/40, at 563 et seq.
990. Barría, 'La responsabilidad objetiva...', cit. at 539.
991. Barría, 'La responsabilidad objetiva...', cit. at 533 et seq.
992. Ramos, *De la responsabilidad* cit., at 74.
993. Alessandri, *Responsabilidad*, cit., at 321.

291. The second paragraph of Article 2328 CC also provides for a collective, preventative action aimed at avoiding any potential damage by allowing any interested party to request that the owner or tenant remove a potentially dangerous object.[994]

§2. Animals

292. Various scenarios come into play when it comes to liability for damage caused by animals, starting with Article 2326 CC on the animal itself. Since 2017, the relevant provisions must be reinterpreted to complement each other, also with regard to the recent law (passed in 2018) on the responsible keeping of pets[995] (i.e., *Ley Cholito*).[996]

293. Prior to the introduction of the *Ley Cholito*, the code provided for two types of liability: a strict liability[997] in the case of fierce animals (*animal fiero*) under Article 2327 CC,[998] and a presumption of fault[999] in relation to other animals under Article 2326 CC. In addition to these cases, there is another case of damage caused by wild animals, which falls outside the scope of the aforementioned rules.

294. Both in the case of Article 2326 CC as well as Article 2327 CC, the liability refers to the person who held the animal and could therefore control or supervise it. The peculiarity of Article 2326 CC is therefore to expressly sanction not only the liability of the owner for his own actions, but also in relation to the person charged with the custody or use at the time of the damage. That person (literally called *dependiente encargado*) is not always liable as, pursuant to the second paragraph of Article 2326 CC, he may be released from liability if the owner has not disclosed

994. E.g., Ramos, *De la responsabilidad* cit., at 74–75; Barros, *Tratado*, I, cit., at 220.

995. Literally it referes to 'Mascotas' and 'animales de compañias': Ley 21.020/2017, of 19 Jul. (DO 2 Aug. 2017): Ley de Tenencia Responsable de Mascotas y Animales de Compañía. The name comes from the name of the brutally beaten dog that was reason for drafting the law.

996. Decreto 1007/2018, of 31 May (Ministerio del Interior y seguridad pública, DO 17 Aug. 2018).

997. Figueroa, *Curso IV*, cit. at 107; Barros, *Tratado*, I, cit., at 220. Nor would Ramos, *De la responsabilidad Civil*, cit. at 72.

998. On the other hand, a minority doctrine, based on Art. 491.2 of the Penal Code, considers that Art. 2314 CC should be applied in the case of the ferocious animal: Javier Barrientos Grandon. *Código Civil, su jurisprudencia e historia. Edición crítica, concordada, comentaday anotada* (Santiago de Chile: Thomson Reuters-La Ley, 2016), tomo II, at 1086.

For a historical reconstruction of the provision, and also in relation to the analogous Colombian Art. 2356 cc: Luis Carlos Sánchez Hernández. 'Una regla de responsabilidad objetiva fundamentada en la creación de peligros extraordinarios: la responsabilidad por effusio vel deiectio y por el hecho del animal fiero del código civil de Andrés Bello', *La vigencia del Código Civil de Andrés Bello* (Felipe Navia Arroyo y Carlos Chinchilla Iambett ed.) (Bogotá: Universidad Externado, 2019), at 431–464, especially at 449 et seq.

999. Barros, *Tratado*, I, cit., at 221.

a particular vice or predisposition of the animal.[1000] Similarly, the owner of the animal may not be liable when the animal is held by a third party, who holds and benefits from the animal.[1001] Such solution is deduced from the second paragraph of Article 2326 CC, which equates with the owner 'any person who makes use of an animal belonging to a third party'. Therefore, the liability of the person who uses the animal and the owner of the same are mutually limiting, although part of the doctrine that considers them jointly[1002] when both parties receive a direct benefit from the use of the animal.[1003]

295. Under Article 2327 CC, a fierce animal (*animal fiero*) is identified as one that 'does not generate any utility in the surveillance or service for the land'. Broadening the scope of this provision, it is not considered applicable to those animals that are ferocious and generate economic utility (e.g., animals used in circuses or zoological parks), in which the doctrine holds the presumption pursuant to Article 2326 CC to be applicable.[1004] It should be noted that the case law has established the responsibility of the non-owner holder/keeper of an elephant in a case involving the death of a minor on circus grounds. More specifically, the court, generally considering Article 2327 CC to be a specific application of Article 2326 CC, applied Article 2326 CC to condemn the non-owner elephant holder/keeper for moral damages related to the death.[1005]

296. Given the above, it can be deduced that a ferocious animal is not the same as a 'wild animal' (*animal bravio*), as the latter is identified by Article 608 CC as an animal that '[lives] naturally free and independent from man', whereas a ferocious animal can be domesticated without prejudice of being able to return to the wild if it is no longer under the control of its keeper. Indeed, the same provision also defines and differentiates domesticated and tamed animals; if domesticated animals are those that 'belong to species that normally live under the dependence of man', tamed animals are those that without being wild animals have become accustomed to domesticity and recognize the commands (literally *el imperio*) of man.

For this reason, it is necessary to analyse the extent of any liability for damage caused by the wild animal and, on the other, how the foregoing provisions can be reconciled with the introduction of the *Ley Cholito*.

297. The *Ley Cholito* expressly includes among its objectives[1006] the aim to regulate the liability for damages caused by *mascotas* (pets) and companion animals. Given that Article 608 CC (in identifying domestic animals) expressly lists

1000. This is how the particularly rebellious horse is referred to: Alessandri, *Responsabilidad*, cit. at 291.
1001. Alessandri, *Responsabilidad*, cit., at 291–292.
1002. Barros, *Tratado*, I, cit., at 221.
1003. Cf. Alessandri, *Responsabilidad*, cit., at 292.
1004. Corral, *Lecciones*, cit., at 246.
1005. The animal was leaning against a wall which caused the damage from its fall: CS 15 Apr. 2014 (rol 555/2014).
1006. Art. 1 number 4) *Ley Cholito*.

chickens and sheep as examples, one must wonder whether the new law complements or partially derogates from the discipline pursuant to Article 2326 CC. Such cause for inquiry derives from the fact that, at the time of the enactment of the Civil Code, the phenomena between man and pets were carried out on different premises.

The problem arises because the definition of *mascotas* (pets) and companion animals is part of the more general category of pets, defined as 'domestic animals of any species kept by people for reasons of companionship or security'.[1007] Thus, the reference to the holding for security reasons could also be partially associated with Article 2327 CC in the event of possession or ownership of particularly dangerous animals. In fact, the special legislation also refers to potentially dangerous[1008] dog species.

298. The matter is particularly relevant since the *Ley Cholito* seems to introduce a different liability scheme.

Specifically, it introduces a system of strict liability for the owners[1009] of the animals and establishes that the person who owned the animal at the time of the damage acts as guarantor (*fiador*).[1010]

The interpretive confusion also stems from the fact that the law states that 'whoever has custody of an animal shall be liable as guarantor for damages caused by it, in the terms established by Title XXXV of the Fourth Book of the Civil Code';[1011] that is, with reference to Article 2326 and 2327 CC. However, it is evident that this system differs from that of Article 2326 CC, which establishes the (potential) liability of the person who has custody of the animal (and not based on the activity of guarantor), while Article 2327 CC establishes the strict liability for any holder.

Ultimately, it should be accepted that the introduction of the *Ley Cholito* is a special application for certain categories of domestic animals. Therefore, considering that it the *Ley* expressly refers to canine and feline species, it should apply to these species of animals and should not be held to derogate from the disciplines of Articles 2326 and 2327, which remain applicable to other types of animals. Given the special law currently considers only the canine species as potentially dangerous animals, for other domestic animals and dangerous pets (such as snakes) the provisions of the Civil Code would apply, and in particular Article 2327 CC.

1007. Art. 2 number 1) *Ley Cholito*.

1008. Art. 6, 21, 25 *Ley Cholito*.; Art. 13 et seq. Regulations of the *Ley Cholito*.

1009. This can be deduced not only from Art. 10 *Ley Cholito* for which it is considered that: 'the holder or the owner will be responsible for pets or animals'. In support of this, there is also Art. 13, which states that the civil liability for damages caused by the action of the animal will always be met, except for the corresponding criminal liability, in which case Art. 144 of the Penal Code will apply.

1010. On the difference between being a guarantor (*fiador*) and subsidiary liability, *see* Andrés Kuncar Oneto. 'La responsabilidad subsidiaria', *Estudios de Derecho Civil XIII* (Claudia Bahamondes Oyarzún, Leonor Etcheberry Court, Carlos Pizarro Wilson ed.) (Santiago de Chile: Thomson Reuters, 2018), at 551 et seq.

1011. Art. 10 *Ley Cholito*.

299. The *Ley Cholito* also refers to certain types of canines that are characteristic of Chile, or the so-called *perro callejero*[1012] (i.e., the dog that roams freely in the public space all or most of the day, without a direct control) and the *perro comunitario*[1013] (i.e., the dog that does not have a specific owner and is fed by and receives basic care from the community). If the civil liability of the owner of the *perro callejero* is evident, the same is not true in the case of the *perro comunitario.* Indeed, this second phenomenon may fall under different liability schemes in the absence of a dedicated discipline. Although a general rule establishes the civil liability of all responsible parties,[1014] application of this rule to the case of the *perro comunitario* would mean that the entire town must be considered liable. This is due to the fact that the town feeds it, despite not ever possessing the animal or consider itself the owner. Accordingly, and also by virtue of an obligation to provide safety and security, it is the municipality that should assume responsibility. The solution is still open,[1015] and some scholars argue that liability must be established on a case-by-case basis. For example, the liable party may be the person who specifically feeds the animal, the general group of people who feed it, or the municipality if there is a specific campaign to protect these animals.[1016]

300. As *Ley Cholito* refers to both physical and material damages,[1017] it is noteworthy that a party can be held civilly liable for damage to the environment, which is expressly sanctioned by the legal provision that states that the owner of the animal 'must ensure compliance with the obligations provided for by law and regulations, in order to prevent the pet from causing damage to the environment'.[1018]

301. The liability for wild animals[1019] (*animal bravío*) remains to be discussed. Since wild animals do not fall into any of the above categories, the doctrine[1020] that equates wild and ferocious animals (*animal bravío* and *animal fiero*) should not be accepted. Namely, although Article 608 CC provides a ferocious animal can also be wild, the contrary is not necessarily true. Consider, for instance, fauna animals or wild boar, ibex or deer. Hence the necessity to identify the party responsible for any damage caused by these animals, for example when leaving a field or hunting preserve, or when entering a public or private road.

1012. This is the one 'whose owner does not make a responsible detention and is kept in the public space during the day or large part of it without direct control'_Art. 2 number 3) *Ley Cholito.*
1013. Art. 2 number 4) *Ley Cholito*; Art. 1) letter u) reglamento *Ley Cholito.*
1014. Art. 13 *Ley Cholito.*
1015. On the application of hunting regulations with respect to stray dogs: Alfredo Ferrante. 'Responsabilidad por daños provocados en accidente vial con un animal bravío', *Revista chilena de Derecho Privado,* 2015/24, at 156.
1016. *See* Emilio José Bécar Labraña. 'El sujeto responsable del daño causados por los 'perros comunitarios': algunas observaciones a partir de la Ley 21.020', *Estudios de Derecho Civil XIV* – (Marícruz Gómez de Latorre Vargas, Gabriel Hernández Paulsen, Fabiola Lathrop Gómez, Mauricio Tapia Rodríguez ed.) (Santiago de Chile: Thomson Reuters, 2019), at 1016–1018.
1017. Art. 1 number 4) *Ley Cholito.*
1018. Art. 4) Reglamento *Ley Cholito.*
1019. *See* Ferrante, 'Responsabilidad por daños provocados...', cit., at 143 et seq.
1020. Corral, *Lecciones,* cit., at 259.

Liability for damage caused by a wild animal could fall under the general rule of Article 2314 CC in cases where some sort of ownership relationship can be identified (e.g., animals found on private land). However, the solution is more complex when the animal is hunted.

In these cases, hunting law[1021] establishes that if the damage occurs on the hunting ground, all the agents involved are jointly liable, including: the owner of the equipment, the owner of the land and the hunters. In this case, however, the owner of the equipment who authorized the hunt can be exempted if he proves that he could not have prevented the event.[1022]

If the animal escapes from the hunting grounds and causes damage, the owner of the hunting grounds shall be liable if it is proved that the fences were not adequate to prevent the animal from escaping.[1023] This provision is broad in scope and does not only apply to hunting grounds, but also to animals escaped from breeding centres.[1024]

302. It should be noted that the owner of a hunting reserve is also subject to specific safety obligations required under the hunting law.[1025] In this context, the owner of the hunting reserve and the person obtaining economic benefits from it are similar.[1026]

303. The law of the road[1027] is generally applicable when a wild animal causes an accident on a public road. The rules according to which animals cannot be left loose to hinder transit[1028] appear particularly relevant, in addition to the obligation to maintain fences to prevent animals from entering a public road.[1029] These provisions are complementary to the aforementioned hunting laws, or may be applied when the former is deemed inapplicable.[1030]

304. In the event of an accident involving a vehicle, it is necessary to examine the relationship between the potential liability of the injured party who was driving the vehicle[1031] and that of the parties responsible for the proper maintenance of the

1021. Ley 19.473/1996, of 4 Sep. (DO 27 Sep. 1996).
1022. Art. 11 Ley 19.473/1996, cit.
1023. First paragraph of Art. 21 Ley 19.473/1996, cit.; Ferrante, 'Responsabilidad por daños provocados...', cit., at 156 et seq.
1024. Second paragraph of Art. 21 Ley 19.473/1996, cit.; Art. 59 of Decree No 5/1998 of 7 December (DO 9 Jan1999).
1025. Art. 37 Hunting Law Regulation: Decree No. 5/1998, cit.
1026. Ferrante, 'Responsabilidad por daños provocados...', cit., at 156–157; cf. Art. 21 Ley 19.473/1996, cit.; Art. 43 Decreto N° 5/1998, cit. y Art. 609 of the CC.
1027. *See* paras 305 et seq.
1028. Art. 160 n. 11 LT.
1029. Art. 200 n. 19 LT.
1030. Ferrante, 'Responsabilidad por daños provocados...', cit., at 157–158.
1031. Art. 167, 170 LT.

road surface[1032] or the subcontractors,[1033] bearing in mind that liability[1034] may also arise for improper maintenance of the road surface or paths,[1035] an aspect which complicates the system also from a procedural perspective.[1036]

1032. Art. 169.4 DFL Nº 1/2009; Art. 106 DFL Nº 1/2009.
1033. CS 17 Aug. 2011 (rol 6.370/2009).
1034. These forms of liability would configure a hypothesis of *responsabilidad concurrente* or *in solidum* for which those responsible would not be jointly and severally liable but would nevertheless have to answer for the total extent of damage: Andrés Kuncar Onero, 'Responsabilidad solidaria versus responsabilidad concurrente', cit. p. 783.
1035. Art. 18 DFL 859/1997 of 12 Sep. (DO 25 Sep. 1998), Art. 42 Ley 18.575, cit.; thus condemning for moral damage the concessionaire and the State for lack of maintenance that caused the collision between a vehicle, causing the death of the driver, and a horse: CS 9 May 2017 (rol 38297/2016).
1036. *See* Ferrante, 'Responsabilidad por daños provocados...', cit., at 159–160.

Part III. Strict Liability

Chapter 1. Road and Traffic Accidents

305. Accidents caused by cars are characterized by the strict liability[1037] of the owner or holder[1038] of the car, and the driver. Liability in these cases is expressly established as joint and several[1039] by the *Ley de Transito,*[1040] despite the owner may be released by demonstrating that the vehicle was taken from him against his will,[1041] such as in the case of theft. The injured party enjoys broad protection due to the possibility of recourse against any liable third parties,[1042] such as the State or the municipality for failure to properly maintain the road surface,[1043] founded on lack of service.[1044] Since 1997,[1045] the person who has entered into a duly transcribed leasing contract is also liable.

306. It is expressly stated that the violation of an administrative rule, such as an infraction of the highway code, does not necessarily affect liability as such violation does not necessarily imply the presence of a causal link between the infraction and the damage.[1046] There are certain presumptions in this sense.[1047]

1037. This is despite the fact that the law associates liability with the culpable conduct of the tenant. In fact, the law effectively transforms it into strict liability, Barros, *Tratado*, II, cit., at 776 In this sense, Corral affirms that it is a system of strict liability of the owner or holder that is based on the fault-based liability of the tenant; Corral, *Lecciones,* cit., at 260.
1038. This is to be understood in a broad sense, regardless of whether it possesses the title to the holding: *see* CS 15 May 2018 (rol 8388/2017).
1039. In relation to Art. 2314, 2317 and 1511 CC, the relationship between *obligaciones in solidum* and the joint and several liability of the principal, contractor and subcontractor for the death of a worker in a road accident during the unloading of a beverage truck: CS 26 Jan. 2017 (rol no 95.110/2016) commented on by *see* Pamela Mendoza Alonzo. 'Obligaciones concurrentes o in solidum (Supreme Court)', *Revista de Derecho, Valdivia*, 2018/31, at 387 et seq.
1040. Art. 165 and 169.2 LT.
1041. Art. 169.2 LT.
1042. This is expressly stated in Art. 169.2 LT. For example, it provides for the joint and several liability of anyone who improperly grants a driving licence (Art. 169.3 LT) or who makes false statements when issuing a vehicle inspection (Art. 169.4 LT).
1043. Art. 169.3 LT.
1044. *See* paras 278 also 303–304.
1045. By virtue of the last sentence of Art. 169 LT, as amended by Law 19.495/1997 of 7 March (DO 8 Mar. 1997). *See* CS 24 Aug. 2010 (rol 1839/2010).
1046. Art. 166 LT.
1047. Art. 167, Art. 168.2 and 168.3 LT. It is debated whether these are presumptions of liability or of causality: *see* CS 21 Aug. 2012 (rol 1004/2010). More extensively, *see* Barros, *Tratado*, II, cit., at 777–783.

307. In the event of an accident between two or more vehicles, the insurance companies are jointly and severally liable for any injuries to pedestrians or when it is impossible to establish which vehicle the injured party was travelling in.[1048] The criterion of *culpa basal*[1049] (which is more general in relation to the fault of the driver/injured party) is used to assess the extent to which two imprudent deeds contribute to the cause of the damage, evaluating the relationship between fault and causation.[1050] In this sense, the norm aims to establish whether conduct or administrative offences were relevant in creating the damage, so as to establish whether Article 2330 CC applies.[1051] Therefore, the norm is instrumental in establishing whether the injured party is entitled to less compensation on account of its own reckless behaviour and/or exposing itself to damage,[1052] and also to exclude liability by establishing a causal relationship between the damage and the third party's behaviour.[1053]

308. Under Chilean law, a pedestrian is presumed to be liable if he has been hit when jaywalking or committing other offences. Likewise, the driver of a vehicle that overtakes another vehicle which is stationary is presumed liable, just as a drunkard or person driving under the influence of drugs is liable.[1054]

309. In Chile, motor vehicle insurance is required, albeit with certain peculiarities. Direct action by the injured third party against the insurance company is provided for in the case of motor vehicle insurance.[1055] Compensation from the insurance[1056] company is also facilitated by the fact that the law expressly considers it sufficient to pay 'only the demonstration of the accident and the consequences of the death or injury that it caused to the victim'.[1057]

However, because compulsory insurance is required to compensate only for bodily injury and not for material damage, some questions arise.

1048. Art. 12 Ley 18.490, cit.
1049. The doctrine, based also on CS 22 Apr. 1998 (*Fallos del Mes*, no. 472, at 342 et seq.) associates the notion of '*causa basal*' with '*causalidad jurídica*' or normative causation, i.e., what, from the criminal law perspective, is considered '*imputabilidad objetiva*': Lilian San Martín Neira, 'La relación entre culpa y causalidad. El ejemplo de la causa basal del accidente de tránsito'. *Presente y futuro de la responsabilidad civil* (Rodrigo Barría Díaz & Alfredo Ferrante & Lilian San Martín Neira ed.) (Santiago de Chile: Thomson Reuters, 2017), at 360.
1050. *See* generally San Martín Neira, 'La relación entre culpa y causalidad....', cit., at 359 et seq.
1051. *See* paras 376 et seq.
1052. For more details: Barros, *Tratado,* II, cit., at 784 et seq.
1053. Thus, the liability of the truck driver who injures a motorcyclist is excluded on the finding that the accident was due to poor maintenance of cables unusually present CS 18 may 2014 (rol 1880/2014), Cf. San Martín Neira, 'La relación entre culpa y causalidad...., cit., at 362.
1054. Art. 171 LT.
1055. This is expressly provided for by Art. 10 Ley 18.490 of 2 Jan. (DO 4 Jan. 1986). On the possibility of action for recovery on the insured in certain cases: *see* Art. 11, *a fortiori* in case of fraud (Art. 16 Ley19.490, cit.).
1056. The action is time-barred in one year, which term is interrupted upon the presentation of the documentation of the accident Art. 13 Ley 18.490, cit.
1057. Art. 6 Ley 18.490, cit.

310. Initially, compulsory insurance coverage was foreseen for physical and material damage. However, with the 1991 reform, the coverage of material damage was eliminated from the compulsory insurance scheme, now called 'SOAP'(*seguro obligatorio de accidentes personales*).[1058] This removal has been considered a real 'mutilation',[1059] although some believe it is justified in order to lower the cost of insurance policies.[1060]

Of course, insured parties may enter into policies with greater or complementary[1061] coverage, also because the vehicle may be subject to a non-possessory lien (*prenda sin desplazamiento*)[1062] in the event of lack of coverage for material damage.[1063]

Therefore, if a non-compulsory policy is taken out, one might wonder whether direct action is possible in such cases. Such query could be based on the inapplicability of Article 10 of Law 18.490, which only provides (indirectly) for physical damage, in accordance with the SOAP.

311. To these effects, although the 2013 reform introduces the discipline of the liability policy in the Commercial Code,[1064] and direct recourse is not expressly provided for (albeit it was included in the draft law of the reform[1065]), the question has been raised whether this is possible.

The possible availability of a direct action has thus been advocated on the basis of the analogical application of other direct actions, such as that provided for by the Commercial Code in the case of maritime liability (Article 1201 CCom) or on the reinterpretation of the 2013 reform (arg. Article 513 letra c, Article 570 CCom).[1066]

1058. This is regulated by Ley 18.490, cit.

1059. Corral, *Lecciones*, cit., at 445.

1060. Eduardo Juan Contardo González, *El seguro automotriz obligatorio* (Santiago de Chile: Metropolitana, 1996), at 88 et seq.; of the same opinion also Barros, *Tratado*, II, cit., at 775.

1061. Permitted by Art. 14 Ley18.490, cit.

1062. In accordance with Art. 1 Ley18.490/1986, cit. Critical of the application of this norm is Corral, *Lecciones,* cit., at 445.

1063. This is done by means of Ley 19.050/1991 of 13 Mar. (DO 22 Mar. 1991), which derogates from Title IV of the Law on Compulsory Insurance (L 18.490/1986, cit.), and in particular from the original Art. 35.

1064. On an overview of the tort policy Corral, *Lecciones,* cit., at 423 et seq.; Barros, *Tratado*, II, cit., at 1175 et seq.

1065. As the doctrine of direct action initially envisaged for both compulsory and voluntary insurance foreseen in the reform project (in what should have been the new Art. 572 Commercial Code) has carefully observed: Osvaldo Lagos Villareal. '¿Se reconoce acción directa de la víctima contra el asegurador en la legislación chilena?', *Estudios de Derecho Civil X*, (Álvaro Vidal Olivares, Claudia Mejías Alondo, Gonzalo Severín Fuster ed, Santiago de Chile: Thomson Reuters, 2015), at 988.

1066. For this position, and more broadly, *see* Hernán Corral Talciani. 'Acción directa de la víctima contra el aasegurador de responsabilidad civil', *Estudios de Derecho Civil IX,* (Susan Turner Saelzar, Juan Andrés Varas Braun ed.) (Santiago de Chile: Thomson Reuters, 2014), at 565 et seq.; Hernán Corral Talciani, 'La interposición de la acción directa implícita del tercero perjudicado en contra del asegurador de responsabilidad civil en el nuevo régimen de seguro chileno', *Revista Chilena de Derecho*, 2/2015, at 397 et seq., especially at 403 et seq.

Opponents of this position critically observe[1067] that the introduction of the current Article 570 CCom would partially overcome many of the issues underlying the position in favour of allowing direct action.

Essentially, it is noted that in accordance with Article 570 CCom, as things stand at present, the third party can claim payment from the insurance company whenever there is a judgment or a judicial or extrajudicial settlement. The only drawback is that it is neither possible to sue the insurance company and the insured jointly, nor is it possible to sue the insurance company directly. Consequently, once the responsibility of the insured has been demonstrated, the latter must pay the corresponding compensation.[1068]

In the final analysis, dichotomies could therefore be envisaged in relation to direct action depending on the damage caused, if such were accepted as inadmissible in the case of compulsory insurance.[1069]

312. The problems in the case of cross-border accidents involving domestic vehicles are different.[1070]

1067. *See* Osvaldo Lagos Villareal. '¿Se reconoce acción directa de la víctima contra el asegurador en la legislación chilena?', *Estudios de Derecho Civil X*, (Álvaro Vidal Olivares, Claudia Mejías Alondo, Gonzalo Severín Fuster ed.) (Santiago de Chile: Thomson Reuters, 2015), at 987 et seq.

1068. These are the interesting observations of Lagos Villareal. '¿Se reconoce acción directa..., cit. at 996–997.

1069. Already denied direct action prior to the 2013 reform of the Commercial Code: Juan Achurra Larraín, *Derechos de Seguros. Escritos de Juan Achurra* (Santiago de Chile: Asociación de Aseguradores de Chile, Univrsidad de los Andes, Centro de Derecho de Seguro, 2005), t. III, at 78.

1070. Alfredo Ferrante, 'La responsabilidad por accidente transfronterizo ocasionado por vehículos motorizados, *Revista chilena de Derecho Internacional Privado*, 3/2017, p. 45 et seq.

Chapter 2. Product Liability

§1. Sale and Consumer Act

313. Unlike in other jurisdictions, a characteristic of Chilean law is that liability for dangerous products does not fall necessarily under strict liability, in certain case it can be subjective.

314. From a contractual perspective, the liability arising from a lack of conformity of goods is governed by the Vienna Convention (CISG) when it comes to the international sale of movable goods, while the rules of the Civil Code relating to the sale of goods, which are based on a subjective non-performance, are generally applicable.[1071] In B2C relations, a *garantia legal*[1072] is applied in relation to lack of conformity where performance can be considered either objective or subjective, depending on the position.[1073] This protection is regulated by the Consumer Protection Act (LPC) and is complemented by a general rule regarding compensation for damages that also applies in tort.[1074]

1071. For all references, *see* Sergio Gatica Pacheco, *Aspectos de la indemnización de perjuicios por incumplimiento de contrato* (Santigo de Chile: Editorial Jurídica de Chile, 1959), Juan Ignacio Contardo, *Indemnización y resolución por incumplimiento* (Santiago de Chile: Legal Publishing, 2015), Patricia Verónica López Díaz, *a autonomía de la indemnización de daños por incumplimiento de un contrato bilateral en el Código Civil chileno* (Santiago de Chile: Thomson Reuters, 2015), Alvaro Vidal Olivares, Iñigo De La Maza Gazmuri, *Cuestiones de Derecho Contractual. Formación, Incumplimiento y remedios* (Santiago de Chile: Thomson Reuters, 2018), más espefiicaamente Alfredo Ferrante, 'Consideraciones críticas sobre la reducción del precio', *Estudios de derecho de contratos en homenaje a Antonio Manuel Morales Moreno* (Álvaro Vidal Olivares, dir, Gonzalo Severin Fuster, ed., Thomson Reuters, Santiago de Chile, 2018), at 877–896.

1072. Alfredo Ferrante, 'La jerarquía de remedios en la compraventa de consumo a partir de sus límites civiles y tributarios', *Revista chilena de Derecho*, 3/2019, at 893–921; Alfredo Ferrante, 'Consideraciones críticas sobre la resolución del contrato de venta de consumo frente a la disconformidad material en el derecho chileno', *Estudios de Derecho Privado en homenaje al profesor Daniel Peñailillo Arévalo* (Santiago de Chile: Thomson Reuters, 2019), at 759–778; Alfredo Ferrante, 'Reducción del precio y garantía legal', *Estudios de Derecho Civil XIV, Ponencias Presentadas en las XVI Jornadas Nacionales de Derecho Civil, Coquimbo 2018*, Marícruz Gómez de Latorre Vargas, Gabriel Hernández Paulsen, Fabiola Lathrop Gómez, Mauricio Tapia Rodríguez ed.) (Santiago de Chile: Thomson Reuters, 2019), at 887–900; Alfredo Ferrante, 'La devolución de la cantidad pagada en la jurisprudencia: desencaje con la garantía legal', *Revista de Derecho* (Universidad Austral), 1/2020, at 141–158; Alfredo Ferrante, 'Servicio técnico y reparación del bien: la alteración de la tutela efectiva del consumidor en caso de disconformidad material. Una visión jurisprudencial', *Revista Ius et Praxis*, no. 3/2020, pp. 65–80; Cristián Aedo Barrena, (Santiago de Chile: Tirant Lo Blanch, 2021), Francisca Barrientos Camus. *Garantía Legal* (Santiago de Chile: Thomson Reuters, 2016).

1073. *See* Alfredo Ferrante, 'Una revisión de los remedios del consumidor chileno en la compraventa con disconformidad a partir de la diferencia entre obligación y garantía', *Revista de derecho privado*, 35/2018, at 165 et seq.

1074. Art. 3 let. e) LPC, in relation to compensation e.g., *see also* Art. 24 let. c), 25 A, 40, 49. 50, Art. 51, LPC. Cf. Gatica Rodríguez, 'Atividades peligrosas y tecnología ... ' cit., at 957 et seq.

315. With regard to compensation for dangerous products,[1075] there is no general regime in the Civil Code and the problem concerning B2C is only partially resolved by the LPC and special legislation for certain types of goods.

The clear lack of concern to regulate this phenomenon is illustrated by the fact that the laws are sometimes completely non-technical. A prominent example is that what is known as the *Responsabilidad Extendida del Productor* (REP) – introduced in 2016,[1076] together with its 2017 regulation[1077] – does not refer to the civil liability of the producer in case the use of such goods causes damage, but to a liability that essentially fits into the environmental one since it relates to the damages caused by the management of hazardous waste.[1078]

316. Prior to modern consumer law (LPC, introduced in 1997), liability for infringement (with administrative or penal sanctions) for the misrepresentation of the quality of goods was already foreseen in a predecessor law.[1079] Confronted with this framework, the doctrine[1080] considered it possible to provide protection in accordance with the Civil Code under the laws on contractual liability for defective products (Articles 1857 et seq. CC[1081]) or the general rules of tort liability (with the disadvantage of requiring the claimant to prove malice and fault, as well as lack of a general rule on civil responsibility relating to goods) with the consequent applicability of Article 2329 CC.[1082]

317. The introduction of the LPC of 1997, however, neither implies the existence of a general statute of liability for products, nor does it indicate the safety that can be expected from them,[1083] and does not therefore contribute to a better or clearer understanding since it does not govern liability for dangerous products.

1075. *See generally* Barros, *Tratado,* II, cit., at 809 et seq. For less recent monographs *see* Erika Isler Soto, *El producto defectuoso* (Santiago de Chile: Librotecnia, 2013); Hernán Corral Talciani, *Responsabilidad por productos defectuosos. Analisis y propuestas para el derecho civil y de consumo en Chile* (Santiago de Chile: AbeledoPerrot, Legal Publishing, 2011).

1076. L. 20920/2016, of 17 May (DO 1 Jun. 2016).

1077. Decree of the Ministry of the Environment 8/2017 of 17 Mar. (DO 30 Nov. 2017).

1078. Art. 43 Ley N° 20.920/2016, cit. *See infra* para. 333.

1079. Art. 7 Ley 18.223/1983, of 24 May (DO 10 Jun. 1983). On an overview of the previous consumer legislation Hernán Corral Talciani. 'Responsabilidad civil por productos defectuosos. analisis desde el punto de vista de la responsabilidad de la empresa en los textos legales de proteccion al consumidor', *Revista de Derecho (PUCV)*, 17/1996, at 294 et seq.

1080. In this sense, the reconstruction of Corral Talciani. 'Responsabilidad civil por productos defectuosos. Analisis...', cit., at 298–299.

1081. Similarly applicable to the B2B report of the national sale in accordance with Art. 1454 Ccom.

1082. On the later application of Art. 2329 also Barros, *Tratado*, II, cit., at 813.

1083. Erika Isler Soto. 'La seguridad esperable en la responsabilidad por productos en la Ley 19.496', *Estudios de Derecho Civil XIV* – (Marícruz Gómez de Latorre Vargas, Gabriel Hernández Paulsen, Fabiola Lathrop Gómez, Mauricio Tapia Rodríguez ed.) (Santiago de Chile: Thomson Reuters, 2019), at 923. In this sense, it is considered that there is no general regime of liability for defective products: Rodrígo Momberg Uribe, 'Responsabilidad por producto defectuoso:¿Estatuto contractual, extracontractual o especial?'. *Presente y futuro de la responsabilidad civil* (Rodrigo Barría Díaz & Alfredo Ferrante & Lilian San Martín Neira ed.) (Santiago de Chile: Thomson Reuters, 2017), at 136.

318. On the one hand, there is a section on 'defective' products (defective in a broad sense: Article 20 LPC) and related to the *garantia legal* (legal guarantee) (Articles 18–21 LPC); on the other, there is a section on provisions related to product safety (Articles 44–49 LPC). Despite this, the legislation is insufficient and poorly structured as there is no precise concept of the product or clear differences between the defects or pathological and safety characteristics that it may present.[1084]

Thus, essentially, the law only establishes specific information obligations where the product is 'potentially dangerous for the health or physical integrity of consumers or for the safety of their goods' (Articles 45.1, 49 bis LPC), where there are possible preventive or corrective measures on the part of the producer who has become aware of the manufacture of an unsafe product (Article 46 LPC),[1085] and where certain precautions must be taken in service contracts (Article 45.2 LPC). Although in the case of toxic or harmful products the joint and several liability of the manufacturer, the importer and the first distributor of the product or the service provider is foreseen (Article 47 of the LPC), (Article 49 of the LPC), the law does not foresee any legal consequences in relation to possible damages despite linking liability to the violation of the foreseen preventive and informative regulations. In this sense, while there is no strict liability for dangerous products, the doctrine considers that in Article 47 there is a presumption of fault.[1086] Although this last norm is relevant[1087] in relation to liability, it is also possible to recall the extensive application of the general provision of Article 3 letter e) which establishes the consumer's fundamental right to compensation for material and moral damage.

A third form of protection is possible. That is, it is possible to claim infractional responsibility linked to the product characteristics. In this last case, having noted the

---

1084. *See* Francisca Barrientos Camus. 'La distinción entre la calidad y la seguridad de los productos. Algunos problemas que presnta la responsabilidad del vendedor en las ventas de consumo, *Estudios de Derecho Civil VI – Jornadas Nacionales de Derecho Civil, Olmué 2010* (Gonzalo Figueroa Yañez; Enrique Barros Bourie, Mauricio Tapia Rodríguez ed.) (Santiago de Chile: Abeledo Perrot, Legal Publishing, 2010) at 683 et seq.

1085. Cf. Corral Talciani. 'Responsabilidad civil por productos defectuosos. Analisis...', cit., at 311.

1086. Figueroa, *Curso IV*, cit., at 107.

1087. Jorge López Santa María, 'La responsabilidad civil por productos', *RDJ*, 2000/97, 2, primera parte, at 117; Hernán Corral Talciani, 'La responsabilidad por incumplimiento y por productos peligrosos en la Ley de protección de los derechos de los consumidores', *La protección de los derecho de los consumidores en Chile. Aspectos sustantivos y procesales luego de la reforma contenida en la Ley n.º 19.955 de 2004 Cuadernos de Extensión Jurídica*, (Jorge Baraona González, Osvaldo Lagos Villareal ed., Santiago de Chile: Universidad de los Andes, 2006) at 104. This last author, however, previously, and further discussing the objectification of Art. 47 LPC, stated that only the damage and the causal link between defect and damage should be proved: Hernán Corral Talciani, 'La relación de causalidad en la responsabilidad por productos defectuosos', *Revista Chilena de Derecho Privado*, 2/2004, at 91–92.

lack of practice in suing the manufacturer,[1088] an attempt has been made to recognize a joint responsibility of the manufacturer and the buyer in accordance with Article 23 LPC.[1089]

319. In response to this situation, part of the doctrine initially sought to extend the liability for defective product to the dangerous products, thus applying the laws on the legal guarantee also to compensate for damages and its prescription (Articles 20 and 21 LPC). It should be recalled that this statute provides for producer liability in certain cases.[1090]

320. Alternately, strict liability for dangerous products is governed by specific rules, whether the product is manufactured or used.

§2. Pharmaceutical and Medical Use Products

321. From another perspective, with the *Ley Ricarte Soto de 2015,*[1091] entered into force in 2017,[1092] introduces in the healthcare code[1093] – via the new title V on the 'responsibility for defective healthcare products' (Articles 111 H–111 N)[1094] – a broad form of strict liability for damage caused by healthcare products that is held to compensate 'all types of damage',[1095] including that arising from both civil and

1088. Francisca Barrientos Camus. 'La ¿Por qué no hay demandas de responsabilidad civil contra el fabricante?', *Estudios de Derecho Civil V – Jornadas Nacionales de Derecho Civil, Concepción 2009* (Departamento de Derecho Privado de la Facultad de Ciencias Jurídicas y Sociales de la Universidad de Concepción ed., Santiago de Chile: Thomson Reuters, 2009) at 687 et seq.

1089. Francisca Barrientos Camus. 'La responsabilidad civil del fabricante bajo el art. 23....', cit., at 1 y ss; more recently on a reinterpretation of at 23 also to favour the evidential burden of the consumer: Gabriel Hernández Paulsen & María Paz Gatica Rodríguez, 'Protección del consumidor y responsabilidad civil por producto o servicio defectuoso', *Revista de Estudios de la Justicia*, 31/2019, at 20 et seq.

1090. Cf. Alfredo Ferrante, 'Una revisión de los remedios...', cit., at 188, 189, 193; Francisca Barrientos Camus. 'La responsabilidad civil del fabricante bajo el art. 23 de la Ley de protección de los derechos de los consumidores y su relación con la responsabilidad civil del vendedor', *Revista Chilena de Derecho Privado*, 147/2010, at 16–18; Hernán Corral Talciani, 'La responsabilidad por incumplimiento y por productos peligrosos en la Ley de protección de los derechos de los consumidores', *La protección de los derecho de los consumidores en Chile. Aspectos sustantivos y procesales luego de la reforma contenida en la Ley n.º 19.955 de 2004 Cuadernos de Extensión Jurídica*, (Jorge Baraona González, Osvaldo Lagos Villareal ed., Santiago de Chile: Universidad de los Andes, 2006) at 100–101.

1091. Ley 20.850/2015 of 1 Jun. (DO 6 Jun. 2015). One of the main goals of the law is to create a system of financial protection for high-cost medicines, in memory of the death from lung cancer of periodical writer Ricarte Soto, hence its name.

1092. Decree of the Ministry of Health (*Decreto Ministerio de Salud*) 17/2017 of 21 Abr (DO 10 Jul. 2017).

1093. DL 725/67, of 11 Dec. (DO 31 Jan. 1968).

1094. *See* Hernán Corral Talciani, 'El primer régimen legal chileno de responsabilidad por productos: daños por defectos de los productos sanitarios', *Estudios de Derecho Civil XI* (Departamento de Derecho Privado Universidad Concepción ed., Santiago de Chile: Thomson Reuters, 2016), at 877 et seq.

1095. Art. 111 I DL 725/67, cit. Corral Talciani, 'El primer régimen legal..., cit., p. 902.

criminal liability.[1096] The regulation is more systematic, not only identifying the product safety standards, but also expressly providing for the effects of liability.

Thus, the healthcare product must combine the characteristics relative to the foreseeable use to be made of it, having as a standard of reference also those of the same series,[1097] establishing that the previous version cannot be considered defective if an improved form of the same is put into circulation.[1098]

322. Related to the liability of healthcare products, the law expressly excludes[1099] liability for cosmetic products, personal hygiene products and deodorant products.[1100] In these cases, the general rules of the Civil Code apply. Pharmaceutical products[1101] and products for medical use[1102] are covered by the law. Expressly included are also food products used for the treatment of certain pathologies or health conditions.[1103] The introduction of this last category creates greater applicative inconveniences since the methods of manufacture must include those of administration or maintenance of the product.

323. A joint and several liability is established between the holder of the product licence or authorization, the manufacturer and the importer vis-à-vis the injured party, with the possibility of recourse 'depending on their respective role in the production of the damage'.[1104]

The injured party is extensively protected by two other measures. First, by the mandatory insurance, endorsement or financial guarantee required of the manufacturer and importer.[1105] Second, a special responsibility of the State is also foreseen, and the *Central de Abastecimiento del Sistema Nacional de Servicios de Salud* is additionally considered responsible for *falta de servicio* (liability for service) in accordance with the law relating to the system of health guarantees,[1106] with the possibility of recourse against the previously mentioned parties.[1107] Generally, the term for filing a claim action is five years,[1108] except in the case of a clinical test, where the term is of nine years from the occurrence of the damage,[1109] while the recourse action (*acción de repetición*) is two years from the payment of compensation.[1110]

1096. On criminal liability of the manufacturer, *see* Lautaro Camilo Contreras Chaimovich, 'La prohibición de colocar en el mercado productos que sean peligrosos en caso de utilización conforme a su finalidad o racionalmente previsible', *Ius et Praxis*, 2/2019, at 19 et seq.
1097. Art. 111.2 and 111.3 H DL 725/67, cit.
1098. Art. 111.4 H DL 725/67, cit.
1099. Art. 111 DL 725/67, cit. Corral Talciani, 'El primer régimen legal..., cit., p. 900.
1100. Art. 106 DL 725/67, cit.
1101. Art. 95 DL 725/67, cit.
1102. Art. 111 DL 725/67, cit.
1103. Art. 102 DL 725/67, cit.
1104. *See* Art. 111 I DL 725/67, cit.
1105. Art. 111 F and Art. 111 M DL 725/67, cit.
1106. The reference is to Art. 38–42 Ley19.966, of 25 Aug. (DO 3 Sep. 2004).
1107. Art. 111 I DL 725/67, cit.
1108. Cf. Art. 111 I and Art. 111 L DL 725/67, cit.
1109. Art. 111 E DL 725/67, cit.
1110. Art. 111 L DL 725/67, cit.

Also important are certain jurisdictional aspects relating to the filing of a claim.[1111]

324. As far as standing is concerned, protection in such cases should certainly be broadened. If it is generally accepted that the protection for defective products should also be extended to the consumer,[1112] then producers of healthcare products should also be responsible for harm to indirect victims.[1113]

325. Liability for medical products is strict, expressly stating that the injured party must prove 'the defect, the damage and the causal link between the first two, with the peculiarity that in cases of clinical trials the law expressly presumes the causal link once the damage is accredited, considering that this has been produced during the research in progress'.[1114] Therefore, the exemption only applies if the party is able to demonstrate that the damage proceeded from facts or circumstances that could not be foreseen 'according to the state of scientific or technical knowledge existing at the time of putting into circulation or use of the product'.[1115]

326. Furthermore, the law also establishes civil liability for the production or distribution of the healthcare product. In fact, it is established that the holders of health licences or authorizations, producers and importers will also be civilly liable in the event that highly expensive treatments carried out with certain medicines cannot be carried out continuously.[1116]

§3. Pesticides

327. This establishes liability for damage caused by pesticides, regardless of whether they were applied accidentally or unavoidably. Compensation may be claimed within the year of discovery of the damage, but within four years of the application of the pesticide.[1117]

1111. Vid. Art. 111 H, *see* Corral Talciani, 'El primer régimen legal..., cit., p. 907 et seq.
1112. With jurisprudential references: Hernández Paulsen & Gatica Rodríguez, 'Protección del consumidor y responsabilidad civil ...', cit., at 21 and 29–30.
1113. Corral Talciani, 'El primer régimen legal..., cit., p. 903 or 904.
1114. Art. 111. J DL 725/67, cit.
1115. Art. 111 K DL 725/67, cit.
1116. Art. 15 Ley 20.850/2015, cit.
1117. Art. 36 DL 3557 29 Dec. (DO 9 Feb. 1981).

Chapter 3. Liability for Service

328. Generally speaking, no strict liability can be recognized. Reference is made to other provisions where these aspects have been dealt with in relation to liability in the State where various aspects of liability for service have already been discussed. However, it should be noted that, in the local context, part of the doctrine has analysed not only liability for service but also compensation for damages in the event of deprivation or limitation of property.[1118]

1118. Pablo Montt Retting, 'Responsabilidad del Estado pro acto ilícitos. ¿Queda espacio para reclamar perjuicios por privaciones o limitaciones de la propiedad?', *Lo Público y lo Privado. Estudios en homenaje al prof. Enrique Barros Bourie*, (Santiago de Chile: Thomson Reuters, 2017), at 759 et seq.

Chapter 4. Environmental Liability

329. A characteristic of the Chilean legal system is that environmental liability,[1119] is also not necessarily a strict liability. Rather, similarly to what has been discussed in the other case, it is maintained to give coherence to the required structure of the section of the law in which it is included.

330. Environmental protection is constitutionally protected,[1120] and the civil liability associated with it is generally regulated by Article 51 de la *Ley sobre Medio Ambiente*[1121] ('Law on the Environment'), which establishes liability shall be based on fault or fraud, cosí l' Article 51 states of 'Anyone who culpably or maliciously causes environmental damage will respond … .'[1122]

Nevertheless the literality of Article 52 states a 'presumption of liability'[1123] in the case of infringements of environmental or emission standards, or any other rule of a preventive nature (in which case it is only necessary to prove the causal link between the infringement and the damage produced).[1124]

Faced with a possible objectification of liability for environmental damage, part of the doctrine[1125] has been critical, arguing that the attempt to reinterpret civil and

---

1119. On this problematic also in relation with a comparison with Colombian law *see* Carlos Pizarro Wilson, 'La responsabilidad por daño ambiental en perspectiva civil', *Estudios de derecho privado: en homenaje al profesor Christian Larroumet* (Fabricio Mantilla Espinosa, Carlos Pizarro Wilson, ed.), (Santiago de Chile/Bogotà: Universidad Diego Portales, Fundación Fueyo Laneri/ Universidad de Rosario, 2008), at 387 et seq.; For one of the first aproximación to this typology of liability Cristián Banfi del Río, 'De la Responsabilidad civil como instrumento de protección ambiental', *Revista Chilena de Derecho Privado*, 2004/2, at 19 et seq.

1120. Thus, Art. 19 n° 8 CPR establishes the right to live in an environment free from contamination, with the obligation of the State to protect such right.

1121. Art. 51 Ley19300/1994, of 1 Mar. (DO 4 Mar. 1994). On such liability vid. Jorge A. Femenías Salas, *Responsabilidad por Daño Ambiental* (Santiago de Chile: Universidad Católica, 2017), in particular at 42 et seq. More generally *see* Pedro Fernández Bitterlich, *Manual derecho ambiental chileno* (Santiago de chile: Thomson Reuters, 5th ed., 2017). Precursor of environmental law studies in Chile was Rafael Valenzuela Fuenzalida: *see* Rafael Valenzuela Fuenzalida, *El derecho ambiental: presente y pasado* (Santiago de Chile: Editorial Jurídica de Chile, 2010).

1122. '*Todo el que culposa o dolosamente cause daño ambiental responderá …* ': Art. 51 Ley 19300/ 1994, cit.

1123. '*Se presume legalmente la responsabilidad del autor del daño ambiental …* ': Art. 52 Ley 19300/ 1994, cit.

1124. For case law e.g., CS 25 Sep. 2019 (rol 13177-2018); CS 25 Jan. 2018 (rol 41417/2017), CS 29 Jun. 2016 (rol 37170/2015), CS 8 Jul. 2016 (rol 13/2015), Corte de Puerto Montt 2 Apr. 2004 (rol N° 11.652-2003).

More extensively on this topic: Alberto Barros Bordeau, 'La resolución de calificación ambiental como fuente y límite de la culpa en la responsabilidad por daño ambiental', *Lo Público y lo Privado. Estudios en homenaje al prof. Enrique Barros Bourie*, (Santiago de Chile: Thomson Reuters, 2017), at 697 et seq.; Jean Paul Dussaubat, 'Daño ambiental y el fracaso de la reparación voluntaria: diagnóstico y propuestas', *Revista de Derecho Ambiental*, 2016/6, at 178 et seq.; Jorge A. Femenías Salas, 'Los daños ambientales como única categoría jurídica cuya reparación regula la Ley n.° 19.300. Comentario a la sententecia Corte Suprema 29 junio 2016, rol 37.170/2015', *Revista Chilena de Derecho*, 2017/ 1, at 295 et seq.; Iván Hunter Ampuero, 'La culpa con la Ley en la responsabilidad civil ambiental', *Revista de Derecho* (Valdivia), 2005/2, at 9 et seq.

1125. Cristián Banfi Del Rio, 'Riesgos en la aplicación del principio precautorio en responsabilidad civil y ambiental', *Revista chilena de derecho*, 2019/3, at 643 et seq.

environmental liability in the light of the precautionary principle risks distorting the essence of the fault and causal link, which may lead to the imposition of a strict liability with no legal basis.

331. Since 2010, the possibility of exonerating oneself from responsibility has been introduced[1126] whenever it is demonstrated that 'the person who committed the damage successfully carried out the (environmental) repair plan approved by Environment Superintendency'.[1127] In this sense, it is of great interest to analyse the standard of conduct related to the compliance of the *Environmental Impact Assessment System*[1128] provided by Article 10 of the law.[1129] So despite the literality of Article 52 about presumption of liability, the reform of Article 53 permits make reference to a presumption of fault.[1130]

332. In addition to claims for damages, the law also provides for *environmental recourse,*[1131] which aims at compensating in kind to restore the environment to its previous state before the damage occurred.[1132] Legal standing is broader since claims may be made both by parties who have been directly affected by the environmental damage, and the State and public entities (who are considered to have a legitimate interest), and especially municipalities (*las municipalidades*) where the damage has occurred and the *Consejo de Defensa Del Estado.*[1133]

Interestingly, the municipality may also be held liable since is jointly and severally liable for any environmental harm caused by the alleged offensive conduct if it

1126. A new paragraph is introduced to Art. 53 Ley 19300/1994, by Ley 20417/2019, of 21 Jan. (DO 26 Jan. 2010).

1127. This is the '*plan de reparación ambiental aprobado por la Superintendencia del Medio Ambiente*'. Art. 53.2 Ley 19300/1994, cit. *See* Bastián Pastén Delich. & Gonzalo Parot Hillmer, 'Diversificación de la reparación del daño ambiental en Chile: Perspectiva para los planes de reparación', *Revista Justicia Ambiental*, 2012/4, at 187 et seq

1128. This is called *Sistema de Evaluación de Impacto Ambiental*: SEIA.

1129. On the point, vid. Jorge A. Femenías Salas, 'La culpabilidad en la responsabilidad por daños ambiental y su relación con el sistema de evaluación de impacto ambiental', *Revista de Derecho (PUCV)* XLVIII/2017, at 233 et seq. The non-introduction to the SEIA of an activity that subsequently produces damage would configure for the author of the infraction of a norm of environmental protection (Art. 8 Ley 19300/1994, cit) and would produce the application of the presumption of the first paragraph of Art. 52 Ley 19300/1994, cit. If, on the contrary, the activities have encroached on the SEIA, various aspects should be evaluated, such as the foreseeability of the damage.

1130. Talking of 'presunción de culpabilidad': Jean Paul. Dussaubat Diban, 'Responsabilidad por daño ambiental: de la presunción de culpabilidad a la presunción de causalidad', *Revista de Derecho Administrativo Económico*, 2016/22, at 147–158; Bastián Pastén Delich. & Gonzalo Parot Hillmer, 'Diversificación de la reparación del daño ambiental en Chile: Perspectiva para los planes de reparación', *Revista Justicia Ambiental*, 2012/4, at 172 .Talking of 'presumption of fault' (*presunción de culpa*): Figueroa, *Curso IV*, cit., at 107; identifying the presumption of liability with the presumption of fault: Corral, *Lecciones,* cit., at 265.

1131. 'Acción ambiental': Art. 53.1, 54 Ley 19300/1994, cit.

1132. Barros, *Tratado*, II, cit., at 875 et seq.

1133. Art. 5.,1 Ley 19300/1994, cit.

does not take a decision within forty-five days of the private party's request to assess the existence of environmental damage.[1134]

333. The provisions of the Law on the Environment must be considered general in nature, being integrated by and subject to specific regulations of special laws. Thus, the general rules of liability provided by the Civil Code will apply in the absence of a specific regulation or special law.[1135] As discussed,[1136] a strict civil liability has been introduced for damages caused to the environment due to the management of hazardous waste.[1137] Another case of strict liability is illustrated by the spillage of hydrocarbons in the sea,[1138] in which case the liability regime provided by the International Convention on Civil Liability for Damages Caused by the Contamination of the Sea by Hydrocarbons, of 29 November 1969, is expressly applicable and the owner, the shipowner or the operator (in any capacity) of the ship or of the naval artefact that produces the spillage or the discharge are jointly and severally liable for the damage. In this case, not only is it presumed that the spillage causes damage, but also exemption from liability is granted only if it is proved that the damage was caused by war (or equivalent) or exceptional, inevitable and irresistible phenomena, or if it is proved that a third party is either negligently or intentionally responsible. In the same way, a strict responsibility is foreseen in the case in which the discharges do not take place at sea but from a land installation; in this case, the owner shall be liable.[1139] Particular interest has been aroused by the liability for environmental damage in the case of State concessionaires in the construction of roads.[1140] For instance, it has been argued that the five-year prescription period for claims relating to environmental protection[1141] is considerably short.[1142]

334. In addition to a claim for damages, there is also a preventive or protective action against environmental damage.

Sometimes recourse is made to Article 937 CC (concerning the *works that corrupt the air and make it conocidamente harmful*[1143]) to cause the cessation of any harmful event. Pursuant to Article 948 CC, it is also possible to initiate a class action

1134. Art. 54.2 Ley 19300/1994, cit.
1135. In this sense, Art. 2314 et seq. CC: Verónica Delgado Schneider, 'La responsabilidad civil extracontractual por el daño ambiental causado en la construcción u operación de las carreteras', *Revista de Derecho* (Valdivia), 1/2012, at 56.
1136. *See* para. 315.
1137. Art. 43 Ley20.920/2016, cit.
1138. Art. 144 Decree Law 2.222/1978 (*Decreto Ley 2.222/1978*), of 21 May (DO 31 May 1978).
1139. Art. 147 Decree Law 2.222/1978 (*Decreto Ley 2.222/1978*), cit.
1140. *See* Verónica Delgado Schneider, 'La responsabilidad civil extracontractual..., cit., at 47 et seq.
1141. This is calculated from the 'obvious manifestation of the damage' in accordance with Art. 96 Ley 19300/1994, cit.
1142. *See* Verónica Delgado Schneider, 'La responsabilidad civil extracontractual..., cit., at 60.
1143. '*Operas que corrumpen el aire y lo hacen conocidamente dañoso*', *see* Barros, *Tratado*, II, cit., at 859–860.

aimed at protecting the environment[1144] or, given its constitutional protection, an *acción de protección* with a preventive function.[1145]

335. The doctrine has begun analysing the relationship between civil liability and climate change.[1146]

1144. *See* CS 21 Oct. 2014 (rol 12.938/2013). In favour of this position by means of a historical reconstruction: Verónica Delgado Schneider, 'La protección del medio ambientea través de las acciones populares del art. 948 del código civil de Andrés Bello. Un estudio histórico comparativo', *Sesquicentenario del Código Civil de Andrés Bello. Pasado, presente y futuro de la codificación* (María Dora Martinic, Mauricio Tapia Rodríguez, ed.) (Santiago de Chile: Lexis Nexis, 2006), at 907 et seq.; this doctrine is also endorsed by Carlos Amunátegui Perello, *Derecho Civil y medio ambiente. Un estudio de la teoría de las inmisiones y su apliabilidad en el derecho chileno* (Santiago de Chile: Thomson Reuters, 2014), at 159 *contra* Barros, *Tratado*, II, cit., at 861–862.
1145. Thus, with jurisprudential references: Barros, *Tratado*, II, cit., at 863 et seq.
1146. *See* Cristián Banfi Del Rio, 'Sobre la responsabilidad civil por cambio climático en Chile', *Acta Bioethica* 2019/2, at 153 et seq.; Gabriel Araya Ahumada, 'La responsabilidad del Estado en relación a la implementación de la política nacional de adaptación', *Actas de las jornadas de Derecho Ambiental VII* (Santiago de Chile: Thomson Reuters, 2014), at 3–23, from the comparative perspective also Mathilde Bouttonet, 'Responsabilidad Civil y cambio climatico', *Actas*...cit., at 53 et seq.

Chapter 5. Others

§1. Liability for Nuclear Damages

336. Strict liability is envisaged for damage caused by nuclear accidents or radioactive substances governed by the Nuclear Safety Act,[1147] which expressly excludes at Article 49 exoneration from liability –not even in cases of force majeure – unless the damage is due to a riot or war.[1148]

337. Thus, those who[1149] derive economic benefit from nuclear substances – not only in the event of a nuclear accident, but also in a series of other specific cases relating to damage occurring inside installations – are liable,[1150] including when damage is caused by third parties with nuclear or radiological materials unlawfully removed. However, if the former is responsible for the express dictate of the special law,[1151] the liability of the latter (i.e., third parties) must follow the general rules of liability.

338. Although liability is strict, it only potentially respects the principle of full compensation for the damage since it is expressly limited in amount according to certain canons that are associated with international standards,[1152] with the requirement of insurance or security to carry out the activity.[1153]
Compensation for personal injury is prioritized. For property damage, if the amounts are insufficient, the reparation will be spread[1154] over a period of ten years from the date of the damaging event or from the corresponding claim.[1155]

§2. Air Carrier Liability

339. Generally speaking, there has been a delay in Chile's incorporation of international law.[1156] Indeed, it was not until 1979 that Chile became a party to the Warsaw Convention, incorporating the Montreal Convention ten years later in 2009.

1147. Ley 18.302/1984, of 6 Apr. (DO 2 May 1984). In relation also to international regulations, *see* Francisco González Cruz y Santiago Acevedo Ferrer, 'Revisión del Estatuto de responsabilidad civil por daños nucleares', *Revista Chilena de Derecho,* 2013/1, at 11 et seq.
1148. Art. 56 Ley 18.302/1984, cit.
1149. If there are several people and there are doubts about the sharing of the benefits of exploitation, joint and several liability is expressly established: Art. 53 Ley 18.302/1984, cit.
The transporter of a nuclear substance or radioactive material is considered one of them until he has delivered it in accordance with Art. 54 of Law 18.302/1984, cit.
1150. Art. 16 and 50 Ley 18.302/1984, cit.
1151. Art. 52 Ley 18.302/1984, cit.
1152. Art. 60 Ley 18.302/1984, cit.
1153. Art. 62 et seq. Ley 18.302/1984, cit.
1154. Art. 61 et seq. Ley 18.302/1984, cit.
1155. Art. 66 et seq. Ley 18.302/1984, cit. A different application is also possible when the injured party has suffered particularly grave damage.
1156. Maximiliano Escobar Saavedra, 'El trasporte aéreo de pasajeros en el derecho chileno ¿un contrato de consumidores?', *Estudios de Derecho Comercial* (Guillermo Caballero Germáin, Osvaldo Lagos Villareal, ed.) (Santiago de Chile: Thomson Reuters, 2015) at 25 et seq.

The Aviation Code[1157] establishes both contractual and tort liability for damages related to the aircraft, also providing for a section related to the collision between aircraft.[1158] The right to claim damages in both cases are time barred in one year from the day of the damaging event, from the day when the aircraft landed or from the moment when the transport was interrupted, depending on the cases.[1159]

340. In cases where it is not possible to apply the Aviation Code or international regulations, express reference is made to common regulations, customs or general principles of law. Some aspects have been refined in this regard,[1160] but it is still necessary to reconcile with consumer law.[1161] It has been noted that the decline in air fares contributes to new problems relating to consumer protection and unfair terms.[1162]

Special regulations or ordinary rules may also apply when the aircraft is neither civil nor commercial. In fact, there are other types of flights that do not fall within the scope of the regulations analysed herein, such as instruction flights made by aeroclubs. In this context, it is possible to identify the liability of other parties, such as the liability of the State in relation to the actions of the *Inspector de vuelo*, an official of the *Dirección General de Aeronáutica Civil.*[1163]

1157. In particular, Art. 112 et seq. Ley N° 18.916/1990, of 19 Jan. (DO 8 Feb. 1990). For some less recent monographic studies, also in relation to international regulations: Rodrigo Hananías Castillo, *La responsabilidad civil en el Transporte Aéreo de Mercancías* (Santiago de Chile, La Ley, 2003); Maximiliano Prado Donoso, *Responsabilidad civil en el Trasporte Aéreo. Daños a los pasajeros en el trasporte internacional*, (Santiago de Chile: LexiNexis, 2005).

1158. Art. 161 et seq. Ley N° 18.916/1990, cit.

1159. Art. 175 Ley N° 18.916/1990, cit.

1160. Art. 6 Ley N° 18.916/1990, cit. *See* Claudia Mejías Alonzo, Angela Toso Milos, 'Fuentes normativas para el tratamiento de la responsabilidad del porteador en el trasporte aéreo. El contenido de las remisiones del código aerenáutico al Derecho Común y a los usos, constumbres y proncipios generales del derecho', *Ius et Praxis*, 2021/2, at 199 et seq.

1161. Maximiliano Escobar Saavedra, 'El trasporte aéreo de pasajeros en el derecho chileno ¿un contrato de consumidores?', *Estudios de Derecho Comercial* (Guillermo Caballero Germáin, Osvaldo Lagos Villareal, ed.) (Santiago de Chile: Thomson Reuters, 2015) at 50.

1162. Maximiliano Escobar Saavedra, 'El trasporte aéreo low const y sus potenciales peligros para los derechos de los pasajeros', *Estudios de Derecho Comercial* (Loren Carvajal Arenas, Angela Toso Milos, ed.) (Santiago de Chile: Thomson Reuters, 2017) at 165 et seq. In relation to one of the first judgments debating the applicability of consumer law to the air transport contract: *see* Rodrigo Momberg Uribe, 'Sentencia sobre la aplicación de la ley de protección de los derechos de los consumidores al contrato de transporte aéreo (Segundo Juzgado de Policía Local de Osorno, Corte de Apelaciones de Valdivia)', *Revista de Derecho* (Valdivia), 2003/2, at 227

1163. Reglamento sobre Operación de Aeronaves, en adelante también Reglamento DAR-06 D.S. [Defensa] N° 52, de 2002, Reglamento sobre licencias al personal aeronáutico, en adelante también Reglamento DAR-01 D.S. [Defensa] N° 51, de 2004, ampliamente refer to the work of Macarena Díaz de Valdés Haase, 'La responsabilidad civil por daños, lesiones y muerte en vuelos de instrucción dentro de Chile. Comentario a tres sentencias de la Corte Suprema', *Ius et Praxis*, 2017/2, at 509 et seq. Others, also with jurisprudential references, also differentiate in case the accident occurred during practices or the real examination, having to differentiate between a contractual liability of the instructor (Art. 1545 y ss CC) from the other possible cases of tort liability (Arts 2314 CC et seq).

341. In tort matters, there are two types of regulation in the case of a single aircraft causing damage,[1164] or in the case of damage caused by a collision of several aircraft.[1165]

342. The legislation attributes liability to the person who benefits economically from the air transport service (*explotador*), opening up the possibility of also identifying other jointly and severally liable persons.

In fact, the *explotador* does not necessarily coincide with the owner of the aircraft. In such case the owner will be jointly and severally responsible, unless he registers the contract by which the economic benefits derived from the use of the aircraft are transferred in the National Register of Aircraft.[1166]

A similar discussion takes place when the *explotador* does not coincide with the carrier. Even here, the law establishes joint and several liability[1167] among all those who can be considered responsible for the damaging event.[1168]

343. In case of charter flight, the liability between the charterer and the lessee is established.[1169] In the event the subleasing of the aircraft is permitted, the assignor (or sub-lessor) shall be free from liability if he registers the contract in the National Register of Aircrafts.[1170]

344. It should be recalled here that the liability of employees during the performance of their duties is enshrined for both the air carrier and the person who benefits financially from the operation.[1171]

345. Without prejudice to the foregoing, where only one aircraft is involved, the tort liability envisaged is strict and falls upon the person who benefits economically from the use of the aircraft (the *explotador*). In these circumstances, the tortfeasor is liable for any damage caused by the aircraft (or a piece of the same that becomes detached from it), including any damage caused on the ground,[1172] except in specific cases, such as an unlawful seizure of the aircraft, as a direct consequence of armed conflicts, and the like.[1173]

346. When the aircraft that caused the damage has been used by a person other than the *explotador,* liability is joint and several unless the *explotador* proves that he took all appropriate measures to avoid the damage or that it was impossible for him to do so.[1174]

1164. Art. 155 et seq. Ley N° 18.916/1990, cit.
1165. Art. 166 et seq. Ley N° 18.916/1990, cit.
1166. Art. 100 Ley N° 18.916/1990, cit.
1167. Art. 174 Ley N° 18.916/1990, cit.
1168. Art. 174 Ley N° 18.916/1990, cit.
1169. Art. 111 Ley N° 18.916/1990, cit.
1170. Art. 102 Ley N° 18.916/1990, cit.
1171. Art. 171 Ley N° 18.916/1990, cit.
1172. Art. 155 Ley N° 18.916/1990, cit.
1173. *See* Art. 156 Ley N° 18.916/1990, cit.
1174. *See* Art. 157 Ley N° 18.916/1990, cit.

347. Compensation for personal injury is given priority over property damage,[1175] with a possible proportional reduction if the amounts do not cover the entire indemnifiable[1176] sum. In fact, the award for damages is limited by parameters related to the type of aircraft, providing a maximum indemnity according to its weight.[1177] However, it is important to note that the limits do not apply if it is proved that the damage is due to the fault or malice of the carrier, the beneficiary or their employees.[1178] In this case, therefore, there is a peculiarity of liability which, although it is objective, is based on parameters that determine not the *an* but the *quantum* of damages. This method of compensation also applies to liability in the event of a collision between aircraft.[1179]

348. A specific provision governs the tort liability arising from a collision of aircraft,[1180] which is strict and operates also in the event of a fortuitous event.[1181]

All involved aircraft and their *explotadores*[1182] are jointly and severally liable for any personal and property damages caused on the ground, without prejudice to the right of the *explotadores* of the various airlines to recover the amount paid in damages (which is prescribed six months from the time the payment[1183]) for damage caused by the culpable operation of the other airlines involved, including any individuals at fault.[1184]

349. As far as the contractual liability of the air carrier[1185] is concerned, certain indemnity limits have been established,[1186] presuming that any person on board the aircraft at the time of the accident is a passenger.[1187] Since liability is strict, proof of liability will be required if the damage is due to the victim, related to his state of health, or caused by a third party who is not a passenger.[1188]

350. Contractual liability is not only established for personal and property damages, but also compensation for delays unless it can be demonstrated that 'all necessary measures were taken to avoid the event that caused the delay or that it was impossible to take such measures', currently set at an amount not exceeding 250

1175. *See* Art. 159 Ley N° 18.916/1990, cit.
1176. *See* Art. 160 Ley N° 18.916/1990, cit.
1177. *See* Art. 158 Ley N° 18.916/1990, cit.
1178. Art. 171 Ley N° 18.916/1990, cit.
1179. *See* Art. 165 Ley N° 18.916/1990, cit.
1180. *See* Art. 166–169 Ley N° 18.916/1990, cit.
1181. Art. 168 Ley N° 18.916/1990, cit.
1182. Art. 166 Ley N° 18.916/1990, cit.
1183. Art. 169 Ley N° 18.916/1990, cit..
1184. Art. 167 Ley N° 18.916/1990, cit.
1185. Art. 143 Ley N° 18.916/1990, cit. In relation to contractual damages in international transport: Rafael Durán Sanhueza 'El ámbito de aplicación de las normas sobre responsabilidad del transportista en el transporteaéreo internacional', database online Microjuris 7.10.2009 (MJCH-_MJD365).
1186. Art. 144 Ley N° 18.916/1990, cit.
1187. Art. 145 Ley N° 18.916/1990, cit.
1188. Art. 146 Ley N° 18.916/1990, cit.

Unidad de Fomento for each passenger.[1189] Additionally, the rights of the consumer in case of flight cancellation, denied boarding or overbooking are also regulated, although in a somewhat defiant manner.[1190]

351. In the case of a collision between aircraft in flight, liability is associated with the conduct of the pilot and his wilful or negligent conduct.[1191] The law sanctions such conduct with the joint responsibility of the *explotadores* of the aircraft involved, who are entitled to recourse against the others for any sums paid in excess of the relative quota,[1192] as compensation is paid in proportion to the negligent conduct in the measure indicated by the judge.[1193]

352. There are a number of exemptions from liability common[1194] to all types of liability envisaged by the law, such that it is expressly provided that the grounds for exemption or mitigation of responsibility are based on the fact that the injured party caused or contributed to the damage, or recklessly exposed himself to it.[1195] The latter case is based on Article 2330 CC.

353. Liability for the acts of employees during the performance of their duties is also established for both the air carrier and the person who benefits financially from the business.[1196] The injured party is entitled to direct recourse[1197] against the employee (in which case, the carrier or *explotador*), except in cases of fault or wilful misconduct by the employee. The carrier or *explotador* may invoke the limits on the amounts established by law.

In the case of contractual liability, it is necessary to coordinate what has been discussed thus far, in the sense that it is stipulated that in the case of several carriers, the action for compensation must be made against the last 'porteador' who carried out the transport, unless the first carrier has expressly assumed responsibility.[1198]

1189. *See* Art. 130 Ley N° 18.916/1990, cit.et seq., *see* Andrés Eduardo Celedón Baeza, 'Tu vuelo está sobrevendido? Derecho a compensación y asistencia en caso de overbooking. Ejercicio al derecho de reclamo', *Estudios de Derecho del Consumidor* (Humberto Carrasco Blanch, ed.) (Santiago de Chile: Rubicon, 2018), at 219 et seq.; In relation to passenger rights in the period relating to Covid-19 also in relation to consumer law: *see* Natanael Peña Calderón, 'El contrato de transporte aéreo y la emergencia por COVID-19: el estatuto aeronáutico chileno frente a la cancelación de vuelos por caso fortuito y la reactivación del tráfico aéreo pospandemia', *Revista Chilena de Derecho Privado,* 2021/36, at 79 et seq.
1190. Art. 147 Ley N° 18.916/1990, cit.
1191. *See* Art. 162 Ley N° 18.916/1990, cit.
1192. *See* Art. 163 Ley N° 18.916/1990, cit.
1193. *See* Art. 164 Ley N° 18.916/1990, cit.
1194. Art. 170–175 Ley N° 18.916/1990, cit.
1195. Art. 170 Ley N° 18.916/1990, cit.
1196. Art. 171 Ley N° 18.916/1990, cit.
1197. Art. 173 Ley N° 18.916/1990, cit.
1198. Art. 128 Ley N° 18.916/1990, cit.

Part IV. Defences and Exception Clauses Liability

Chapter 1. Limitation of Claims

§1. General Aspects

354. Apart from the statute of limitations, tort liability is discharged in accordance with the standard rules applicable to obligations, subject to the peculiarities of contractual autonomy and relative agreements. Thus, the doctrine illustrates how it is possible to extinguish such obligations by novation, compensation, confusion, remission, transaction and by renunciation by the holder.[1199]

355. The doctrine[1200] categorizes and summarizes the main characteristics of the action to claim damages as being of a 'personal' nature (Article 578 CC), *mueble*, to refer to a pecuniary reparation (Article 580 CC) or the performance of certain acts to cease or prevent the damage (Article 581), and 'patrimonial' in that it is susceptible to pecuniary appreciation (in the case it is not of personal nature).

In the event that the damage is incidental (*daño contingente*, cf. Articles 932, 948, 2333, 2334) the holder of the action may be either a determinate or an indefinite person.[1201]

356. In addition to the specific limitation periods provided by certain special rules,[1202] the limitation period for actions for damages relating to tort liability arising out of negligence or wilful misconduct is governed by Article 2332 CC.[1203] Despite the provision prescribing a period of four years from the 'performance of

1199. It is not possible to compensate a tort due to violence or fraud (Art. 1662.2 CC). Alessandri, *Responsabilidad,* cit., at 374–375, has clearly pointed this out. Similarly e.g., Tapia, *De la responsabilidad*, cit., at 326 et seq.; Barros, *Tratado*, II, cit., at 1027–1028.

1200. Alessandri, *Responsabilidad*, cit., at 327, 378; similarly, *see also* Abeliuk, *Las Obligaciones*, *I*, at 323–324.

1201. Alessandri, *Responsabilidad*, *supra*, cit. at 328 Thus, this doctrine affirms that, in this sense, Art. 2315 CC, in identifying the persons, is not exhaustive but develops the general principle of Art. 2314 CC.

1202. In general, *see* Ramón Domínguez Águila, La *prescripción extintiva: Doctrina y Jurisprudencia* (Valparaiso: Prolibros, 2021).

1203. For a historical analysis of the norm: Luis Valentin Ferrada Walker. 'Aspectos históricos del Art. 2332 del Codigo Civil. Hacia la recta interpretación del precepto', *Estudios de Derecho Civil VI*

the act', it is considered that if it is a matter of *daño contingente* (and therefore relating to preventive liability actions under Articles 2333 and 2334 CC, as well as under Article 2328 CC[1204]), the action would be imprescriptible in accordance with Article 950.2 CC.[1205] In this regard, preventive actions are possible as long as the threat of damage persists.

The statute of limitations of Article 2332 CC refers to the action for compensation, as other limitation periods must be applied when other actions are taken (e.g., the claim for theft,[1206] subrogation of the insurer or the jointly liable party, or the reimbursement claim[1207]).

357. The literal meaning of Article 2332 CC in relation to the *dies a quo* has been questioned since in some cases it would lead to a paradoxical time-barring of the action. Accordingly, case law has recently established that the prescriptive term begins from the moment in which the damage[1208] occurred, or when the victim became or was able to become aware of it,[1209] instead of the moment in which the event occurred. In this sense, partly following an initial orientation in favour of a more open interpretation of Article 2332 CC,[1210] there is a change of direction compared to the position that literally applies[1211] the norm (which is based on the traditional Chilean doctrine[1212] and does not assign relevance to the effects that the liability may generate). Rather, the reinterpretation of the *dies a quo* of Article 2332

– *Jornadas Nacionales de Derecho Civil, Olmué 2010* (Gonzalo Figueroa Yañez; Enrique Barros Bourie, Mauricio Tapia Rodríguez ed.) (Santiago de Chile: Abeledo Perrot, Legal Publishing, 2010) at 719 et seq.

1204. José Luis Díez Schwerter, 'La acción de daño contingente del artículo 2333 del Código Civil chileno: sus elementos y ámbito de aplicación', *Revista de Derecho* (PUCV), 2016/46, at 131. More broadly and with practical application: José Luis Díez Schwerter, 'La acción por daño contingente del art. 2333 del Código Civil en movimiento: tres casos de la jurisprudencia reciente', *Estudios de Derecho Privado. En homenaje al prof. Daniel Peñailillo Arévalos*, (Santiago de Chile: Thomson Reuters, 2019), p. 723 et seq.

1205. Corral, *Lecciones,* cit., at 414.

1206. Abeliuk, *Las Obligaciones*, *I*, at 324; in the sense of limited application to such actions for compensation also Tapia, *De la responsabilidad*, cit.,at 319 et seq.

1207. *See* Arts 1522 and 2515 CC, on the *dies a quo* of the redemption claim (since it revoked the benefit): CS 30 Jan. 2013 (rol 6302/2010), Barros, *Tratado*, II, cit., at 1037–1038; Corral, *Leciones,* cit., at 404–405.

1208. CS 21 Mar. 2016 (Rol 8106/2017), CS 20 Mar. 2020 (Rj 23.241/2019), *see* Ramón Domínguez Águila, 'Inicio de la prescripción en caso de cuasidelito civil', *Revista de Derecho* (Universidad de Concepción), 2020/247, at 247 et seq.

1209. CS 4 Dec. 2017 (rol 58.987/2016); CS 19 May 2016 (rol 22.878/2015); CS 13 Aug. 2015 (rol 3968/2015); on the point Barros, *Tratado*, II, cit., at 1031.

1210. Alessandri, *Responsabilidad,* cit., at 23, 40, 327,377; Tapia, *De la responsabilidad*, cit., at 319–320.

1211. For this strand relating to the literal interpretation of Art. 2332 CC, e.g., CS 28 Mar. 2017 (rol 38.283), commented by Ramón Domínguez Águila, 'Comentario de Jurisprudencia. Prescripción extintiva de la acción de responsabilidad extracontractual, *Revista de Derecho* (Universidad de Concepción), 2017/241, at 166 et seq.

With more extensive reference to Ramón Domínguez Águila, La *prescripción extintiva: Doctrina y Jurisprudencia*, cit., passim.

1212. Alessandri, *Responsabilidad,* cit., at 23, 40, 327,377; Tapia, *De la responsabilidad*, cit., at 1319-320, *contra* en la doctrina clásica Abeliuk, *Las Obligaciones*, *I*, at 245, Ramón Domínguez Águila in the works cited here, *passim.*

CC is based on the observation that there is no illicit fact without damage,[1213] and that, therefore, the latter must be considered or else the remedy available to the damaged party may be time-barred if the damage is produced considerably after the causal event.[1214] Thus, it is argued that application of the principle *actioni non natae non praescribitur*[1215] prevents the statute of limitations from running in cases when the action has not yet been filed.

Notwithstanding the tendency to reinterpret the rule, this orientation has not yet been consolidated. Consequently, the rule continues to be literally interpreted. For example, in the case of civil liability arising from a crime, it has been established that in these cases the *dies a quo* for the action of contractual liability starts from the damaging event and not from the criminal judgment.[1216] In the case of civil liability of the State, the period starts to run from the moment of the event, in accordance with special regulations.[1217]

Still, albeit the solution is not unanimous,[1218] it is significant that modern Chilean doctrine[1219] tends to favour the non-literal interpretation of the norm.

1213. Ramón Domínguez Águila, 'Comentario de jurisprudencia: Prescripción en materia de responsabilidad
extracontractual. Momento del inicio del cómputo. Artículo 2332 del Código Civil. Perpetración del acto. Distinción entre hecho ilícito y daño. Daños continuados, Revista de Derecho Universidad de Concepción, 2001/ 210, at 337.

1214. Ramón Domínguez Águila, 'Plazo de prescripción de la acción de responsabilidad extracontractual debe contarse desde el hecho dañoso y no desde la sentencia penal condenatoria', *Revista de Derecho* (Universidad de Concepción), 2018/243, at 150.

1215. Ramón Domínguez Águila, 'Inicio de la prescripción en caso de cuasidelito civil' cit., at 250.

1216. CS 19 Apr. 2018 (rol 12.221/2017), Ramón Domínguez Águila, 'Plazo de prescripción de la acción de responsabilidad extracontractual debe contarse desde el hecho dañoso y no desde la sentencia penal condenatoria', cit., at 147 et seq.

1217. Thus complicating the application of Art. 2332 CC in the area of state liability, this position is also confirmed by relying on Art. 40 Ley 19.966: CS 25 May 2017 (rol 25.427/2016).

1218. In favour of the literal interpretation: José Pablo Vergara Bezanilla, 'Aceptación jurisprudencial de la doctrina de que la prescripción extintiva de que la responsabilidad extracontractual empieza a correr desde la perpetración del acto ilícito y no a contar de la producción del daño', *Prescripción extintiva. Estudios sobre su procedencia y funcionamiento en Derecho Público y Privado, Cuadernos de Extensión Jurídica*, (Hernán Corral Talciani, ed.) (Santiago de Chile: Universidad de los Andes, 2011), at 25 et seq.

1219. Fabián Elorriaga de Bonis, 'Del día de inicio del plazo de prescripción de una acción indemnizatoria cuando el perjuicio se ha manifestado con posterioridad al hecho que lo origina', *Estudios de Derecho Civil III* (Alejandro Guzmán Brito ed.), (Santiago de Chile: Legal Publishing, 2008), at 771 et seq.; Corral, *Lecciones*, cit., at 401, Barros, *Tratado*, II, cit., at 1030–1033. The latter author, also taking the German order as a source of inspiration, proposes a maximum temporal application in all cases, considering that in any case it should meet the maximum limitation period provided by the code in cases of special prescriptions: that of ten years from the commission of the damage. This term, which is not applicable to moral damage, would be applied by the author to deferred damage. In the case of continuous damage, the term should be calculated from the end of the harmful event, which is also applicable in the case of connected events or an instantaneous event with damage prolonged in time. It is also considered that the aggravation of the initial damage is not a reason to start a new limitation period with respect to the initial one.

§2. Suspension of the Claim for Damages

358. The possibility to suspend the course of the statute of limitations for liability actions is debated in both the doctrine[1220] and the courts.

On the one hand, it has been argued that the suspension is inadmissible on the grounds that the limitation period set out in Article 2332 CC is a short prescription term,[1221] meaning that (unlike the general prescription period) it does not satisfy all the preconditions for admission and therefore cannot be applied.[1222]

On the other hand, there are those who argue that the rule prohibiting suspension refers to contractual liability and not to tort liability, which is not referenced by the relevant provision. In fact, Article 2524 CC refers to actions arising from deeds and contracts. Consequently, the statute of limitations could be interrupted[1223] in certain circumstances, making Article 2509 n. 1 and n. 2 CC applicable.[1224]

§3. Interruption of Damages Claims

359. The third paragraph of Article 2518 CC states that the statute of limitations is interrupted either civilly (i.e., by the recognition of an obligation) or upon the filing of a legal claim before the court, except in the cases of Article 2503 CC. As noted,[1225]

Article 2503 no. 1 CC does not require notification of the claim for interruption; rather, it only indicates that the claim must have been served to substantiate the interruption. However, based on the above-mentioned provision, it was traditionally considered as a matter of priority[1226] that the statute of limitations cannot be interrupted without the counter party being properly notified of the claim within the relevant term.

Be that as it may, following a 2016 decision,[1227] there has been a tendency to establish that the mere filing of a claim for damages with the court (and not its notification) is sufficient for the interruption of the statute of limitations. The Supreme

1220. By way of example, for the traditional doctrine, against the suspension of the prescriptive term and its inapplication in favour of the persons indicated in Art. 2509 CC: Alessandri, *Responsabilidad,* cit., at 381 in favour instead of Tapia, *De la responsabilidad*, cit., at 323.

1221. Art. 2523 and 2524 CC, on the point *see* Carlos Pizarro Wilson, 'Acerca de la suspensión del término de prescripción de la accion de demanda extracontractual', *Estudios de Derecho Civil XI,* (Departamento de Derecho Privado, Universidad de Concepción ed., Manuel Barría Paredes coord.) (Santiago de Chile: Thomson Reuters, 2015) at 913 et seq.

1222. CS 21 Jun. 2017 (rol 101.758/2016), CS 4 Apr. 2016 (rol 3952/2015CS 11 Jul. 2012 (rol 8879/2010), CS 7 Nov. 2001, *RDJ*, 98, s. 1ª, at 245, Barros, *Tratado*, II, cit., at 1036–1037; Tapia, *De la responsabilidad*, cit., at 322–323.

1223. Art. 2520, 2524, 2509 CC.

1224. CS 31 May 2012 /rol 4593/2009), CS 14 Jul. 2016 (rol 11085/2015); Barros, *Tratado*, II, cit., at 1037.

1225. Ramón Domínguez Águila, 'Sobre la interrupción civil de la prescripción extintiva … ', cit., at 245.

1226. The trend has essentially been constant, e.g., CS 10 Apr. 1929, *RDJ*, 1930/27, s. 1st, at 240; CS 8 Jun. 1945, *RDJ*, 1946, 46, s. 1st, at 18; CS 26 Nov. 1991, *RDJ*, 1991/88, s. 1st, at 102 contra CS 26 Dec. 1910, *RDJ*, 9, s. 1st, at 97.

1227. Route opened by CS 31 May 2016 (rol 6900/2015).

Court is divided on this point and there have been a series of contradictory decisions regarding whether interruption of the prescription period is achieved with the submission of a claim for damages[1228] or whether such claim must be served on the relevant parties.[1229]

This has generated an intense academic discussion,[1230] also animated by the court decision.[1231] It has been noted that part of the problem stems from the lack of coordination between civil and procedural law and the absence of a rule that prevents the prescription period from being indefinitely interrupted by the claimant who does not notify the counter party.[1232]

360. The debate appears to have been partially resolved – at least in relation to Article 2332 CC. Indeed, an authentic interpretation is provided by the legislator in law no. 21.226,[1233] which refers to the statute of limitations of legal proceedings, albeit in the context of COVID-19.

This law states that, for the duration of the state of emergency (....) and any extension periods, the statute of limitations for claims shall be understood to be interrupted by the mere filing of the claim, provided that the same is not declared inadmissible and is duly notified within fifty business days following the date on which the state of emergency has ceased to be in force, or within thirty business days from the date the claim was filed, whichever occurs last.[1234] Although applicable to a specific historical context, the legislator's message is clear in the sense of making notification necessary for the interruption of the statute of limitations.

1228. Follows 2016 e.g CS 16 Apr. 2019 (rol 10.170/2019, CS 4 Jul. 2018 (rol 43.350/2017); CS 7 Jun. 2017 (rol 7407/2016).
1229. For example, CS 9 Jul. 2019 (rol 28,280/2018); CS 29 Jan. 2019 (rol 24,854/2018), CS 30 Oct. 2018 (18,624/2018); CS 3 Aug. 2017 (rol 8147/2'17), CS 20 Feb. 2017 (rol 41.190/2017, CS 28 Dec. 2016 (rol 87.787/2016).
1230. Ramón Domínguez Águila, 'Sobre la interrupción civil de la prescripción extintiva. Basta la sola interposición de la demanda', *Revista de Derecho* (Universidad de Concepción), 2017/239, at 245 et seq.; Ruperto Pinochet Olave, 'La notificación de la demanda debe efectuarse dentro del plazo de prescripción para interrumpir civilmente la prescripción', *Estudios de Derecho Civil XII* (Hernán Corral Talciani, Pablo Manterola Domínguez ed.) (Santiago de Chile: Thomson Reuters, 2017), at 173 et seq.; Jaime Alcalde Silva, 'Sobre la eficacia procesal de la demanda que interrumpe la prescripción extintiva', *Estudios de Derecho Civil XII* (Hernán Corral Talciani, Pablo Manterola Domínguez ed.) (Santiago de Chile: Thomson Reuters, 2017), at 189 et seq.; Rodrigo Barcia Lehmann, '¿Desde cuándo se cuenta la interrupción de la prescripción', *Estudios de Derecho Civil XIV* – (Marícruz Gómez de Latorre Vargas, Gabriel Hernández Paulsen, Fabiola Lathrop Gómez, Mauricio Tapia Rodríguez ed.) (Santiago de Chile: Thomson Reuters, 2019), at 439 et seq.; Rodrigo Barría Díaz, 'Revisión crítica de la alteración convencional de los plazos de prescripción extintivas', *Estudios de Derecho Civil XIV* – (Marícruz Gómez de Latorre Vargas, Gabriel Hernández Paulsen, Fabiola Lathrop Gómez, Mauricio Tapia Rodríguez ed.) (Santiago de Chile: Thomson Reuters, 2019), at 451 et seq.
1231. Professor Pizarro drafted the judgment of 31 May 2016, cit., as integrating counsel in the Supreme Court, *see* Carlos Pizarro Wilson, 'La interrupción civil de la prescripción por la mere presentación de la demanda', *Estudios de Derecho Civil XII* (Hernán Corral Talciani, Pablo Manterola Domínguez ed.) (Santiago de Chile: Thomson Reuters, 2017), at 161 et seq.
1232. Barros, *Tratado,* II, cit., at 1035, on the point and with jurisprudential discussion at 1033–1036.
1233. Ley 21.226/2020, of 1 of Apr. (DO 2 Apr. 2020).
1234. Art. 8 Ley 21.226/2020, cit.

361. In criminal matters, the mere filing of a claim or the appearance as a civil party interrupts the statute of limitations. The same is true even when the relative civil action is brought before the civil judge within sixty days of the continuation or termination of the criminal proceedings. If, however, the civil claim is not presented within this term, the statute of limitations will continue as if it had not been interrupted.[1235]

362. It is also possible to exceptionally achieve interruption by submitting a claim before the *Juez de Policia Local.*[1236]

1235. Art. 61.3 and 68 CPP; Barros, *Tratado*, II, cit., at 1035–1036; Corral, *Lecciones,* cit., at 403–405.
1236. Art. 9.5 Ley 18.287 Corral, *Lecciones,* cit., at 404. The author states that this is a case of interruption although the literalness of the provision speaks of suspension.

Chapter 2. Grounds of Exemption

363. It has been said that, in general, the purpose of exemptions is to exclude the illicit nature[1237] (*ilicitud*) or unlawfulness (*antijuridicidad*) of the offence under the premise that the relationship between fault and unlawfulness is two-fold;[1238] what is certain is that they relate to the conduct of the subject under the assumption of a case of subjective responsibility. Accordingly, it is held that an exemption exists[1239] when the damage is caused by a fact that is not attributable to the agent's intent or fault. The exemption must be the sole and exclusive cause of the damage, the application of Article 2330 CC being possible if the victim recklessly exposed himself to the damage.[1240]

364. Part of the doctrine[1241] does not consider the causes of exemption to be applicable in the case of Articles 2321 and 2327 CC (i.e., when damage is caused by a minor as a result of repetitive misconduct due to bad manners or habits, and damage caused by an *animal fiero* on the grounds that, in these cases, there is a presumption of liability).

365. The exemptions from liability in civil law are not identical and do not necessarily coincide with those enshrined in criminal law. If the former are deduced from the general principles of law,[1242] the latter are typified by Article 10 CP;[1243] there are also exceptions such as state of necessity[1244] or self-defence.[1245] The burden of proof of grounds for exemption follows the general rule and falls on those who allege it.[1246]

1237. Corral, *Lecciones,* cit., at 121.

1238. Barros, *Tratado,* I, cit., at 138–139. Although also for this author guilt is related to illegitimacy: Barros, *Tratado,* I, cit., at 99.

1239. Así Alessandri, *Responsabilidad,* cit., at 433.

1240. Así Alessandri, *Responsabilidad,* cit., at 454, and at 449–450; also Corral, *Lecciones*, cit., at 127.

1241. Tapia, *De la responsabilidad*, cit., at 268; Alessandri, *Responsabilidad*, cit., at 454.

1242. Alessandri, *Responsabilidad*, cit., at 433; Tapia, *De la responsabilidad*, cit., at 250; Barros, *Tratado*, I, cit., at 141.

1243. On the non-application of the exemptions and aggravating circumstances of Art. 11 and 12 CP: Abeliuk, *Las Obligaciones*, *I*, at 238.

1244. For example, *see* Javier Wilenmann Von Bernath, 'El fundamento del estado de necesidad justificante en el derecho penal chileno. Al mismo tiempo, introducción al problema de la dogmática del estado de necesidad en Chile', *Revista de derecho* (Valdivia), 2014/1, at 213 et seq.; Juan Pablo Castillo Morales, 'El estado de necesidad del artículo 10 n° 11 del Código penal chileno: ¿Una norma bifronte? Elementos para una respuesta negativa', *Politica Criminal*, 2016/22, at 349 et seq.; Juan Pablo Mañalich Raffo, 'El estado de necesidad exculpante. Una propuesta de interpretación del artículo 10 n° 11 del Código penal chileno', *Humanizar y renovar el Derecho penal. Estudios en memoria de Enrique Cury* (Alex Van Weezel (ed.) (Santiago de Chile: Legal Publishing, 2013), at 715 et seq.

1245. *See e.g.*, Patricia Tapia Ballestreros, 'Legítima defensa. Requisitos y aplicabilidad en supuestos de violencia de género', *Revista Doctrina y Jurisprudencia penal. Legítima defensa. Límites sustanciales y procedimentales*, 2014/14, at 37 et seq.

1246. Applying the general rule of Art. 1698 CC, Tapia, *De la responsabilidad*, cit., at 268; Alessandri, *Responsabilidad*, cit., at 455, Barros, *Tratado*, I, cit., at 140; Corral, *Lecciones*, cit., at 131.

§1. CONSENT

366. Consent of the injured party exempts the other party from liability, although the application in tortious liability is limited. However, since consent can be given by a unilateral act,[1247] not only can it be associated with contractual covenants or agreements, it also applies to tort liability.

367. This aspect is interpreted and associated with a form of acceptance of the risk.[1248] Thanks to the brocardo *volenti non fit injuria*, it is sometimes accepted that the aggrieved party's consent or acceptance of the risk exonerates the damaging party from liability in the absence of its wilful misconduct.[1249]

368. Of particular importance are the hybrid situations where both contractual and tort liability can arise, such as in the case of medical liability. In such circumstances, the question arises as to the efficacy of a freely given informed consent[1250] in the case of medical services, insofar as the requirements for attributing both contractual and tort liability are met.

If consent to performance is associated with the acceptance of risk, the grounds for justification could also be extended to the case of performance by a third party. However, in such cases, it is necessary to take particular care to ensure that consent is not only freely given, but that the patient is adequately informed of the possible and effective risks involved. Thus, in this last case, the abusiveness of any clauses signed and the duties of the parties to inform and be informed play an important role.

§2. NECESSITY

369. It is necessary to assess whether compensation should be paid for damage caused in a state of necessity (i.e., to avoid a threat to oneself or a third party).[1251] In civil law, liability is exempted[1252] if one has acted to avoid a harm that is imminent and there is no other viable solution or lesser harm. For this reason, the exemption provided for in criminal law is not necessarily applicable in civil law,[1253] leading to its more limited application.

1247. Barros, *Tratado*, I, cit., at 143.
1248. Alessandri, *Responsabilidad,* cit., at 449–450; Corral, *Lecciones,* cit., at 127.
1249. Barros, *Tratado*, I, cit., at 143 and 463 et seq.; Cf. Corral, *Lecciones,* cit., at 127–128.
1250. On the point from a contractual perspective: Gabriel Hernández Paulsen & Felipe Chahuán Zedan, 'Consentimiento informado en las prestaciones de salud', *Acta Bioethica*, 2021/1, at 22 et seq., more generally Iñigo de la Maza Gazmuri, 'Consentimiento informado, una visión panorámica', *Ius et Praxis*, 2010/2, at 89 et seq.; Rodolfo Figueroa García Huidobro, 'Consentimiento informado en la nueva ley de derechos de los pacientes', *Revista Médica de Chile*, 2012/2010, at 1347 et seq.; Carlos Pizarro Wilson, 'En oposición al consentimiento hipotético infomado', *Revista de Derecho* (PUCV), 2015/44, at 97 et seq.
1251. Abeliuk, *Las Obligaciones*, *I*, at 236.
1252. Tapia, *De la responsabilidad*, cit., at 264; Corral, *Lecciones,* cit., at 122; Alessandri, *Responsabilidad*, cit., at 442.
1253. Con particiolare rifermiento alle causali del n. 11 del art. 10 CP; Corral, *Lecciones,* cit., at 123.

If applied, the injured party (who is nevertheless entitled to restitutionary protection for any unjustified enrichment[1254]) must bear the lesser harm according to a proportional weighing[1255] of the damages caused and those prevented.

However, the exemption will never apply if the offence results from culpable conduct,[1256] and does not apply in cases of personal injury since 'there is nothing more valuable than human life'.[1257]

§3. Self-Help and Self-Service

370. Unlike the state of necessity, self-defence in civil matters operates in the same way as in criminal[1258] matters. However, this does not mean that an acquittal in criminal matters automatically entails exoneration in civil matters.[1259]

In determining whether to apply this exemption in civil matters, the requirements established in criminal matters are applied (such as the existence of an unlawful aggression or the lack of provocation of such conduct), replacing the 'rationality of the means employed'[1260] – which is required in criminal law – with the (de)proportionality of the response.[1261] However, if there is no rationality (or proportionality) and therefore it is not possible to apply the exemption in its entirety, a reduction in damages may still be applied if the victim has recklessly exposed himself to harm as per Article 2330 CC.[1262] This[1263] applies to both personal injury and property damage.

§4. Others

I. Irresistible Force or Insuperable Fear

371. Article 10 n. 9 CP establishes an exemption from criminal responsibility if the crime is prompted by irresistible force or insuperable fear. Part of the doctrine considers this exemption applicable also in the civil sphere, provided it is proved that an ordinary person would have done the same thing.[1264] For others, this would not constitute grounds for the exclusion of the illegitimacy of the fact; rather, it

1254. Corral, *Lecciones,* cit., at 122; Barros, *Tratado,* I, cit., at 146.
1255. Alessandri, *Responsabilidad,* cit., at 443; Barros, *Tratado,* I, cit., at 145.
1256. Tapia, *De la responsabilidad*, cit., at 268; Alessandri, *Responsabilidad*, cit., at 443.
1257. In this sense Tapia, *De la responsabilidad*, cit., at 265; similarly Alessandri, *Responsabilidad*, cit., at 443.
1258. Barros, *Tratado,* I, cit., at 146.
1259. *See* Art. 179.2 CCP.
1260. *See* Art. 10 no. 4 CP.
1261. Corral, *Lecciones,* cit., at 122; Abeliuk, *Las Obligaciones, I*, at 236; Tapia, *De la responsabilidad*, cit., at 267.
1262. CS 8 Apr. 1982, *RDJ*, 1982/79, s. 4ª, at 22; Corral, *Lecciones,* cit., at 122; Tapia, *De la responsabilidad*, cit., at 268.
1263. Tapia, *De la responsabilidad*, cit., at 267; Alessandri, *Responsabilidad*, cit., at 440; Barros, *Tratado*, I, cit., at 146, Corral, *Lecciones*, cit., at 122.
1264. Alessandri, *Responsabilidad,* cit., at 439–440.

could relate to the will or intent to commit the fact, since in such cases the volition would be clearly 'reduced or even completely non-existent'.[1265]

The same applies if the damage is caused under duress by physical or moral violence,[1266] unless the act is committed under the advice or insistence of others.[1267]

II. Error

372. Damage committed in error produces liability, although part of the doctrine[1268] holds that liability could be exempted if it is shown to be excusable in the sense that a person in the same circumstances would have committed the same error.

III. Activity Proceeding from Legal Order or Legitimate Authority

373. Some conventional scholarship has also argued that another cause of exoneration is when a legal order is being carried out or comes from a legitimate authority,[1269] certainly in the case of proceeding from a public authority,[1270] but not in the case of damage caused despite an administrative authorization.[1271]

374. The most recent doctrine, also bearing in mind that in this case the exemption is in line with Article 10 no. 10 CP,[1272] tends to agree as far as acts authorized by the law are concerned (although within the limits of the exercise of rights).[1273] However, some doubts have arisen, especially when a manifestly unlawful order is received.[1274]

IV. Breaking Off of an Engagement

375. There is also no liability for breach of betrothal/engagement (*esponsales*) in the event of a repentance of marriage. This is supported by doctrine,[1275] both from a contractual and tort perspective, on the basis of Article 98.2 CC.

1265. Corral, *Lecciones,* cit., at 124.
1266. Tapia, *De la responsabilidad*, cit., at 261.
1267. Alessandri, *Responsabilidad,* cit., at 440.
1268. Alessandri, *Responsabilidad,* cit., at 453; followed by Corral, *Lecciones,* cit., at 124.
1269. Tapia, *De la responsabilidad*, cit., at 262.
1270. This would tend not to be the case in the case of private authority: Alessandri, *Responsabilidad,* cit., at 438–439.
1271. Alessandri, *Responsabilidad,* cit., at 453.
1272. Corral, *Lecciones,* cit., at 124.
1273. Thus, a policeman can in certain cases deprive a person of liberty or in accordance with the law produce a seizure: Barros, *Tratado,* II, cit., at 141–142.
1274. Thus Barros, *Tratado*, II, cit., at 142–143.
1275. Corral, *Lecciones,* cit., at 125–126.

Chapter 3. Contributory Fault

§1. Overview

376. It has been explained that the Chilean legal system essentially provides for a system of subjective liability (and, consequently, liability linked to the conduct of the damaging party) and, as a result, the fault or malice of the parties involved plays a key role, whereby an event (linked to the negligent conduct) results in damage and there is a causal relationship between them.

In this sense, contributory fault is associated with Article 2330 CC, which refers to the imprudent exposure of the victim to the damage, despite being sometimes termed by the doctrine as *culpa concurrente*.

According to this scheme, whether malice or negligence exists may help establish liability or allow it to be imputed.

Traditionally, the (exclusive) fault of the victim or the fact of the third party,[1276] together with force majeure, are considered conditions for exemption from liability of others to sever the causal link.

However, it is necessary to highlight the nuance between the 'fact' committed by the victim and the third party from any 'fault' of these parties.

This nuance not only helps to better understand the exoneration of liability as a result of the fact of the victim or third party in cases of strict liability, but also allows a better understanding of a problem that Chilean doctrine has posed in analysing the aggrieved party's conduct within the causal event (and therefore the liability that may derive from it). This problem also arises because there is no criterion for distribution among the parties liable according to the interests at stake,[1277] unlike in contractual matters (Article 1522 CC).

377. Thus, the actions of the injured party, the third party or force majeure/unforeseeable circumstances are traditionally considered causal factors which exonerate liability by severing the causal link between the event and the damage.

The situation is partly complicated by the presence of Article 2330 CC, which deals with contributory fault and states that 'the assessment of the damage is subject to reduction if who suffered it recklessly exposed himself to it'.

Although the black letter of this provision affects the quantification/extent of the damage, the doctrine has questioned whether the reduction in compensation should be related to the causal connection or, instead, should be associated with the culpable conduct of the party (and therefore relating it to the event).

This possible alternative interpretation has considerable practical aspects insofar as it could potentially lead to different results. Specifically, if it is considered that the victim's conduct operates in the causal relationship, it could lead to the total

1276. *See* paras 407 et seq.

1277. Barros, *Tratado,* II, cit., at 446. For a comparative view and a partial review of Art. 1522 Hernán Corral Talciani, 'Nueva tendencias en la comprensión y funcionamiento de la obligación solidaria. Un análisis desde los intrumentos de armonización del derecho de contratos y su posible recepción en le derecho civil chileno', *Revista Chilena de Derecho*, 2018/31, at 155 et seq., especially at 182.

exclusion of liability (it would operate from the perspective of the *an)*. Conversely, if it is considered that it has bearing on the event, it might be held that the victim's conduct has contributed, through his own fault, to the damage and there would be an interpretative problem of assessing the extent or proportion to which the conduct or the contributory factors relating to the parties involved have had an effect. Consequently, if the damage is due to a single cause, Article 2330 CC would not be applicable.[1278]

378. A further premise should be made. The assessment of the injured party's culpable conduct or concurrent fault is different from the joint and several liability envisaged by Article 2317 CC.

This last rule establishes the joint and several liability (except for Articles 2323 and 2328 CC and the other hypotheses discussed earlier) of those who have participated in the same unlawful act, which is different from the causal intervention of multiple negligence.[1279]

In the case analysed here, several behaviours may intervene to generate (possible) independent faults that could have produced the damage.

This also differs from obligationes *in solidum* for which, although there is no joint and several liability, certain persons are obliged to indemnify the totality of the amounts.[1280]

The hypothesis analysed here is also different from cases of alternative causation: that is, when two or more simultaneous events occur and each of them is sufficient to produce the damage.[1281]

379. The fact or the exclusive fault of the injured party or of the third party in terms of absolute exoneration of liability will be dealt with in the section on the causal link.[1282] In this sense, the injured party's fault has a double effect: it alters or exonerates[1283] the liability of the party who is deemed to have caused the damage. For this reason, it is important to distinguish *culpa exclusiva* ('exclusive fault') of the victim from *culpa concurrente* ('concurring fault').[1284]

1278. It would only be the if there are (at least) two causes: Ramón Domínguez Águila, 'El hecho de la víctima como causal de exoneración de responsabilidad civil', *Revista de Derecho* (Universidad de Concepción), 1966/136, at 42 et seq.

1279. Clear in this distinction is Barros, *Tratado,* II, cit., at 443.

1280. *See e.g.*, Kuncar Onero, 'Responsabilidad solidaria versus responsabilidad concurrente', cit., at 779 et seq.

1281. Here the problem would be more associated with the theory of *conditio sin qua non*: *see* Barros, *Tratado,* II, cit., at 444–445.

1282. *See* paras 407 et seq.

1283. Abeliuk, *Las Obligaciones*, *I*, at 235, also Jorge Baraona González, 'La culpa de la víctima en los accidentes del trabajo: dogmática y jurisprudencia chilenas', *Responsabilidad civil del empresario por accidentesdel trabajo y enfermedadesprofesionales*, (Sara Rodríguez Pinto, Francisca Barrientos Camus ed.) *Cuadernos de Extensión Jurídica*, 2011/20, at 137.

1284. Lilian San Martín Neira, 'La frontera entre culpa exclusiva y concurrente de la víctima en la producción del daño a la luz de la jurisprudencia chilena', *Revista chilena de derecho privado*, 2016/27, at 9 et seq.; Lilian San Martín Neira, 'La culpa de la victima en la estructura de la responsabilidad civil extracontractual', *Estudios de Derecho Civil XI* (Departamento de Derecho privado de Concepción ed., Manuel Barría Paredes, coord.) (Santiago de Chile: Thomson Reuters, 2016), at 922 et seq. and 939.

§2. Specific and Problematic Aspects

380. Following these important premises, it is necessary to evaluate at this point how the Chilean legal system,[1285] and in particular Article 2330 CC, treats cases in which the injured party has played a role in causing the damage suffered, triggering a reduction that originates from Roman law.[1286]

In relation to contributory fault,[1287] the doctrine has taken two positions.[1288] On the one hand, it has framed the problem as relating to fault.[1289] On the other, the doctrine has associated it with causation.[1290] In this latter case, the general rule applies and the imprudent exposure to harm must be proven for there to be *culpa concurente* (Article 1698 CC),[1291] provided that it is possible to apply certain presumptions.[1292]

381. Since compensation is reduced in the case of concurrent fault, it is considered[1293] that Article 2330 does not apply in the case of fraudulent intent by one of the parties, as this would exclude the possibility of concurrent fault. Nevertheless, since in Chilean law *culpa grave* is expressly equated with wilful misconduct (Article 44 CC), the question arises as to whether it is possible to offset *culpa leve* and *culpa lata.*[1294]

If, on the contrary, one wished to eliminate the reference to 'exclusive fault', in this sense it would be the 'hecho de la víctima' that refers to the cause of total exoneration: Domínguez Águila, 'El hecho de la víctima como causal ...', cit., at 30–31.

1285. For a comparative view *see* Lilian San Martín Niera, *La carga del perjudicado de evitar o mitigar el daño: estudio histórico-comparado* (Bogotà: Universidad Externado, 2012); Carmen Domínguez Hidalgo, 'El Deber de minimizar los daños de la víctima o del acreedor. Análisis comparado', *El Principio de Reparación Integral en sus Contornos Actuales. Una Revisión desde el derecho Chileno, Latinoamericano y Europeo* (Carmen Domínguez Hidalgo, ed.) (Santiago de Chile: Thomson Reuters, 2019), at 273 et seq.

1286. For a reconstruction in this sense vid. Lilian San Martín Neira, 'La reducción del resarcimiento por culpa de la víctima: reflexiones a la luz del análisis de algunas fuentes romanas', *Revista de Derecho Privado* (*Universidad Externado de Colombia*), 2014/27, at 35 et seq.

1287. For a systematic reconstruction of the various traditional positions, *see* Cristian Aedo Barrena, 'El tratamiento dogmático de la culpa de la víctima en la responsabilidad civil: un enfoque desde la imputación objetiva', *Estudios de Derecho Civil VIII* (Carmén Domínguez Hidalgo, Joel González, Javier Barrientos, Juan Luis Goldemberg, ed.) (Santiago de Chile: Thomson Reuters, 2012), at 505 et seq.

1288. On a jurisprudential study of the positions. *See* San Martín Neira, 'La frontera...', cit., at 26 et seq.

1289. *See* Lilian San Martín Neira, 'La frontera entre culpa exclusiva y concurrente de la víctima en la producción del daño a la luz de la jurisprudencia chilena', *Revista chilena de derecho privado*, 2016/27, at 21 et seq.

1290. Claudia Bahamondes Oyarzún, Carlos Pizarro Wilson, 'La exposición de la víctima al daño: desde la culpabilidad a la causalidad', *Revista de Derecho* (PUCV), 2012/39, at 39 et seq.

1291. Diez Schwerter, *El daño extracontractual,* cit., at 233–234.

1292. Barros, *Tratado*, I, cit., at 456–457.

1293. Barros, *Tratado*, I, cit., at 460; confirmed and expanded by San Martín Neira, 'La frontera entre culpa exclusiva y concurrente de la víctima en la producción del daño a la luz de la jurisprudencia chilena', *Revista chilena de derecho privado*, 2016/27, at 33 et seq.

1294. San Martín Neira, 'La frontera...', cit., at 37.

382. The main practical problems that may arise relate to the extent by which the compensation should be reduced and the applicable criterion (which is not established by the rule), and the reductions applicable in cases of incapacitated persons, heirs and victims of consequential damage (*daño por rebote o repercusión*),[1295] highlighting a heterogeneous application of criteria even in the case law.[1296]

383. As far as the calculation criterion is concerned, it is unclear as to how the reduction of Article 2330 CC should operate,[1297] revealing an argumentative shortfall[1298] in the judgment that applies the reduction. Indeed, the application of the reduction is sometimes based on causation or on the possible graduation or gravity of the fault, 'attributing such gravity in proportion to the gravity of the behaviour,[1299] or oscillating in the division into equal shares or through equitable or proportional shares'.[1300]

384. In relation to the determination of the *quantum* (amount) to be reduced in cases of subjective liability, there are different doctrinal positions. Indeed, it has been argued (by those who associate Article 2330 CC not with causation but with damage) that the reduction criterion should be calculated according to the gravity of the fault. This argument is based on the idea that the greater the gravity of the *culpa* the greater the damage, and where this is not possible the judge should reduce the compensation by half or apply an equitable criterion.[1301]

Alternately, the division of the compensation in two parts is criticized by those who associate the rule with causation, thus avoiding the theory of equivalence of conditions (which would lead to such a solution) and going so far as to argue that it is necessary to refer to the theory of adequate causation and to flexible parameters linked to predictability and reasonableness.[1302]

1295. For example, *see* Fabian Elorriaga De Bonis, 'El daño por repercusión o rebote', *Revista Chilena de Derecho*, 1999/2 at 390 et seq.; Verónica Wegner Astudillo., '¿Es verdaderamente la acción de la víctima por repercusión o rebote una acción autónoma e independiente?', *Estudios de derecho civil IX* (Susan Turner Saelzer, Susan & Juan Andrés Varas Braun, ed) (Santiago de Chile: Legal Publishing- Thomson Reuters, 2014), at 743 et seq.

1296. On the jurisprudential analysis *see* San Martín Neira, 'La frontera...', cit., at 9 et seq.; Lilian San Martín Neira, 'Culpa concurrente de la víctima y daño por rebote o repercusión, *Revista de Derecho* (PUCV), 2016/ XLVII, at 151 et seq.; also Diez Schwerter, *El daño extracontractual,* cit., at 225 et seq.

1297. Diez Schwerter, *El daño extracontractual,* cit., at 225 et seq., and277.

1298. *See* David Quintero Fuentes, 'El efecto reductor del hecho concurrente de la víctima en la determinación del monto indemnizatorio', *Estudios de Derecho Civil XII* (Hernán Corral Talciani, Pablo Manterola Domínguez ed.) (Santiago de Chile: Thomson Reuters, 2017), at 517 et seq.

1299. Bahamondes Oyarzún & Pizarro Wilson, 'La exposición de la víctima al daño ...', cit., at 44 et seq.

1300. *See* David Quintero Fuentes, 'El efecto reductor del hecho...', cit., at 519 et seq.

1301. This is the position of Lilian San Martín Neira, 'El quantum indemnizatorio en caso de culpa concurrente de la víctima. Su posible revisión via casación, *Revista de Derecho* (Concepción), 2016/ 240, at 68.

1302. Bahamondes Oyarzún & Pizarro Wilson, 'La exposición de la víctima al daño ...', cit., at 46.

In the case of strict liability, the causation and damage theories coincide and support the need to identify the criteria of objective imputation for calculation purposes, when one cannot refer to fault and conduct.[1303]

385. The fact that the extent of damages tends not to be reviewable in cassation[1304] did not prevent such a review from being proposed in relation to the reduction of the *quantum* relating to Article 2330 CC.

Therefore, those who associate the rule with the damage[1305] have argued that in the case of the reduction of the amount of compensation under Article 2330 CC, the determination of the amount of compensation is a matter of law and hence reviewable in Cassation. This is based on the consideration that the reduction of damages, which must be justified by the judge.[1306] Accordingly, the judge must first determine the damage and then apply the reduction in proportion to the assumption of the victim's contribution to the damage. The review in cassation is also supported by those who associate Article 2330 to problems of randomness, based on the observation that the problem is not factual but normative, since it affects the causation.[1307]

386. With respect to the application of the reduction in the case of an incapacitated person, there are various positions.

Some scholars[1308] argue that the reduction should not operate based on the observation that, in the traditional system of subjective liability, there is a close relationship between fault and causation whereby 'he who is at fault is considered to be the cause of the damage'.[1309] This would lead to the assertion that the reduction could not be made in the absence of fault, and therefore Article 2330 CC is inapplicable whenever the person who causes the damage is an incapable person, given that incapable people cannot be at fault.[1310]

A different solution is to allow the reduction in the case of an incapacitated person, based on another finding and giving relevance to causation. Thus, although it

1303. This is the position of Lilian San Martín Neira, 'El quantum indemnizatorio...', cit., at 68; Bahamondes Oyarzún & Pizarro Wilson, 'La exposición de la víctima al daño ...', cit., at 46.
1304. Ramos, *De la responsabilidad Civil*, cit. at 93. In the same sense e.g., also with jurisprudential references: Pino Emhart, 'La situación económica de las partes...', cit., at 499; Corral, *Lecciones*, cit., at 161.
1305. Lilian San Martín Neira, 'El quantum indemnizatorio en caso de culpa concurrente de la víctima. Su posible revisión via casación, *Revista de Derecho Privado* (Concepción), 2016/240, at 41 et seq.
1306. Under Art. 170(4) of the CPC.
1307. Bahamondes Oyarzún & Pizarro Wilson, 'La exposición de la víctima al daño ...', cit., at 46.
1308. *See* Veronika Wegner Astudillo, '¿Es verdaderamente la acción de la víctima por repercusión o rebote una acción autónoma o independiente?', *Estudios de derecho civil IX* (Juan Andrés Varas Braun, Susan Turner Saelzer ed.) (Santiago de Chile: Thomson Reuters, Legal Publishing, 2014) at 752; Lilian San Martín Neira, *La culpa de la víctima en la responsabilidad civil* (Santiago de Chile: Der, 2018), *passim*. The monograph essentially reworks and systematizes the author's own writings cited here.
1309. San Martín Neira, 'La culpa de la victima en la estructura ...', cit., at 940.
1310. *Ibid.*, pú ampliamente *see* Lilian San Martín Neira, 'La imputabilidad o capacidad como elemento de la responsabilidad extracontractual. Un Debate pendiente', *Ius et Praxis*, 2018/1, at 554 et seq.

is agreed that Article 2330 CC does not apply in the case of an incapacitated person,[1311] this does not prevent a reduction being made under Article 2314 CC. According to this second interpretation, the reduction can be applied whenever the intervention of the (incapable) actor is involved in the cause of the damage, with causation[1312] playing a key role.

In this case, since the incapacitated person affects the causal relationship in the creation of the damage, the other person 'is liable only for his share according to the parameters of causation'.[1313]

387. According to these positions, the concurrent fault is, on the one hand, associated with negligence (albeit in its close interrelation with causation), leading to a more favourable interpretation for the incapable person since the reduction of compensation is inapplicable. On the other, the causal nature and the general application of Article 2314 are invoked with the aim of applying the law more strictly in these cases and allowing for a possible reduction.

388. In relation to the heirs, it is held that the reduction applies if the damages are claimed *iure hereditatis,*[1314] whereas the position is more open where the heirs claim damages *iure proprio.*[1315]

389. The application in cases involving incapacitated persons requires further discussion since these individuals are required to have someone look after them. It is therefore discussed whether the reduction pursuant to Article 2330 CC can also be applied to the secondary victims, such as those people charged with the care (have the *cuidado*) of the primary, incapacitated victim.

Consider, for example, a parent of a (incapacitated) minor who has suffered an injury. Here, too, a distinction must essentially be made as to whether the claim operates in relation to compensation in favour of the parent or the incapacitated minor.

Hence, for the proponents of the view[1316] that associates contributory fault with conduct, it is possible to apply the reduction of compensation when the incapable person has acted culpably while under the supervision of the guardians: this is the case if they claim compensation *iure proprio*, while, on the contrary, the reduction could not be applied to claims *iure hereditatis* of the supervised incapable person.

1311. Bahamondes Oyarzún & Pizarro Wilson, 'La exposición de la víctima al daño ...', cit., at 48.
1312. *Ibid.*, at 40.
1313. *Ibid.*, at 50.
1314. Diez Schwerter, *El daño extracontractual,* cit., at 236 et seq.; Bahamondes Oyarzún & Pizarro Wilson, 'La exposición de la víctima al daño ...', cit., at 49; Barros, *Tratado, I*, cit., at 461.
1315. Diez Schwerter, *El daño extracontractual,* cit., at 236 et seq., Bahamondes Oyarzún & Pizarro Wilson, 'La exposición de la víctima al daño ...', cit., at 49–50.
1316. San Martín Neira, 'Culpa concurrente de la víctima y daño por rebote o repercusión' cit. at 163 & 170–171.

This position is substantially supported by that part of the doctrine[1317] which does not follow the rules of fault but of causation. This means that 'not having exercised the care that was required of them, they cannot receive the full compensation'.[1318]

The situation is more complicated, however, when the supervisory activity is carried out with regard to a minor capable of discernment. In this situation, the doctrine that frames the problem of Article 2330 CC from the perspective of the causal nexus excludes[1319] the possibility of reduction due to the fault of the supervising adult ('guardian'), since the relevant fault is that of the minor. However, it does support the reduction if the supervisor's conduct is involved in the causal link.

390. If, in contrast, the person is killed instead of injured, thereby creating a situation where the person is both a secondary victim and an heir, the doctrine clarifies that the full extent of damages is not recoverable if the injurer's estate has been accepted.[1320]

391. It is held[1321] that an act of valour does not constitute an imprudent act or imprudent exposure to harm (Article 2330 CC), and therefore the reduced compensation amounts are not applicable where a person deliberately takes a risk for the sake of saving another person's property or physical integrity, unless such activity was unnecessary or obviously performed carelessly (*torpe*).

392. It has also been argued that Article 2330 CC is applicable to contractual matters, and in particular to accidents at work (under labour law) or generally to integrate a duty of protection and any damage relating to non-performance.[1322]

1317. Bahamondes Oyarzún & Pizarro Wilson, 'La exposición de la víctima al daño ...', cit., at 48.
1318. *Ibid.*
1319. *Ibid.*
1320. *Ibid.*
1321. Alessandri, *Responsabilidad,* cit., at 452.
1322. This is the position of Lilian San Martín Neira, 'Deberes de Proteción y culpa de la víctima: reducción de la indemnización por exposición imprudente al daño en la responsabilidad contractual', *Estudios de Derecho Civil XII* (Hernán Corral Talciani, Pablo Manterola Domínguez ed.) (Santiago de Chile: Thomson Reuters, 2017), at 527 et seq. *See also* Jorge Baraona González, 'La culpa de la víctima en los accidentes del trabajo: dogmática y jurisprudencia chilenas', *Responsabilidad civil del empresario por accidentesdel trabajo y enfermedadesprofesionales*, (Sara Rodríguez Pinto, Francisca Barrientos Camus ed.) *Cuadernos de Extensión Jurídica*, 2011/20, at 147 et seq.; Jorge Baraona González, 'La culpa de la víctima en los accidentes del trabajo: dogmática y jurisprudencia chilenas, *La responsabilidad por accidentes del trabajo* (Jorge Baraona y Pedro Zelaya Etchegaray ed.). *Cuadernos de Extensión Jurídica*, 2005/10, at 123 et seq.

Chapter 4. Exemption Clauses

393. It should be noted that it is possible[1323] to contractually exclude[1324] tort liability except in cases of fraud or gross negligence, or when the tort involves personal injury or damage to non-tangible property.[1325] Therefore, in general, such exclusions are only allowed for material damage committed in the absence of fault or intent.[1326] Accordingly, if an agreement contains exclusions of liability which should be null and void[1327] (such as the clause which excludes liability for both material damage and bodily harm), the solution should be partial nullity[1328] and the rest of the agreement should be deemed valid.

394. One part of the doctrine[1329] believes that covenants to exclude a duty of *cuidado* are admissible since such a covenant would not exclude liability; rather, a greater risk is assumed.

It is not an agreement by which a limit is set on the amount of compensation once the damage has been done, but a waiver by the victim or a settlement.[1330]

1323. For example, as in a case of a sporting event or car race Abeliuk, *Las Obligaciones*, *I*, at 239.

1324. For an overview also in relation to contractual liability: Joel González Castillo, 'Las cláusulas limitativas, agravantes o exonerativas de responsabilidad en materia contractual. Validez y límites', *Estudios de Derecho Civil VI – Jornadas Nacionales de Derecho Civil, Olmué 2010* (Gonzalo Figueroa Yañez; Enrique Barros Bourie, Mauricio Tapia Rodríguez ed.) (Santiago de Chile: Abeledo Perrot, Legal Publishing, 2010) at 543 et seq.; Carlos Pizarro Wilson, 'El control de las cláusulas exclusivas y limitativas de responsabilidad. Algunas pistas para su régimen legal, *Estudios de Derecho Civil VI – Jornadas Nacionales de Derecho Civil, Olmué 2010* (Gonzalo Figueroa Yañez; Enrique Barros Bourie, Mauricio Tapia Rodríguez ed.) (Santiago de Chile: Abeledo Perrot, Legal Publishing, 2010), at 557 et seq.; Sebastián Ríos Labbé, 'Cláusulas limitativas y exonerativas de responsabilidad. Un balance', *Estudios de derecho civil en homenaje a Gonzalo Figueroa Yáñez* (en Mauricio Tapia Rodríguez, María Paz Gatica Rodríguez, Javiera Verdugo Toro (coord.) (Santiago de Chile: Thomson Reuters-La Ley, 2014), at 530 et seq.

1325. Abeliuk, *Las Obligaciones*, *I*, at 240, Corral, *Lecciones*, cit., at 127.

1326. Alessandri, *Responsabilidad*, cit., at 464.

1327. It is established that those which exclude fraud and serious negligence, personal injury and express legal prohibitions would be null and void for illicit object (Art. 1682 CC): Alessandri, *Responsabilidad*, cit., at 462–463. More extensively Barros, *Tratado*, II, cit., at 1196 et seq.

1328. In this sense Barros, *Tratado*, II, cit., at 1207.

1329. Barros, *Tratado*, II, cit., at 1201–1202. This doctrine also considers as admissible covenants by which the damage is conventionally accepted, such as that whereby it is agreed that the neighbour makes disturbing noises for a certain period Barros, *Tratado*, II, cit., at 1202; Barros, *Tratado*, I, cit., at 466.

1330. Alessandri, *Responsabilidad*, cit., at 457–458. We could also admit clauses of attenuated responsibility, that is where a limit of compensation is established in case of possible damage, but here we would enter the field of contractual responsibility: Alessandri, *Responsabilidad*, cit., at 466; Barros, *Tratado*, II, cit., at 1202 et seq.

395. Scholar considers that in B2C contract, the clauses that reverse the burden of proof to the detriment of the consumer will be void.[1331]

1331. Thus it could not be established a clause that the consumer must prove the fault in the case of Art. 46 LPC since this establishes a presumption of fault: Hernán Corral Talciani, 'Clausula de exención, limitación y agravación de responsabilidad civil', *Estudios de derecho civil VI*, (Gonzalo Figueroa Yañez, Enrique Barros Bourie, Mauricio Tapia Rodríguez ed.) (Santiago de Chile: Abeledo Perrot, Legal Publishing, 2011) at 674–675. On limitative covenants and agreements in consumer contracts *see also* Claudia Bahamondes Oyarzún & Leonor Etcheberry Court, 'Cláusulas limitativas y exonerativas de responsabilidad en la compraventa y en el derecho común y de consumo', *La compraventa: Estudios* (Juan Ignacio Contardo González & Íñigo de la Maza Gazmuri, dir.), (Santiago de Chile: Thomson Reuters, 2017), at 503 et seq.

Part V. Causation

Chapter 1. Introduction

396. Some features of the joint and several liability, the scope of Article 2317 CC – which application must be limited[1332] – and its difference with the joint and several liability (aspects which also cover the necessary correlation between civil and procedural law[1333]) have already been discussed,[1334] as well as the possibility for several persons (including the injured party himself) to be liable, based on the causal link, in certain cases.[1335]

397. In this section, the main theories of causation recognized by the doctrine and their practical application in the case law will be briefly analysed, followed by a discussion of the main causes of exoneration of civil liability on the basis of an interpretive construction of the causal link, and in particular through the introduction of a 'strange cause' (*causa extraña*) which generates a mediated causal relationship[1336] between the event and the damage.

398. The causal link between the event and the damage can be deduced from the Civil Code itself. Thus, the doctrine observes how Article 2314 CC uses the expression *inferir* the damage (*ha inferido un daño al otro*, has caused damage to other), whereas Article 2316 CC refers to '*el que hizo el daño...*' ('whoever did the damage') to then consider, in Article 2329 CC that 'por regla general todo daño que pueda imputarse a malicia o negligencia de otra persona (As a general rule, any damage that can be attributed to malice or negligence of another person must be repaired)'.[1337]

1332. Ramos, *De la responsabilidad Civil*, cit., at 120.
1333. *See* Alejandro Romero Segue, 'La Obligación Solidaria pasiva Y Debido Proceso', *Revista Chilena de Derecho*, 1/2019, at 99 et seq.; questúltimo and several of the works cited in the previous apartati are brought together in the work: Hernán Corral Talciani, Alejandro Romero Seguel, *Solidaridad Obligacional. Diez estudios sobre sus aspectos civiles y procesales*, (Valencia: Tirant Lo Blanch, 2019).
1334. *See e.g.*, paras 79, 82, 107, 177, 207, 224, 259, 260, 282, 286, 287, 378.
1335. *See* paras 376 et seq.
1336. Alessandri, *Responsabilidad*, cit., at 180. Another part of the doctrine refers to an exclusion of the culpability of the subject in cases where the behaviour of the victim is the exclusive cause of the damage: Domínguez Águila, 'El hecho de la víctima como causal ...', cit., at 31.
1337. Tapia, *De la Responsabilidad*, cit., at 242; A similar discourse can also be found in Alessandri, *Responsabilidad*, cit., at 174.

Chapter 2. Determination of Causation

399. Traditional doctrine[1338] has taken a narrow view toward causation, essentially delineating the theory of equivalence of conditions (or *conditio sine qua non*).
This leads to, in the mid-sixties, the establishment of the theory of equivalence of conditions, which has become accepted as the primary and most widespread theory of causation in Chile[1339] ever since.[1340]

400. Nonetheless, over time and especially since the beginning of the 2000s, the application of the theory of equivalence of conditions has been undermined such that it is no longer considered 'solid'.[1341] Indeed, new theories have been elaborated, although apparently treating these topics more superficially. So judgments begin to clarify the difference between factual and legal causation.[1342]
The gradual introduction by doctrine (through so-called legal transplants), contributes to this process, identifying and describing new criteria based on the reasoning of foreign scholarship, including relevant theories applicable in criminal law. This phenomenon contributes to broadening the range of criteria by means of which the presence of a causal link between the event and the damage can be identified. Thus, for example, the theory of proximate causation, the theory of adequate causation, also in relation to the predictability,[1343] the theory of finality, risk[1344] and

1338. Thus, Alessandri essentially alludes to the theory of equivalence of conditions and does not deal with criteria of objective imputation: *see* Alessandri, *Responsabilidad*, cit. at 174 et seq.
1339. Domínguez Águila, 'El hecho de la víctima como causal ...', cit., at 36.
1340. As indicated in the third edition from 2007 of the manual by Tapia, whose first edition is from 1941: Tapia, *De la Responsabilidad*, cit., at 247.
1341. Jorge Baraona González, 'La Causa del daño en la jurisprudencia', *Revista Chilena de Derecho*, 2003/2, at 379. In this sense it is stated that in Chile 'mon sire could be adhered to a determined teoría!' (op. cit. 347), refer for an análisis of the rulings of that period.
1342. Pionieer in contractual liability is CS 26 enero 2004 (rol 2497/2002), comented by Carlos Pizarro Wilson, 'Jurisprudencia comentada' *Revista Chilena de Derecho* Privado, 2004/2, at 175 et seq.; *see also* Hugo Cárdenas Villareal, 'Reflexiones sobre la teoría de la imputación objetiva y su aplicabilidad en el ámbito del derecho de daños', *Estudios de derecho civil* (Juan Andrés Varas Braun, Susan Turner Saelzer ed.) (Santiago de Chile: Thomson Reuters, Legal Publishing, 2005) at 533 et seq.
1343. In relation to predictability and comparative aspects: Vvaa, *La relación de causalidad, Cuadernos Jurídicos* 2008/15 (Tatiana Vargas Pinto, ed.) (Santiago de Chile: Universidad los Andes, 2008); Iñigo de la Maza Gazmuri, Previsibilidad y causalidad', *Estudios de derecho civil XIII* (Carlos Pizarro Wilson, Leonor Etcheberry Court, Claudia Bahamondes Oyarzún ed.) (Santiago de Chile: Thomson Reuters, 2018) at 635 et seq.; Joaquín Ugarte Godoy, 'Relación de causalidad y previsibilidad en la responsablidad extracontractual. Jurisprudencia', *Estudios de derecho civil X* (Álvaro Vidal Olivares, Gonzalo Severín Fuster, Caludia Mejías Alonso ed.) (Santiago de Chile: Thomson Reuters, 2015) at 847 et seq.
1344. On probabilistic causation and increased risk *see* Daniela Accatino Scagliotti, 'Incertidumbre, probabilidad y prueba de la causalidad en el derecho de daños. Análisis de la doctrina del incremento del riesgo a más del doble', *Lo Público y lo Privado. Estudios en homenaje al prof. Enrique Barros Bourie*, (Santiago de Chile: Thomson Reuters, 2017), at 697 et seq. Reference should also be made to Cristian Aedo Barrena, La recepción de la creación de riesgos no permitidos en el derecho chileno, como criterio de imputación objetiva. ¿Puede distinguirse de la culpa?, *Revista Chilena de Derecho Privado,* 2019/35, at 117 et seq.

objective imputation are explained and introduced in greater depth, highlighting their merits and defects.[1345] An illustrious author has dedicated his doctoral thesis to this topic.[1346]

401. The concrete application of the various theories of causation is in part attenuated by the protection in case law of the injured party. Indeed, subjective liability has become objectified due to the fact that fault and causation are considered strictly dependent variables.[1347] Thus, it has been carefully observed[1348] that the courts' scant regard for causal relations is attributable to the preponderance in Chile of a subjective system which resolves this problem through the criteria of subjective imputation (i.e., the fault or malice of the defendant).

402. Causation and fault are linked whenever the causal relationship is liable or unclear, offering the judge certain flexibility and a margin of autonomy.[1349] In fact, it has long been held that, in terms of causation, the judges' criterion will be decisive.[1350]

Hence, in a number of cases, the causal link is shown by proof of negligence. In other cases, the judge may use other general criteria, such as legal or judicial

---

1345. In this sense Barros, *Tratado*, I, cit., at 395 et seq. and 408 et seq. and499 et seq.; Corral, *Lecciones*, cit., at 175 et seq. Brief treatises with references to the theories are also to be found in Tapia, *De la Responsabilidad*, cit., at 241–248; Figueroa, *Curso IV*, cit., at 123 et seq.; if these essentially rely on French and German doctrine, the one who relies on Argentine doctrine is Ramos, *De la responsabilidad Civil*, cit., at 102 et seq. Also Rodrigo Barcia Lehmann, 'Algunas consideraciones de la relación de causalidad material y jurídica en la responsabilidad médica', *Cuadernos de análisis jurídico* (*ejemplar dedicado a la Responsabilidad medica*, Iñigo de la Maza ed.), 2010/VI, at 85 et seq. *See also* Joaquín Ugarte Godoy, 'La relación de causalidad en la responsabilidad extracontracutal. Su naturaleza, sus grados y su protección en la contribución de la deuda', *Estudios de derecho civil IX* (Juan Andrés Varas Braun, Susan Turner Saelzer ed.) (Santiago de Chile: Thomson Reuters, Legal Publishing, 2014) at 691 et seq.

1346. Ramón Domínguez Águila, *La causalité dans la responsabilitè en droit comparé fraçais et chilien*, (Toulouse: Universitè de Toulouse, 1967); *see also* Ramón Domínguez Águila, 'Aspectos de la relación de causalidad en la responsabilidad civil con especial referencia al derecho chileno', *Revista de Derecho* (Universidad de Concepción), 2001/209, at 7 et seq.

1347. On the ascertainment of this interrelation San Martín Neira, 'La culpa de la victima en la estructura ...', cit., at 940; Cristian Aedo Barrena, 'La culpa como criterio de distribución de riesgos sociales ¿Hay en la culpa una infracción a un deber jurídico?', *Estudios de Derecho Civil X* (Álvaro Vidal Olivares, Gonzalo Severin Fuster, Claudia Mejías Alonso (coord..) (Santiago de Chile: Thomson Reuters, 2015), at 61 et seq.

1348. Jorge Baraona González, 'La Causa del daño en la jurisprudencia', *Revista Chilena de Derecho*, 2003/2, at 379.

1349. On the convergence of causation and fault: Aedo Barrena, La recepción de la creación de ...', cit., at 117 et seq.; Renzo Munita Marambio, 'Causalidad incierta, alternativa y flexibilidad probatoria', *Estudios de derecho civil XIII* (Claudia Bahamondes Oyarzún, Leonor Etcheberry Court y Carlos Pizarro Wilson, ed.) (Santiago de Chile: Thomson Reuters, 2018), at 737 et seq., in partcolare 744 et seq.

1350. Alessandri, *Responsabilidad*, cit., at 181.

presumptions, sound criticisms or the like.[1351] It is claimed that occasionally the use of presumptions plays a palliative[1352] role, but that they are nevertheless applied.

403. In general, there has sometimes been talk of *presunción de responsabilidad* ('presumption of liability'), presumptions which can be seen from two points of view.

More specifically, the term 'presumption of liability' has been used with two different meanings. On the one hand, it has been associated with a 'presumption of fault'; on the other hand, it has been associated with a kind of *presuncion de causalidad* ('presumption of causality').[1353] Accordingly, some rules are associated with presumptions of 'presumptions of liability' (as in the case of parental liability for the tort of minors under Article 2321 CC) without necessarily linking it to a presumption of causation; rather it is linked to a liability manifesting a certain 'rigour of interpretation'.[1354]

What is established operates either by means of legal presumptions (*presunciones legales*) and therefore associated with certain provisions, or by means of judicial presumptions (*presunciones judiciales*) on the ascertainment of reasoning of the judges and evidentiary criteria.[1355]

404. Presumptions of causation can move in the context of both strict and subjective liability, especially in the case of legal presumptions.

Consider, for example, a case of strict liability in the healthcare profession versus a case of subjective liability for harm to the environment.

Hence, it is expressly provided that in the event of clinical test damage, it is 'presumed to have occurred on the occasion of the test'.[1356]

The issue in environmental matters is more controversial, as Chilean law treats liability as subjective. It is thus debated whether the 'presumption of responsibility' should be considered a presumption of fault or causality whereby 'the liability of

1351. In this sense is important the jurisprudential study and conclusions in Lilian San Martín Nieria & Jorge Larroucau Torres, '*El razonamiento probatorio en la causalidad en la responsabilidad civil: Los criterios jurídicos en que se funda la jurisprudencia chilena*', *Revista de Derecho Privado* (*Universidad Externado de Colombia*), 2021/ 40, at 329 et seq.

1352. Munita Marambio, 'Causalidad incierta, alternativa y flexibilidad probatoria', cit., at 744.

1353. For example, it refers to a presumption of culpability in the jurisprudential application of Article 2328: Barría, La responsabilidad objetiva..., cit. at 539.

1354. Thus Barros, *Tratado*, I, cit., at 178–179.

1355. *See* San Martín Nieria & Larroucau Torres, '*El razonamiento probatorio en la causalidad...* ', cit., at 329 et seq.; Munita Marambio, 'Causalidad incierta, alternativa y flexibilidad probatoria', cit., at 744 et seq.; Barros, *Tratado*, I, cit., at 438–441.

1356. Art. 111. J DL 725/67, cit. *See supra* 321 et seq.

the author of the environmental damage[1357] is legally presumed' when certain standards of prevention are violated. In this case, some scholars identify the 'presumption of liability' with a presumption of fault,[1358] while others with a presumption of causality.[1359]

405. On the liability for activities related to Article 2329 CC, which has already been partially discussed,[1360] the question has been raised as to whether this could be regarded as a 'presumption of liability' rather than a presumption of fault, considering that for some it would be a presumption of causality[1361] to avoid tautology with Article 2314 CC.

406. It should be recalled that in other cases the law expressly establishes that administrative offences are not necessarily causally related to the damage, such as in the case of traffic accidents.[1362]

407. Loss of opportunity is an additional problem associated with causation and/or damage. However, this will be discussed in greater detail later.[1363]

408. Causation has also been studied with particular reference to the abestos liability and mesothelioma.[1364]

1357. Art. 52 Ley19300/1994, cit. In case law *see* CS 25 Sep. 2019 (rol 13177-2018); CS 25 Jan. 2018 (rol 41417/2017), CS 8 Jul. 2016. Corte de Puerto Montt 2.4.2004 (rol N° 11.652-2003).
1358. Discussing the presumption of fault Figueroa, *Curso IV*, cit., at 107; and the presunción de culpabilidad: Hunter Ampuero, 'La culpa con la Ley en la responsabilidad civil ambiental', cit., at 9 et seq.; Pastén Delich. & Parot Hillmer, 'Diversificación de la reparación del daño ambiental ... ', cit., at 172.
1359. Jean Paul. Dussaubat Diban, 'Responsabilidad por daño ambiental: de la presunción de culpabilidad a la presunción de causalidad', *Revista de Derecho Administrativo Económico*, 2016/22, at 147 et seq., especially at 153 et seq.; also San Martín Nieria & Jorge Larroucau Torres, '*El razonamiento probatorio...* ', cit., at 341.
1360. *See supra* paras 146 et seq.
1361. Corral, *Lecciones*, cit., at 225–226; Barros Bourie, 'Análisis histórico y comparado de la presunción de la responsabilidad... ', cit., at 619 et seq. Per un analisi de la jurisprudencia que opta por la tesis de la presunción véase Carolina Schiele Manzor &Tocornal Cooper, 'Artículo 2329 del Código Civil. ...', cit., at 123 et seq.
1362. Art. 166, 167, 168.2 y 168.3 LT In general on the relation of causation in road accidents San Martín Neira, 'La relación entre culpa y causalidad. EL ejemplo de la causa basal del accidente de tránsito'. cit., at 349 et seq.
1363. Barros, *Tratado*, I, cit., at 309 et seq. *See* paras 466 et seq.
1364. Cristián Banfi del Río, 'La causalidad en casos de responsabilidad civil por mesotelioma: una mirada al derecho chileno e inglés', *Lo Público y lo Privado. Estudios en homenaje al prof. Enrique Barros Bourie*, (Santiago de Chile: Thomson Reuters, 2017), at 721 et seq.; Rodrigo Barría Díaz, 'Asbesto y silicosis: acerca de la recepción jurisprudencial de una forma de daños diferidos', *Estudios de Derecho Civil XI,* (Departamento de Derecho Privado, Universidad de Concepción ed., Manuel Barría Paredes coord.) (Santiago de Chile: Thomson Reuters, 2015), at 877 ct scq.

Chapter 3. Grounds for Exoneration of Liability: Interruption of Causation

§1. 'Exclusive Fault of the Injured Party' Versus 'Fault of the Injured Party as Grounds for Excluding the Damage'

409. 'Exclusive fault of the injured party' (*Culpa exclusiva de la víctima*) or 'fault of the injured party as grounds for excluding the damage' (culpa de la víctima como cáusa excluyente del daño)?

The terminology in these cases has hardly been univocal. For instance, part of the traditional doctrine has identified a blurring of lines between *hecho de la víctima*[1365] – which it used to identify the grounds for exoneration of liability as the breaking of the causal link – and that of *culpa della víctima*[1366] (also called *culpa común*[1367]), which it associated instead with the reduction under Article 2330 CC.

Instead others do not distinguish between the injured party's 'fact' and 'culpa' and have used the expression '*culpa de la víctima* indiscriminately[1368] for both hypotheses.

A third approach refers generally to the *culpa de la víctima* for both cases, then distinguishes between the *culpa comun* related to Article 2330 CC and *culpa exclusiva* as grounds for total exoneration.[1369]

It is comprehensible, then, how such lack of clarity could create confusion also with regard to the relationship between culpability, cause and causation. This is precisely why another part of the doctrine contends that the expression *culpa della victima* should not be used as it is essentially inaccurate.[1370]

Still, some modern scholars continue to use the expression and refer to the *culpa exclusiva de la vívtima* in relation to the total exclusion of liability, and of *culpa concurrente* in relation to the reduction under Article 2330 CC.[1371] Additionally, there are others still who continue to sometimes perceive nuances between the 'fault' and 'fact' of the injured party,[1372] and speak (with more propensity) of *culpa de la víctima como causa excluyente del daño* (fault of the injured party as grounds for excluding the damage) – an expression which should be preferred to the others.[1373]

1365. Así Alessandri, *Responsabilidad*, cit., at 180.
1366. Así Alessandri, *Responsabilidad*, cit., at 412.
1367. Así Alessandri, *Responsabilidad*, cit., at 175.
1368. Abeliuk, *Las Obligaciones*, *I*, at 235.
1369. Tapia, *De la responsabilidad*, cit., at 251, 258–259.
1370. David Quintero Fuentes, 'El efecto reductor del hecho... ', cit., at 522–523.
1371. Emblematic is the title of the paper of San Martín Neira, 'La frontera... ', cit., at 26 et seq. He also speaks of 'concurrencia de la culpa de la victima' Corral, *Lecciones*, cit., at 195.
1372. Thus part of the doctrine associates *culpa de la víctima* with Art. 2330 CC, while the 'act of the victim' ('hechos de la víctima') with the consent and the assumption of the risk of the latter as exoneration Barros, *Tratado*, I, cit., at 43.
1373. Barros, *Tratado*, I, cit., at 459.

Thus, it has been carefully observed[1374] that the latter circumstance implies the total exclusion of liability of the offender without a legal analysis of the injured party's behaviour, just a mere factual explanation in relation to the offender's conduct.

§2. Acts of Third Parties

410. As concerns liability for the acts of third parties, the expression *hecho de tercero*[1375] is used instead of 'fault of the third party.[1376] The relevance of the intervention of the third party may thus render irrelevant the culpable conduct previously carried out by the defendant, whenever his behaviour substantially affects the ordinary course of events (this is called *prohibición de regreso*),[1377] although it is debated whether the fact that the latter did not adopt the appropriate measures to prevent the damage excludes this circumstance.[1378]

411. The 'act' of the third party is also grounds for exoneration provided that it alone[1379] causes the harm inflicted on the injured party and provided that it arises from a tort (i.e., it was committed negligently or maliciously).

If, on the other hand, it derives from the offender's lawful conduct, this shall be deemed[1380] to operate as a fortuitous event to exonerate the defendant.

If the act of the third party is not the only circumstance that caused the damage, it will be a hypothesis of passive solidarity and Article 2317 CC will apply.[1381]

412. Similarly, the voluntary acceptance of risk (not of the damage) could also result in the exoneration of liability. Consider, for example, the case where a person decides to participate in a particularly dangerous sporting activity,[1382] or one agrees to engage in prohibited conduct.[1383]

1374. Domínguez Águila, 'El hecho de la víctima como causal ... ', cit., at 36 et seq.; taken up and reworked by Lilian San Martín Neira, 'La frontera entre culpa exclusiva y concurrente de la víctima en la producción del daño a la luz de la jurisprudencia chilena', *Revista chilena de derecho privado,* 2016/27, at 9 and 38.
1375. E.g., Abeliuk, *Las Obligaciones, I,* at 235; Tapia, *De la responsabilidad,* cit., at 258; Barros, *Tratado,* I, cit., at 145; Corral, *Lecciones,* cit., at 193.
1376. Barros, *Tratado,* I, cit., at 434–435.
1377. In support of this the exclusion or inclusion of subjects should be carried out according to the theory of adequate causation: Barros, *Tratado,* I, cit., at 435. For a jurisprudential application CS 20 Aug. 2012 (rol 2282/2010); CS 21 Oct. 2002 (*Fallos del Mes,* 503, at 3182.
1378. *See* CS 26 Jun. 2013, rol 3579/2012), Corral, *Lecciones,* cit., at 194.
1379. Tapia, *De la responsabilidad,* cit., at 258–259.
1380. Tapia, *De la responsabilidad,* cit., at 259; Abeliuk, *Las Obligaciones, I,* at 236.
1381. Tapia, *De la responsabilidad,* cit., at 259; Abeliuk, *Las Obligaciones, I,* at 236.
1382. Barros, *Tratado,* I, cit., at 144 and 464.
1383. This is how the doctrine formulates the example of an injury after entering a place where access is prohibited, as Alessandri, *Responsabilidad,* cit., at 451. The author also gives the example of a thief who is injured for security reasons. On the point and the possible insurance coverage: *see* Alfredo Ferrante 'El ladrón desventurado y la historia de su muerte asegurable', *Revista chilena de Derecho Privado,* 2016/26, at 269 et seq.

§3. Unforeseeable Circumstances/Force Majeure

413. Article 45 CC defines both unforeseen circumstances and force majeure as 'unforeseeable events that cannot be avoided'. As such, the doctrine has been concerned with reinterpreting or elaborating on the requirements, demanding that the intervention is significant.[1384] Clearly, it should not come from the parties involved,[1385] focusing in particular on contractual liability.[1386]

414. Some scholars consider the fortuitous event as a causal exoneration, not only for the lack of a causal link between the fact and the damage but also for lack of fault; this view is shared by other scholars who consider it as 'grounds for eliminating the volition to act'.[1387] In an effort to clarify this position, it helps to differentiate between the scope of the fortuitous event or force majeure, depending on whether the case at issue deals with subjective tort liability (and therefore relatable to behaviour) or strict liability. It has been argued[1388] that in cases of subjective liability, the existence of a fortuitous event excludes fault and, consequently, the causal link. Instead, when there is strict liability, since culpability has no role in the imputation of procedural liability, the fortuitous event directly breaks the causal link.

415. If a culpable act is committed and subsequently a fortuitous event occurs, the offending party will be held liable whenever it is deemed that the imprudent conduct would have caused the damage regardless of the presence (or occurrence) of the fortuitous event or force majeure.[1389]

However, if such liability is recognized, the question arises as to whether it is proportionately reducible.

1384. Initially, for example, only three requirements were required: unforeseen, insuperable and external, i.e., coming from a cause external to the will of the person claimed to be responsible: e.g., Tapia, *De la Responsabilidad*, cit. at 254.

1385. For all, *see* Mauricio Tapia Rodríguez, *Caso fortúito o fuerza mayor*, 3rd ed., (Santiago de Chile: Thomson Reuters, 2020); María Graciela Brantt Zumarán, 'La exigencia de exterioridad en el caso fortuito: su construcción a partir de la distribución de los riesgos del contrato', *Revista de Derecho* (PUCV), 2009/33 at 39 et seq.

1386. For an extensive discussion on the subject e.g.,. : Raul Letelier Wartenberg, La fuerza mayor en la responsabilidad extracontractual de la administración del Estado (Santiago de Chile: Conosur, LexisNexis: 2001); María Graciela Brantt Zumarán, *El caso fortuito y su incidencia en el derecho de la responsabilidad civil contractual : concepto y función del caso fortuito en el Código Civil chileno* (Santiago de Chile: Legal Publishing, 2010),; Sebastian Campos Micin, *Caso fortuito y teoría de la imprevisión en el derecho de contratos*, (Santiago de Chile: Der, 2020); Iñigo de la Maza, Álvaro Vidal Olivares, *Caso Fortuito e incumplimiento* (con concordancias, doctrina, jurisprudencia y medidas excepcionales en Colombia, por Jorge Oviedo Albán, Bogotá: Tirant lo Blanch, 2021).

1387. In this sense the author considers that in the case of force majeure or fortuitous event 'There is no illegality, no fault, no causation': Corral, *Lecciones,* cit., at 107.

1388. Lilian San Martín Neira, 'El caso fortúito en la responsabilidad civil exracontractual', *Revista Ius et Praxis*, Año 27, N° 2, 2021/2, at 3 et seq.

1389. Corral, *Lecciones,* cit., at 193.

According to the traditional approach whereby the fortuitous event is understood as a cause of complete exoneration, the concurrence (and therefore the accumulation of the fault of the liable party and the fortuitous event) is impossible; these would be self-excluding and therefore no proportional convictions would be possible.

Fairly recently, however, a more open doctrinal position has emerged (not supported by case law), according to which the fault of the damaging party and existence of a fortuitous event can, in certain circumstances, be considered concurrent causes. As such, it is possible to arrive at a proportional compensation.[1390] It was also observed that the inability to moderate any compensation is also due to the fact that the causal relationship is often conceived in terms of equivalence of the conditions.[1391]

416. Although Andrés Bello expressly includes earthquakes as an example of force majeure under Article 45 CC, part of the doctrine has reconsidered the concept of force majeure in relation to natural events. More specifically, it has argued that natural disasters can be framed as events that give rise to incidental damage (*daño contingente*), associating natural disasters with the availability of the preventive protection under Article 2333 CC, which would be useful in these cases also with respect to potential State liability.[1392]

1390. Corral, *Lecciones,* cit., at 193; Also apparently partially receptive to this openness: Lilian San Martín Neira, 'Desastres naturales y responsabilidad civil. Identificación de los desafíos que presenta esta categoría de hechos dañinos', *Revista de Derecho* (Valdivia), 2019/2, at 132–134.
More critical of this possibility is Barros who, although he does not seem justified in certain cases in attributing extreme solutions such as the totality of damages or its exclusion, states that 'this question remains open': Barros, *Tratado,* I, cit., at 437 (at footnote 157).

1391. Jorge Baraona González, 'La Causa del daño en la jurisprudencia', cit., at 367.

1392. Lilian San Martín Neira, 'Desastres naturales y responsabilidad civil... ', cit., at 134 et seq.

Part VI. Remedies

Chapter 1. General Principles

417. It has already been discussed[1393] that the principle of full compensation[1394] aims to repair the full extent of damage in accordance with the principle of *neminem laedere*. However, because it is not always possible to place the victim in the same position as he was in before the damage occurred, different safeguards have emerged, such as the admissibility of non-asset damage.

The different functions[1395] of tort law also affect the possibility of providing a broader range of remedies, since there is not only an action for damages, but also different types of actions such as actions in kind. These two actions will be dealt with in this section and the possibility of actions in restitution will be dealt with elsewhere.[1396]

418. In recent years, notwithstanding the principle of full compensation has been analysed, outlining its contours in contract and tort matters,[1397] as well as questioned,[1398] the important role that this principle plays within the social function of civil law[1399] has nonetheless been highlighted. It has been noted that despite of it is

1393. *See supra* paras 47 et seq.

1394. For a comparative perspective *see* Vvaa, *El Principio de Reparación Integral en sus Contornos Actuales. Una Revisión desde el derecho Chileno. Latinoamericano y Europeo* (Carmen Domínguez Hidalgo, ed.) (Santiago de Chile: Thomson Reuters, 2019), in particolare at 551 et seq.

1395. Over a decade ago, the assimilation of several functions seemed more stagnant and it was feared that the acceptance of other purposes of civil liability could transform the claim for damages into a 'super action' that could be exercised for any purpose: Carmen Domínguez Hidalgo, 'Algunas consideraciones en torno a la función de la responsabilidad civil', *Estudios de derecho civil II,* (Hernán Corral Talciani, María Sara Rodríguez Pinto ed.) (Santiago de Chile: Thomson Reuters, 2011) at 603.

1396. *See supra* paras 539 et seq.

1397. Carmen Domínguez Hidalgo, 'El principio de reparación integral del daño: sus contornos', *Estudios de derecho civil VIII*, (Carmen Domínguez Hidalgo, Joel González Castillo, Marcelo Barrientos Zamorano, Juan Luís Goldeberg Serrano, ed.) (Santiago de Chile: Thomson Reuters, Legal Publishing, 2013), at 564 et seq.

1398. In this sense it has been considered that sometimes integral reparation is used in non-pecuniary matters as a 'pseudo principle' and as an excuse to derogate from general rules of civil liability Gonzalo Ruz Lártiga, 'La reparación integral del daño: ¿Mito o realidad?', *Estudios de derecho civil IV*, (Carlos Pizarro Wilson ed.) (Santiago de Chile: Thomson Reuters, 2009) at 672.

1399. Ruperto Pinochet Olave, 'El principio de reparación integral de daño y su relación con la función social del Derecho Civil', *Estudios de derecho civil VIII,* (Carmen Domínguez Hidalgo, Joel

not always possible to fully compensate the injured party for damage suffered in extramarital matters, compensation must be as integral as possible also in these cases, in application of a canon of reasonableness (*reparación razonable*).[1400] For this reason, the principle of full compensation is sometimes limited.[1401] For example, some scholars argue it only operates in cases of fraud or serious fault,[1402] and in any case it must be particularly commensurate in the repair of collective or objective[1403] moral damages. The question has also been raised as to whether the principle of full compensation may be applied in the context of civil liability for adultery.[1404]

§1. Action for Damages

419. Although the claim for damages is the best known and most widely used remedy in matters of tort liability, there are other legal remedies to protect the interests of the injured party and which are in part also associated with the function of civil liability. While it is true that the purpose of compensation within the meaning of the principle of full compensation is based on the action for damages – the purpose of which is to put the victim in the position he was in beforehand, to the extent possible – other remedies are available.

420. There is no real organization of these actions within the structure of the Civil Code. However, Chilean doctrine[1405] has made some effort in this direction,

González Castillo, Marcelo Barrientos Zamorano, Juan Luís Goldeberg Serrano, ed.) (Santiago de Chile: Thomson Reuters, Legal Publishing, 2013), at 585 et seq.

1400. Carmen Domínguez Hidalgo, 'El principio de reparación del daño y su contneido: algunas consecuencias para el derecho chileno', *Estudios de derecho civil V*, (Departamento de Derecho Privado de la Universidad de Concepción ed.) (Santiago de Chile: Legal Publishing, 2010) at 671 et seq.

1401. Ramón Domínguez Águila, 'Los limites al principio de reparación del daño', *Revista Chilena de Derecho Privado*, 2010/15, at 11 et seq.; Ramón Domínguez Águila, 'Límites del principio de repapación integral del daño', *El Principio de Reparación Integral en sus Contornos Actuales. Una Revisión desde el derecho Chileno. Latinoamericano y Europeo* (Carmen Domínguez Hidalgo, ed.) (Santiago de Chile: Thomson Reuters, 2019), at 181 et seq.

1402. Cristián Banfi del Río, 'Por una reparación integral de dalo extracontractual limitadas a los hechos dolosos o gravemente negligentes', *Ius et praxis*, 2012/2, at 3 et seq.

1403. Carmen Domínguez Hidalgo, 'Los derechos de la personalidad y el principio de reparación integral del daño', *Estudios de derecho civil IV*, (Carlos Pizarro Wilson ed.) (Santiago de Chile: Thomson Reuters, 2009) at 658.

1404. In favour of its application and critical of a decisión that denied its application (SAP Santiago 10 Nov. 2009, rol 7738/207): Mario Opazo González, Èl principio de reparación integral de dalo y los daños causados por adulterios', *Estudios de derecho civil VII*, (Fabián Elorriaga De Bonis ed.) (Santiago de Chile: Thomson Reuters, Abeledo Perrot, 2012), at 589 et seq.; *see* paras 528–529.

1405. With the exception of Barros, *Tratado*, II, cit., at 973 et seq..; in limited part also Alessandri, *Responsabilidad*, cit., at 385 et seq.; Corral, *Lecciones*, cit., at 376 et seq.; Tapia, *De la responsabilidad*, cit., at 271 et seq.

and select special laws expressly provide for additional remedies. Thus, it appears necessary to classify available remedies, for example, in the case of protection against unfair competition.[1406]

As such, it is possible to observe that in addition to the action for damages, there is an action for compensation in kind (*in natura*), as well as the possibility to remedy certain harm through application of the principle of unjustified enrichment via the action for restitution.

421. While a claim for damages aims to make the injured party whole by monetary means and expresses the concept of 'in kind' repair, such an action is associated with the preventive function of compensation in order to avoid or prevent damage from occurring.[1407]

The exercise of these actions for general purposes is limited by the prohibition to abusively exercise one's rights, which is also rooted in the principle of proportionality.[1408]

422. Associated with the restitutionary (and not compensatory[1409]) purpose is the action of a procedural nature which allows the current and continuing damage to be stopped (Article 608 CPC).

§2. Compensation in Kind

423. If compensation (for equivalent) repairs the damage, compensation in kind stops damage from persisting in the future.[1410] For this reason, the remedy *in natura* is considered the "most perfect'"[1411] form of action associated with reparation.

424. Remedial action in favour of third parties, such as that obtained by means of an out-of-court settlement, by handing over goods to other consumers in lieu of compensation for collusion relating to the high price of the goods, is relevant.[1412]

1406. As expressly set out in a provision of the law on unfair competition, which not only provides for an action for compensation but also the possibility, 'jointly or separately', to bring an action of cessation/removal of the act of unfair competition: Art. 5 Ley 20.169.
1407. Barros, *Tratado*, II, cit., at 974; Alessandri, *Responsabilidad,* cit., at 385; Corral, *Lecciones,* cit., at 376.
1408. As argued by Barros, *Tratado,* II, cit., at 984. Cf. Abeliuk, *Las Obligaciones*, *I*, at 230.
1409. Barros, *Tratado*, II, cit., at 980.
1410. Adopting the French doctrine: Alessandri, *Responsabilidad,* cit., at 386.
1411. Tapia, *De la responsabilidad*, cit., at 272.
1412. Concretely a collusion case related to diapers *see* para. 256.

I. Cessation or Repair of Damages

425. The primary action of this type applies, for example, in cases of environmental damage[1413] where claimants may file the *acción ambiental* aimed at repairing the damage, as envisaged both in the specific legislation[1414] as well as is inferable from select provisions of the Civil Code.[1415]

426. Among the duties to compensate in kind for the damage suffered, the doctrine[1416] finds – for example in cases involving prejudice to the right to honour – that the repair may also be achieved through the correction or the publication of the ruling containing the relevant (correct) information. Similar aspects can be found in intellectual property law.[1417] In this context, besides an action for compensation or cessation, it is also possible to publish an extract of the judgment in a periodical,[1418] with certain aspects being discussed which may be framed as restitutory rather than compensatory.[1419]

427. This protection of intellectual property is complemented[1420] by that of industrial property (IPR), which provides a similar mechanism of protection[1421] and a triple form of protection, defined by Article 108 as compensatory.[1422]

428. The Chilean system expressly foresees a broad possibility in favour of the injured party in the event of a ruling involving an obligation to act. This is made explicit in both substantial and procedural laws, whereby the rules intuitively associated with breach of contract may be applied (where compatible).[1423] To this end, there is a whole series of measures that are not only compensatory. Reparation in

---

1413. *See* paras 329 et seq.
1414. Arts 53–54 Ley 19.300/1994, cited above.
1415. Arts 937, 948 CC.
1416. Barros, *Tratado*, I, cit., at 643 et seq. Rights of rectification are also provided for in periodicals in case of untruthful information: Arts 16 y 17 Ley 19.733.
1417. *See* Rodrigo Barría Díaz, 'Configuración del derecho moral de autor en la Ley de propiedad intelectual', *Estudios de derecho civil X* (Álvaro Vidal Olivares, Gonzalo Severín Fuster, Caludia Mejías Alonso ed.) (Santiago de Chile: Thomson Reuters, 2015) at 941 et seq.; Alberto Pino Emhart, 'Las acciones civiles por infracciones al derecho de propiedad intelectual', *Revista Chilena de Derecho y Tecnologia*, 2019/2, at 33 et seq.
1418. Art. 85 B Ley 17.366. *See also* Arts 85 C et seq. On issues of prior non-consent: CS 22 Mar. 2016 (rol 3798/2015); CS 15 May 2018 (rol 55082/2016); CS 14 Aug. 2013 (rol 4649/2013). *See* paras 58–59.
1419. *See* Rodrígo Barría Díaz, 'La acción de enriquecimiento injustificado por la intromisión en los derechos de propiedad intelectual', *Estudios de derecho civil XII* (Hernán Corral Talciani, Pablo Manterola Domínguez, ed.) (Santiago de Chile: Thomson Reuters, 2017) at 399 et seq.; also Pino Emhart, 'Las acciones civiles por infracciones al derecho de propiedad intelectual', cit., at 33 et seq.
1420. Rodrigo Barría Diáz, 'La función preventiva o disuasoria de la responsabilidad civil', cit., at 177.
1421. Here too, Art. 106 IPR provides for the possibility of ceasing the harmful acts (and taking the necessary measures not to continue them), compensation for damages and publication of the judgment. Ley 19.039/1991, of 24 Jan. (DO 25 Jan. 1991), now DFL 3/2006, (DO 20 Jun. 2006).
1422. *See* paras 454 and 543 et seq.
1423. Art. 530 CPC et seq.; Arts 1553 CC et seq. On the point extensively Claudia Bahamondes Oyarzún, *El cumplimiento específico de los contratos.* (Santiago de Chile, Der, 2018).

kind may be more appropriate in cases involving failure to act, when it is necessary to remove or destroy what has been created.[1424]

429. Another action that allows for the cessation of an activity or the reinstatement of the previous situation[1425] concerns water that has flowed onto another person's property, or the closing of another person's well[1426] in cases where no benefit has resulted or the benefit is less than the damage caused.[1427]

II. Damages Prevention and *Daño Emergente*

430. Important preventive actions may be merely civil or provide a different protection when a constitutional right has been violated.

431. Whenever a constitutional right (such as property or many of the rights protected by Article 19 CPR) is perceived as being under threat, it is possible to file a protective (and thus partially preventative) action under Article 20 CPR.[1428]

432. Civil actions having a preventive function and which for part of the doctrine[1429] represent the expression of a repair in kind are those based on the *obra ruinosa* claim in accordance with Article 932 CC, as well as those whereby an element located in the upper part of a building is removed in order to avoid any damage resulting from its fall (Article 2328 CC).

433. An important preventive measure is the people's action.[1430] This action relates to contingent damages (*daño contingente*) and is aimed at eliminating or correcting certain situations which may cause damage due to imprudence or negligence (Article 2333 CC). The preventative function of contingent damage has already been discussed.[1431] Here, it should be noted that it has effectively been applied in a manner which has allowed the doctrine[1432] to identify the differences between contingent damage and the recourse to protection from threats (*recurso de protección por amenazas*). In cases of harassment in connection with construction

1424. Cf. Abeliuk, *Las Obligaciones, I*, at 386.
1425. Art. 123 Código de Aguas (repealed Art. 936 CC).
1426. Art. 56.1 Código de Aguas (repealed Art. 945 CC).
1427. Tapia, *De la responsabilidad*, cit., at 272–273; Abeliuk, *Las Obligaciones, I*, at 229.
1428. *See e.g.*, Francisco Javier Leturia Infante. 'Las acciones cautelares y el recuerso de protección ¿Es necesaria una diplicidad de instituciones? notas para una mejor garantía de los derchos fundamentales, *Estudios Constitucionales* 2018/1, at 227 et seq.
1429. Alessandri, *Responsabilidad*, cit., at 387.
1430. In this sense Andrés Bello is influenced by popular Roman action: Barros, *Tratado*, II, cit., at 1053.
1431. *See* paras 56 et seq., 355 et seq., 416.
1432. In this case, significant is the study of José Luis Diéz Schwerter, 'La acción por daño contingente del art- 2333 del codigo civil en movimiento: tres casos de la jurisprdencia reciente, *Estudios de Derecho Privado. En homenaje al prof. Daniel Peñailillo Arévalos*, (Santiago de Chile: Thomson Reuters, 2019), p. at 723 et seq.

of a building,[1433] although part of the doctrine has accepted the applicability of the former, it rejects the possibility of applying the latter. This is because the latter requires culpable or negligent conduct to award damages, and it is not possible to bring legal action in cases of licit conduct.[1434] Additionally, it has clarified certain jurisdictional aspects in regard to environmental problems or contamination, asserting that the Environmental Court (not the ordinary court) is competent[1435] to decide cases relating to the application of Article 2333 in environmental matters. This assertion is based on the observation that the relevant events have already occurred (and therefore have already caused environmental damage), specifying that the ordinary court would be competent if the action were compensatory (in accordance with Article 2314 CC rather than with Article 2333).[1436]

§3. Restitutionary Action and Unjustified Enrichment

434. In addition to actions for damages and reparation *in kind,* it is also possible to receive restitutionary protection,[1437] which will be discussed below in a designated section.[1438]

1433. SAP Concepcion Apr. 18, 2019 (rol 574/2018).
1434. CS 25 Sep. 2017 (rol 15519/2017).
1435. Art. 60 Ley 19.300/1990, cit. The doctrine instead had manifested itself in favour of the ordinary jurisdiction: Diéz Schwerter, 'La acción por daño contingente del art- 2333 del codigo civil en movimiento... ', cit., at 737.
1436. CS 21 Dec. 2020 (rol 22893/2019).
1437. *See* para. 70.
1438. *See* paras 539 et seq.

Chapter 2. Types of Damages

§1. General Aspects

435. The concept of damage can be considered in two different ways: it is not only a condition for which civil liability arises, but it is also the object of the liability[1439] itself since it is what is concretely requested in the claim (*petitum*). Thus, it has been established[1440] that damage is both an element and a presupposition of tort liability.

436. Although there is no consensus[1441] on the conditions and characteristics of the harm,[1442] it has traditionally been held[1443] that the harm must be: (a) certain, (b) significant (serious), (c) direct (i.e., linked to the event giving rise to it) and, clearly, must not have already been repaired, in order to avoid unjust enrichment.

The position as to whether a legitimate interest must be violated is more open.[1444] However, even requirements such as certainty or that damage must be direct are questionable.[1445]

437. Some consideration must also be given to the foreseeability of the damage.

In contractual matters, the Chilean legal system differentiates between intentional and negligent conduct. In the case of fraudulent conduct, Article 1558 CC stipulates that, in the case of negligence, the foreseeable damages are to be compensated[1446] unless otherwise agreed, whereas in the case of fraudulent conduct the unforeseeable damages are also to be compensated.

1439. Barros, *Tratado*, I, cit., at 223.
1440. For example, Diez, *El daño,* cit., at 26–27.
1441. Figueroa, *Curso IV*, cit., at 135.
1442. For a view in relation to foreign law: Ramón Domínguez Águila, 'Consideraciones en torno al daño en la responsabilidad civil. Una visión comparatista', *Revista de Derecho* (Universidad de Concepción), 1990/188, at 150 et seq.; Carmen Domínguez Hidalgo, 'Algunas consideraciones entorno al daño como elemento de la responsabilidad civil', *Revista de Derecho* (PUCV), 1998/19, at 237 et seq.
1443. Ramos, *De la responsabilidad Civil*, cit., at 80 et seq.; Figueroa, *Curso IV*, cit., at 133 et seq.; Diez, *El daño*, cit., at 30 et seq.; Tapia, *De la Responsabilidad*, cit., at 190 et seq. *See also* Gastón Salinas Ugarte, 'Requisitos comunes del daño como elemento de la indemnización de perjuicios' *Estudios de derecho civil III*, (Alejandro Guzmán Brito ed.) (Santiago de Chile: Thomson Reuters, 2008) at 735 et seq.
1444. For example, on the various positions regarding the necessity or otherwise of the violation of a legitimate interest in the traditional doctrine *see*: Diez, *El daño*, cit., at 22–24; also Corral, *Lecciones,* cit., at 133 et seq.; Barros, *Tratado*, I, cit., at 229 et seq. For the classical position Alessandri, *Responsabilidad*, cit., at 153 et seq.
1445. *See* paras 466 et seq.
1446. On contractual matters, *see* Lilian San Martín Neira, 'La previsibilidad como límite al resarcimiento del daño por incumplimiento contractual', *Estudios de derecho civil IX* (Juan Andrés Varas Braun, Susan Turner Saelzer ed.) (Santiago de Chile: Thomson Reuters, Legal Publishing, 2014) at 649 et seq.

A part of modern doctrine seems to consider that such provisions do not apply to tort liability, since compensation in tort can also be awarded for foreseeable damage.[1447] However, there are some perplexities since the damage, being unforeseeable, may not be fully in line with the causal link that is required to be compensated for the damage.[1448] Thus, another part of the doctrine favours applying the provisions of Article 1558 CC also in tort cases, and asserts that unforeseeable damage is recoverable only in the event of malice or gross negligence.[1449]

438. Regarding the significance or severity of the harm, some scholars[1450] argue that the severity of harm is an element of damage and not a requirement. However, if the damage must consist of an abnormal disturbance or molestation,[1451] then the damage must be significant and the lesser harm must be tolerated.[1452] In this sense, a reciprocal tolerance is necessary.[1453]

§2. Individual and Collective Damages

439. It is indisputable that the damage must be 'personal', meaning that it must be claimed by the person who has suffered such harm, without prejudice to possible actions *iure proprio* or *iure hereditatis.*[1454]

There is no provision in the Civil Code for actions for collective interests, except for the people's actions mentioned above relating to the *daño contingente* and Articles 2333 and 2334 CC[1455] and there is no real *class action*[1456] in Chile, but there is protection of collective and diffuse interests especially in matters of consumption, although there are other protections also in some special laws.[1457]

1447. Barros, *Tratado*, I, cit., at 243.
1448. Corral, *Lecciones,* cit., at 137.
1449. Cristián Banfi del Río, 'Por una reparación integral de dalo extracontractual limitadas a los hechos dolosos o gravemente negligentes', *Ius et praxis*, 2012/2, at 3 et seq.
1450. Figueroa, *Curso IV*, cit., at 135.
1451. Diez, *El daño*, cit., at 30.
1452. Corral, *Lecciones,* cit., at 140–141.
1453. This is what the doctrine points out, extending to the matter of compensation the principle applied at the stage of an appeal for protection (*recurso de protección*) by some jurisprudential resolutions: e.g., CS 4 mayo 1983, *Fallo del* Mes, 294, at 192, Barros, *Tratado,* I, cit., at 236.
1454. Barros, *Tratado*, I, cit., at 249, *see* paras 483 et seq. and 517 et seq.
1455. *See* also paras 56 et seq., 355 et seq., 416, 433.
1456. In this sense the doctrine has been critical in relation to the reform of the LPC: Iñigo de la Maza Gazmuri, 'La indemnización del daño en las acciones colectivas: ¿masivas una promesa incumplida', *Estudios de derecho civil XV* (Fabian Elorriaga De Bonis ed.) (Santiago de Chile: Thomson Reuters, 2020) at 783 et seq.
1457. A brief categorization is found in Barros, *Tratado,* I, cit., at 250 et seq.

440. The greatest protection against such interests is provided by consumer law,[1458] and specifically by special legislation which envisages particular procedures (which were additionally reformed in 2004,[1459] 2011[1460] and again in 2018[1461]) that reformed the LPC[1462] and established the possibility for injured parties to file a claim for kind of joint moral damage.[1463]

441. The National Consumer Defense Service (SERNAC) has set out a number of interpretative circulars in relation to the judicial exercise of general consumer interests,[1464] on alternative mechanisms for the distribution of damages, devolution and compensation in such cases,[1465] on the legal duties, and good practices of litigants during the handling of such proceedings.[1466]

442. Similar protection is provided by other laws. For instance, as discussed above, in cases of environmental damage it is possible to bring an action in kind,[1467] which can also be pursued, for example, by the State or municipalities. Although a part of the doctrine holds such protection inapplicable to associations,[1468] there is no express limit in this sense as the law also provides standing to any 'natural or legal, public or private person who has suffered damage or prejudice'.[1469]

443. Following the earthquake of 2010, an action for collective interests has also been allowed in the case of construction damage. Such allowance has been made in accordance with Article 19 of the *Ley General de Urbanismo y Construcciones* ('General Law on Urbanism and Construction'), which refers in terms of proceedings to the above-mentioned consumer legislation.[1470]

1458. For a jurisprudential overview: *see* Iñígo de la Maza Gazmuri, Hugo Ojeda-Montoya,' Eel interés general de los consumidores y su tutela en las decisiones de los tribunales Superiores de Justicia' *Revista de Derecho* (Universidad de Concepción), 2017/242, at 105 et seq.
1459. Ley 19.955/2004, of 29 Jun. (DO 14 Jul. 2004).
1460. Ley 20.543 /2011, of 11 Oct. (DO 21 Oct. 2011).
1461. Ley 21081/2018, of 13 Jul. (DO 13 Sep. 2018).
1462. *See* Arts 51 et seq. LPC. *See* Alfredo Ferrante, *Ley sobre protección de los derechos de los consumidores. Edición anotada, concordada, indice analítico y nota preliminar* (Santiago de Chile: Tirant Lo Blanch, 2021).
1463. Mauricio Tapia Rodríguez, 'Daño moral colectivo', *Estudios de derecho civil XV* (Fabian Elorriaga De Bonis ed.) (Santiago de Chile: Thomson Reuters, 2020) at 1015 et seq.; Fabían González Cazorla, 'Daño moral colectivo en el derecho del consumo chileno: situación actual y proyecciones', *Latin American Legal Studies*, 2021/8, at 122 et seq.
1464. Resolución Exenta 932/2019, of 22 Nov.
1465. Resolución exenta 759/2020, of 6 Nov.
1466. Resolución exenta 71/2021, of 5 Feb.
1467. Art. 53, 54 Ley 19300/1994, cit. *See supra* paras 329 et seq.
1468. Barros, *Tratado*, I, cit., at 257.
1469. Art. 54 Ley 19300/1994, cited above.
1470. Art. 19 DFL 458/1975, cited above, as amended by Ley 20.443/2010, of 16 Nov. (DO 23 Nov. 2010).

444. Copyright law provides another example of how collective interests may be legally protected, given that an action may be brought by 'entities of collective management' (*entidades de gestión colectiva*), for example to recover royalties or, in some cases, to protect copyrights. However, this is usually carried out by the Chilean society of authors and musical interpreters (*Sociedad Chilena de Autores e Intérpretes Musicales*).[1471]

445. Hybrid situations are those cases where a single person both represents collective interests and also has legal responsibilities (which may give rise to liability) of his or her own – such as the case of the property manager of a condominium who represents collective interests in relation to the preservation and management of the common property. In this context, however, the condominium manager also has precise duties from which liability[1472] may arise.

Likewise for the liquidator of a group of creditors in a bankruptcy proceeding since, although the liquidator may represent the creditors in court, he may also be liable in some cases for *culpa levissima.*[1473]

446. Actions of collective and diffuse interests should not be confused with actions exercisable jointly by several persons for the benefit of a single interest. As it has been noted,[1474] claims for damages brought by at least 5% of the shareholders against the directors and managers of an SPA (*sociedad anónima*)[1475] represents a single interest (i.e., the company's interests) in relation to dealings contrary to such interests.

§3. Direct and Indirect

447. In tort matters, most of the legal doctrine asserts that only direct damage is recoverable (i.e., damage that has a direct relationship with the wrongful act).[1476] Such requirement of direct damage is perceived by the doctrine as mere reiteration of the causal link.[1477]

However, there is another position which, based on the observation[1478] that Article 2329 CC literally refers to 'any damage' (*todo daño*), posits there is no distinction between direct and immediate damage and indirect or mediated damage.

1471. Arts 67, 91, 102 LEY 17.336/1970, of 28 Aug. (DO 2 Oct. 1970). *See* CS 15 Jan. 2001, GJ 247, at 41,as pointed out by Barros, *Tratado*, I, cit., at 256.
1472. In this sense Article 23 *Ley copropiedad inmobiliaria* (Ley 19.537/1996, of 5 Dec, DO 16 Dec. 1997).
1473. Cf. Art. 35–36 L 20.720/2013 (DO 9 Jan. 2014).
1474. Barros, *Tratado*, I, cit., at 255.
1475. Article 133 bis *Ley de Sociedades Anónimas* (Ley 18.046/1981, cited above).
1476. Abeliuk, *Las Obligaciones*, *I*, at 256; Alessandri, *Responsabilidad*, cit., at 170–171; followed by Corral, *Lecciones,* cit., at 137. In relation to this jurisprudential position Diez, *El daño*, cit., at 72 contra Abeliuk, *Las Obligaciones*, *I*, at 310 y 377.
1477. Figueroa, *Curso IV*, cit., at 136.
1478. In this sense, the distinction made in contractual matters, pursuant to which Art. 1558 CC is applicable, would be irrelevant in tort matters: Tapia, *De la Responsabilidad*, cit., at 199, 310, 377.

If, it is assumed that the mediated damage may or may not necessarily be indirect (i.e., they are not necessarily synonymous), there may be another cause in addition to that relating to the act carried out by the person entrusted with the task. In this sense, the presence of other causes may not prevent the attribution of liability, albeit with different canons, depending, in this sense, also on the theory of causation that is taken into consideration.[1479]

§4. Pecuniary and Non-pecuniary Losses

448. Damages are primarily divided into pecuniary and non-pecuniary loss, although a traditional distinction has been made between *material* (in relation to pecuniary or patrimonial loss,[1480] including loss to persons and things[1481]) and moral damages (*daño moral*).[1482]

Non-pecuniary damage does not necessarily respect the principle of full compensation, especially in cases of personal injury, in that the injury suffered is not fully repaired.

I. Pecuniary Damage

449. The distinction between expectation (positive interest) and reliance (negative interest) does not seem recognized by Civil Code. Pecuniary damage includes *daño emergente* and *lucro cesante* (loss of profit). In this sense, a parallel can be drawn with contract law. Accordingly, the rule governing recoverable damages in cases of breach (Article 1556 CC) is held to apply also to tort situations.[1483] *Daño emergente* is the concrete loss occurred and it is the monetary substitute of non-performed obligation.

450. The concrete loss or diminution of assets[1484] is associated with *Daño emergente*, while with the loss of profit it is associated with the impossibility to make an expected profit, calculated based on a future and hypothetical situation but which is in any case concrete.[1485]

451. The loss of profit will be dealt with under the heading of future damage.[1486]

1479. Cf. Barros, *Tratado*, I, cit., at 243, 257 and 272.
1480. Tapia, *De la responsabilidad*, cit., at 219.
1481. Alessandri, *Responsabilidad,* cit., at 161.
1482. *See* paras 452 et seq.
1483. For all Alessandri, *Responsabilidad*, cit., at 395; Tapia, *De la responsabilidad*, cit., at 305; Diez, *El daño*, cit., at 57.
1484. For example, Alessandri, *Responsabilidad,* cit., at 395.
1485. On this point, refer to the study by Daniel Peñailillo Arévalo, 'Sobre el lucro cesante', *Revista de Derecho* (Universidad de Concepción), 2018/243, at 7 et seq.
1486. *See infra* paras 459 et seq.

II. Moral/Non-patrimonial Damage

452. It is noteworthy that there is still no clear understanding of what exactly constitutes moral damage (*daño moral*). The confusion partly stems from the doctrine that considers moral damage with patrimonial repercussions and moral damage involving material damage as two distinct categories.[1487]

Although the evolution of moral damage has been highlighted – passing from a concept related to the *pretium doloris*[1488] to other aspects while attempting to highlight both the nuances and the differences between moral and non-pecuniary damage[1489] – it is still treated as basically synonymous[1490] to non-pecuniary damage despite traditional doctrine generally distinguishes between material damage and moral damage without reference to non-pecuniary damage.[1491]

Still, notwithstanding the nuances between non-pecuniary damage and moral damage are not well defined in the Chilean legal system, there may be a general/special relationship between the two. This generates a restrictive approach to the subject matter in terms of indemnification of such damages (such as in the case of personal injury), without prejudice to the fact that the concept of moral damage includes loss of quality of life, aesthetic damage and other items of damage.[1492]

The doctrine has been critical in finding that many decisions do not respect the constitutional principles underlying liability.[1493]

453. In the absence of a specific norm that expressly allows compensation for non-pecuniary or moral damage, in tort liability, the opening up to various categories of damage is based on the broad interpretation of Article 2329 CC. More specifically, as Article 2329 CC states that 'any damage' must be compensated, damages for non-pecuniary loss arising out of tort have been awarded since the beginning of 1900.[1494] Recognition of non-pecuniary damage for breach came

---

1487. In this way a distinction was made between purely moral damage ('*daño meramente moral*') and ordinary damage (*daño ordinario*, the latter also involving material damage): Alessandri, *Responsabilidad*, cit., at 164.

1488. This association was clear from the traditional doctrine which affirmed that moral damage 'consists in the pain, harassment that the person suffers in his physical sensibility, feelings, beliefs and affections': Alessandri, *Responsabilidad*, at 160–161.

1489. On the point: Marcelo Barrientos Zamorano, 'Del daño moral al daño extrapatrimonial : la superación del pretium doloris', *Revista chilena de derecho*, 2008/1, at 35 et seq.

1490. For example, Figueroa, *Curso IV*, cit., at 137, as does Barros who states that moral damage is extra-patrimonial or non-patrimonial damage, also with references to case law: *see* Barros, *Tratado*, I, cit., at 299.

1491. Alessandri, *Responsabilidad*, cit., at 160.

1492. Classic monograph of reference in Chile on moral damage: Carmen Domínguez Hidalgo, *El daño Moral* (Santiago de Chile: editorial Jurídica de Chile, 2000). *See* also Cristian Aedo Barrena, *El daño moral en la responsabilidad contractual y extracontractual* (Valparaiso: Libromar, 2001).

1493. Eduardo Court Murasso, 'Análisis crítico de los criterios de valoración del daño moral en Chile', *Estudios de derecho civil XV* (Fabian Elorriaga De Bonis ed.) (Santiago de Chile: Thomson Reuters, 2020) at 916 et seq.

1494. Compensation begins with some train accidents that result in death: CS 8 Aug. 1902, Gceta de los Tribunales, 1902/2274, at 94; CS 22 Sep. 1905, RDJ, 3, s. 1ª, at 124; CS 10 Oct. 1906, RDJ, 3, s. 1ª, at 412 In 1907, giving relevance also to Corte de Apelación Santiago 27 Jun. 1907 RDJ tomo 4 s. 2ª, at 139, consolidating definitively with CS 16 Dec. 1922 *RDJ* tomo 21, s. 1ª at 1053: *See*

later,[1495] which is why the rules of tort have been preferred in cases involving both tort and contract damages.[1496]

454. At present, various special laws specifically provide for compensation of moral damages. For instance, moral damages are recognized in relation to work-related accidents or occupational diseases,[1497] as well as in B2C relationships.[1498] They are also recognized in cases where the right to health (except in cases where the damages were unforeseeable according to modern science[1499]) or the right to privacy[1500] has been jeopardized. Violations of the right to freedom of information[1501] and (since 2010) infringements of the original 1970 law on intellectual property[1502] may also give rise to awards for moral damages. Additionally, such damages have been recognized in cases involving harm caused to minors by negligent care on the part of the State.[1503]

455. Legal persons can also claim non-pecuniary damage, especially in cases of damage to name, reputation and image.[1504]

Carmén Domínguez Hidalgo, 'La indemnización por daño moral. Modernas tendencias en el derecho civil chileno y comparado', *Revista chilena de derecho*, 1998/1, at 35 y seq: also Barros, *Tratado*, I, cit., at 306–309; *See* Carmen Domínguez Hidalgo, 'Responsabilidad civil y principio de reparación integral del daño', cit., at 33 et seq.

1495. Although also recognized in isolation in some earlier judgments, in contractual material the consolidation of the compensability of moral damage essentially takes place with CS 20 Oct. 1994 RDJ, t. 91, s. 1ª, at 100 et seq. although the consolidation takes place in the nineties. On a systematic excursus *see* Iñigo de la Maza Gazmuri, 'El daño moral en materia contractual: la mirada de la Corte Suprema', *Revista Chilena de Derecho*, 2018/2, at 275 et seq. *See also* Luís Diez Schwerter,' La resarcibilidad del daño no patrimonial en Chile, Colombia, Ecuador y El Salvador. Del modelo de Bello a nuestros días', *Revista de Derecho Privado* (Universidad Externado), 2005/9, at 177 et seq.

1496. *See* paras 92 et seq.

1497. Art. 69 letra b) Ley 16.744, cited above.

1498. Arts 3 letra e); 37, 51, 54C, LPC. In the field of consumers it has been seen that it is possible to speak of a joint moral damage: *See supra* paras 439 et seq., Tapia Rodríguez, 'Daño moral colectivo', cit., at 1015 et seq.; González Cazorla, 'Daño moral colectivo en el derecho del consumo chileno: ...', cit., at 122 et seq.

1499. Art. 41 Ley 19.966/ 2004, cit.

1500. Art. 23 Ley 19.628/1999, cit.

1501. Art. 40.2 Ley 19.733/2001, cit.

1502. Art. 85 B letra b), 85 E, 85 K, Ley 17.336/1970, of 28 Aug. (DO 2 Oct. 1970), thanks to the rigour operated for the Ley 20.435/2010, of 23 Apr. (DO 4 May 2010). *See* Barría Díaz, 'Configuración del derecho moral ...', cit., at 941 et seq.; Pino Emhart, 'Las acciones civiles por infracciones al derecho de propiedad intelectual', cit., at 33 et seq.

1503. Art. 2a L 21.302/2020 of 22 Dec. (DO 5 Jan. 2021).

1504. For a categorization of the different positions: Mauricio Tapia Rodríguez, 'Daño moral de las personas jurídicas en el derecho chileno', *Estudios de derecho civil VIII*, (Carmen Domínguez Hidalgo, Joel González Castillo, Marcelo Barrientos Zamorano, Juan Luís Goldeberg Serrano, ed.) (Santiago de Chile: Thomson Reuters, Legal Publishing, 2013), at 621 et seq., although with a more critical stance *see* Cristián Larraín Páez, 'Daño moral a personas jurídicas: una aprente consolidación jurisprudencial', *Estudios de derecho civil V*, (Departamento de Derecho Privado de la Universidad de Concepción ed.) (Santiago de Chile: Legal Publishing, 2010) at 751 et seq., also Cristián Larraín Páez, 'Jurisprudencia reciente en materia de responsabilidad civil por ejercicio no autorizado del derecho a la imagen. En particular sobre el daño', *Estudios de derecho*

456. The uncontrolled, albeit limited, compensation of moral damage related to things has been noted.[1505] For example, compensation has been awarded for depression and suffering for the loss of one's car,[1506] or for the loss of jewelry following an investigation related to a theft.[1507]

457. Although damage (including moral damage) must be proven by whoever alleges to have incurred a loss (Article 1698 CC), the burden of proof for moral damages appears to benefit from certain flexibility.[1508] This flexibility is manifested above all in consumer relations,[1509] where the court grants compensation[1510] as a remedy[1511] in the face of inadequate protection by the consumer legislation.

§5. Pure Economic Loss

458. Chilean doctrine has analysed the subject essentially from the point of view of foreign law (namely common law and German[1512] law). As such, it defines pure economic loss (*daño patrimonial puro*) as that which produces a patrimonial harm without injury to property or the person (e.g., injury in matters of unfair competition,[1513] liability arising from false, erroneous or inaccurate information from

---

civil VIII, (Carmen Domínguez Hidalgo, Joel González Castillo, Marcelo Barrientos Zamorano, Juan Luís Goldeberg Serrano, ed.) (Santiago de Chile: Thomson Reuters, Legal Publishing, 2013), at 573 et seq.

In this critical sense the doctrine is inclined to disallow it for those with an animus of profit Cristian Larraín Páez, 'Daño moral a personas jurídicas: prevenciones teorícas y propuestas de solución', *Estudios de derecho civil IX* (Juan Andrés Varas Braun, Susan Turner Saelzer ed.) (Santiago de Chile: Thomson Reuters, Legal Publishing, 2014) at 593 et seq. In a partially critical sense *see also* Barros, *Tratado*, I, cit., at 309 et seq.

1505. He also observes and counters this with a categorization of decisions of merit: Barros, *Tratado*, I, cit., at 378–379.

1506. CS 10 Jun. 1969, *RDJ*, 66, s. 1ª, at 85; CS 10 Nov. 2015 (rol 30456/2014).

1507. CS 22 May 2017 (rol 97726/2016).

1508. Corral, *Lecciones*, cit., at 157 et seq.

1509. Carmen Domínguez Hidalgo, 'En torno a la reparación del daño moral en el ámbito del derecho del consumo: distinción entre problemas comunes y especiales', *Estudios de derecho civil XV* (Fabian Elorriaga De Bonis ed.) (Santiago de Chile: Thomson Reuters, 2020) at 885 et seq.

1510. For some recompilations in the case law in the field of consumer law: Juan Ignacio Contardo González, Hernán Felipe Cortes López, *Cuantificación del daño moral de los consomidores*. Tendencias y Sentencias, (Santiago de Chile, DER, 2019); Fabían Gonzáñez Cazorla, *Daño moral el derecho del consumidor*, (Santiago de Chile, DER, 2019).

1511. As in the case of the legal guarantee (protection in the case of lack of conformity): Alfredo Ferrante, 'Servicio técnico y reparación del bien: la alteración de la tutela efectiva del consumidor en caso de disconformidad material. Una visión jurisprudencial', *Ius et praxis*, 20020/3, at 73–74.

1512. Cristián Banfi del Río, 'Reflexiones del daño puramente patrimoniale', *Estudios de derecho civil VII*, (Fabián Elorriaga De Bonis ed.) (Santiago de Chile: Thomson Reuters, Abeledo Perrot, 2012), at 685 et seq.; Adrían Schopf Olea, 'Él ámbito de protección de la responsailidad extracontractual y los daños puramente patrimoniales', *Estudios de derecho civil X* (Álvaro Vidal Olivares, Gonzalo Severín Fuster, Caludia Mejías Alonso ed.) (Santiago de Chile: Thomson Reuters, 2015) at 921 et seq.; also Barros, *Tratado*, I, cit., at 295 et seq.

1513. Barros, *Tratado*, I, cit., at 272, 295 et seq.; Cristián Banfi del Río, 'Reflexiones del daño puramente patrimoniale', *Estudios de derecho civil VII*, (Fabián Elorriaga De Bonis ed.) (Santiago de Chile: Thomson Reuters, Abeledo Perrot, 2012), at 685; Schopf Olea, 'Él ámbito de protección...', cit., at 926–927.

experts in relation to a business choice[1514]), noting that the pure economic loss is concealed between the categories of *daño emergente* and loss of profit, essentially in the latter.[1515] In this context, the arguments discussed in relation to loss of profit and unfair competition[1516] are repeated. The genesis of such damage has been identified implicitly in some decisions,[1517] and in general the doctrine considers that abuse, malice or gross negligence is required for its recoverability.[1518]

§6. Actual and Future Damages (Lost Profits)

459. The certainty of the damage has essentially been associated with its existence at the time of the claim. However, it will be seen that it is possible to compensate future damages,[1519] but that also the requirement of actuality and certainty of the damage may encounter new flexibilities in relation to the loss of chance.[1520]

I. Future Damages and Loss of Profits (*Daño Futuro and Lucro Cesante*)

460. It has been long established by traditional doctrine that future damage is indemnifiable both in the case of *daño emergente*[1521] as well as loss of profit. This may occur, for instance, in cases involving lost wages due to the loss of an arm or other bodily injury.[1522] In such hypotheses, the jurisprudence has allowed such damages since the second half of the 1800s.[1523] Thus, although future damage and loss of profit are similar, they do not necessarily coincide. The same is true for actual damage and *daño emergente*.[1524]

1514. Adrían Schopf Olea, 'Responsabilidad extracontractual de expertos por información falsa, errónea o inexacta', *Estudios de derecho civil XI* (Departamento de Derecho Privado Universiad de Concepción, ed.) (Santiago de Chile: Thomson Reuters, 2016) at 943 y ss. Generally on liability for bad advice Enrique Barro sBourie, Andrés Rioseco López, 'Responsabilidad de quien da un mal consejo', *Estudios de derecho civil X* (Álvaro Vidal Olivares, Gonzalo Severín Fuster, Caludia Mejías Alonso ed.) (Santiago de Chile: Thomson Reuters, 2015) at 633 et seq. *See* Arts 2012, 2018, 2119 CC.

1515. Cristián Banfi del Río, 'Reflexiones del daño puramente patrimoniale', cit., at 698–699.

1516. *See* paras 251 et seq.

1517. *See* CS 15 Nov. 1919 (RDJ, 18, 2, at 164); CS 31 Aug. 2009 (rol 3516/2009), relating to SAP Concepción 30 Dec. 2008 (rol 360/2005), commented by Iñigo De la Maza Gazmuri, Carlos Pizarro Wilson, *Responsabilidad civil casos prácticos* (Santiago de chile: Abeledo Perrot, Legal Públishing, 5th ed, 2010), at 245 et seq., *see* Cristián Banfi del Río, 'Reflexiones del daño puramente patrimoniale', cit., at 699.

1518. Cf. Cristián Banfi del Río, 'Reflexiones del daño puramente patrimoniale', cit., at 702; Schopf Olea, 'Él ámbito de protección...', cit., at 935, also Barros, *Tratado*, I, cit., at 168 et seq.

1519. *See* paras 460 et seq.

1520. *See* paras 466 et seq.

1521. On *daño emergente futuro*, for example, *see* CS 14 Sep. 2017 (rol 400/2017) concerning a medical negligencia relating to a preventive medical examination (contractual liability), annoted by Tomás Frenck, 'Daño emergente futuro. Corte Suprema de fecha 14 de septiembre de 2017', *Revista justicia & Derecho*, 2020/3, at 1 et seq.

1522. As noted, Alessandri, *Responsabilidad*, cit., at 157.

1523. A jurisprudential overview can be found in Alessandri, *Responsabilidad*, cit., at 157–158.

1524. Gastón Salinas Ugarte, 'Requisitos comunes del daño...', cit. at 737.

Accordingly, the loss of profit where certainties of its production are compensable, such claims are more problematic in ambiguous situations where the burden of proof plays a fundamental role.

461. Hence, compensation for loss of profit is generally more complicated and must be accompanied by a concrete assessment,[1525] or at least be characterized by the 'reasonable probability'[1526] that such profit would materialize. Therefore, although traditional doctrine has tended to exclude its indemnifiability, this is not entirely the case, at least in the field of tort liability, which is more ardent in contractual liability.[1527]

462. As such, future damage can be compensated provided it is certain and not merely hypothetical.[1528] For this reason, it should be noted that certain damage and actual damage are not synonymous,[1529] as future damage can be certain since the future nature of the damage essentially refers to its effects.[1530] From this perspective, the biggest problem may be in defining the amount recoverable.[1531]

463. In establishing the extent of damages, various parameters or variables are considered.[1532] These are often freely reinterpreted by the judge to include economic parameters (e.g., the previous work situation and income), personal situations (e.g., the age of the injured party) and technical aspects (e.g., expert opinions, whether of a medical or economic nature). In terms of quantifying the loss of earnings, the Supreme Court uses flexible parameters, taking into account, for example, the 'expectation of development of professional activity', specifically that of a professional driver.[1533]

1525. For example, Alessandri, *Responsabilidad,* cit., at 398.
1526. Barros, *Tratado*, I, cit., at 247.
1527. *See* Sergio Gatica Pacheco, *Aspectos de la indemnización de perjuicios por incumplimiento de contrato (estudio de los artículos 1535 a 1544, 1556, 1558, 1559 y 1535 a 1544 del Código Civil)*, (Santiago de Chile: Editorial Jurídica, 1959).
1528. Tapia, *De la responsabilidad*, cit., at 311.
1529. As evidenced by Tapia, *De la responsabilidad*, cit., at 195.
1530. In this sense, in relation to the effects, the *lucro cesante* (lost profit) is always relative to a future damage: Abeliuk, *Las Obligaciones*, *I*, at 245. On current and future damage *see* Diez, *El daño*, cit., at 65 et seq.
1531. In relation to future damages for welfare benefits *see* Hugo Cárdenas Villarreal, 'Los daños futuros en el Derecho chileno: de las condenas pecuniarias a las prestaciones asistenciales', *Estudios de derecho civil XV* (Fabian Elorriaga De Bonis ed.) (Santiago de Chile: Thomson Reuters, 2020) at 901 et seq.
1532. A brief analysis in Joaquín Andrés Muñoz Ayarza, *El lucro cesante en la responsabilidad civile, Su prueba y determinación en el proceso* (Santiago de Chile: Editorial Metropolitana, 2020).
1533. As noted in CS 24 Nov. 2014 (Rol 2547/2014). Although the case relates to contractual liability, it can be extended to tort liability in terms of reasoning. Note that here it refers to an amputation of an artery (example traditionally provided by the doctrine) during work activity.

464. Another particularly relevant issue is the loss of profit associated with liability for unfair competition.[1534] However, the doctrine[1535] has observed that, in general, the problem with attributing liability in competition law torts stems, on the one hand, from difficulties in identifying who has standing and, on the other hand, from the difficulties in determining appropriate compensation methods and extent of relevant damages. Progress has been made in this direction given that some decisions establish the relevance of economic relations in the quantification of lost profits,[1536] which the Chilean doctrine has begun to categorize.[1537]

465. It is likewise conceivable that damage may be caused to the property of indirect victims, regardless of whether the primary claimant lives or dies.[1538]

II. Loss of Chance and Certain of Damage

466. Although 'related' concepts,[1539] loss of chance and loss of profit are different[1540] and cannot be treated identically.[1541] Whereas compensation for loss of profit involves harm that has not yet occurred and requires a sufficiently certain loss with reference to future profits (which extent is uncertain), in the case of loss of chance, the damage has already occurred. Therefore, in this latter case, it is necessary to assess damage with regard for the past and according to the statistical probability[1542] that such an event would have occurred. Nonetheless, this is not the approach adhered to by the courts (*see infra*).

1534. *See* DFL 1/2004, 18 Oct. (DO 7 Mar. 2005): consolidated, coordinated and systematized text of the Decree Law (*Decreto Ley*) 211/1973; Ley 20.945/2016, of 19 Aug. (DO 19 Aug. 2016).

1535. *See* Andrés Fuchs Nissin, Álvaro Vives Martens, 'Dos problemas en torno a la responsabilidad civil derivada de ilícito anticompetitivos', *Estudios de derecho civil X* (Álvaro Vidal Olivares, Gonzalo Severín Fuster, Claudia Mejías Alonzo ed.) (Santiago de Chile: Thomson Reuters, 2015) at 963 et seq.

1536. For example, *see* JPI Santiago, 10º, 17 Dec. 2019 (Rol 1940/2013).

1537. In this sense, the analysis made in Jorge Fantuzzi Majulis is very interesting. Victoria Edwards Vial, *Determinación de lucro Cesante. Una mirada económica* (Cizur Menor: Thomson Reuters, 2019).

1538. CS 4 Apr. 2019 (rol 27948/2017), CS 12 Mar. 2019 rol 2609/2018), CS 28 Sep. 2016 (rol 7237/2015), such concession being made long ago: CS 9 Sep. 1946 (*RDJ*, tome 44, s. 1ª, at 130); CS 4 Aug. 1933 (*RDJ*, tome 30, s.1 ª, at 524): Barros, *Tratado*, I, cit., at 364 et seq.

1539. The differences are observed, although it is noted that the Civil and Commercial Code of the Argentine nation treats them together in Articles 1738 and 1739: Daniel Peñailillo Arévalo, 'Sobre el lucro cesante', *Revista de Derecho* (Universidad de Concepción), 2018/243, at 15–16. Sobre una asocciazione tra lucro cessante e perdita di opportunità: Barros, *Tratado*, I, cit., at 247–248.

1540. Daniel Peñailillo Arévalo, 'Sobre el lucro cesante', *Revista de Derecho* (Universidad de Concepción), 2018/243, at 7 et seq.; Fabián Elorreaga Bonis, 'Daño físico y lucro cesante', *Derecho de daños* (Santiago de Chile, LexisNexis, 2002), at 53 et seq.

1541. On some nuances, *see* Ramón Domínguez Águila, 'Notas sobre el lucro cesante y el perjuicio económico futuro', *Estudios de derecho civil V*, (Departamento de Derecho Privado de la Universidad de Concepción ed.) (Santiago de Chile: Legal Publishing, 2010) at 655 et seq.

1542. The reasoning is also interesting in economic terms in Fantuzzi Majulis. Edwards Vial, *Determinación de lucro Cesante.* cit., at 69 et seq.

467. Recently, the certainty requirement has been partially challenged by the possibility to recover damages from loss of chance.

Traditionally, it has been considered that 'certain means that it is a question of a current or future damage',[1543] such that 'there is the certainty that the damage has necessarily occurred or will occur',[1544] 'because it is the prolongation of a state of affairs that already exists or because certain circumstances have occurred that make it inevitable'.[1545] This requirement was also based on wording of the Civil Code, which makes reference to 'damage suffered' (*daño sufrido*) at Article 2315 CC and to 'damage occasioned' (*daño ocasionado*[1546]) at Article 2323 CC. Thus, the certainty of the damage has led to the recoverability of future damage as well,[1547] and the difference between certainty and uncertainty of damage impacts the *an* rather than the *quantum* of compensation. For this reason, for the purposes of establishing its certainty, it is irrelevant that the extent of damages is difficult to determine.[1548] If it is easy to identify existence of this requirement for pecuniary damage, it is also clear that this requirement may be met in relation to moral damage by means of presumptions.[1549]

468. Based on this finding, compensation for eventual[1550] or hypothetical[1551] damage was denied. The doctrine has not dealt directly with the subject, but it is symptomatic that part of the doctrine argued, at the end of 1997 and in relation to awards for damages for loss of chance, that 'up to now [compensation in such cases] has been unheard of in our courts. Hence, we will not comment further'.[1552] In spite of this, a couple of years later, another part of the doctrine considered that the loss of chance 'is not equivalent to the repair of a hypothetical damage, but a certain one, since the probability can be a significant pecuniary value with monetary value'.[1553]

469. This view appears to be changing. Indeed, despite – based on the requirement of certainty of damages – traditionally damages for loss of chance have not been recoverable, in the last few decades (and particularly since the 2015–2016 biennium,[1554] although some judgments[1555] have even implicitly admitted loss of chance, in the past[1556]), the Supreme Court has been more receptive to such a view.

1543. Figueroa, *Curso IV,* cit., at 135.
1544. Figueroa, *Curso IV*, cit., at 135.
1545. Alessandri, *Responsabilidad*, cit., at 156–157.
1546. Tapia, *De la Responsabilidad*, cit., at 195, note no. 461; also Diez, *El daño,* cit., at 55.
1547. Also Alessandri, *Responsabilidad*, cit., at 156; Barros, *Tratado,* I, cit., at 245.
1548. Alessandri, *Responsabilidad*, cit., at 156.
1549. Barros, *Tratado*, I, cit., at 244.
1550. Ramos, *De la responsabilidad Civil*, cit., at 81.
1551. Diez, *El daño*, cit., at 55.
1552. Diez, *El daño*, cit., at 81.
1553. Ramón Domínguez Águila, 'Comentarios de Jurisprudencia . Accidente del trabajo. Aplicación de reglas de derecho común Prescripción. Lucro cesante Pérdida de una chance.' *Revista de Derecho* (Universidad de Concepción), 1999/2006 at 169.
1554. Initiating this trend: CS Dec. 3, 2015 (rol 29365/2014), CS 22 Sep. 2016 (rol 9481/2016).
1555. For example, CS 11 Apr. 2007 (rol 3291/2005); CS 20 Jan. 2011 (rol 2074/2009) contra CS 27 Oc 2008 (rol 1021/2007).
1556. *See* Mauricio Tapia Rodríguez, 'Pérdida de una chance: ¿Un perjuicio indemnizable en Chile?', *Estudios de derecho civil VII* (Santiago de Chile, Abeledo Perrot, 2012), at 645 et seq.; Mauricio

This view has been accepted essentially in relation to the death of the victim in cases of medical malpractice and compensation for the victims of the earthquake and tsunami of February 27, 2010 – and therefore essentially in relation to non-pecuniary damages, which tends to be mixed with moral damages in Chile.

However, in some cases, provided that the chance is actual and significant, it also refers to an economic profit. However, in this case, again, its nuance and difference with the profit is blurred.[1557]

470. Although loss of chance is treated here in association with harm, there are two strands of interpretation. For one part of the doctrine,[1558] the loss of chance must be associated with the element of damage and not with the causal relationship. This position is opposed by another part of the doctrine[1559] that frames the loss of chance within the discussion of causation, since in this case the causal aspects that could have avoided the damage already produced would be more relevant.[1560] In some cases, the doctrine has been critical of both views.[1561]

It will be illustrated later that although some case law (especially in the case of medical liability) associates it with causation, other case law associates it with damage. For instance, loss of chance has been framed as a recoverable damage in cases involving the victims of tsunamis.

Tapia Rodríguez, 'Pérdida de una chance. Su indemnización en la jurisprudencia chilena', *Revista de Derecho* (Escuela de Postgrado de la Universidad de Chile), 2012/2, at 251 et seq.

1557. Of 'possibility de profitto eventuale' speaks CS 30 Sep. 2015 (rol 2795/2015), of 'obtaining a profit or avoiding a pérdita' speaks CS 3 Dec. 2015 (rol 29365/2014); we refer to the interesting study and analysis of Mauricio Tapia Rodríguez, 'Pérdida de una opportunidad de negocio como daño indemnizable en el Derecho Chileno', *Estudios de derecho civil XIV* (Maricruz Gómez de la Torre Vargas, Gabriel Hernández Paulsen, Fabiola Lathrop Gómez, Mauricio Tapia Rodríguez ed.) (Santiago de Chile: Thomson Reuters, 2019) at 1071 et seq.; Ramón Dóminguez Águila, 'El principio en relación con el lucro cesante: tensione', *El Principio de Reparación Integral en sus Contornos Actuales. Una Revisión desde el derecho Chileno. Latinoamericano y Europeo* (Carmen Domínguez Hidalgo, ed.) (Santiago de Chile: Thomson Reuters, 2019), at 159 et seq.

1558. For example, Mauricio Tapia Rodríguez, 'Pérdida de una chance: ¿Un perjuicio indemnizable en Chile?'., *Estudios de derecho civil VII* (Santiago de Chile, Abeledo Perrot, 2012), p. 645 et seq.; It frames the loss of chanche within the damage in relation to certeza: Ignacio Ríos Erazo, Rodrigo Silva Goñi, 'Pérdida de la chance u oportunidad como nuevo capitulo indemnizatorio', *Estudios de derecho civil II,* (Hernán Corral Talciani, María Sara Rodríguez Pinto ed.) (Santiago de Chile: Thomson Reuters, 2011) at 281, *see also* Rìos Erazo, Ignacio & Silva Goñi, Rodrigo, *Responsabilidad civil por pérdida de la oportunidad* (Santiago de Chile: Editorial Jurídica de Chile, 2014), at 91 et seq.

1559. *See* Barros, *Tratado,* II, cit., at 1290; Barros, *Tratado*, I, cit., at 399 et seq.

1560. For example, with respect to the loss of profit where the gains are more important: Barros, *Tratado,* I, cit., at 247 et seq.

1561. It has been argued that this would lead to a 'denaturation' of the concept of damage that would result in excessive civil liability: Claudia Mejias Alonzo, 'La pérdidad de una chance. Una revisión a partir de los daños indemnizables', *Estudios de derecho civil XIV* (Maricruz Gómez de la Torre Vargas, Gabriel Hernández Paulsen, Fabiola Lathrop Gómez, Mauricio Tapia Rodríguez ed.) (Santiago de Chile: Thomson Reuters, 2019) at 1079–1080.

471. While it is noted that in some cases the full extent of damages is awarded, in others it is reduced[1562] on the grounds that the same amount cannot be awarded for harm as would be awarded in the case of death of the injured party, since there is no causal link with the latter. In any event, without a binding indemnity table, the assessment of any amount is relative, making the above statement also relative. Consequently, the judge is the one that actually performs the assessment of damage on a prudential basis.[1563] Moreover, many decisions that award a reduced amount of damages compared to damages claimed merely state that 'it is not possible to assess the proven loss in the same terms as the patient's death'.[1564] Some peculiarities will be mentioned regarding awards for full compensation in cases of tsunami or earthquake victims (*see infra*).

472. It should be noted that just as for compensation for the loss of chance relating to the death of the victim, damages may also be claimed both by the injured party itself as well as its family members for any non-pecuniary damage. If, initially, such damages are awarded to the son, the daughter-in-law and the granddaughter[1565] without further specification, subsequently it is considered that the compensation is owed to the spouse, and the son should be compensated 'for not having counted on having had the presence of your family member for a longer period of time'[1566] – a line of reasoning that generally applies also in the case of a sister and grandchild,[1567] father and brother,[1568] or spouse and mother.[1569] Non-pecuniary damages may also be claimed by 'parents who can no longer enjoy the company of their child'.[1570]

A. *Medical Liability*

473. In the area of medical malpractice,[1571] indemnification for loss of chance began catching on following a 2015 judgment relating to the attention in the emergency room of a cardiac problem that resulted in the patient's death,[1572] and another

1562. Hugo Cárdenas Villareal, 'La perdida de la chance en la reciente jurisprudencia médica', *Estudios de derecho civil XIV* (Maricruz Gómez de la Torre Vargas, Gabriel Hernández Paulsen, Fabiola Lathrop Gómez, Mauricio Tapia Rodríguez ed.) (Santiago de Chile: Thomson Reuters, 2019) at 1029 et seq.
1563. Ignacio Ríos Erazo, Rodrigo Silva Goñi, 'Pérdida de la chance u oportunidad como nuevo capitulo indemnizatorio', *Estudios de derecho civil II,* (Hernán Corral Talciani, María Sara Rodríguez Pinto ed.) (Santiago de Chile: Thomson Reuters, 2011) at 286–287.
1564. For example, CS Dec. 3, 2015 (rol 29365/2014); CS Dec. 26, 2017, (rol 11526/2017).
1565. CS 22 Sep. 2016 (rol 9481/2016).
1566. CS 29 Aug. 2017 (rol 101769/2016), in the same sense CS 25 Oct. 2016 (rol 22751/2015),in relation to loss of daughter also CS 24 Apr. 2019 (rol 7108/2017).
1567. CS 6 Nov. 2017 (rol 62104/2016).
1568. CS 3 Apr. 2019 (rol 13129/2018).
1569. CS 27 Feb. 2018, (rol 21599/2017).
1570. CS 26 Dec. 2017, (rol 11526/2017).
1571. For an overview of some judgments in relation to the loss of chance *see* Hugo Cárdenas Villareal, 'La perdida de la chance en la reciente jurisprudencia médica', cit., at 1027 et seq.;Vidal Olivares, *Responsabilidad civil Medica*, cit. at 224 et seq.
1572. CS Dec. 3, 2015 (rol 29365/2014).

decision from 2016 relating to medical negligence involving a patient suffering from VIH/SIDA.[1573] Although both decisions refer to the loss of the possibility of a longer life[1574] and coincide in denying the causal link between mala praxis médica and the death of the subject, they differ in part. In fact, if the first decision does not associate the chance to a problem of causation, stating that 'they deprived the person of a worthy life'[1575] and 'they deprived him of any possibility, even minimal, to be subjected to adequate, relevant and timely treatment, by virtue of which he could, possibly, save his life',[1576] the 2016 judgment establishes that there can be a causal relationship between the medical implementation and a potentially longer life, which would have been achieved had it not been for the negligent behaviour.[1577]

474. The trend of the 2016 judgment is followed, and partially amplified, by a series of decisions which expressly associate chance with causation.[1578] Thus, strangely, although the court does not consider there to be a causal relationship between the hospital's conduct and the death of the patient, it states that it cannot be discarded either,[1579] thus giving effect to chance and the related compensation. For this reason, it is stated that the relevant causal link 'is not related to the death of the patient – as there are degrees of uncertainty that prevent the causal link from being established – but rather to the circumstance of depriving him of the opportunity to obtain effective treatment at an early stage'.[1580] which gives rise to the right to damages for the loss of the chance to live longer (*sobrevida*). This last concept related to the possibility of living a longer life is realized in the following cases: whooping cough,[1581] pulmonary embolism,[1582] myocardial infarction,[1583] failure to detect hypovolemic[1584] shock or pancreatitis where there is a lack of 'possibility to have promptly started a targeted treatment to cope with the development of pancreatitis'.[1585]

Similar considerations are made in another judgment for which it is expressly stated that it is not possible to establish the causal relationship between incorrect diagnosis and appropriate treatment and death, but that 'it is undoubtedly possible

1573. CS 22 Sep. 2016 (rol 9481/2016).
1574. The 2015 judgment speaks of '*pérdida de oportunidad de sobrevida*', the 2016 judgment speaks of '*posible sobrevida*' or '*chances de sanar o sobrevivir*'.
1575. CS 3 Dec. 2015 (rol 29365/2014). Interesting that this judgment speaks in terms of patrimonial loss since it speaks of obtaining a profit or avoiding a loss (' conseguir una ganancia o evitar una pérdida').
1576. CS 3 Dec. 2015 (rol 29365/2014).
1577. CS 22 Sep. 2016 (rol 9481/2016).
1578. Thus, it is considered that 'it is relevant to invoke the loss theory of chance to determine the causal relationship': CS 29 Aug. 2017 (rol 101769/2016).
1579. This is because the patient's intracranial haemorrhage had a direct cause in the embolic complication developed by the patient.
1580. CS 29 Aug. 2017 (rol 101769/2016).
1581. CS Nov. 9, 2017 (rol 1745/2017).
1582. CS Apr. 3, 2019 (rol 13129/2018).
1583. CS 25 Oct. 2016 (rol 22751/2015).
1584. CS 27 Feb. 2018, (rol 21599/2017).
1585. CS Apr. 24, 2019 (rol 7108/2017).

to state that such treatment would have given the patient a clear possibility of a longer life',[1586] arriving at the same conclusions regarding the causal link as described above.[1587]

475. Some judgments do not affect such reasoning expressed in terms of causation and the possibility of a better life. However, awarding damages for loss of opportunity to have had 'a better quality of life'[1588] or condemning a party to pay compensation 'not for deprivation of life but of the opportunity to fight worthily for it',[1589] or 'loss of chance for the patient to have received adequate treatment according to the degree of progression of the disease'.[1590]

B. Liability Arising from Tsunami

476. It is important to discuss the consolidation of compensation for loss of earnings in the event of the peculiar seismic phenomenon of 27 March 2010, which was also linked to a tsunami that caused the death of several individuals. This circumstance resulted in the filing of many lawsuits against the Chilean State due to its lack of adequate warning of the possible danger of a tsunami.

An important study[1591] analyses the events and observes noteworthy conclusions. It is observed that the Supreme Court, in resolving the questions, changes its opinion and reverses its first position that appeared to deny the claims for damages for lack of causal link between the conduct of the State and the death of the victims.[1592]

Subsequently, this trend is reversed by two lines of argumentation: one that considers the existence of the causal link and another that considers the presence of a loss of chance as an autonomous form of damage in its own right (therefore not related to the causal link).

1586. Considering that the chances of fighting the disease – hospital pneumonia – increase early treatment with broad-spectrum antibiotics started: CS 6 Nov. 2017 (rol 62104/2016).

1587. Thus, it is considered that 'the causal link is not related to the death of the patient – since there are degrees of uncertainty that prevent the causal link from being established –, but rather to the circumstance of depriving him of the opportunity to obtain effective treatment early': CS 6 Nov. 2017 (rol 62104/2016).

1588. Prescribing neuroleptic drugs with various contraindications including fatigue and involuntary movements (dystonia) : CS 11 May 2017 (rol 47936/2016).

1589. Loss that the court considers 'certain and actual' that caused death due to diagnostic error in emergency room: CS 26 Dec. 2017, (rol 11526/2017).

1590. In relation to a diagnostic relating to breast cancer. CS 2 Oct. 2018 (rol 41890/2017).

1591. Rodrigo Barría Díaz, 'La pérdida de una oportunidad en la jurisprudencia de la Corte Suprema sobre juicios indemnizatorios derivados del terremoto y tsunami de 27 de febrero de 2010', *Revista de Derecho* (Universidad de Concepción), 2019/245, at 235 et seq.

1592. CS 23 Jan. 2013 (rol 1250/2012), CS 29 Apr. 2014 (rol 16.920/2013 & rol 16.885/2013, CS 4 Oct. 2016 (rol 24.306/2016). Also posteriorly isolated CS 28 Jun. 2018, (rol 31.757/2017).

477. According to the first line of argumentation, the court's prior orientation is completely subverted and the State should be held liable for the deaths of the victims on the grounds of lack of service (*falta de servicio*) for having communicated incorrect information (e.g., that there was no danger of tsunami after the earthquake).[1593]

The second line of argumentation, instead, submits that the State is liable not so much for the deaths as for having deprived such individuals from the possibility of survival. In this context, the lack of adequate preparation or prevention policies in relation to seismic phenomena become relevant. In this sense the damages for loss of chance are established, not by framing them in terms of causation but by compensating the loss of opportunity to have survived the tsunami (which is considered an autonomous damage) and considering that the causal relationship occurs between the lack of service and the missed opportunity to save one's life.[1594]

478. In analysing the solutions offered by the Supreme Court to the claims brought, the doctrine[1595] carefully noted that the courts moved away from dogmatism in favour of compensating victims for the particular event experienced. Thus, the pragmatic and functional view of the courts has allowed increased protection for the victims, although some legal solutions, such as the judicial presumptions used to establish the causal relationship between the lack of service provided by the State and the death of the victims are questionable.[1596]

479. In this pro-victim context, one understands the 'conceptual confusion'[1597] of jurisprudence in understanding loss of opportunity and their peculiar inconsistency. For example, rulings that frame the damage as loss of chance without proportionately reducing the award (and thus failing to formally reduce the amount to be compensated) often result in substantially awarding full compensation.[1598]

1593. *Ex pluris* CS 18 Dec. 2013 (rol 1.629/2013); CS7 Jun. 2016 (rol 32.262/2015); CS 27 Jul. 2017 (rol 68.818/2016), CS 12 Dec. 2017 (rol 172/2107); CS, 26 Mar. 2018 (rol 10.165/2017), CS 4 Dec. 2018 (45.305/2017), CS 18 Mar. 2019 (rol 4185/2018).

1594. CS 9 Nov. 2017 (rol 12,169/2017); CS 16 Nov. 2017 (rol 4.658/2017), CS 17 Jan. 2018 (rol 5.094/2017); CS 17 apr2018 (rol 18.225/2017); CS 8 Nov. 2018 (rol 871/2018); CS21 Jan. 2019 (rol 40.166/2017). For a comment to CS 9 Nov. 2017 *see* also Sonia Inostroza Adasme, 'Análisis de la sentencia CS rol 12169/2017 a la luz de la pérdida de la chance', *Revista de Derecho* (Universidad Externado), 2019/39, at 309 et seq.

1595. These are the interesting conclusions of Rodrigo Barría Díaz, 'La pérdida de una oportunidad en la jurisprudencia de la Corte Suprema sobre juicios indemnizatorios derivados del terremoto y tsunami de 27 de febrero de 2010', *Revista de Derecho* (Universidad de Concepción), 2019/245, at 265–266.

1596. In this sense Barria affirms that the causal relation should not have been between negligent informative communication and death, but between the former and the bad behavioural choice of the victim or the fact that the latter did not adopt a different behaviour: Rodrigo Barría Díaz, 'La pérdida de una oportunidad en la jurisprudencia de la Corte Suprema sobre juicios indemnizatorios derivados del terremoto y tsunami de 27 de febrero de 2010', *Revista de Derecho* (Universidad de Concepción), 2019/245, at 246.

1597. Barría Díaz, 'La pérdida de una oportunidad en la jurisprudencia...', cit., at 265.

1598. *Ibid.*, at 263–264. In general, the author observes that in the judgments approximate calculations are made confirming those of the first instance (op. cit. at, 250).

§7. Other Costs

480. Compensation for damage to tangible property also includes compensation for indirect or related expenses, such as repair estimates.[1599]

481. Interest is applied to pecuniary compensation even though there is no fixed criterion relating to the time of quantification.[1600]

Without a similar provision for contract matters that envisages interest on arrears,[1601] the doctrine has questioned whether such a rule would be applicable in tort cases. Based on the observation that Article 1551 n. 3 CC establishes the debtor is in default from the moment of a judicial claim, it is possible to arrive at this solution and reject the notion that the debtor is in default from the moment of the decision, given the declaratory nature of the same.[1602] Nevertheless, the Supreme Court seems to award interest starting them from the moment of the final judgment.[1603]

§8. Mitigation of Damages

482. In non-contractual liability matters, for a part of doctrine it is 'possible to question'[1604] the duty to mitigate the damage, despite another part of the doctrine allows such mitigation.[1605] Furthermore, it should be noted that the doctrine[1606] has pointed out that damage which can reasonably be avoided cannot be claimed by claiming reimbursement of the expenses incurred to minimize damage. The problem of mitigation of damages in part is that it can be related to the Article 2330 CC and the imprudent exposure of the victim to the harm, this issue can be framed both as an aspect relating to the damage and as associated with causation.[1607] Some precautionary and conservation measures have also been associated with the duty to mitigate and Article 2330 CC.[1608]

1599. Barros, *Tratado*, I, cit., at 286.

1600. For example, they are granted either from the moment of the event, the damage or the judgment of first instance. Reference is made to the interesting study of Ruperto Pinochet Olave, Francisca Concha Le Beuffe, 'Criterios para el cálculo de intereses y reajustes en casos de condenas judiciales en juicios de indemnizaciones civiles por responsabilidad civil extracontractual', *Revista de Derecho*, 237/2015, at 119, en particular at 136 et seq.; also Schwerter, *El daño extracontractual*...cit., at 218 et seq.

1601. Art. 1559 CC.

1602. Barros, *Tratado*, II, cit., at 996.

1603. Interesting on point is the CS 20 May 2021 judgment (rol 8738/2018).

1604. Carlos Pizarro Wilson, 'Contra el fatalismo del perjuicio. A propósito del deber de mitigar el daño', *Revista de Derecho* (PUCV), 2013/41, at 69.

1605. Corral, *Lecciones*, cit., at 383. More widely it is opportune to consult San Martín Neira, *La carga del perjudiciado de evitar o mitigar el daño. Estudio histórico comparado*, cit., *passim*, especially at 357 et seq.

1606. Ramón Domínguez Águila, 'Notas sobre el deber de minimizar el daño', *Revista Chilena de Derecho Privado*, 2005/5, at 76.

1607. *See supra* paras 376 et seq.

1608. In relation to some precautionary or conservation measures related to the duty to mitigate: Orlando Palominos Aravena, 'Aproximaciones al reconocimiento de la carga de mitigar el daño en el derecho chileno', *El Principio de Reparación Integral en sus Contornos Actuales. Una Revisión desde*

§9. Compensation *Iure Proprio* to Victims by Reflection (Indirect Victims)

483. Traditionally, moral damages have been awarded to the relatives of the deceased,[1609] thus materializing a *iure proprio* right to the so-called victims by reflex or rebound victims (defined for example *por rebote*, *por repercusión*) or indirect victims.

484. The action of the indirect victim (who is not necessarily an heir) is an autonomous and dependent action[1610] with respect to that of the principal victim. Hence, it has been stated[1611] that the damages settlement of the primary victim does not extend to any settlements or payments of other damages.

However, the dependence of the action of the secondary victim on the other would mean that, according to some scholars,[1612] its amount should be reduced whenever the primary victim does not claim the total amount of damages (e.g., when s/he has contributed to the production of the damage pursuant to Article 2330 CC).

In more detail, another part of the doctrine[1613] asserts that the problem differs according to whether Article 2330 CC is associated with a problem of damage or causation. Understanding it in terms of damage leads to the possibility of being able to compensate the indirect victim even though the primary victim is responsible for his own death. This is because the damage for the indirect victim would remain unaltered. Framing the issue in terms of causation would yield the opposite result.

---

el derecho Chileno. Latinoamericano y Europeo (Carmen Domínguez Hidalgo, ed.) (Santiago de Chile: Thomson Reuters, 2019), at 311 et seq.; On the precautionary principle and the principle of full reparation: Ramón Domínguez Águila, 'Principio de reparación integral y principio de precaución', *El Principio de Reparación Integral en sus Contornos Actuales. Una Revisión desde el derecho Chileno. Latinoamericano y Europeo* (Carmen Domínguez Hidalgo, ed.) (Santiago de Chile: Thomson Reuters, 2019), at 329 et seq.

1609. An initial approximation for Chilean law: Fabián Elorriaga De Bonis, 'Novedades judiciales en torno al daño moral por repercusión', *Estudios de derecho civil II*, (Hernán Corral Talciani, María Sara Rodríguez Pinto ed.) (Santiago de Chile: Thomson Reuters, 2011) at 229 et seq.; Fabián Elorriaga De Bonis, 'Del daño por repercusión o rebote', *Revista Chilena de Derecho*, 1999/2, at 369 et seq., Alessandri, *Responsabilidad*, cit., at 329 et seq.

1610. On autonomy and dependence: Kuncar Oneto, '¿Es el estatuto de responsabilidad extracontractual aplicable a las víctimas por repercusión o rebote?', *Estudios de derecho civil VII*, (Fabián Elorriaga De Bonis ed.) (Santiago de Chile: Thomson Reuters, Abeledo Perrot, 2012), at 714; also Barros, *Tratado*, II, cit., at 1054.

1611. Alessandri, *Responsabilidad*, cit., at 376.

1612. On autonomy and dependence: Veronika Wegner Astudillo, '¿Es verdaderamente la acción de la víctima por repercusión o rebote una acción autónoma o independiente?', *Estudios de derecho civil IX* (Juan Andrés Varas Braun, Susan Turner Saelzer ed.) (Santiago de Chile: Thomson Reuters, Legal Publishing, 2014) at 743 et seq.; in this sense also Kuncar Oneto, '¿Es el estatuto de responsabilidad extracontractual aplicable a las víctimas por repercusión o rebote?', *Estudios de derecho civil VII*, (Fabián Elorriaga De Bonis ed.) (Santiago de Chile: Thomson Reuters, Abeledo Perrot, 2012), at 714 y ss, in particular at 754.

1613. Claudia Mejias Alonzo, 'Posibles límites al daño por repercusión o rebote', *Estudios de derecho civil X* (Álvaro Vidal Olivares, Gonzalo Severín Fuster, Caludia Mejías Alonso ed.) (Santiago de Chile: Thomson Reuters, 2015) at 885–887.

Before such clarification, decisions to fully compensate indirect victims pursuant to Article 2330 CC had been criticized both by those who defended its association with the damage and by those who associate the provision with causation.

According to the former perspective, it is unfair not to consider the fault of all injured parties, including indirect victims, so they may have participated in the causation of the damage itself; their contribution, if any, must be included in the assessment of the fault of the damaging party.[1614] Anyway, if the injured party has imprudently exposed itself to the harm, the indirect victims' compensation has to reduce.

The latter perspective, which associates Article 2330 CC with causation, also supported reducing the degree of liability of the damaging party on grounds of equity.[1615]

The case law still has not taken a clear position.

In some cases, the courts have associated the issue with causation and rejected damages claims made by the widow and children on the grounds that the negligent and reckless behaviour of the deceased had caused the death by electrocution, despite being proven that the employer had failed to inform the deceased injured party about the risks existing in the tunnel or had falsely communicated that the power plant was disabled.[1616] In other cases, however, the courts have awarded full compensation to the indirect victim even the primary victim had imprudently exposed himself to harm.[1617] The commentaries on Article 2330 CC are also illustrative.[1618]

485. Certainly, to be an indirect victim, one must prove an emotional relationship with the primary victim.[1619] An attempt is being made to restrict[1620] the scope of indirect victims to victims who have been harmed in criminal matters, in connection with Article 108 CPP.[1621] In this sense, indirect victims are the spouse or cohabiting partner, children, relatives in the ascending line, siblings, adoptees and adopting parents. However, this list should be considered in abstract terms since it is essentially, in part, a rule related to criminal procedure. In fact, the second paragraph of the provision states that these individuals are subject to a particular order in which they can appear before the court, a kind of graduated standing, in the event

---

1614. In this sense Barros who also states that it would be absurd for the defendant not to dispose with these an exception that he would have with respect to the direct victim: Barros, *Tratado*, I, cit., at 461.

1615. Domínguez Águila, 'El hecho de la víctima como causal ...', cit., at 50.

1616. CS 23 de diciembre de 2014 (rol 24546/2014).

1617. The judgment clarifies that the reduction in relation to Art. 2330 CC applies, instead, when the parties do not claim *iure propio* but rather *iure hereditatis*: CS 28 Sep. 2016 (rol 7237/2015). This confirms the independence of the two actions. On the point *see* Manuel Barría Paredes, 'Algunos aspectos que plantea la aceptación de la teiss de la trasmisibilidad de la acción indemnizatoria por daño moral', *Estudios de derecho civil XIII* (Carlos Pizarro Wilson, Leonor Etcheberry Court, Claudia Bahamondes Oyarzún ed.) (Santiago de Chile: Thomson Reuters, 2018) at 680–681.

1618. *See* paras 376 et seq.

1619. Domínguez Hidaldo, *Daño moral,* cit., at 738.

1620. In this sense Claudia Mejias Alonzo, 'Posibles límites al daño por repercusión o rebote', *Estudios de derecho civil X* (Álvaro Vidal Olivares, Gonzalo Severín Fuster, Caludia Mejías Alonso ed.) (Santiago de Chile: Thomson Reuters, 2015) at 877.

1621. Cf. *see* para. 72.

of the death of the victim and that 'the intervention of one or more persons belonging to a category excludes those included in the following categories'. Hence, the case law[1622] ultimately establishes that problems related to demonstrating the actual affective relationship is a probative problem. Such finding is based on the observation that Articles 2314 and 2329 CC do not impose any limitation of a substantial nature. So, despite damage having been compensated, the spouse and children cannot be excluded *a priori* from any damages paid or awarded to the extended family (parents and siblings). At the same time, this can be used as a double-edged sword. Indeed, it has been submitted that the extension of the scope of compensation does not mean that those who are part of this family nucleus must always be compensated. There are multiple hypotheses that can be presented. But to name a few, it has been argued that: damages should not be awarded when it can be demonstrated that no damage exists; there should also be some distinction when the family member is related by blood or by law; damages should not be awarded in the cases where the parties are related by blood but have never physically met (in which there is no emotional relationship that has been harmed by the event).[1623] Therefore, this interpretation broadens the scope of the law, allowing a flexibility which also moves on certain burdens of proof which widen or narrow the fields of compensation relating to subjects inside and outside the family nucleus. In this sense, not only could the defendant provide evidence to dismantle the emotional bond, but it could also be possible to establish certain emotional bonds by presumptions.[1624] In this way, it has also been possible to award damages *iure proprio* to the posthumous child (*hijo postumo*), i.e., the child born after the death of the father.[1625]

Notwithstanding the above remarks, however, the approach established by the traditional doctrine is maintained and damages are awarded only to those who claim to have suffered a profound and genuine pain.[1626] So if in the case of the parents, spouse and children it is presumed that it is natural for them to suffer pain for the loss, it is not necessarily so in the case of the grandchild.[1627]

Interesting is that it is possible to grant a compensation for non-patrimonial damages not only in the case of death but in favour of the parents in respect of the damage suffered by the child who in the process of childbirth, suffered a severe asphyxia which caused irrecoverable neurological damage.[1628]

1622. CS 9 Dec. 2013 (rol 9428/2013).

1623. CS 14 Dec. 2017 (rol 18982/2017).

1624. It is established that certain relatives (parents and siblings) of the deceased worked with the deceased and were present at the sad event during the working day, and compensation was paid accordingly: CS 28 Oct. 2014 (rol 23369/2014).

1625. An important analysis of some judgments is made by Manuel Barría Paredes, 'Algunos aspectos que plantea la aceptación de la tesi de la transmisibilidad ...', cit., at 681–682. Barría considers that, in any case, it would have been more appropriate to request compensation *iure hereditatis* (also based on Articles 77 and 962 CC) in order to avoid evidential problems in relation to the certainty of the damage. In spite of what the author has affirmed, it should be remembered that for the reasons stated above these actions would be compatible except for the limitations in terms of prescription.

1626. Alessandri, *Responsabilidad*, cit., at 334.

1627. That presumption is established by CS 16 Dec. 2015 (rol 1561/2015).The solution can be different in the case of grandchild.

1628. CS 2.8.2016 (rol 16002/2016).

In the case of more than one indirect victim, it has been argued that there is no active consortium necessary in claiming compensation,[1629] and the transition or waiver of one does not affect the others.[1630] Accordingly, the action may be exercised either jointly or severally.[1631]

486. The doctrine[1632] has addressed some of the problems that could arise from combining liability of direct and indirect victims also in relation to the relevant jurisdiction[1633] and the contractual versus tort nature of the actions.[1634]

1629. Alessandri, *Responsabilidad*, cit., at 335.

1630. Alessandri, *Responsabilidad*, cit., at 336.

1631. For some reflections along these lines *see* Barría Paredes, 'Algunos aspectos que plantea la aceptación ...', cit., at 682–683; *see also* Susana Espada Mallorquín, Alberto Pino Emhart, 'La transmisibilidad del crédito indemnizatorio por daño moral de la víctima fallecida: análisis del caso chileno', Vniversitas, 2020/69, ID 2011-1711.

1632. Domínguez Águila, 'Sobre la transmisibilidad de la acción por daño moral', *Revista Chilena de Derecho*, 2004/3, at 502.

1633. José Luís Diéz Schwerter, 'Víctimas directas y por repercusión en la responsabilidad civil derivada de accidentes de trabajo o enfermedades profesionales en nuestra jurisprudencia reciente: del problema de la competencia a las distorsiones sustanciales', *Estudios de derecho civil* (Juan Andrés Varas Braun, Susan Turner Saelzer ed.) (Santiago de Chile: Thomson Reuters, Legal Publishing, 2005) at 563 et seq.; José Luís Diéz Schwerter, 'Responsabilidad civil por muertes en accidentes del trabajo: vacilaciones que persisten', *Estudios de derecho civil II*, (Hernán Corral Talciani, María Sara Rodríguez Pinto ed.) (Santiago de Chile: Thomson Reuters, 2011) at 273 et seq.

1634. Andrés Kuncar Oneto, '¿Es el estatuto de responsabilidad extracontractual aplicable a las víctimas por repercusión o rebote?', *Estudios de derecho civil VII*, (Fabián Elorriaga De Bonis ed.) (Santiago de Chile: Thomson Reuters, Abeledo Perrot, 2012), at 705 et seq.

It should be noted that in 2018 one of the reference rules, Article 420 of the Labour Code, was reformed. In this sense, the amendment to Article 420(f) expressly introduced the possibility for the heirs of the deceased worker to claim contractual compensation for damages caused by the work accident. *See* para. 103.

Although it has been observed that the reform does not expressly solve the problem of the transmissibility of moral damage still giving the possibility of different interpretations: *see* Manuel Barría Paredes, 'Algunos aspectos que plantea la aceptación de la teiss de la trasmisibilidad de la acción indemnizatoria por daño moral', *Estudios de derecho civil XIII* (Carlos Pizarro Wilson, Leonor Etcheberry Court, Claudia Bahamondes Oyarzún ed.) (Santiago de Chile: Thomson Reuters, 2018) at 676 et seq.

Chapter 3. Assessment and Compensation for Damages

§1. Objective Versus Subjective

487. The method of pecuniary compensation is objective, so that the pecuniary damage covers all the expenses which may have been paid in relation to the damage. In this context, provided expenses can be accounted for, issues relating to proof of such expenses are not particularly problematic as concerns establishing the existence and extent of any damage. In relation to loss of profit, *see* the relevant section.[1635]

For non-pecuniary damage, subjective factors (e.g., the age of the victim) can be taken into account depending on the specific case (*see infra*).

§2. Concrete Versus Abstract

488. Without prejudice to what will be discussed in terms of equity in the case of non-pecuniary damage, the method of quantifying economic loss must be concrete.

§3. Methods of Assessing Damages

I. Property Damage

489. In relation to damage to goods, a distinction must be made between whether the good has been damaged or destroyed. In the first case, the injured party is entitled to bring a pecuniary claim for the value of the repair or the lesser value that the good holds in relation to the damage.[1636] This approach is based on the German and French doctrine, which maintains that compensation should be limited in cases where the repair is technically impossible, with costs disproportionate to the value of the replacement, or when the injured party refuses cure or repair. In this latter case, the damage would be equivalent to the total loss, namely the value of the replacement of the good.[1637] For this reason, it will also be necessary to rely on estimates of the actual or estimated repair costs, depending on the case, bearing in mind that compensation must put the injured party back in the same position as he was in prior to the occurrence of the damage.[1638] This means that if the asset has diminished in value following the repair, such loss must be taken into account when determining the extent of damages owed.[1639] The same is true in reverse terms, since the cost of repair cannot be greater than the damage suffered;[1640] although, in

1635. Cf. *see* paras 459 et seq.
1636. Barros, *Tratado*, I, cit., at 282.
1637. Barros, *Tratado*, I, cit., at 282–283.
1638. Barros, *Tratado*, I, cit., at 284.
1639. Alessandri, *Responsabilidad,* cit., at 397–398.
1640. Alessandri, *Responsabilidad,* cit., at 399.

this latter circumstance, it is arguable that compensation cannot be denied on the grounds of unjust enrichment as the repair is rooted in a tort.[1641] Where it is impossible to replace the damaged property, as in the case of an non-fungible good, compensation must equal the property's market value at the time of the damage.[1642]

II. Non-pecuniary Damage

490. The difficulty of quantifying moral damage is an issue that has interested the doctrine.[1643] Specifically, it has been highlighted that moral damage is difficult to prove, as well as to clearly determine the content and concept of such damage. This is especially true when it comes to torts.[1644]

491. In the absence of a consolidated tabular method, such determination and quantification is left to the discretion of the judge, with the finding that the extent established by the relevant court on the merits is not reviewable in cassation.[1645] Despite this, some laws establish certain *ad hoc* parameters.

492. Thus, despite a lack of any definite parameter for assessment (even though express reference is made to compensation for moral damage),[1646] awards for damages involving rights of intimacy and private life must be 'prudentially established by the judge, taking into account the circumstances of the case and the gravity of the facts'.[1647] In this context, it should be noted that the traditional doctrine has found that to quantify the damage, the court should not refer to the severity of the facts but to the extent of the damage.[1648]

Consumer law refers to the moral damage as prejudice not only to physical and mental integrity, but also to dignity,[1649] by providing that in moral damages for consumers the judge may appoint an expert to establish a minimum amount. It appears

1641. Barros, *Tratado*, I, cit., at 285.
1642. Barros, *Tratado,* I, cit., at 287. On the moment of assessment of patrimonial and non-patrimonial damage Barros, *Tratado,* II, cit., at 989 et seq.
1643. Refer, for example, to Domínguez Águila, 'Consideraciones en torno al daño en la responsabilidad civil. Una visión comparatista', *Revista de Derecho* (Universidad de Concepción), 1990/188, at 154 et seq.; Carmen Domínguez Hidalgo, 'Hacia una uniformidad y trasparencia de la fijación del quantum indemnizatorio por daño moral', *Estudios de derecho civil II*, (Hernán Corral Talciani, María Sara Rodríguez Pinto ed.) (Santiago de Chile: Thomson Reuters, 2011) at 215 et seq.; Paulina González Vergara, Hugo Cárdenas Villareal, 'Sobre la prueba de la existencia del daño moral', *Estudios de derecho civil II*, (Hernán Corral Talciani, María Sara Rodríguez Pinto ed.) (Santiago de Chile: Thomson Reuters, 2011) at 671 et seq.
1644. Carmen Domínguez Hidalgo, 'Naturaleza, evaluación y prueba del daño moral: aspetos a desarrolar en el estado actual de su reparación', *Estudios de derecho civil X* (Álvaro Vidal Olivares, Gonzalo Severín Fuster, Claudia Mejías Alonzo ed.) (Santiago de Chile: Thomson Reuters, 2015) at 919.
1645. Ramos, *De la responsabilidad Civil*, cit., at 93.
1646. Art. 69 letra b) L16.744, cit.; Art. 40.2 L 19.733/2001, cit.
1647. Art. 23 Ley 19.628/1999, cit.
1648. Alessandri, *Responsabilidad,* cit., at 394.
1649. Art. 51.2 LPC.

significant that such establishment is not subject to a petition by the injured party but may also be established *de oficio* by the judge.[1650]

Particularly relevant are the parameters in the case of compensation in the event of health-related guarantees[1651] (AUGE), as it is stipulated that age or physical condition must be considered.

It is worth mentioning the most recent regulation on moral damage, which, in 2021, quantifies the moral damage caused to minors during activities related to the lack of service caused by the *Servicio nacional de proteción especializada a la niñez y adolecencia.*[1652] In the latter case, a very detailed rule is reached since practically all the parameters just highlighted are combined. Thus, the judge will have to consider 'the seriousness of the damage and the modification of the conditions of existence of the person affected and the consequence of the damage produced, taking into account his age, physical and mental conditions, in accordance with the general rules applicable. This is without prejudice to other remedial measures for violations of rights that may proceed as appropriate, in the available public offer, in particular medical benefits for mental health consequences'.[1653]

Where general compensation provisions apply (e.g., Articles 2314, 2329 CC), it has traditionally been argued that this should be determined according to the principles of equity.[1654] However, despite it has been noted that the principles of proportionality and equality should also be taken into account,[1655] case law has considered relevant factors for the quantification of damages, their intensity and the seriousness of the fault.[1656]

The future consolidation of the statistical framework,[1657] albeit indirectly based on the previous canons, may change this trend by producing a partial homogenization of the amounts, which has not happened so far due to the subjectivity[1658] in the determination of moral damage.

1650. Art. 51.2 LPC.
1651. Art. 41 L 19.966/ 2004, cit.
1652. For a case in which a minor committed suicide inside an installation, with condemnation of the Servicio Nacional (which on that occasion received the name SENAME): CS 25 Oct. 2019 (rol 26.680/2018).
1653. Art. 2a L 21.302/2020 of 22 Dec. (DO 5 Jan. 2021).
1654. Ramos, *De la responsabilidad Civil*, cit., at 94.
1655. *See* Barros, *Tratado*, I, cit., at 333.
1656. We refer with extensive case law to Barros, *Tratado*, I, cit., at 323.
1657. In favour of the creation of a baremo: Court Murasso, 'Análisis crítico de los criterios de valoración....', cit., at 913; Cárdenas Villarreal, 'Los daños futuros en el Derecho chileno...', cit., at 908–910. For some critical aspects of baremo Francisco Rubio Varas, 'El principio de reparación integral y la valoración del daño moral: el baremo estadístico jurisprudencial chileno', *El Principio de Reparación Integral en sus Contornos Actuales. Una Revisión desde el derecho Chileno. Latinoamericano y Europeo* (Carmen Domínguez Hidalgo, ed.) (Santiago de Chile: Thomson Reuters, 2019), at 235 et seq.
1658. An important jurisprudential review with relevant amounts can be found in Barros, *Tratado*, I, cit., at 326–332.

§4. Equitable Limitation of Damages

493. Apart from the considerations that have been made about the possible equitable quantification of non-pecuniary damage, the question has been raised whether in certain cases the damage may be limited by other factors.

I. Economic Capacity of the Parties

494. It is significant that some scholars have considered whether economic canons (i.e., estate of the liable party) impact the determination of an obligation to pay damages.

There is no consensus neither in the traditional doctrine nor in more recent literature.

Part of the traditional doctrine rejects the notion that the economic capacity of the damaged party is a relevant factor, just as it denies the relevance of the value of the estate of the damaging and injured party respectively.

Thus, the circumstances that the damaging party happens to be economically better off than the injured party (and therefore more capable of paying a higher award) should not be grounds for increasing the amount of compensation owed.[1659] This reasoning is based on the traditional idea that civil liability is compensatory and not punitive in character.

The opposite viewpoint, however, argues that a comparison should be made between the value of the estate of the two parties.[1660]

495. More modern doctrine has also taken up the debate, arriving at a number of alternative solutions.

The restrictive position, which is opposed to taking into account economic capacity for the purposes of quantifying damages, has proposed a series of criticisms, including the possible distancing from the principle of full compensation, producing a measured discretionary power of the judge tending towards different functions of responsibility such as punitive, and also considering that a redistribution of wealth is being carried out which is not the purpose of compensation.[1661] To adopt the economic capacity of the parties as a parameter for determining the extent of an award would also be contrary to the preventive function and to the possibility of

1659. Alessandri, *Responsabilidad,* cit., at 408.

1660. Jorge, López Santa María, 'La posición económica de la víctima y del autor del daño como elemento para la fijación del monto de la indemnización', *Revista de Ciencias Jurídicas,* 1971/1, at 95 et seq., cf. Fernando Fuyo Laneri, *Istituciones de Derecho Civil Moderno* (Santiago de Chile: Editorial urídica, 1990), at 110.

1661. These are the interesting arguments of Rodrígo Barría Diáz, 'La capacidad económica de las partes como criterio de cuantificación del daño moral en la jurisprudencia chilena', *Estudios de derecho civil IX* (Juan Andrés Varas Braun, Susan Turner Saelzer ed.) (Santiago de Chile: Thomson Reuters, Legal Publishing, 2014) at 524 et seq.

applying Article 2330 CC (which would be obscured by the greater amount attributable by the judge, and creating a new element of unforeseeability in the resolution of the conflict).[1662]

496. This position is followed by a contrary one which justifies the application of the criterion relating to the economic situation of the parties. This perspective is based on the retributive justice function that civil liability can fulfil, as well as the need to guarantee the principle of equality of the parties before the law,[1663] also considering that it would not lead to greater uncertainty and unpredictability as claimed by the contrary thesis since this aspect already characterizes compensation in the context of tort liability.[1664]

497. As far as the case law is concerned (and especially jurisprudence on the merits), there is a tendency to consider the economic situation of the parties.[1665] This is partially because the amount of the damage tends not to be revisable in cassation[1666] (except for what has been said in relation to Article 2330 CC).[1667]

Nevertheless, the courts have not expressed a clear position.

For instance, in some cases the courts have reduced the compensation because the damaging party was not very financially sound,[1668] while in others the wealth of the damaging party[1669] was considered irrelevant and for this reason the extent of damages awarded was unaffected given it is the damage and its extent that justifies the amount of the award. This position has been reinforced by the finding that the economic situation of the country or the economic capacity of the parties as criteria for reducing moral damage distracts from its nature.[1670]

498. A different and independent aspect of the previous situation is the fact that the judge may take into consideration the actual financial status of the victim, albeit separately and not relative to the wealth of the injured party.[1671] In this sense, in the case of non-pecuniary damage, a standard more in line with the canons of equity

---

1662. Rodrígo Barría Diáz, 'La capacidad económica ...cit', at 528–529. This doctrine considers that this criterion would distort not only extracontractual liability but also contractual liability.
1663. Alberto Pino Emhart, 'La situación económica de las partes y la avaluación del daño moral. Al rescate de una vieja tesis', *Estudios de derecho civil XIII* (Carlos Pizarro Wilson, Leonor Etcheberry Court, Claudia Bahamondes Oyarzún ed.) (Santiago de Chile: Thomson Reuters, 2018) at 497 et seq.
1664. Pino Emhart, 'La situación económica de las partes ...', cit. at 509.
1665. For example, SAP Santiago 27 Mar. 2019 (rol 4028/2019). For a brief jurisprudential review along these lines, *see* Rodrígo Barría Diáz, 'La capacidad económica ...cit',at 520.
1666. Already Ramos, *De la responsabilidad Civil*, cit. at 93. In the same sense e.g., also with jurisprudential references: Pino Emhart, 'La situación económica de las partes...', cit., at 499; Corral, *Lecciones,* cit., at 161.
1667. *See* para. 384.
1668. In favour of that view is the one which considers that the non-pecuniary damage of insult should be measured by 'the economic faculties of the person who caused the injury' CS 19 Apr. 1984, *RDJ*, 81, s. 4, at 81.
1669. CS 29 Nov. 1968, *RDJ*, 65, s. 4, at 323.
1670. CS 21 Mar. 2016 (rol 21061/2014). Cf. Court Murasso, 'Análisis crítico de los criterios de valoración....', cit., at 924–925.
1671. Alessandri, *Responsabilidad,* cit., at 409.

would be applied, establishing that in relation to the quantification of moral damage 'the current economic situation of the injured party must be taken into consideration'.[1672]

Despite this, it should be noted that some less recent rulings have gone in the opposite direction and have reduced the compensation in view of the neighbourhood where the victim lived. Such was done based on the finding that the compensation awarded for the breakage of furniture was excessive in view of the location of the property.[1673]

II. *Compensatio Lucre Cum Damno*

499. In some circumstances, damage actually produces or generates a gain for the injured party.

The doctrine[1674] favours commensuration (*compensatio*), as illustrated even in historical judgments. More precisely, it is argued that the surplus value received as a result of payment of damages should be deducted from the amount of the award, so as to avoid overcompensation or compensating the damage twice.[1675] To provide a practical example: in the case of broken dishes, the extent of the damage must be calculated within the limits of their purchase price (meaning that compensation cannot exceed market value).[1676] In the absence of a dedicated provision, the doctrine has elaborated three requirements; namely, that: the benefit and damage must have the same source, the benefit must be causally linked to the illicit fact and the benefit must have a legal nature similar to the injury suffered[1677] (i.e., the benefit must be compensatory and therefore applicable to both pecuniary and non-pecuniary damage).

500. Emblematic is the case where the injured party is entitled to make a claim with his insurance provider. Since the scope of life insurance is to cope with future incapacity[1678] (and not to compensate loss), the death of the insured individual potentially generates a gain for the beneficiary of the policy.[1679]

The most debated argument is in the case of injury or illness since insurance is meant to cover relevant costs and medical expenses. In these cases, part of the doctrine argues that damages and compensation are not accumulable and therefore submits that, pursuant to Article 534 CCom, the insurance company can file an action

1672. CS 24 Sep. 1986, *RDJ*, 83, s. 4ª, at 191.
1673. Thus a judgment of the year 1869 (*Gaceta de Tribunales*, 1869, at 649) cited by Alessandri, *Responsabilidad*, cit., at 409.
1674. Corral, *Lecciones*, cit., at 138.
1675. Alessandri, *Responsabilidad*, cit., at 400. Citing a judgment of año 1919.
1676. Alessandri, *Responsabilidad*, cit., at 400. Citing a judgment of año 1919.
1677. In this sense Fabian Elorriaga De Bonis, 'Conflictos de aplicación de la *compensatio lucri cum damno*', *Estudios de derecho civil VI* (Gonzalo Figueroa Yañez, Enrique Barros Bourie, Mauricio Tapia Rodríguez, ed.) (Santiago de Chile: Abeledo Perrot: 2011), at 571 et seq.
1678. Barros, *Tratado*, I, cit., at 1013.
1679. Corral, *Lecciones*, cit., at 138–139, formerly Tapia, *De la responsabilidad*, cit., at 207 et seq., especially 211–213.

of subrogation in the rights of the insured.[1680] Another part of the doctrine, instead, is more concerned with cases involving social security institutions (ISAPRE), arguing that such institutions must indemnify no matter what any benefit received by the injured party. And, according to these scholars, this is especially true[1681] since the applicable law (Ley 18.933) is silent on the matter and does expressly provide for the application of the general law.

501. Commensuration is also possible with regard to work-related accidents where the employer has an express right of recovery against the person responsible for the accident,[1682] as well as with regard to road accidents.[1683] Ultimately, the commensuration or offsetting of the amounts depends on whether the sources of the obligations have the same compensatory nature. If both their purpose is not compensatory, or if they are hybrid (such as the case of social security pension), the solution is not so clear-cut.[1684]

In addition to having the same compensatory nature as that of the damage caused, it will not be possible to accumulate damages if one also has insurance for damage to property or if one has established insurance for loss of profit (‘*seguro de lucro cesante*’).[1685]

502. The potential for a damaging fact to produce income for the damaging party (rather than the injured party) should also be considered. The enrichment of the damaging party does not justify a claim by the injured party for greater compensation, as enrichment of the damaging party does not match the harm suffered by the injured party.[1686] Any future admission of a different concept of unjustified enrichment could open the door to further grounds for compensation, since this justification would disappear.

1680. Barros, *Tratado*, I, cit., at 1015 cf. Corral, *Lecciones*, cit., at 140.
1681. Elorriaga De Bonis, ‘Conflictos de aplicación de la *compensatio lucri cum damno* ..., cit., at 575 et seq.
1682. *See* Art. 69 Ley 16.744, cit.; Elorriaga De Bonis, ‘Conflictos de aplicación de la *compensatio lucri cum damno* ..., cit., at 573; Barros, *Tratado*, I, cit., at 1015.
1683. *See* Arts 15–16 Ley 18,490, cit.; Elorriaga De Bonis, ‘Conflictos de aplicación de la *compensatio lucri cum damno* ..., cit., at 573; Barros, *Tratado*, I, cit., at 1015.
1684. On the point *see* Elorriaga De Bonis, ‘Conflictos de aplicación de la *compensatio lucri cum damno* ..., cit., at 577 et seq., Barros, *Tratado*, I, cit., at 1017–1019.
1685. As Barros notes, *Tratado*, I, cit., at 1019–1020.
1686. Alessandri, *Responsabilidad*, cit., at 400.

§5. Methods of Payment

I. Lump Sum

503. Traditional doctrine[1687] has already established that compensation can be paid by lump sum or annuity, including a combination of the two.[1688] Legal scholars do not consider judicial discretion as to the method of payment as a case of *ultra petita.*[1689]

504. As noted above, the Chilean legal system expressly sanctions the right to pay damages in a single lump sum when the relevant infringement pertains to intellectual or industrial property rights.[1690]

II. Annuities

505. Annuities may be granted for life or monthly.[1691]

506. There have been judgments awarding non-pecuniary damage in the form of an annuity,[1692] which would be facilitated if there were a tabular method of quantifying personal injury that expressly provided for it.

507. Such mechanisms, together with compensation in kind, have been suggested by the doctrine in the case of future damages relating to personal injuries, which would be enabled by the introduction of appropriate legislation in this sense.[1693]

508. In the context of an insurance policy, the insurance contract expressly envisages the possibility for compensation to be paid by way of a lump sum or annuity (Article 512 Ccom).

III. Others

509. If monetary compensation is not chosen, protection may be extended by reparation in kind or restitutory remedies.[1694]

1687. Alessandri, *Responsabilidad,* cit., at 390.
1688. CS 8 Nov. 1971, RDJ, 68, s. 4ª, at 274, *see* Barros, *Tratado*, I, cit., at 295.
1689. Cf. Alessandri, *Responsabilidad,* cit., at 391.
1690. *See* paras 454 and 543 et seq.
1691. Alessandri, *Responsabilidad,* cit., at 390.
1692. CS 16 Apr. 1998, *Fallo del mes,* 473, at 301, *see* Barros, *Tratado*, I, cit., at 295.
1693. Cárdenas Villarreal, 'Los daños futuros en el Derecho chileno...', cit., at 908–910.
1694. *See* paras 543–544.

Chapter 4. Personal Injury and Death

§1. Pecuniary Losses

510. Personal injury cases are peculiar in that they may involve pecuniary damages (e.g., medical or surgical expenses) and non-pecuniary damages (e.g., relating to the loss of functionality of a limb or quality of life, as well as issues inherent to loss of earnings). Despite this, it is not its own category of damages in the Chilean legal system given its relatively scarce study,[1695] both from a conceptual and dogmatic point of view. Therefore, there is no specific or proper category of damage in the nuances that, for example, could be present in Spanish or Italian law.

511. In this panorama, which has yet to evolve and consolidate, it is interesting to observe efforts to categorize certain aspects[1696] or to evaluate future pecuniary damage in the case of injuries (e.g., costs of prostheses, new operations or the like). For instance, part of the doctrine believes that future damages related to a person's life is related to problems with causation, and that it may be difficult to quantify the extent of damages despite an expert opinion. Accordingly, the system of life annuities or compensation in kind is appropriate.[1697]

§2. Non-pecuniary Losses

512. Personal injury[1698] (*daño a la persona*) in its non-material aspect is traditionally a part of 'moral damage' (*daño moral*). A clear example of recoverable damage in this regard is represented by the possibility to claim damages for prejudice to the impossibility of living in the situation prior to the harm (defined as *perjuicio de agrado*[1699]).

513. However, this kind of prejudice is of clear relevance. The effort to work on a project for calculating the quantification of damages since June 2012 is appreciable. This project is directed by the University of Concepcion, led by Professor Luís Diez, and the *Sala Tercera* of the Supreme Court, propelled by the support of Minister Eugenia Sandoval.

1695. Thus the reference of the doctrine has been essentially to foreign law: *see* Fabian Elorriaga De Bonis, 'Configuración, consecuencias y valorización de los daños corporares', *Cuadernos Jurídicos* (Universidad Adolfo Ibañéz, 1995/1, at 1 et seq.; *see also* Barros, *Tratado*, I, cit., at 288 et seq.
1696. *See* Fabian Elorriaga De Bonis, 'El perjuicio patrimonial por daños físicos en la doctrina y jurisprudencia chilenas', *Revista Anales de Derecho UC – Temas de Responsabilidad Civil*,, 2006/1, at 231 et seq.
1697. Cárdenas Villarreal, 'Los daños futuros en el Derecho chileno...', cit., at 901 et seq.
1698. Barros, *Tratado*, I, cit., at 241 et seq., for an analisis of the foreign tabular system (at 343 et seq.).
1699. On this point e.g. Barros, *Tratado,* I, cit., at 339 et seq.

A tabular method on moral damage from death (‘*baremo estadístico jurisprudencial sobre indemnización del daño moral por muerte*’) was created, with results initially published towards the end of 2013 and updated periodically afterwards.[1700] Subsequently, a further scale (*baremo*) was introduced[1701] concerning the moral damage from bodily injuries in work-related accidents (‘*baremo relativo a la indemnización de daño moral por lesiones*’). The *baremo* can be consulted in the official page elaborated by the Supreme Court.[1702]

514. The *baremo* is merely referential and non-binding, and has been elaborated on statistical criteria with reference to qualitative factors, such as the age of the victim and the compensation amounts. The effort is clearly significant, although some problems persist as statistical data are developed on a moral damage that has often been understood and identified using separate criteria that rely on subjective parameters or equity; in certain cases, they may move from different factual premises in granting its compensation and its amount.

515. There is a progressive application of the amounts fixed by the tables. The first application by the Supreme Court was in 2014[1703] to compensate the victims of the earthquake of 2010. In spite of this, it can be observed that sometimes it is desirable to grant amounts higher than those foreseen.[1704]

516. It has been observed that personal injury can cause pecuniary or moral/non-pecuniary damage to persons close to the victim, in which case it is possible to speak of reflected damage (*daño reflejo o por repercusión*) as discussed above.

§3. Transferability of Damages to Heirs

517. The action for damages is of a patrimonial nature and therefore assignable to third parties by deed *inter vivos*, both for pecuniary and non-pecuniary damage.[1705] Greater problems arise instead with regard to the transferability *mortis causa* of non-pecuniary damage.

1700. For example, in the first update as of May 2015, there were 1,130 recompiled sentences.
1701. In 2015, a new protocol was signed between the Supreme Court and the University of Concepción: ‘Protocolo de elaboración de Baremo jurisprudencial estadístico sobre indemnización de daño moral por lesiones derivadas de infortunios laborales’: https://baremorm.pjud.cl/file/ProtocoloBLesion.pdf.
1702. Available at: https://baremorm.pjud.cl/
1703. CS 19 junio 2014 (rol 5817/2013).
1704. Thus, although a compensation of 50 million Chilean pesos was granted (tendentially in consonance with the statistical *balance*), a dissenting vote proposed a compensation of 80 million: CS 11 May 2017 (rol 47396/2016). The judgment is particularly important because it associates the compensatory standard of damages for death, in a compensation for loss of chance, which as we have seen sometimes escapes from this reference point, associating more with the loss of lack of life.
1705. Alessandri, *Responsabilidad*, cit., at 342; Barros, *Tratado*, II, cit., at 1054; Corral, *Lecciones*, cit., at 359.

518. This has created real problems in the realm of compensation for non-pecuniary damage resulting from death.

Nevertheless, compensation to indirect victims can also be awarded in cases where the victim does not die. Thus, in some cases sentimental compensation ('*perjuicio de afección*') has been awarded for the suffering of a family member in the face of incidents of particular relevance and relevant gravity, such as having seen their child as a victim of sexual abuse or sodomy.[1706]

519. Article 2315 CC allows not only to the victim to claim damages, but expressly provides damages may be claimed by the heirs of injured parties, and more generally also to other parties who benefit from certain goods or rights at the time of the relevant event. Article 2315 CC states that 'not only the owner or possessor of the thing that has suffered the damage, or his heir, but also the usufructuary, the inhabitant or the user, if the damage affects their right of usufruct or habitation or use, can ask for compensation. He who has the thing with the obligation to answer for it may also claim it in other cases; but only in the absence of the owner'.

The problem that arises in the case of non-pecuniary damage is whether the heir can also claim damages for the victim's non-pecuniary damage, and in particular for the victim's death. This is also because a compensation table system has not yet been developed in relation to non-pecuniary damage for permanent and temporary injuries.

520. The death of the injured party (generally a non-pecuniary damage) is traditionally qualified in Chile as *pretium doloris* or *daño moral*, which may be framed in two perspectives. The damage or suffering that generates a right to claim damages in favour of certain family members,[1707] and a lethal injury *iure proprio* belonging to the victim himself. Traditionally it has been debated whether this damage from death is indemnifiable and consequently transmissible, and therefore whether it is claimable *iure hereditatis*.

521. Cases of procedural succession[1708] envisaged by Article 1097.1 CC are outside this context. This is also because death does not terminate the lawyer's mandate (Article 529 COT) for which the heirs who have already been instituted (following a valid claim of such rights by the living heir) succeed in the judgment, which can refer to pecuniary or non-pecuniary damage relating, for example, to temporary or permanent injury.

There is also no doubt (*nulla quaestio*) in the case of death occurring after the judgment condemning the deceased, as this circumstance does not give rise to a

1706. CS 27 Jan. 1998 (*GJ*, 211, at 57), CS 27 Mar. 2003 (Fallo del mes, 508, at 198), For a review also of case law on the merits: Barros, *Tratado*, I, cit., at 369 et seq.

1707. *See supra* paras 483 et seq.

1708. In this sense there is no problem and the doctrine is in agreement: Ramón Domínguez Águila, 'Sobre la transmisibilidad de la acción por daño moral', *Revista Chilena de Derecho*, 2004/3, at 497; Ramos, *De la responsabilidad Civil*, cit., at 113.

question relating to the transmission of the right; rather, it concerns the successor transmission of a liquidated credit and therefore whether the rights are included in the relevant party's estate.[1709]

522. Influenced by other European legal systems concerning the right to be compensated for death, two visions have emerged: one in favour of its compensability and one against.

The negative view was based on the fact that at the time of death legal personality was extinguished and therefore no successor right could be incorporated into the estate.

The doctrine is divided on transmissibility.

523. Even when it is accepted that such a right can be established during the life (*iure propio*) of the deceased person, the doctrine and jurisprudence[1710] have denied its transmissibility on the grounds that the right is strictly personal and that the scope of moral damage (unlike in the case of pecuniary damage) would be distorted if it were paid out to a person other than the deceased.[1711] In cases of death following a work-related incident, the argument was strengthened by the fact that the same labour code (at Article 88) states that rights arising pursuant to such provision are strictly personal and therefore inalienable.[1712] In this sense, this part of the doctrine has denied the possibility of claiming *iure hereditatis* such damage. This thesis has been confirmed in doctrine[1713] to the point that authoritative doctrine has changed its position; if before such doctrine initially allowed the compensability, it now generally denies it.[1714]

524. Another part of the doctrine, instead, allows such transmissibility. Although there is a thesis that allows compensation despite the injured party has passed away (whether or not by immediate death), given the significance of the right to life and its constitutional protection,[1715] traditional

1709. Already: Ramón Domínguez Águila, 'Sobre la transmisibilidad de la acción por daño moral', *Revista Chilena de Derecho*, 2004/3, at 497–498; Ramos, *De la responsabilidad Civil*, cit., at 113.

1710. For example, CS 23 Jun. 2007 (rol 309/2006), CS 27 Nov. 2007 (rol 6196/2006); CS 29 Sep. 2011 (rol 2073/2009).

1711. And therefore limiting the heirs' active legitimacy under Art. 2315 CC only to moral damages Ramón Domínguez Águila, 'Sobre la transmisibilidad de la acción por daño moral', *Revista Chilena de Derecho,* 2004/3, at 501 et seq.; in a substantially identical sense *see also* Ramón Domínguez Águila, 'Por la intrasmisibilidad de la acción de daño moral', *Estudios de derecho civil* (Juan Andrés Varas Braun, Susan Turner Saelzer ed.) (Santiago de Chile: Thomson Reuters, Legal Publishing, 2005) at 607 et seq.

1712. Domínguez Águila, 'Sobre la transmisibilidad de la acción por daño moral, *Revista Chilena de Derecho*, 2004/3, at 501.

1713. Barros, *Tratado*, II, cit., at 1059. The author maintains his position with respect to the first edition of the work (at 947).

1714. In this sense Corral who modifies his position with respect to his two editions, if he initially admitted it in the 2003 edition (at 320–321), now denies it Corral, *Lecciones,* cit., at 356–359.

1715. This is the position of Rodríguez who admits it 'although a tiny fraction of time passes': Rodríguez, *Responsabilidad Extracontractual*, cit. at 366. This position is criticized by

scholars[1716] have allowed it within certain limits. That is, transmissibility is not allowed when the person died instantaneously; rather, damages may be recovered only if a period of time has passed between the injury and the death, and provided that during that time and before death the injured party had become aware of his fate. In this case, he may be entitled to damages and would be aware of such rights. Thus, it has been argued that although the claim pursuant to Article 2315 CC only applies to property damage, the standing of the claimant-heir stems from general principles of succession where the injured party has survived for a period. Such argument is additionally supported by the fact that there is no rule that denies such transmissibility in application, therefore, of Article 1097 CC and the general provision of the law of succession set out in Article 951 CC.[1717] Accordingly, the right is transmissible every time the injured party has died following a period of injury (or suffering) irrespective of the advancement of any claim in this regard.[1718] Practically speaking, adhering to this theory would allow transmission of the right to claim damages to heirs only for pecuniary damages and not for non-pecuniary damages in cases where the injured party has died instantaneously. The argument in favour of transmissibility has also recently been defended on other grounds. In particular, it has been stated that – to the extent the right is personal – the right to compensation is transmitted and not the right to claim damages.[1719] However, this is limited by the requirement to demonstrate when this type of claim (if not already claimed in life by the future deceased) can be transferred. It is particularly relevant in work-related accidents given the principle in favour of workers' protection,[1720] or generally based on the observation that the concept of moral damage is broad and exceeds the scope of the *pretium doloris* to encompass also any prejudice to a life project.[1721]

525. The recent trend in case law seems to allow transmissibility. Essentially, it is allowed in cases of death due to work-related accidents and has been allowed in a 2016 appeal to render case law and doctrine more coherent,[1722] which additionally dismantled any argument that the tenor of Article 88 of the Labour Code establishes 'the rights of this law are non-waivable and non-transferable'. Therefore, it is considered that this provision does not apply to the claim for damages pursuant to

---

Domínguez Águila who states that constitutional values do not affect the problem of transmissibility: Domínguez Águila, 'Sobre la transmisibilidad de la acción por daño moral', *Revista Chilena de Derecho*, 2004/3, at 501.

1716. Thus Alessandri, *Responsabilidad*, cit., at 337–338.

1717. Thus Alessandri, *Responsabilidad*, cit., at 337–338.

1718. Abeliuk, *Las Obligaciones*, *I*, at 247.

1719. Thus Susana Espada Mallorquín, Alberto Pino Emhart, 'La transmisibilidad del crédito indemnizatorio por daño moral de la víctima fallecida: análisis del caso chileno', Vniversitas, 2020/69, ID 2011-1711.This doctrine also speaks of a transmissibility absoluta and a relative one, the first would always be admitted, the second only if the deceased had manifested in life the desire to activate for the claim of the damage.

1720. Thus one would speak of a principle of '*in dubio pro operario*': *See* Benjamín Andrés Vico Gárate, 'Sobre la transmisibilidad de la acción indemnizatoria del daño moral en sede laboral: una propuesta en base al principio protector', *Ius et praxis*, 2021/2, at 217 et seq.

1721. Denisse Díaz Duarte, 'Por la transmisibilida de la acción a favor de los herederos para reclamar el daño moral de su causante, *Revista de Derecho* (Universidad de Concepción), 2017/241, at 121

1722. CS 27 Sep. 2016 (rol 33.990/2016).

Article 69 B) Labour Code, since it is held that in Article 88 'it refers to those of a social nature, in particular medical, disability, invalidity and survivor's benefits (...) but does not cover the indemnity actions provided for in article 69' (*se alude a aquellos de índole social, en particular las prestaciones médicas, por incapacidad, invalidez y por supervivencia (...) pero no alcanza a las acciones indemnizatorias previstas en el artículo 69*).[1723]

The same aspect is confirmed in civil court (by the civil section and not the employment law section) again in relation to a work-related accident, albeit with a dissenting opinion.[1724] Indeed, as we have seen, the presence of a civil and labour jurisdiction sometimes has to be coordinated.[1725]

526. Although this aspect seems to be consolidated as concerns work-related accidents, at present there do not appear to be any consolidated solutions offered in other contexts; there continue to be decisions which allow transmissibility and those which deny it.

For example, it has recently been confirmed that transmissibility is allowed also in the case of a non-work-related death. Although the grounds were contractual, it is significant that the case involved the death of a guest who drowned in a hotel swimming pool, which event generated 'helplessness and anguish when sinking into the pool and perceiving the beginning of a process of asphyxia until losing consciousness'.[1726] In that case the victim, unconscious, was taken to hospital where he died.

In contrast, another decision holds that the strictly personal nature of this right prevents its transmissibility in case of death caused by crimes of humanity.[1727]

527. It has sometimes been argued that actions *iure propio* and *iure hereditatis* are not concurrent. This assertion is found on the fact that such persons would have been excessively enriched by receiving compensation for the same event.

In this sense, supporters of this notion hold that allowing both forms of action potentially generates a situation of unjustified enrichment, and is also contrary to the principle of *no bis in idem*[1728] where the same damage is compensated. However, this latter approach must be considered unfounded as it confuses two statuses: that of family member (who can claim damages on his own behalf as an indirect victim) and that of heir, who is not necessarily a family member.[1729]

1723. CS 27 Sep. 2016 (rol 33.990/2016).
1724. CS 30 ag 2017 (rol 4670/2017). *See* Vico Gárate, 'Sobre la transmisibilidad de la acción...', cit., at 217 et seq.
1725. *See supra* para. 486.
1726. CS Mar. 1, 2018 (rol 27842/2017).
1727. CS 22 May 2018 (21614-17). *See* Vico Gárate, 'Sobre la transmisibilidad de la acción...', cit., at 225 et seq.
1728. Domínguez Águila, 'Sobre la transmisibilidad de la acción por daño moral', *Revista Chilena de Derecho*, 2004/3, at 502.
1729. Barros, *Tratado*, I, cit., at 249.

Chapter 5. Various Damages

§1. Family

528. The existence of any damage suffered within the family unit has also been analysed. Indeed, it has been argued[1730] that the liability for breach of marital obligations between spouses would be of a tort nature, also noting that essentially the claims in relation to this liability concern the claim for non-pecuniary damages.[1731] However, the procedure is debatable, especially in the case of breach of the duty of fidelity.[1732]

529. The law on *Acuerdo de Unión Civil* provides for an action for damages in favour of the cohabitee for damage caused by third parties to the other cohabitee.[1733]

1730. Yasna Otárola Espinoza, 'E estatudo de reparación del daño derivado del incumplimiento de deberes matrimoniales', *Estudios de derecho civil XII* (Hernán Corral Talciani, Pablo Manterola Domúnguez ed.) (Santiago de Chile: Thomson Reuters, 2017) at 543 et seq.
1731. Susan Turner Saelzer, 'El daño en la jurisprudencia nacioal sobre resposabilidad civil entre cónyuges', *Estudios de derecho civil XII* (Hernán Corral Talciani, Pablo Manterola Domúnguez ed.) (Santiago de Chile: Thomson Reuters, 2017) at 557 et seq.; *see also* Susan Turner, Saelzer, 'Indemnización de perjuicios a propósito del divorcio por culpa', *Presente y futuro de la responsabilidad civil* (Rodrigo Barría Díaz, Alfredo Ferrante, Lilían San Martín Niera eds.) (Santiago de Chile: Thomson reuters, 2017), at 215 et seq.
1732. A systematization of the different positions can be found in Alfredo Ferrante, 'Perfectos desconocidos', *Cine y derecho de Familia* (Graciela Medina, Cristián Lepin Molina, ed.), (Buenos Aires, Santa Fe: Rubinzal-Culzoni), 2020, at 359 et seq.; for a deepening *see also* e.g Gabriel Hernández Paulsen, 'Las consecuencias de la infracción de de deberes matrimoniales no dan lugar a indemnización, en *Revista Chilena de Derecho Privado*, 2016/, at 95 et seq.; Susan Turner Saelzer, 'Infidelidad, culpa, divorcio e indemnización de perjuicios en el derecho matrimonial argentino y chileno', *Revista Derecho Privado* (Universidad del Externado), 2018/35, at 105 et seq. *See supra* para. 418.
1733. Art. 20 Ley 20.830/2015, of 13 pr (DO 21 ar 2015). On the point Hernán Corral Talciani, 'Responsabilidad Civil por daños causados por un tercero a uno de los integrantes de la unión civil', *Estudios de Derecho Familiar I* (Cristián Lepín Molna, Maricrúz Gómez de la Torre Vargas, ed.) (Thomson Reuters: Santiago de Chile, 2016), at 295 et seq.; Eduardo Court Murasso, 'Acuerdo de Unión Civil y acciones indemnizatorias del convivente civil por daños causados por terceros al otro conviviente', *Estudios de derecho civil XII* (Hernán Corral Talciani, Pablo Manterola Domúnguez, ed.) (Santiago de Chile: Thomson Reuters, 2017) at 576 et seq.

§2. Property

530. Part of the doctrine has been concerned with analysing, within the context of damage to property, compensation for the restriction of property,[1734] which is a possibility for the State for an illicit act,[1735] especially in the case of expropriation.[1736]

§3. Asbestos Liability

531. It should be noted that liability for silicosis and asbestos has been considered a form of deferred damage.[1737]

1734. Gonzalo Montory Barriga,'¿Indemnización por excesivas restricciones al derecho de propiedad?', *Estudios de derecho civil VI,* (Gonzalo Figueroa Yañez, Enrique Barros Bourie, Mauricio Tapia Rodríguez ed.) (Santiago de Chile: Abeledo Perrot, Legal Publishing, 2011) at 595 et seq.

1735. Pablo Montt Retting, 'Responsabilidad del Estado por acto ilícitos. ¿Queda espacio para reclamar perjuicios por privaciones o limitaciones de la propiedad?', *Lo Público y lo Privado. Estudios en homenaje al prof. Enrique Barros Bourie*, (Santiago de Chile: Thomson Reuters, 2017), at 759 et seq.

1736. Andrés Kuncar Oneto, 'Alcances doctrinarios y jurisprudenciales al daño patrimonial efectivamente casusado por una expropiación (Art. 38 del Decreto Ley n. 2186', *Estudios de derecho civil VI,* (Gonzalo Figueroa Yañez, Enrique Barros Bourie, Mauricio Tapia Rodríguez ed.) (Santiago de Chile: Abeledo Perrot, Legal Publishing, 2011) at 595 et seq.

1737. Rodrigo Barría Diáz, Àbesto y silicosis: acerca de la recepción y consolidación jurisprudencial de una forma de daños diferidos', *Estudios de derecho civil XI* (Departamento de Derecho Privado Universiad de Concepcióned.) (Santiago de Chile: Thomson Reuters, 2016) at 877 et seq.

Chapter 6. Interference with Collateral Benefits

§1. Insurance

532. The 2013 reform of the insurance system in relation to third-party liability policies[1738] is significant, as it amended several provisions of the Commercial Code.[1739] Additionally, although insurance policies are filed with the *Comision de Mercado Financiero*, there is no longer a general control on the policy's content.[1740]

533. Compensation for contractual and non-contractual damages is covered by insurance which, as seen in part, sometimes leads to problems of possible accumulation of compensation.[1741]

It should be noted that while intent is not covered by the policy, it is possible to take out a policy which includes such element in the case of gross negligence. As such, it is possible to circumvent – pursuant to Article 542 CCom – the criterion of *culpa lata dolo aequiparatur* in civil matters falling within the scope of Article 44 CC.[1742]

§2. Social Security

534. The social security system in Chile is based on a pension system providing an old-age, disability and death pension; a health system providing protection in case of illness and pregnancy; insurance against accidents at work and occupational diseases; occupational health and safety; and insurance in case of unemployment.[1743]

535. In fact, both the Chilean pension system and its health guarantees tend to be private, with the insurance system playing an important role in health coverage.

1738. *See* Rodrigo Sapag Álvarez, *La Ley del Seguro, Regulació del mercado y del contrato de Seguro en Chile* (Santiago de Chile: Tirant Lo Blanch, 2021); Maria Fernada Vásquez Palma, *Contrato de Seguro. Doctrina y Jurisprudencia* (Santiago de Chile: Tirant Lo Blanch, 2018). Vvaa, *El contrato de Seguro. Comentarios al título VII, Libro II, del Código de Comercio* (Roberto Ríos Ossa dir., Carolina Schile Manzor, ed),(Santiago de Chile: Thomson Reuters, 2015), Sergio Arellano Iturriaga, *La Ley De Seguro* (Santiago de Chile: Legal Publishing, Thomson Reuters, 2nd ed., 2014).

1739. Art. 512 et seq. as amended by Ley 20667/2013, of 9 May (DO 9 May 2013).

1740. The policies can be consulted on the page of the Comisión del Mercado Financiero at the following url: https://www.cmfchile.cl/institucional/mercados/deposito_polizas.php?mercado=S

1741. *See* paras 499 et seq., 310–311.

1742. On the point Ferrante, Alfredo, '¿Hacia un concepto unitario de dolo u otra identidad? Sobre los deberes de información y el dolo en el contrato de seguro', *Estudios de Derecho Comercial, VIII Jornadas chilenas de Derecho Comercial, 7 y 8 de septiembre de 2017* (Departamento de Derecho de la empresa, Pontificia Universidad Católica de Valparaíso, Lorena Carvajal Arenas, Ángela Toso Milos edd.), (Santiago de Chile: Thomson Reuters, 2018) at 43 et seq.

1743. *See* the webpage of the *Supeintendencia de la Seguridad Social*: *see* www.suceso.cl.

It is also important to recall the system *Administradoras de fondos de pensiones* (AFP) and the 'individual capitalization system', regulated by DL 3500/1980.[1744]

536. The Supreme Court[1745] has ordered an audit company (in this case Price Waterhouse Coopers) to compensate a pension fund administered for an AFP under the legislation on pension funds following a mere formal and non-fundamental check on the relevant documentation. Indeed, the legislation allows AFPs to bring an action in the event of damage to pension funds.[1746]

537. Just as AFPs can claim damages, they can be ordered to pay them, as in the case of liability due to negligence in the collection of the relevant contributions. In fact, the Supreme Court[1747] finds that the law expressly establishes hypotheses of negligence on the part of the social security institutions[1748] (providing for certain hypotheses by way of example), and that the defendant can submit as a defence[1749] that such hypotheses set out by the law are non-exhaustive.

538. In April 2021, DL 3.500 on the pension system was reformed[1750] by reshaping the part relating to the *Entidades de Asesoria Previsional* and Entidades de *Asesoría Financiera Previsional*,[1751] i.e., for those entities whose task is to provide consultancy services in relation to forecasting systems and any related investments. Article 177 provides that those entities – which are controlled by the *Superintendencia de Pensiones* and by the *Comisión para el Mercado Financiero* – will be liable even for *culpa leve* (*hasta la culpa leve*) for compensation in respect of the breach of their advisory duties in relation to social security matters, which will be in addition to any administrative sanctions.

Article 177 also expressly sanctions the civil, administrative and criminal liability of the partners, shareholders and directors of such an entity 'unless it appears that they did not participate or opposed the fact constituting the infringement or default'.[1752]

1744. Decreto Ley 3500/1980, of 4 Nov. (DO 13 Nov. 1980).
1745. CS 3 Sep. 2021(rol 8,429-18): CS 3 sept 2021 (rol 7.888/19).
1746. Art. 148 Decreto Ley 3500/1980, cit.
1747. CS 7 Feb. 2020 (rol 29.260/2018).
1748. Pursuant to the third paragraph of Article 4a of Law 17.322/1970 of 10 Aug. 1970 (DO 19 Aug. 1970).
1749. Thus, the fourth paragraph of Article 4 *bis* provides that there will be a negligent implementation when (1) does not file an enforcement action within the statute of limitations, in the case of contributions declared and not paid, or does not continue the enforcement action initiated by the worker, (2) does not request the special precautionary measure provided *ad hoc* (*see* Art. 25 bis) this generates a direct damage to the worker or 3) does not file the relevant legal remedies that the law allows and this results in direct pension damage to the worker.
1750. *See* Ley 21314/2021, of 1 Apr. (DO 13 Apr. 2021).
1751. *See* Arts 171 et seq. DL 3.500.
1752. Art. 177 LMV.

Chapter 7. Other Remedies

§1. Restitution for Unjust Enrichment

539. Although restitutory action[1753] can be associated with unjustified enrichment,[1754] there is no normative categorization. Indeed, some provisions provide for it and others are interpreted in this sense by doctrine, despite the reference to its indemnifying character.

540. In general, an action for restitution may also be brought in the case of property stolen or misappropriated unlawfully, since a suitable civil action may be brought under criminal law (189 CPC).[1755]

I. Malice and Profit of Others

541. Articles 1458.2 and 2316.2 CC are a noteworthy and peculiar feature of the Chilean legal system.

Among other things, these rules provide that the party who benefits from the malice of another is also obliged to compensate the damage even if he is not an accomplice, being obliged only up to the amount of what the benefit is worth.

Legal scholars have debated the legal nature of such circumstance. For some, it entitles the relevant party to claim damages[1756] or, in other cases, bring an action for restitution,[1757] with the consequence of *actio in rem verso* and the possibility[1758] to bring such action only following a claim for damages (and therefore in a subordinate phase of the proceedings).[1759]

1753. More generally *see* Javier Barrientos Grandón, *Las condictiones en el Código Civil. El pago de lo no debido y otros supuestos de su procedencia* (Santiago de Chile: Thomson Reuters, 2018).
1754. Ramón Domínguez Águila, 'Sobre el artículo 2316 inciso segundo del código civil y la acción contra el que recibe provecho del dolo ajeno', *Revista de Derecho* (Universidad de Concepción), 2009/225–226, at 218–220; *see* Barros, *Tratado*, II, cit., at 1038 et seq.
1755. Cf. Art. 189 CPC with Arts 59, 83 letra c), 187, 188, 217 CPC. *See e.g.*, Barros, *Tratado*, I, cit., at 1062 et seq.
1756. For example, Ruperto Pinochet Olave, & Ricardo Concha Machuca, (2015). 'Las prestaciones mutuas en caso de nulidad de contrato: carácter indemnizatorio o restitutorio en el Derecho Civil chileno', *Revista de Derecho Privado* (Universidad Externado), 2015/28, at 137.
1757. For example, Alberto Pino Emhart, 'La restitución de ganancias ilícitas y la acción del provecho por dolo ajeno', *Ius et Praxis*, 2016/3, at 229.
1758. On the subsidiary character *see* Alberto Pino Emhart, 'El (supuesto) carácter subsidiario de las acciones restitutorias', *Fundamentos Filosóficos del Derecho Civil Chileno* (Esteban Pereira Fredes, ed.) (Santiago de Chile: Rubicón Editores, 2019), at 465 et seq.
1759. For a detailed analysis on these points *see* Alfredo Ferrante, 'Provecho del Dolo Ajeno y Dolo de tercero: dos visiones diferentes de la indemnización', en *Estudios de Derecho Civil XV* (Fabián Elorriaga De Bonis *et al.* ed.), (Santiago de Chile: Thomson Reuters, 2020), at 929 et seq.

542. These provisions have been specifically applied in a number of judgments in the last decade.[1760]

II. Infringement of an Industrial Property Right

543. Furthermore, the black letter of Article 108 LPin provides for 'compensation' for damages by establishing a threefold mechanism in favour of the relevant party. Thus, it is possible to claim the benefits which the holder has ceased to perceive as a consequence of the infringement; those which the infringer has obtained; or the price which the infringer would have had to pay to the holder of the licence. Despite such literalness the doctrine does not consider it necessarily compensatory; in some cases it may be restitutory.[1761]

544. A recent amendment[1762] to the Law on Intellectual Property adds a second paragraph to Article 108 and introduces, in cases of counterfeiting of a trademark, the option to bring an 'action for damages' (this is the literal wording of the provision) to be replaced by a 'single comprehensive sum' (*somma única comprensatoria*) determined by the judge up to 2,000 monthly tax units.

In this sense, the same approach is taken as that already adopted in 2010 in the law on intellectual property,[1763] which is influenced by the US system and linked to statutory damages.[1764] The difference is that Article 108 LPInd expressly provides that the right of option must be exercised 'in the claim for damages' (i.e., at the time of initiation of litigation). This partially affects the trend in case law that, referring to the similar Article 85 K of the law of intellectual property, held the right must be exercised at the time the judgment was executed.[1765] In intellectual property matters, the nature of this amount has been debated; more precisely, it is submitted that

1760. CS 30 Jan. 2013 (rol 6302/2010), CS 17 Apr. 2013 (rol 10347/2011); CS 12 Sep. 2013 (rol 11.723/2011): CS 30 Sep. 2013 (rol 4871/2012); CS 3 Mar. 2016 (rol 7.179/2015); CS 25 May 2017 (rol 62.041/2016). STC 12 Apr. 2018 (rol 2985/16-INA).

1761. Alberto Pino Emhart, 'Las acciones civiles por infracciones al derecho de propiedad industrial', *Estudios de Derecho Privado. En homenaje al prof. Daniel Peñailillo Arévalos*, (Santiago de Chile: Thomson Reuters, 2019), p. at 795 et seq.; Marcelo Barrientos Zamorano 'Triple cómputo en la Ley de Propiedad industrial', *Estudios de derecho civil IV*, (Carlos Pizarro Wilson ed.) (Santiago de Chile: Thomson Reuters, 2009) at 739 et seq.; also Marcelo Barrientos Zamorano, 'El sistema indemnizatorio del triple computo rn la ley de Propiedad industrial', *Ius et Praxis*, 2006/1, at 123 et seq.; Carlos Urquieta Salazar, 'La acción de indemnización de daños de la Ley de Propiedad Industrial y la regla especial de deteterminación del *quantum* indemnizatorio por lesión de bienes inmatriales', *Estudios de derecho civil XIV* (Maricruz Gómez de la Torre Vargas, Gabriel Hernández Paulsen, Fabiola Lathrop Gómez, Mauricio Tapia Rodríguez ed.) (Santiago de Chile: Thomson Reuters, 2019) at 1181 et seq.

1762. Thanks to the introduction in the LPInd of the second paragraph of Art. 108 operated by Ley 21.335/2021, of 22 Jun. (DO 5 Jul. 2021).

1763. Art. 85 K. 17.366.

1764. It is highlighted that this norm comes into play by virtue of the free trade treaty with the United States and derives from 17 Code of Laws of the United States § 504(c): Elisa, Walker Echenique, *Manueal de propiedad intelectual* (Santiago de Chile: Thomson Reuters, 2014), at 328; Pino Emhart, 'Las acciones civiles por infracciones al derecho de propiedad intelectual', cit., at 49.

1765. CS 16 May 2017 (rol 16,627/2016).

since the sum is a single compensatory sum (*suma única compensatoria*) that cannot be cumulated with other compensation, it can be exercised together with an action for restitution of profits.[1766]

545. Another important safeguard for intellectual property has recently been added by the new Article 50 *bis*, which allows for the possibility to claim compensation from a person who has obtained a patent without being entitled to it.[1767]

III. Miscellaneous

546. In other cases, the restitutive character of the action has been discussed. For example, despite Article 669.1 CC expressly provides for *indemnizaciones* (indemnities), there is a strong argument that the action is restitutory in cases involving the claim for reimbursement of benefits enjoyed brought by a person who has sowed and planted on someone else's land against the landowner.[1768]

§2. Punitive Damages

547. Traditional legal doctrine has not considered punitive damages, which belong to the category of non-pecuniary damages,[1769] within the context of the Chilean legal system. For this reason, punitive damages have been associated only with criminal cases.[1770] Subsequently, however, also in relation to the scope of civil liability,[1771] punitive damages has been denied.[1772] Although a part of scholar arguments that civil liability is never punitive,[1773] another consider that the sanctioning function (which is not necessarily completely punitive) sometimes concurs with the

1766. Pino Emhart, 'Las acciones civiles por infracciones al derecho de propiedad intelectual', cit., at 49. This doctrine considers that the 'suma *única compensatoria*' rather than resartirorio character can be considered as a private fine in favour of the holder of the right.
1767. Thanks to the introduction in the LPInd of Art. 50 bis operated by Ley 21.335/2021, of 22 Jun. (DO 5 Jul. 2021).
1768. Ricardo Núñez Cádiz, 'La naturaleza jurídica y caracteres de la acción del art. 669 inciso 1º del código civil chileno', *Latin American Legal Studies,* 2021/8, at 207 et seq.
1769. Barros, *Tratado,* I, cit., at 323. An overview of foreign law can be found here (op. cit. 317 et seq.) also Cristián Larraín Páez, 'Aproximación a los punitive damages', *Estudios de derecho civil IV,* (Carlos Pizarro Wilson ed.) (Santiago de Chile: Thomson Reuters, 2009) at 707 et seq.
1770. Alessandri, *Responsabilidad,* cit., at 63.
1771. *See* paras 52–53.
1772. Rodriguez Grez, *La responsabilidad....,* cit., at 341.
1773. Carmen Domínguez Hidalgo, 'Los derechos de la personalidad y el principio de reparación integral del daño', *Estudios de derecho civil IV,* (Carlos Pizarro Wilson ed.) (Santiago de Chile: Thomson Reuters, 2009) at 657.

restorative one.[1774] However, the debate has recently been rekindled, also in the field of consumer law,[1775] and part of the doctrine appears to be changing its position.[1776]

548. It is possible to associate in part monetary sanctions (*penas privadas*) with punitive damages insofar as they allow the injured party to recover a greater amount of compensation than the damage suffered. This is attributable to the typification of rules that authorize the judge to impose a monetary sanction in cases of certain prejudicial behaviours.[1777]

1774. Corral, *Lecciones,* cit., at 63.

1775. *See* Aldo Molinari Valdés, Improcedencia del daño moral como categoría compensatoria de la afectación al interés colectivo frente al reconocimiento del daño punitivo', *Estudios de derecho civil XIII* (Carlos Pizarro Wilson, Leonor Etcheberry Court, Claudia Bahamondes Oyarzún ed.) (Santiago de Chile: Thomson Reuters, 2018) at 515 et seq.

1776. *See* Esteban Pereira Fredes, 'Un alegato a favor de las consideraciones punitivas en el derecho privado', *Revista de Derecho Escuela de Postgrado*, 2015/ 7, 61 et seq. Despite this, the traditional view against the punitive function also persists Court Murasso, 'Análisis crítico de los criterios de valoración....', cit., at 920.

1777. The doctrine that has found that they cannot be established *de oficio* by the judge and highlighted some examples such as in the case of usufruct rights in case of serious deterioration of the property (*see* Art. 809 CC), the loss of benefit of inventory for the drafting in bad faith of the same (Art. 1256 CC), the sanctions for the heir (Art. 1231) or the spouse (Art. 1768) who has taken away goods respectively from the hereditary axis or from the conjugal society, the revocation for ingratitude (Art. 1428): Alessandri, *Responsabilidad*, cit., at 401–402.

Selected Bibliography

Basic General Handbooks

René Abeliuk Manasevich, *Las Obligaciones.* I (Santiago de Chile: Thomson Reuters, 6th ed., 2014).
Cristián Aedo Barrena, *Responsabilidad extracontractual* (Santiago de Chile: Librotecnia, 2006).
Arturo Alessandri Rodríguez, *De la responsabilidad extracontractual en el derecho chileno* (Santiago de Chile: Editorial Jurídica de Chile, 1943 reprint, 2011).
Arturo Alessandri Rodríguez, *De la compraventa y de la promesa de venta I-1* (Santiago de Chile: Editorial Jurídica de Chile, 1917 reprint 2003).
Rodrigo Barcia Lehmann, *Lecciones de derecho civil chileno. II. De las Fuentes de Obligaciones* (Santiago de Chile: Editorial Jurídica de Chile, 2010).
Rodrigo Barcia Lehmann, *Lecciones de derecho civil chileno. I. Del acto jurídico* (Santiago de Chile: Editorial Jurídica de Chile, 2010).
Enrique Barros Bourie, *Tratado de Responsabilidad Civil Extracontractual* II vol. (Santiago de Chile: Editorial Jurídica de Chile, 2nd ed., 2020).
Rubén Célis Rodríguez, *La responsabilidad extracontractual* (Santiago de Chile: Universidad Central de Chile, 2003).
Hernán Corral Talciani, *Lecciones de Responsabilidad Civil Extracontractual* (Santiago de Chile: Legal Publishing, Thomson Reuters, 2nd ed., 2013).
José Luis Diez Schwerter, *El daño extracontractual. Jurisprudencia y doctrina* (Santiago de Chile: Editorial Jurídica de Chile, 1997, reprint, 2016).
Gonzalo Figueroa Yáñez, *Curso de Derecho Civil,* IV (Santiago de Chile: Editorial Jurídica de Chile, 2012).
Ramón Meza Barros, *Manual de Derecho Civil. De las Obligaciones* 2 vol. (Santiago de Chile: Editorial Jurídica de Chile, 9th ed., 2010).
René Ramos Pazos, *De la responsabilidad civil extracontractual* (Santiago de Chile: Legal Publishing, 5th ed., 2009).
Pablo Rodríguez Grez, *Responsabilidad Extracontractual* (Santiago de Chile: Editorial Jurídica de Chile: 2nd ed., 2010).
Gonzalo Ruz Lártiga, *Explicaciones de Derecho Civil. Contratos y responsabilidad extracontractual,* IV (Santiago de Chile: Abeledo Perrot, Legal Publishing, 2011).
Adrían Schopf Olea, & William García Machmar, *La responsabilidad extracontractual en la jurisprudencia* (4ed., Santiago de Chile: Legal Publishing, 2009).

Selected Bibliography

Orlando Tapia Suárez, *De la Responsabilidad civil en general y de la responsabilidad delictual entre los contratantes* (Santiago de Chile: Legal Publishing, 3rd ed., 2007).

Function of the Law of Tort

Rodrigo Barría Díaz, 'La función preventiva o disuasoria de la responsabilidad civil, a propósito de las leyes de Propiedad Intelectual y de Propiedad Industrial'. *Presente y futuro de la responsabilidad civil* (Rodrigo Barría Díaz & Alfredo Ferrante & Lilian San Martín Neira ed., Santiago de Chile: Thomson Reuters, 2017), at 177–214.

Carmen Domínguez Hidalgo, 'Algunas consideraciones en torno a la función de la responsabilidad civil', *Estudios de Derecho Civil Código y dogmática en el Sesquicentenario de la Promulgación del Código Civil* (Juan Andrés Varas & Susan Turner, coords.), (Santiago de Chile: LexisNexis, 2005), at 585–607

Aldo Molinari Valdés, *De la responsabilidad civil al derecho de daños y tutela preventiva civil*, (Santiago de Chile: LexisNexis, Ia edición, Santiago, 2004).

Adrían Schopf Olea, *'Las diferencias funcionales entre la responsabilidad civil contractual y extracontractual'*. in *Presente y futuro de la responsabilidad civil* (Rodrigo Barría Díaz & Alfredo Ferrante & Lilian San Martín Neira ed.) (Santiago de Chile: Thomson Reuters, 2017), at 61–86.

Alberto Pino Emhart, 'No sólo quieren dinero: La función expresiva de la responsabilidad extracontractual'. *Presente y futuro de la responsabilidad civil* (Rodrigo Barría Díaz & Alfredo Ferrante & Lilian San Martín Neira ed.) (Santiago de Chile: Thomson Reuters, 2017), at 159–176.

Enrique Barros Bourie, 'Justicia y eficiencia como fines del derecho privado patrimonial', in *Estudios de Derecho Civil Código y dogmática en el Sesquicentenario de la Promulgación del Código Civil* (Juan Andrés Varas & Susan Turner, coords.) (Santiago de Chile: LexisNexis, 2005), at 15–24.

Alberto Pino Emhart, 'Justicia distributiva, responsabilidad civil y terremotos. Reflexiones en torno a los fundamentos de la responsabilidad civil'. *Derecho y Justicia*, 2011/1, at 1–28.

Alberto Pino Emhart, 'Entre reparación y distribución: La responsabilidad civil extracontractual como mecanismo de distribución de infortunios', *Revista Chilena de Derecho Privado*, 2013/21, at 89–135.

Gian Franco Rosso Elorriaga, 'El principio de la responsabilidad civil objetiva limitada: un elemento de equilibrio sistémico que no contradice al denominado principio de la reparación integral del daño', *Revista de Derecho Privado (Externado)* 2014/26, at 449–497.

Relationship between torts and criminal Law

Alex Carocca Pérez,'Algunas consideraciones sobre los efectos de las sentencias penales absolutorias en los procesos civiles'. *Revista Procesal Penal* 2006/54, at 35–48.

Carlos Pizarro Wilson, 'Mirada de un civilista a la reparación en el nuevo proceso penal'. *Gaceta Jurídica*, 2003/296, at 59–75.

Carlos Pizarro Wilson, 'Acción civil en el nuevo proceso penal. Legitimación activa. Víctimas por rebote', *Revista Chilena de Derecho Privado*, 2005/3 at 155–159

Carlos Achiardi Echeverría, 'Sobre la procedencia de la responsabilidad civil ex delicto en ciertas hipótesis penales', *Revista de Derecho de la Universidad Católica de Valparaíso* (1999/20), at 195–210.

Rafael Fontecilla Riquelme, 'La responsabildad civil derivada de delito', *Revista de Derecho y Jurisprudencia*, 1945/42, at 121 et seq.

Juan Carlos Marín González, 'La acción civil en el nuevo código penal procesal penal chielno: su tratamiento procesal', *Revista de Estudios de la Justicia*, 2005/6, at 11–44.

Carlos Pizarro Wilson, 'El caso de Aaron Vásquez y la responsabilidad por el hecho ajeno. Corte Suprema, Santiago, 22 de agosto de 2012. Rol 2830–2012 y Corte de Apelaciones de Santiago, 19 de enero de 2012, rol 6427–2010', *Revista Chilena de Derecho Privado*, 2012/19, at 205–208.

Ignacio Ried Undurraga, 'El efecto de la cosa juzgada de la sentencia penal absolutoria y del sobreseimiento definitivo en el proceso chileno de responsabilidad civil'. *Revista Chilena de Derecho Privado*, 2015/24, at 9–57.

Ignacio Ried Undurraga, 'El efecto de la sentencia condenatoria del procedimiento abreviado en el juicio indemnizatorio por responsabilidad civil ex delicto'. *Ius et praxis*, 2017/1, at 579–626.

Relationship between contract and delictual responsibility

Carlos Pizarro Wilson, 'Responsabilidad contractual y extracontractual: Desde el problema de la opción al dilema del derecho común y especial'. *Presente y futuro de la responsabilidad civil* (Rodrigo Barría Díaz & Alfredo Ferrante & Lilian San Martín Neira ed.) (Santiago de Chile: Thomson Reuters, 2017), at 49–59.

Cumul/no cumul

Carlos Pérez Bravo, 'Concurrencia de responsabilidades', *Art boni et aequi,* 2000/4, at 111–146.

Hernán Corral Talciani, 'Concurrencia de acciones de responsabilidad civil contractual y extracontractual en los daños causados por accidentes del trabajo', *Rev. Chilena de Derecho Privado*, 2010/14, at 69–107.

María Teresa Alonso Traviesa, *El problema de la concurrencia de las responsabilidades* (Santiago de Chile: Lexis Nexis, 2006).

Carmen Domínguez Hidalgo, 'La concurrencia de responsabilidades o el mal llamado cúmulo de responsabilidades en el derecho chileno: estado actual', *Estudios de Derecho Civil III* (Alejandro Guzmán Brito ed., Santiago de Chile: Legal Publishing, 2008), at 717–734.

Hernán Corral Talciani, 'El concurso de responsabilidades en el derecho de daños chileno: defensa y delimitación de la teoría de la opción', *Estudios de Derecho Civil V* (Departamento de Derecho Privado Universidad de Concepción ed.) (Santiago de Chile: Abeledo Perrot Legal Publishing, 2010), at 639–653.

Bruno Caprile Biermann, 'Las acciones del comprador insatisfecho: el cúmulo actual y la tendencia al deber de conformidad', *Estudios de derecho civil II*,

(Hernán Corral Talciani & Mª Sara Rodríguez Pinto ed.) (Santiago de Chile: Thomson Reuters y La Ley, 2007), at 629–650.

Bruno Caprile Biermann, 'Las acciones del comprador insatisfecho: el cúmulo actual (ley de protección al consumidor, vicios redhibitorios, error sustancial, resolución por incumplimiento), y la tendencia al deber de conformidad en el derecho comparado', *Estudios de derecho privado en homenaje a Christian Larroumet*, 561–602 (Fabricio Mantilla Espinosa & Carlos Pizarro Wilson, ed.) (Santiago de Chile: Fundación Fernando Fueyo Laneri, 2008), at 561 et seq.

Pedro Zelaya Etchegaray, 'El cúmulo de responsabilidad en la nueva ley de protección al consumidor. Estudios sobre la ley N° 19.496 y las principales tendencias extranjeras in Cuadernos de Extensión de la Universidad de los Andes'. *Derecho del consumo y protección del consumidor*, (Hernán Corral Talciani ed.).1999/3, at 213–250.

Precontractual liability

Hugo Rosende Álvarez, 'La responsabilidad precontractual en la formación del consentimiento en los contratos reales y solemnes', *Instituciones modernas de derecho civil: Homenaje al profesor Fernando Fueyo Laneri* (Santiago de Chile: Conosur, 1996), at 337 et seq.

Hugo Rosende Álvarez, *Algunas consideraciones sobre la responsabilidad precontractual* (Valparaíso; Valparaíso editorial Universitaria, 1979).

Iñigo De la Maza Gazmuri, 'El retiro unilateral como un caso de responsabilidad precontractual', *Cuadernos de análisis jurídico. Temas de Contratos* (Iñigo De la Maza Gazmuri ed.), 2006/III, at 131–158

Isabel Margarita Zuloaga Ríos, *Teoría de la responsabilidad precontractual. Aplicaciones en la formación del consentimiento de los contratos*, (Santiago de Chile: Legal Publishing, 3rd ed., 2008).

Lilian San Martín Neira, 'Responsabilidad precontractual por ruptura injustificada de negociaciones', *Rev. Chil. Derecho*, 2013/1. at 317–324.

Manuel Risueño, *De las obligaciones precontractuales* (Santiago de Chile: Litografía Universo, 1933).

Marcelo Barrientos Zamorano, *Daños y deberes en las tratativas preliminares de un contrato* (Santiago de chile, Editorial Legal-Publishing, 2008).

Marcelo Barrientos Zamorano, 'Culpa in contrahendo en mutuo hipotecario', *Revista Chilena de Derecho* 2012/3, at 829–847.

Patricia Verónica López Díaz, 'La indemnización precontractual y contractual: Divergencias y eventuales zonas de confluencia'. *Presente y futuro de la responsabilidad civil* (Rodrigo Barría Díaz & Alfredo Ferrante & Lilian San Martín Neira ed., Santiago de Chile: Thomson Reuters, 2017), at 87–127.

Patricia Verónica López Díaz, '*La tutela precontractual y contractual del acreedor en el código civil chileno: dos sistemas estructuralmente diversos pero, ¿plenamente coherentes y convergentes*', *Rev. Chilena de Derecho Privado*, 2017/29, at 9–98.

Patricia Verónica López Díaz, 'Los supuestos y el alcance de la indemnización de daños como medio de tutela precontractual en el Código Civil chileno y su eventual confluencia con la indemnización por incumplimiento contractual', *Ius et Praxis* 2018/1, at 243–292.

Patricia Verónica López Díaz, 'La nulidad como un medio de tutela precontractual en el Código Civil chileno: configuración, modalidad de ejercicio y eventual concurrencia con la resolución por incumplimiento', *Revista de Derecho (Coquimbo)*, 2019/26, e3697.

Patricia Verónica López Díaz, 'La indemnización de daños por vicios redhibitorios como medio de tutela precontractual autónomo en el Código Civil chileno: un tópico cuya procedencia y alcance aún permanecen difusos', *Estudios de Derecho Civil XI* (Derecho Privado de la Universidad de Concepción ed. Santiago de Chile: Thomson Reuters-La Ley, 2016) at 659–683.

Patricia Verónica López Díaz, 'La protección del acreedor por vicios redhibitorios en el Código Civil chileno: entre la fase precontractual y contractual', *Revista de Derecho de la Pontificia Universidad Católica de Valparaíso* 2016/47, at 57–90.

Patricia Verónica López Díaz, 'Las relaciones entre la tutela precontractual y contractual del acreedor: la conexión y la proyección-absorción', *Revista de Derecho de la Pontificia Universidad Católica de Valparaíso*, 2018/30, at 51–91.

Patricia Verónica López Díaz, *La tutela precontractual del acreedor* (Santiago de Chile: Thomson Reuters, 2019).

Ramón Domínguez Benavente & Ramón H. Domínguez Águila, & Carmen Domínguez Hidalgo, 'Responsabilidad precontractual. Responsabilidad extracontractual. Retiro immotivado de las negociaciones preliminares. Comentario de jurisprudencia: Corte de Apelación Concepción 5 de junio de 1996', *Revista de Derecho (Universidad de Concepción)* 1996/199, at 179–185.

Ramón Domínguez Benavente & Ramón H. Domínguez Águila, & Domínguez Hidalgo, Carmen, 'Responsabilidad precontractual. Ruptura injustificada de Negociaciones Avanzadas. Daño Causados. Comentario a Corte de Apelaciones de Concepción, 30 de junio de 1999, rol 1530-96', *Revista de Derecho Universidad de Concepción*, 1998/204, at 187–188.

Raymond Saleilles, 'De La Responsabilité Précontractuelle. A propos d' un étude nouvelle sur la matière', *Revue Trimestrielle de Droit Civil*, 1907/6, at 697–751.

Roberto Ríos Ossa, *El deber precontractual de declaración del riesgo en el seguro de daños* (Santiago de chile, Editorial Legal-Publishing, 2008).

Rosario Celedón Förster, & Patricia Silberman Veszpremi, *Responsabilidad precontractual por ruptura de negociaciones contractuales* (Santiago de Chile: Editorial Jurídica de Chile, 2010).

Francisco Segura Riveiro, 'El interés contractual indemnizable en las hipótesis de responsabilidad precontractual', in *Estudios de Derecho Civil II. Jornadas Nacionales de Derecho Civil, Olmue, 2006* (Hernán Corral Talciani & María Sara Rodríguez ed., Santiago de Chile, Abeledo Perrot, 2007) at 345–362.

Pedro Pablo Vergara Blanco, 'La responsabilidad precontractual un necesario desafío para enfrentar la cultura del litigio'. *Estudios jurídicos en homenaje a profesores Fernando Fueyo Laneri, Avelino León Hurtado, Francisco Merino Scheihing, Fernando Mujica Be-zanilla, Hugo Rosende Subiabre* (Santiago de Chile: Universidad del Desarrollo, 2007), at 115 et seq.

Selected Bibliography

Medical Malpractice

Hugo Cardenas Villarroel & Jaime Moreno Molinet, *Responsabilidad médica. Estándares jurisprudenciales de la falta de servicio* (Santiago de Chile. Legal Publishing, 2011).

Guajardo Carrasco, Baltazar, *Aspectos de la responsabilidad civil médica. Doctrina y* Jurisprudencia, Santiago de Chile: Librotecnia, 2002.

Jorge Larrocau Torres, '¿Cómo se prueba la responsabilidad civil médica en la justicia chilena?', *Revista de Derecho* (Valdivia), 2014/2, at 43–79.

Carlos Pizarro Wilson, *La responsabilidad civil medica* (Santiago de Chile: Thomson Reuters, 2017).

Álvaro Vidal Olivares, *Responsabilidad civil medica* (Santiago de Chile: (Cuadernos Jurídicos de la Academia Judicial, 2019).

José Miguel Valdivia Olivares, 'La responsabilidad por falta de servicio en la administración hospitalaria en la jurisprudencia chilena', *Revista de derecho (Universidad de Concepción)*, 2019/243, at 213–246.

Legal practitioners

Aavv *Cuadernos de extensión jurídica* (ejemplar especial sobre Derecho Notarial y Registral: contribuciones académicas para su futura reforma, GianFranco Rosso Elorrieaga ed.), 2018/30.

Luis Eduardo Álvarez Díaz, 'Extensión de las obligaciones emanadas de las instrucciones notariales y responsabilidad civil del notario por su incumplimiento', *Revista Chilena de Derecho Privado*, 2015/25, at 77–114.

Sebastían Bozzo Hauri & Gonzalo Ruz Lártiga, 'El deber precontractual de información del abogado', *Ius et Praxis*, 2019/1, at 49–88.

Sebastían Bozzo Hauri & Gonzalo Ruz Lártiga, 'Responsabilidad por incumplimiento del deber de información del abogado', Ius. *Revista del Instituto de Ciencias Jurídicas de Puebla*, 2020/46, at 223–240.

Sebastían Bozzo Hauri & Gonzalo Ruz Lártiga, 'El deber contractual de información del abogado', *Ius et Praxis*, 2021/1, at 121–142.

Joel González Castillo, 'La responsabilidad civil de notarios y conservadores de bienes raíces: régimen de responsabilidad y culpa de que responden', *Revista de derecho (Coquimbo)*. 2019/26, e3595.

Carlos Pizarro Wilson, 'La responsabilidad civil de los notarios en Chile', *Revista de Derecho, Universidad Católica del Norte*, 2011/22, at 137–149.

Builders and Architects

Pablo Cornejo Aguilera, 'Incentivos para la conservación y reglas de responsabildidad: la responsabilidad del Dueño de la edificación por los daños ocasionados por su ruina'. *Revista Chilena de Derecho*, 2012/1, at 33–56.

Hernán Corral Talciani, 'Daños causados por la ruina de edificios y responsabilidad civil del empresario y de los profesionales de la construcción', *Revista de Derecho y Jurisprudencia*, 1996/93, also en Vvaa, *Doctrina Esencial Responsabilidad Civil* (edición bicentnario Revista de Derecho y Jurisprudencia, Raul Tavolari Olivero, ed) (Santiago de Chile: Editorial Jurídica, 2009), at 905–959.

Hernán Corral Talciani, 'La responsabilidad civil de los empresarios constructores y arquitectos por ruina o construcción defectuosa de edificios', *Revista de Derecho y Jurisprudencia*, 1995/92, also en Vvaa, *Doctrina Esencial Responsabilidad Civil* (edición bicentnario Revista de Derecho y Jurisprudencia, Raul Tavolari Olivero, ed) (Santiago de Chile: Editorial Jurídica, 2009), at 827–872.

Hernán Corral Talciani, 'Responsabilidad civil en la construcción de viviendas. Reflexiones sobre los regímenes legales aplicables a los daños provocados por el terremoto del 27 febrero de 2010', *Revista Chilena de Derecho*, 2010/3, at 459–475.

Juan Eduardo Figueroa Valdés, *Contrucción y arbitraje* (Santiago de Chile: Rubicon, 2019).

Patricio, Figueroa Velasco & Juan Eduardo Figueroa Valdés, *Urbanismo y Construcción* (Santiago de Chile: LexisNexis, 2006)

Carlos Pizarro Wilson, 'Daños en la construcción, fuerza mayor y terremotos'. *Revista de Derecho de la Universidad Católica de Valparaíso*, 2010/34, at 171–186.

Sergio Urrejola Santa María, *La responsabilidad profesional de los agentes de la construcción* (Santiago de Chile: LexisNexis, 2nd ed. 2007).

Liability of Public Authorities

Pedro Pierry Arrau, 'Repetición del Estado contra el funcionario', Revista de Derecho Universidad Católica de Valpraiso 1995/XVI, at 349–360.

Hugo Cárdenas Villaroel, 'La acción de repetición del Fisco en contra del personal médico-sanitario', *Estudios de Derecho Civil V (VII Jornadas Nacionales de Derecho Civil, Concepción, 2009)* (Santiago de Chile: Legal Publishing, 2010), at 527–554.

Luís Cordero Vega, Responsabilidad extracontractual de la administración del Estado (Santiago de Chile: Der, 2017).

Juan Carlos Ferrada Bórquez, 'La responsabilidad patrimonial del Estado de Chile: una revisión panorámica después de casi veinte años de jurisprudencia de la Corte Suprema'. *Revista de Administración Pública*, 2020/211, at 373–406.

Hernán García Mendoza, La responsabilidad extracotractual del Estado. Indemnización del error judicial (Santiago de Chile: Conosur, 1997).

Patricio Rondini Fernández-Dávila, *Responsabilidad patrimonial del Estado Juez en Chile* (Santiago de Chile: Lexis Nexis, 2008)

José Miguel Valdivia Olivares, 'La responsabilidad por falta de servicio en la administración hospitalaria en la jurisprudencia chilena', *Revista de derecho (Universidad de Concepción)*, 2019/243, at 213–246.

Vvaa, *La falta de servicio* (Raúl Letelier Wartenberg coord) (Santiago de Chile: Abeledo perrot, 2012).

Liability for Others

Rodrigo Barría Diaz. 'La responsabilidad objetiva del artículo 2328 del código civil', *Estudios de Derecho Civil VI – Jornadas Nacionales de Derecho Civil,*

Olmué 2010 (Gonzalo Figueroa Yañez; Enrique Barros Bourie, Mauricio Tapia Rodríguez ed., Santiago de Chile: Abeledo Perrot, Legal Publishing, 2010) at 521–541.

Alfredo Ferrante, 'Ilícito del menor ¿quién paga?'. *Presente y futuro de la responsabilidad civil* (Rodrigo Barría Díaz & Alfredo Ferrante & Lilian San Martín Neira ed., Santiago de Chile: Thomson Reuters, 2017), at 251–264.

Alfredo Ferrante. 'Responsabilidad por daños provocados en accidente vial con un animal bravío', *Revista chilena de Derecho Privado*, 2015/24, at 143–164.

Patricia López Díaz. 'Responsabilidad civil extracontractual por bullying o acoso escolar. Infracción del art. 16 b de la Ley general de educación. Presunción de culpabilidad por hecho propio. Responsabilidad del guardían. Obligación concurrente. Indemnización de daños. Daños moral', *Revista de Derecho Privado*, n. 1/2018, at 321–338.

Pamela Mendoza Alonzo. 'Responsabilidad del empresario por hechos dañosos de sus dependientes: ¿obligación concurrente o in solidum?', *Estudios de Derecho Civil XIV* – (Marícruz Gómez de Latorre Vargas, Gabriel Hernández Paulsen, Fabiola Lathrop Gómez, Mauricio Tapia Rodríguez ed., Santiago de Chile: Thomson Reuters, 2019), at 1083–1098.

Renzo Munita Marambio. 'Daños derivados del Bullying: consideraciones sobre la naturaleza de la responsabilidad de los establecimientos privados de enseñanza y su estándar de diligencia exigible', *Estudios de Derecho Civil XIV* – (Marícruz Gómez de Latorre Vargas, Gabriel Hernández Paulsen, Fabiola Lathrop Gómez, Mauricio Tapia Rodríguez ed., Santiago de Chile: Thomson Reuters, 2019), at 1113–1134.

Lucia Rizik Mulet. *Responsabilidad civil de los padres por los daños ocasionados por sus hijos menores de edad* (Santiago de Chile: Universidad Diego Portale, 2019).

Gian Franco Rosso Elorriaga. 'El sistema de la responsabilidad de los empresarios por el hecho de los dependientes en el Código de Bello y las dificultades en su interpretación y aplicación', *La vigencia del Código Civil de Andrés Bello* (Felipe Navia Arroyo y Carlos Chinchilla Iambett ed, Bogotá: Universidad Externado, 2019), at 391–428.

Pedro Zelaya Etchegaray, 'La responsabilidad civil del empresario por el hecho de su dependiente. Un intento por sistematizar la jurisprudencia chilena', *Revista de Derecho de la Universidad de Concepción*, n. 197/1995, at 101–145.

Product Liability

Francisca Barrientos Camus. 'La responsabilidad civil del fabricante bajo el art. 23 de la Ley de protección de los derechos de los consumidores y su relación con la responsabilidad civil del vendedor', *Revista Chilena de Derecho Privado*, 147/2010, at 1–50.

Lautaro Camilo Contreras Chaimovich, 'La prohibición de colocar en el mercado productos que sean peligrosos en caso de utilización conforme a su finalidad o racionalmente previsible', *Ius et Praxis*, 2/2019, at 19–66.

Hernán Corral Talciani, 'El primer régimen legal chileno de responsabilidad por productos: daños por defectos de los productos sanitarios', *Estudios de Derecho*

Civil XI (Departamento de Derecho Privado Universidad Concepción ed.) (Santiago de Chile: Thomson Reuters, 2016), at 877–895.
Hernán Corral Talciani, *Responsabilidad por productos defectuosos. Analisis y propuestas para el derecho civil y de consumo en Chile* (Santiago de Chile: AbeledoPerrot, Legal Publishing, 2011).
Erika Isler Soto, *El producto defectuoso* (Santiago de Chile: Librotecnia, 2013).

Environmental Liability

Verónica Delgado Schneider, 'La responsabilidad civil extracontractual por el daño ambiental causado en la construcción u operación de las carreteras', *Revista de Derecho* (Valdivia), 1/2012, at 47–76.
Jorge A. Femenías Salas, *Responsabilidad por Daño Ambiental* (Santiago de Chile: Universidad Católica, 2017).

Air carrier liability

Macarena Díaz de Valdés Haase, -'La responsabilidad civil por daños, lesiones y muerte en vuelos de instrucción dentro de Chile. Comentario a tres sentencias de la Corte Suprema', *Ius et Praxis*, 2017/2, at 509–546.
Claudia Mejías Alonzo, Angela Toso Milos, 'Fuentes normativas para el tratamiento de la responsabilidad del porteador en el trasporte aéreo. El contenido de las remisiones del código aerenáutico al Derecho Común y a los usos, constumbres y proncipios generales del derecho' *Ius et Praxis*, 2021/2, at 199–216.

Defences and Exception clauses

Claudia Bahamondes Oyarzún, Carlos Pizarro Wilson, 'La exposición de la víctima al daño: desde la culpabilidad a la causalidad', *Revista de Derecho* (PUCV), 2012/39, at 39–52.
Ramón Domínguez Águila, 'El hecho de la víctima como causal de exoneración de responsabilidad civil', *Revista de Derecho* (Universidad de Concepción), 1966/136, at 29–54.
Ramón Domínguez Águila, La *prescripción extintiva: Doctrina y Jurisprudencia* (Valparaiso: Prolibros, 2021).
Lilian San Martín Neira, *La culpa de la víctima en la responsabilidad civil* (Santiago de Chile: Der, 2018)

Causation

Cristian Aedo Barrena, La recepción de la creación de riesgos no permitidos en el derecho chileno, como criterio de imputación objetiva. ¿Puede distinguirse de la culpa?, *Revista Chilena de Derecho Privado*, 2019/35, at 117–145.
Jorge Baraona González, 'La Causa del daño en la jurisprudencia', *Revista Chilena de Derecho*, 2003/2, at 345–379.
Lilian San Martín Neria & Jorge Larroucau Torres, '*El razonamiento probatorio en la causalidad en la responsabilidad civil: Los criterios jurídicos en que se funda la jurisprudencia chilena*', *Revista de Derecho Privado* (Universidad Externado), 2021/ 40, at 329–359.

Selected Bibliography

Mauricio Tapia Rodríguez, *Caso fortúito o fuerza mayor*, 3rd ed., (Santiago de Chile: Thomson Reuters, 2020).

Remedies

Rodrigo Barría Díaz, 'La pérdida de una oportunidad en la jurisprudencia de la Corte Suprema sobre juicios indemnizatorios derivados del terremoto y tsunami de 27 de febrero de 2010', *Revista de Derecho* (Universidad de Concepción), 2019/245, at 235–269.

Rodrígo Barría Diáz, 'La capacidad económica de las partes como criterio de cuantificación del daño moral en la jurisprudencia chilena', *Estudios de derecho civil IX* (Juan Andrés Varas Braun, Susan Turner Saelzer ed.) (Santiago de Chile: Thomson Reuters, Legal Publishing, 2014) at 519–531.

Fabian Elorriaga De Bonis, 'Conflictos de aplicación de la *compensatio lucri cum damno*', *Estudios de derecho civil VI* (Gonzalo Figueroa Yañez, Enrique Barros Bourie, Mauricio Tapia Rodríguez, ed.) (Santiago de Chile: Abeledo Perrot: 2011), at 567–583.

José Luis Diéz Scwerter, 'La acción por daño contingente del art- 2333 deñ codigo civil en moviemento: tres casos de la jurisprdencia reciente, *Estudios de Derecho Privado. En homenaje al prof. Daniel Peñailillo Arévalos*, (Santiago de Chile: Thomson Reuters, 2019), at 723–741.

Alfredo Ferrante, 'Provecho del Dolo Ajeno y Dolo de tercero: dos visiones diferentes de la indemnización', en *Estudios de Derecho Civil XV* (Fabián Elorriaga De Bonis *et al.* ed.), (Santiago de Chile: Thomson Reuters, 2020), at 929–955.

Alberto Pino Emhart, 'La situación económica de las partes y la avaluación del daño moral. Al rescate de una vieja tesis', *Estudios de derecho civil XIII* (Carlos Pizarro Wilson, Leonor Etcheberry Court, Claudia Bahamondes Oyarzún ed.) (Santiago de Chile: Thomson Reuters, 2018) at 497–513.

Vvaa, *El Principio de Reparación Integral en sus Contornos Actuales. Una Revisión desde el derecho Chileno. Latinoamericano y Europeo* (Carmen Domínguez Hidalgo, ed.) (Santiago de Chile: Thomson Reuters, 2019).

Index

The numbers here refer to paragraph numbers.

Index

Index

www.ingramcontent.com/pod-product-compliance
Ingram Content Group UK Ltd.
Pitfield, Milton Keynes, MK11 3LW, UK
UKHW020137290926
13471UKWH00003B/544

9 789403 549316